A Pacific Basin Institute Book

THE PACIFIC BASIN INSTITUTE AT POMONA COLLEGE

Now entering its twentieth year of service, the Pacific Basin Institute at Pomona College remains dedicated to its original goal of furthering intelligent communication between the nations of the Pacific Basin and increasing knowledge among Americans of the cultures, politics and economics of the Asia/Pacific countries.

Since moving to Pomona College in 1997, PBI has greatly extended the scope of its activities. Our Pacific Basin Archive of film, video and documentary material, based on the footage used for *The Pacific Century* TV series, has expanded to include more documentary and feature films. PBI's on-going Library of Japan, the first in a planned program of translations from Asian languages, has just published its seventh volume, Mishima Yukio's *Silk and Insight*, with two more planned for 1999-2000.

Pacific Basin Institute Books published by M.E. Sharpe

SENSŌ: The Japanese Remember the Pacific War
Letters to the Editor of Asahi Shimbun
Frank B. Gibney, editor
Beth Cary, translator

Silk and Insight: A Novel
by Mishima Yukio
Frank B. Gibney, editor
Hiroaki Sato, Translator

The Nanjing Massacre:
A Japanese Novelist Confronts Japan's National Shame
by Honda Katsuichi
Frank B. Gibney, editor
Karen Sandness, translator

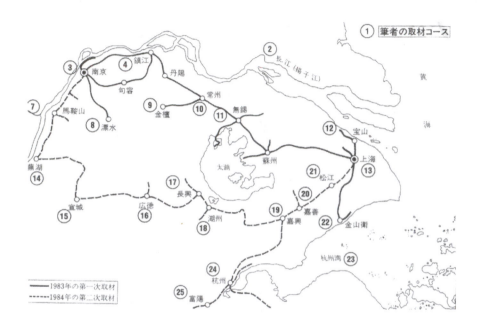

1. The author's research trip
2. Changjiang (Yangtze River)
3. Nanjing
4. Zhenjiang
5. Jurong
6. Danyang
7. Ma'anshan
8. Lishui
9. Jintan
10. Changzhou
11. Wuxi
12. Baoshan
13. Shanghai
14. Wuhu
15. Xuancheng
16. Guangde
17. Changxing
18. Huzhou
19. Jiaxing
20. Jiashan
21. Songjiang
22. Jinshanwei
23. Hangzhou Bay
24. Hangzhou
25. Fuyang
26. First research trip, 1983.
27. Second research trip, 1984.
28. Third research trip, 1987.

The NANJING MASSACRE

A Japanese Journalist Confronts Japan's National Shame

HONDA KATSUICHI

Edited by Frank Gibney

Translated by Karen Sandness

AN EAST GATE BOOK

M.E. Sharpe
Armonk, New York
London, England

An East Gate Book

Copyright © 1999 by The Pacific Basin Institute

The source of the main text of this translation is
Nankin e no Michi (The Road to Nanjing) by Honda Katsuichi
Copyright © 1987 by Honda Katsuichi. Published by Asahi Shimbun Publishing Co., Ltd.

The selections translated in the Appendix are taken from:
Chukogu no Tabi (Journey to China) by Honda Katsuichi. Copyright © 1971
by Honda Katsuchi. Published by Asahi Shimbun Publishing Co., Ltd.
Nankin Daigyakusatsu (The Nanjing Massacre) by Honda Katsuichi. Copyright © 1997
by Honda Katsuichi. Published by Asahi Shimbun Publishing Co., Ltd.

English translation rights arranged with Honda Katsuichi through
Japan Foreign Rights Centre.

Library of Congress Cataloging-in-Publication Data

Honda, Katsuichi, 1931—
[Nankin e no michi. English]
The Nanjing massacre : a Japanese journalist confronts Japan's national shame /
by Honda Katsuichi ; translated by Karen Sandness ; edited by Frank Gibney.
p.   cm.
"An East Gate book."
Includes index.
ISBN 0-7656-0334-9 (alk. paper).   ISBN 0-7656-0335-7 (pbk. : alk. paper)
1. Sino-Japanese Conflict, 1937—1945–Atrocities.
2. Atrocities–China–Nan-ching shih.   3. Nan-ching shih (China)–History.
I. Gibney, Frank, 1924— . II. Title.
DS777.5316.N36H6613   1998
951.04'2--dc21
98-40563
CIP

Printed in the United States of America

The paper used in this publication meets the minimum requirements of
American National Standard for Information Sciences–
Permanence of Paper for Printed Library Materials,
ANSI Z 39.48-1984.

∞

CONTENTS

Appendix

EDITOR'S INTRODUCTION
BY FRANK GIBNEY

"Excellency," the voice of a Sixth Division officer came over the field telephone at the Intelligence Section of China Area Army Headquarters, "We have 12,000 or 13,000 Chinese penned up here. What do we do with them?"

The answer from Lieutenant Colonel Cho Isamu was angry and short: *Yatte Shimae. Katazukerunoda* (Be done with it. I'll clean it up).

The date was December 18, 1937. The place: the outskirts of Nanjing, China. The order was no case of an isolated atrocity triggered by a single extremist, nor was it the first that Cho and others like him gave. Handed down five days after the fall of Nanjing to the Japanese Imperial Army, the order to kill was part of a pattern of deliberate extermination, sanctioned by local commanders in an effort to terrorize the government and people of China into surrender. Their atrocities were perpetrated in defiance of the orders of their commander-in-chief, General Matsui Iwane, who had expressly ordered that no prisoners were to be killed. (Ironically, Matsui was hanged as a war criminal after his trial by the International War Crimes Tribunal in Tokyo, although others far guiltier than he remained unpunished.)

Nor was the storied "Rape of Nanking" merely the sudden sacking of one city rendered defenseless. For several months—from November through January—and throughout the area of the Japanese advance, its inhabitants—civilians and disarmed prisoners-of-war alike—were raped, tortured, and indiscriminately slaughtered by soldiers who were themselves brutalized by their superiors and released to vent their rage on a helpless population. Living off the country, dirty, hungry, and still smarting from losses sustained in their action against Chinese regulars in Shanghai, Japanese troops behaved like a huge armed mob bent on revenge.

Apart from their systematic slaughter of their war prisoners, the raping and killing of innocent Chinese women and children remains a permanent stain on Japan's history—eclipsing even the later brutalities inflicted on Allied war prisoners and thousands of Chinese, Filipino, and Korean women forced into mass prostitution as the "comfort women" attached to the military (*jugun ianfu*) of the Emperor's Army. Over the six decades intervening, the disgrace has been compounded by the arrogant refusal of many postwar

Liberal Democratic Party politicians—including cabinet officers—and alleged "historians" of Japan's right wing, to admit the monstrousness of the Massacre. Some were bold enough to challenge the fact that it had happened.

It is simple justice that recent books in Japan, China, Germany, and the United States—most obviously Iris Chang's best-selling *The Rape of Nanking*—have brought these events the worldwide attention they deserve. Unfortunately, many of them (including, sadly, Ms. Chang's) are flawed, inaccurate, or incomplete; and the attention given them has been uncritical. It is more than fitting, therefore, that Honda Katsuichi's book on these events, which here appears in English translation as *The Nanjing Massacre,* is the work of a Japanese journalist. Honda's writing on this subject includes ample testimony from both Chinese and Japanese sources and presents for the first time this dreadful spoliation in its true context, as he follows the path of the Imperial Army's troops, from their landings in Hangzhou Bay through their murderous advance not only into Nanjing but other towns, cities, and villages along their route.

Contrary to widespread American belief, the story of the Nanjing atrocities is by no means unknown in Japan. In fact, recent literature on the Massacre in Japanese is far, far greater than publications about it elsewhere. If the diehard politicians of Japan's far right have continually tried to cover up the truth about the atrocities in China, some courageous Japanese journalists and historians have been writing about it for more than a quarter-century, from scholarly monographs to lengthy articles in mass publication monthlies and dailies.

They have not had an easy time of it, however. At the time of the Massacre, in late 1937 and 1938, the few reports about the atrocities in China by foreign correspondents—the *New York Times* correspondent Tillman Durdin among them—served to intensify the work of Japan's censors. Japanese newspaper correspondents found it impossible to get any word of the killings past the military's red pencils—not that any of them tried very hard. The need for a cover-up seemed all too obvious. For years thereafter even novels about the China war were subject to the most rigorous scrutiny. As a result, the Japanese public was largely unaware of the widespread murders. News reports of the time were little more than echoes of the Army communiqués. (Honda quotes many of these in his books.) Thus Japanese on the home front read only of heroic battles, their soldiers' hardships, and victories over the enemy troops. Nor did Americans make much of the few atrocity reports to hit their local newspapers. The Japanese bombing of the American gunboat *U.S.S. Panay* that same month of December 1937 drew most of the headlines.

The only word of the Nanjing atrocities that reached most Japanese came years later, after the close of World War II, when the International War Crimes Tribunal held its proceedings in Tokyo. To the average Japanese newspaper reader, the Tribunal's judgments about the Rape of Nanjing and its perpetrators seemed suspiciously like victor's justice—as Honda points out in his preface to the book. In the years following, with the U.S. occupation ended, the subject was not pursued. Protected by America's Cold War umbrella and basking in the sunny world of its surging GNP, the Japanese public turned its attention in the sixties and seventies to economic subjects. The hardships of World War II receded into the past, and for the younger generation, especially, the earlier Fifteen Year War, so-called, with China from 1931 to 1945, was a dead issue.

Indeed, as far as the war was concerned, most Japanese, mindful of Hiroshima and Nagasaki, logically thought of themselves as the principal victims. A conservative nationalist government and an even more conservative Education Ministry saw to it that the record of Japan's rape, pillage, and murder in China and Southeast Asia was neatly swept under the postwar rug.

By contrast, modern Germany has done its collective best to face up to the Nazi crimes of the past and to atone for them, wherever possible. Over the years German visitors to Japan—former Chancellor Helmut Schmidt notable among them—have been astonished at the apparent historical amnesia of most Japanese about the wartime misdeeds of their troops.

When diplomatic relations with China were restored in 1972, however, the misdeeds of the "China Incident" were brought forcibly to public notice. In a formal joint declaration, Japan expressed its "deep regret" over the damage inflicted on the Chinese people. That same year, in his book *Journey to China,* and in an earlier series of articles in Japan's leading newspaper *Asahi* the year before that, Honda Katsuichi, one of the *Asahi's* top reporters, had written an extensive exposé of his countrymen's atrocities in Nanjing and elsewhere. Right-wing apologists were quick to deny his facts, but appearing as they did in the mass circulation press, based as they were on intensive interviews with surviving Chinese victims, Honda's articles had a deep and shocking effect on some, at least, of the newspaper's ten million readers.

Quite obviously, something like a conspiracy of silence had existed for many years among people who had participated in the Nanjing atrocities, or had some knowledge of them. Few veterans of the Imperial Army were up to admitting complicity in the Massacre—at first from fear of becoming defendants at the War Crimes trials. At the time the rapes and murders took place, divisional commanders generally favored a policy of "take no prisoners"— to put it mildly. Diaries and reports of officers, enlisted men, and reporters accompanying the military bear this out. In his book Honda provides copious quotations and excerpts that prove this point. The excuse generally given was that the Japanese Army, itself living off the country, had no room for prisoners, while to release them would allow them to rejoin Chiang Kai-shek's retreating army. Yet those in charge were fully aware of the Geneva Convention's safeguards for war prisoners, not to mention innocent civilians. It is hardly surprising that no formal orders were later found ordering or even mentioning the atrocities. For Japanese participants the whole affair remained a huge guilty secret, conveniently forgotten.

By the 1980s, however, the wartime soldiers were well into their sixties and many felt a desire to confess or at least repent what they had done. In the summer of 1986 *Asahi* asked its readers to write some of their recollections about the war days for the newspaper's op ed page. In response to the invitation, "Let's talk about the war," *Asahi* received an unprecedented flood of letters—over 4,000—and continued to print selections for more than a year! Some 1200 of the letters were later published as a book, in two volumes. I read some of the letters in Japanese. In 1995 the Pacific Basin Institute published a selection of these, in English translation, under the original *Asahi* title of *Sensō* (War) (M.E. Sharpe, 1995). I wish we could have published more. For the letters, volunteered by war survivors—men and women from every walk of life—offer a revealing look at some of the terrible deeds done in the Emperor's name.

Predictably, right-wing apologists—and in Japan they can be very vocal—dismissed such revelations as isolated incidents. When they organized a movement to produce new history textbooks offering totally sanitized versions of Japan's "advance" into China, Honda and other scholars denounced them. By the end of the eighties, almost twenty books had appeared exposing the Nanjing atrocities. Since then Honda has written much more about these events, in an effort to make his countrymen aware of this bad past history. In this episode, as with his earlier writing on Vietnam, he has been a lightning rod for controversy.

Although his work is here translated and published for the first time in the United States, in Japan he continues to be widely read, as one of his country's most prominent journalists. The complete edition of his works, comprising some thirty volumes, was published by the Asahi Press in 1997. A few words of background about him for American readers would be appropriate.

Born in 1932, Honda Katsuichi started as a reporter for *Asahi* in 1958 and continued working for that newspaper until his retirement in 1992. His first books were about mountaineering, exploration, and the lives of primitive peoples, from northern Canada's Eskimos to the Bedouins of the Middle East to Japan's own aboriginal Ainu. In 1966 he made his first trip to Vietnam to cover the war there, and he returned on several occasions. His books on Vietnam and later on Cambodia, sharply critical of the U.S. military, centered on the plight of Vietnamese villagers in a war-ravaged country. He also chronicled the genocide of Pol Pot and the Khmer Rouge. Published by *Asahi,* these works guaranteed him a wide audience. As a hard-hitting left-wing reporter, he enjoyed a reputation in Japan comparable to something between Teddy White, David Halberstam, and the crusading revisionist Izzy Stone in the United States.

After chronicling the depredations of the U.S. military in Vietnam, however, he was led to reflect on what Japan's soldiery had done in China. His book, *Journey to China*, published in 1972, included a now famous section on the Rape of Nanjing. Inspired by the textbook controversies of 1982 and later, when liberal journalists and scholars in Japan complained about the Ministry of Education's official whitewash of the China invasion—labeled by the textbook censors as merely an "advance"—Honda returned to Nanjing in the following year and made another reporting trip there in 1984. His lengthy interviews with Chinese victims of the Massacre in Nanjing and the surrounding towns are incorporated into the present book. Their accuracy is unquestionable.

The controversy over his writings has gone on in Japan to the present day. Right-wing nationalists have continued to attack his version of the atrocities in China, Meanwhile government spokesmen and an angry press in Korea and China denounced the clumsy efforts of various Japanese officials to diminish the extent and severity of the Nanjing atrocities. Within Japan Honda received support from numbers of liberal scholars and journalists, whose revisionist attacks on the Nanjing cover-up of past years have increased in number and intensity. Japan's right-wing nationalists may be noisy, but they are very much in the minority.

Over the past few years middle and high school textbooks have been issued that convey to students a correct, if underplayed, statement of the wholesale killing that went on. In the summer of 1998 the magazine *Sekai* ran a three-part series detailing the admissions of atrocities by senior Japanese military commanders under interrogation at war crimes trials in the People's Republic of China. Japanese government apologies for the atrocities perpetrated in China—including the Massacre—have been made on several occasions, but they tend to be guarded and perfunctory. More disgraceful, however, has been official refusal, until very recently, to acknowledge that the wholesale drafting of unsuspecting teenage girls in China, Korea, and elsewhere to serve as "comfort women"—actually prostitutes—for the soldiery was official Japanese Army policy. It was left for a Japanese scholar, Yoshimi Yoshiaki, working on his own, to track down the paper trail of proof.

In 1997, as previously mentioned, a young Chinese-American author named Iris Chang published an account of the Massacre, *The Rape of Nanking,* which became a best-seller in the United States. In so doing she performed a great service. The wide readership of the book ensured that Nanjing would no longer remain, as her subtitle noted, a "forgotten holocaust." An emotionally charged indictment of the Imperial Army's brutality, shocking in its details of rapes and murders, the book contained a comprehensive witness to the massacre not only by Chinese survivors, but by foreign residents in Nanjing.

Chang's research uncovered the diary of a heroic German businessman, John Rabe, who saved probably thousands of Chinese lives. With a few American and European foreign residents (including some heroic doctors), Rabe established an International Safety Zone, which provided a kind of sanctuary for Chinese fleeing rape, torture, or killing by bands of unrestrained Japanese soldiers. Rabe's story is a fascinating one. Newly translated and annotated in English, it has been published in America as *The Good Man of Nanking* (Knopf, 1998.) Although a Nazi Party member, living far enough from Germany, he and others fought successfully to keep the sex- and loot-obsessed Japanese troops out of this area. They and their Chinese charges owed their safety to the Japanese military's reluctance to antagonize Westerners at that time. (The Bataan Death March and the horrors of the Thai/Burma railway were five years in the future.)

Unfortunately, Chang's book is badly and needlessly flawed—badly enough to enable Japanese right-wing critics to dismiss it as biased and untrustworthy. She hopelessly exaggerates an "atmosphere of intimidation" in Japan, which prevents scholars from researching details of the Massacre. (Sample comment: "I was told in Nanking that the People's Republic of China rarely permits scholars to journey to Japan, for fear of jeopardizing their physical safety.") On the contrary, as pointed out above, the sober books, articles, and editorial comment discussing (and denouncing) the Massacre far outweigh the views of traditionalist diehards still trying to defend it. Rabe's diary itself is a good example. Published in Japan by Kodansha, the country's largest publisher, as *Nankin no Shinjitsu* (The Truth about Nanjing), it quickly became a best seller. There remains in Japan a purposeful historical amnesia about the war and the "China Incident," but in recent years, past wartime atrocities have been much discussed. In fact, most of the exposé writing on them has been done by Japanese historians and journalists.

Serious reviewers of Chang's book—Joshua Fogel in the *Journal of Asian Studies* for one—have justly criticized her simplistic character analyses of "the Japanese," in terms redolent of Michael Crichton's unconsciously racist images in *Rising Sun*. Japanese history she reduces to an absurd emperor-to-shogun-to-*bushido*-to-conformity-to-atrocity syndrome, her facts muddled and her principal reference work, apparently, the faded daguerreotypes of Ruth Benedict's arm's-length sociology in *The Chrysanthemum and the Sword*. She mentions "official denials of wartime atrocities by the Government. . . ;" (there have been apologies, but no denials), and baldly states that "screeners at the Education Ministry" ordered all numerical references to Chinese killed in the Massacre "eliminated." (On the contrary, most middle school textbooks in current use give the figures as 150,000 to 300,000 killed.) A military police general is grandly described as "chief of the Japanese secret police for Emperor Hirohito"! Facts about the Japanese military's people and activities—bad as they were—are seriously distorted. The Lieutenant Colonel Cho quoted at the beginning of this Introduction is referred to, amazingly, as Taisa Isamo! (*Taisa* is the Japanese word for "colonel" and *Isamo* an incorrect spelling of Cho's first name.) The story of his forging a mass execution order for Prince (Lieutenant General) Asaka is unsubstantiated, although according to some later Japanese accounts he did worse, sabering Japanese soldiers reluctant to shoot the Chinese prisoners. Bad as these men were, anyone writing about their deeds should get the facts straight. Questions have also been raised, it must be added, about the time and place of some of the atrocity photographs used.

Worst of all is Chang's cavalier treatment of the numbers of those raped and killed. The sources of her figures, which range from 260,000 to 350,000, are presented in a slapdash fashion; no attempt is made to evaluate them, or produce a considered estimate. This looseness has allowed Japanese right-wing apologists—including, unfortunately, Ambassador to the United States Saito Kunihiko—to cast aspersions on the totality of the work. Writers in the right-wing magazines *Bungei Shunju* and *Shokun* had a veritable field day playing a self-serving numbers game with Chang's figures.

A veteran reporter, Honda in contrast is very careful with his facts and precise in his source materials about both the Japanese military and their Chinese victims. As for the actual numbers of the Massacre's victims, they keep fluctuating. Hata Ikuhiko, a respected Japanese military historian, has come up with a figure of 40,000 based on his study of Imperial Army unit histories of that time, in his book *Nanking Jiken* (Chuo Koron-sha, 1986) which I have read, while the researches of the Kaikosha, an organization of retired Japanese officers, set the figure at 32,000 in a 1989 study. Other Japanese writers have given far larger estimates, ranging up to 300,000. When I talked with Honda in Tokyo in 1997, I asked him for his latest appraisal. "*Ju su man,*" he said. That is, something a bit over 100,000, but not approaching 200,000.

The correct number of victims will never be known. Records are confusing, with many destroyed, and human recollection, at a distance of years, is hard to quantify. The important thing about the Massacre is that it occurred. All responsible writers on the subject, Japanese and foreign, agree that tens of thousands of innocent people were killed, in the most reprehensible of circumstances. The rapes and tortures of Chinese women, if uncountable, were no less appalling in their random viciousness. A pervasive fact which keeps running through all the available testimony about the Massacre—that of Chinese survivors, foreign witnesses, Japanese Army unit reports, and soldiers who later owned up to their own complicity—was the difficulty the troops had in killing so many people at one time. It was, by any account, indiscriminate mass murder, made all the worse by the torments and tortures inflicted on the victims.

One would think that the government of China would have continuously investigated the matter and made the strongest kind of representations to Tokyo. But the Communist Party leadership, from Mao Zedong down to Jiang Zemin, has used the facts of Nanjing rather fitfully—never letting recrimination or disclosure interfere with its Japanese policy of the day. At some points in the past, Beijing even put a damper on local commemorations of the Massacre. One cannot help thinking that an organization with so much blood on its hands—going back well beyond the Tiananmen Massacre to the millions starved, tortured, and killed in the famines and the ideological persecutions (Anti-Rightist campaign, Great Leap Forward, Great Cultural Revolution, etc.) of Mao Zedong's long governance—is not overly eager to discuss other people's massacres.

The question remains: Why did they do what they did? Looking back through the shifting historical fog of six decades, the Massacre seems to us an incomprehensible relic of a distant, because different, past. This behavior of their grandfathers is as puzzling to the new Japanese generation as it is to anybody. They know only little about it and that they would like to forget–far more remote from them, it would seem, than *their* elders' random violence against Vietnamese or Korean civilians may seem to today's American college students or, for that matter, than the killings and beatings, of the innocent by their Red Guard uncles and aunts may seem to young Chinese computer experts. Yet the whys and hows of the Massacre still cry out for answers. Some are obvious, others less so.

Most obviously, the atrocities on the road to Nanjing were the work of soldiers who were ordered to live off the land. They had brought with them lots of ammunition, but few supplies. Thus looting was condoned, even encouraged in the China Area Army. When units arrived in Nanjing or smaller places, they would split up into small groups, searching for what food and housing they could find. Like most invading armies anywhere, they were also looking for liquor and women. Living under wretched conditions, unleashed to charge under fire in punishing landings and attacks, they were literally out for blood. They were angered by unexpected losses from Chinese regulars. Eager for vengeance, they were urged on by their officers, not restrained.

In strictly military terms, the divisions entering Nanjing were in a difficult situation. There was no preparation for the hordes of Chinese soldiers who had surrendered and expected to be treated decently. As one unit reported, "The prisoner stockades are full. There is no food for them. And they keep coming. There are too many of them to shoot. . . . "[1]

If the army stopped to incarcerate the prisoners, offensive momentum would be lost. If the prisoners were released, they might rejoin Chiang's army. Staff officer Cho put it this way, according to his biographer: "In the hell of the battlefield it is a virtue for a man to become a beast. In a dog-eat-dog war between poor countries, manners, morals, decency and humanitarian concerns lose their importance. . . . Pillage leads to violence and rape comes with that. . . . "

Well aware of the violence developing, General Matsui had issued orders that the prisoners were not to be killed. He told his officers this in no uncertain terms. He gave the same order directly to Cho, an Army intelligence officer. But his orders were not obeyed by Cho or others. Ill at the time and at his headquarters away from the immediate action, Matsui was in no position to enforce them personally.

Throughout the militarist thirties, most aggressive moves of the Imperial Army in China and Manchuria had been provoked by its middle management—fire-eating colonels like Isamu Cho, with the High Command generally backing their initiatives, after the fact. The behavior of regimental and divisional commanders in the Nanjing area bore out the syndrome called *gekokujo*—literally, "the top deferring to the bottom," which had become characteristic. Moreover, geopoliticians among the staff officers—and there were more than a few—were well aware that the High Command in Tokyo believed heavy Chinese losses would force Chiang Kai-shek's government to sue for peace, thus relieving Japan of an increasingly expensive war. What better way than mass slaughter to frighten the foe!

Although a few officers like Matsui hoped to have a workable truce (after they won) and ultimately a constructive peace with China (albeit under Japanese control), the soldiers and officers of Japan's China Army looked on Chinese with contempt. They thought them a mass of inferior people, to be handled as they wished. China was theirs for the picking. After all, this was the Emperor's Army, the troops who couldn't lose, shooting their way into

---

1. The quotation, as well as the references to Cho Isamu, was taken from *Goutan no Hito* ("Tough Guy"), an oddly admiring biography of this officer by Abe Makio (Shotensha, 1997).

Japan's new tributary. There is nothing so bad as racist imperialists with a sense of mission.

Other colonial powers had behaved similarly in China—British, French, Germans, and Russians. Nor was the American record all that much better by contrast—as Filipinos, Koreans, and Vietnamese could later testify. What made the Japanese far worse was the peculiar identity and practices of the Japanese armed forces.

While the young reformers who achieved the 1868 Meiji Restoration–the startling and to this day unique self-modernization of Japan–acted in concert, they ultimately shook down into two groups. On the one hand were the makers of cultural revolution, the sponsors of what they hoped would be the Asian Enlightenment. They included intellectuals like Fukuzawa Yukichi and Nakae Chomin and politicals like Okubo Toshimichi, Itagaki Taisuke and Japan's Constitution maker, Ito Hirobumi. Although they differed widely on many things, they all worked to establish a Japanese nation-state with a representative government structured on the European model. They wanted some strong traditional ballast to strengthen it. They found this in the Imperial institution.

To destroy the legitimacy of the old Tokugawa shoguns, Ito and his fellow reformers had needed a stronger, unassailable symbol of national authority. Building on the researches of scholars into the country's historic origins, they revived and revised the Imperial cult. They took the teenage emperor Mutsuhito out of his ornamental closet in Kyoto, dusted him off, put him in a resplendent Western-style military uniform and established him in the new capital, Tokyo, as the centerpiece of the new era named after him—Meiji, which means "illustrious rule." Practical men, they wrote the emperor into their new Constitution as sign and seal of its legitimacy—something even better, perhaps, than the mixtures of Christianity and kingship that they admired on their European fact-finding tours.

The other group was the soldiers. Military men among the reformers liked the imperial idea, but wanted it developed even further. They were equally receptive to modern technology, but their objectives centered on building a strong military, able to work its will on its neighbors through a mixture of power and idealized tradition. Saigo Takamori and Yamagata Aritomo were generals first and modern statists second. Borrowing from the samurai tradition, they set out to build the new Emperor's Army, protective of the state but independent of it.

For many years both sides—civilian and military—worked well in harness. Japan won its early modern wars, beating first China, then Russia, to become a first-rate military power. At the same time the country was evolving into a constitutional monarchy, with democratic elections, a capitalist economy and the rule of law. By the 1920s Japan could call itself a democracy. But beneath the surface a new generation of militarists, growing strong on national conscription, was fashioning the structure of a garrison state. These militarists profited hugely from the one great flaw of Meiji reform: the armed forces came to report directly to the Emperor, subject to civilian budget cutting but essentially independent of all political authority.

A modern officer class grew up to lead the new conscript army and navy. Unlike the feudal clan levies of the Shogunate, officer candidates need not be samurai. By 1930, in fact, barely 15 percent of those passing the military academy's entrance examinations were of samurai stock. Their education, however, was dominated by the classic ideals of traditional *Bushido*— "the way of the samurai warrior"—but revived in a modern reinterpretation, drained of whatever fairness or chivalry the old *Bushido* possessed. Loyalty and personal sacrifice were stressed, but the loyalty was defined as total loyalty, not to the country but to the Emperor, as the embodiment of Japan. Drilled inside a closed world of more than Spartan austerity and steeped in the writings of hare-brained supernationalists like Kita Ikki, the young officers passed on their indoctrination to their conscript troops, most of whom had simple country backgrounds.

By tradition and into the present day, Japanese society sets a premium on single-minded loyalty to one's superior—along with the corresponding obligation of the superior to his charges. "Sincerity" even today remains a highly prized virtue. (In modern Japanese corporations, it is often advanced as a reason for promoting a dull but company-loyal incompetent.) In the old Imperial Army "sincerity" could cover up almost any shortcoming. Loyalty was the great virtue. Obedience was enforced by a brutal system of slaps, beatings and severe punishments. Captains would hit lieutenants, and lieutenants would slap sergeants for slight infractions of discipline. The noncommissioned officers of Japan's army—a notably rough bunch—pummeled the lower ranks without mercy. Essentially, it was a gang of uniformed bullies. Every man could take out his rage and frustration on the rank below him. Even the lowly second class private could beat up on helpless "comfort women," prisoners, or, in the occupied areas, Chinese.

In my first book, *Five Gentlemen of Japan* (Farrar Straus, 1953) I noted that "Japanese ethics are founded on the social contract, not the abstract value. . . . The system of contracts and commitments threads its way like a giant steel web through every segment of Japanese society." I have never found it necessary to retract this description. In many ways it is as valid today as it was then. Nonetheless, as Japan grew into an industrialized country, with political parties, businesses, unions, and near-democratic institutions, the old web ties gradually relaxed. The "Taisho democracy" of the 1920s was real. The right to vote was continually expanded—although not yet to women. The press was reasonably free and often critical of authority. The courts prescribed the rule of law.

In the army, however, things were different. The young officers found the modern world outside their garrisons unruly, irreverent, and disgustingly rich. Most of them from poor or lower-middle-class families, they railed against the post–World War I depressions and financial scandals as the fault of foreigners, politicians, and rich capitalists. Their web was all too tightly woven. Their loyalty to the Emperor was virtually a religion. It became obsessive, as they plotted a new "restoration"—led by a docile Emperor under military control—that would restore harmony, redistribute the wealth, and gain new colonial conquests for their country.

It was the young officers' cliques, so called, that provoked first the occupation of Manchuria, then the China Incident of 1931. Their superiors generally supported them, behind the scenes. Top-ranking generals and young captains and majors—Nanjing staff officer Cho conspicuous among them—bonded in the *Sakurakai* (Cherry Society) or similar secret societies, pledged to overthrow the civilian government. True to an old tradition, the generals were content to let the young men do their dirty work for them.

The Japanese governments of the twenties and early thirties were largely internationalist and antiexpansionist. Against them the militarists now planned a series of assassinations and attempted *coups d'état*. Prime Minister Hamaguchi was killed in 1931, and in the next year a group of young Army and Navy assassins killed Prime Minister Inukai and other political leaders. In 1936 came the infamous February 26 coup, when rebellious officers led soldiers of several Tokyo regiments in an effort to take over the government. In the process Finance Minister Takahashi Korehiko and several others were killed, Prime Minster Okada barely escaping with his life.

Emperor Hirohito, in one of his few decisive acts during a long reign, ordered the mutiny suppressed—despite the foot-dragging actions of generals sympathetic to the rebels. Loyal Army forces ultimately surrounded the mutineers, and the young officer ringleaders were summarily executed.

Despite its suppression, the February 26 mutiny effectively signaled the end of civilian rule in Japan. After that, few politicians had the courage to disagree with the military. The full-scale invasion of China followed in the next year. It was by no means unpopular. Big business was pleased with the opportunity to develop Manchuria and the occupied areas of China. (The alternative could be unpleasant, as the 1932 assassination of Baron Dan Takuma, the head of the Mitsui companies, suggested.) National pride and the promise of prosperity seemed to go hand in hand. The news of continual victories stirred a revival of patriotism. Songs like *Aikoku koshinkyoku* ("The Patriotic March") became popular hits, and crowds of cheering citizens saw their newly conscripted sons off on the trains.

Emperor Hirohito, carefully uniformed and astride his white horse *Shirayuki,* took the cheers of troops marshaled on the Imperial Palace plaza. Schoolchildren's textbooks celebrated the joys of soldiering under the Rising Sun flag. Trade unions and political parties alike were subsumed into the all-embracing Imperial Rule Assistance Association. Prominent intellectuals wrote approvingly of Japan's mission. Some became correspondents with the troops and recorded each new victory (while any mention of atrocities was carefully censored out).

Dissenting voices were almost unheard. Communists, along with many Socialists and union leaders, had been jailed by an increasingly obvious police power. Press criticism became muted, particularly after rightist goon squads had savaged the offices of *Asahi.* The amazing thing about the militarization of Japan was that it happened so fast and so completely. There was no "underground" nor any real popular opposition on which to base one. The Meiji reformers, for all their democratic ideas, had encouraged the build-up of a strong military. *Fukoku kyohei*—"Rich country, strong army"—had been one of their most popular slogans. Japanese were proud of their soldiers. For years the strong army had behaved and by and large kept to its barracks. (The navy high command, less insular than the soldiers, had been a force for moderation.) By the mid-thirties, however, the mixed sounds of children's *Banzais* at school, patriotic songs on the radio, and the gunfire of uniformed assassins told the world that General Yamagata's Frankenstein monster had finally escaped from the castle.

It was against this background that Japanese troops landed in Hangzhou Bay for the march on Nanjing. Their morale was high. With the arrogance of a conquering army, they were out to teach the Chinese a lesson. They were all too eager to loot and pillage. After all, these Chinese were the emperor's enemies. And the women—they were theirs for the taking!

A word should be said here about the position of women in 1930s Japan, and the attitudes of men toward them. In the ancient Heian society women played strong roles. Court ladies like the famed Murasaki Shikibu (author of *The Tale of Genji*) wrote sophisticated poetry and prose, and indeed were courted by their men. At least one empress reigned alone. For centuries, women of humbler estate had their voice in the rough democracy of the toiling village. But the civil wars of the middle ages were hard on family life and unprotected girls. The samurai cult of *Bushido* had no place for women, except as hostages or spoils of war. And the neo-Confucianism which the Tokugawa shoguns adopted as Japan's ideology treated women as total subordinates. Although some of the Meiji reformers–Fukuzawa Yukichi among them–wanted women educated and treated as equals, the Meiji legal system, when it was adopted, merely codified existing practices. Women could not own property, nor could a wife initiate a divorce, while her husband could do so with a mere written statement.

In the countryside, where most of the China Army soldiers came from, the position of women was abjectly low. Female babies were often smothered at birth and in hard times it was by no means unusual for hard-pressed peasant families to sell a daughter into prostitution. In the urbanizing Taisho democracy the *moga*—the abbreviated term for "modern girl"—was slowly improving her status, as educational opportunities widened and international contacts increased. But to most of the men in Japan's peasant army, women were chattels, to be used at a man's convenience. This was especially true of Chinese women—who, according to many of their officers, were a subrace.

Once looting was allowed, rape was sure to follow. And it did. One could expect it from a field army whose men were regularly released to take their pleasure, by platoons, in fenced-off enclosures with the unfortunate Korean "comfort women" attached to their units. The gang rape was treated as a kind of sport. Many years after the Massacre, going through captured stores on Peliliu and Okinawa, I found a quantity of the condoms regularly issued by the army to its soldiers. On the wrapping of each was a picture of a Japanese soldier charging with the bayonet. The caption below read simply *Totsugeki*—"Charge!" That little piece of paper told a lot about the Rape of Nanjing.

There were sensitive men in this army, who hated the rapes and murders and, on occasion, spoke out against them. But most kept silent. In the Imperial Army dissenting opinions were not encouraged. But gradually, over the postwar years the cumulative testimony of wartime soldiers and their families offered further confirmation of what had been done.

In *Sensō*, the book of Japanese wartime reminiscences previously cited, the most shocking testimony came from a middle-aged Japanese housewife. Staying overnight in an improvised dormitory in 1945, not long after the war ended, she overheard the conversation of some recently discharged soldiers, drinking.

"It was unbearable to listen to them," she wrote, "They laughed coarsely about the many Chinese women they had raped, and one told about seeing how far into a woman's body his arm would go. . . . "

"I tried to rush out of the room, tearing at the mosquito netting. In a panic, my mother grabbed me and told me to stay quiet, because who knows what might happen. . . . And still the men went on and on, telling stories about their experiences. . . . "

"'Where was that?'" [one asked].

"'Nanking. We had the most fun in Nanking. We could do anything we wanted. . . .'"

"I remembered joining in the parade to celebrate the fall of Nanking, waving a handmade flag. I had used things we needed dearly to fill comfort bags for our soldiers. I had made talismans and thousand-stitch belts. I had written letters every day to thank and encourage our soldiers. Now I couldn't bear it. . . ."

Let me add to this a final and personal note. I served for almost two years in the Pacific area as an intelligence officer interrogating Japanese prisoners of war, and for a year thereafter in the U.S. Occupation of Japan.[2] I got to know many of them and in some cases continued our acquaintanceship for long after the war. Although a few POWs were at first defiant, full of *Nippon seishin*— "Japanese spirit," as we translated it—the effects of their military indoctrination wore off with varying degrees of speed. The more thoughtful among them regarded themselves as people released from a huge but tight compression chamber. Many of them had recently come from China with their units and told us in detail of their experiences there. But no one ever talked about Nanjing.

Now the extensive researches of Honda Katsuichi and other journalists and historians in Japan—as well as former soldiers and their relatives—have resulted in this tragic episode of Asian history finally and comprehensively revealed. Wartime atrocities were by no means restricted to Japanese. All of us, Americans conspicuously included, share their guilt. It is our fervent hope, however, as the author states in his preface, that telling this story, as it happened, can lift what remains of the veil of silence unwisely put over this by self-proclaimed Japanese spokesmen.

---

2. In the course of my work on Okinawa, I gathered considerable information about the past history of Cho Isamu, who served there as a lieutenant general, chief of staff of the Japanese 32d Army. Near the close of the fighting there, Cho committed suicide, along with his commanding general, Ushijima Mitsuru, slitting his own belly in the time-honored samurai ritual suicide of *seppuku*. At least he was consistent. It was there that I learned from POWs something of Cho's activities as a staff lieutenant colonel at Nanjing. My own later researches confirmed his key role in the Massacre.

TRANSLATOR'S NOTE

All Asian names are given family name first. Thus Liu Meiling is a member of the Liu family with the given name of Meiling. Similarly, the author of this book, Honda Katsuichi, is a member of the Honda family.

As a rule, I have transcribed Chinese proper names in the *pinyin* romanization. The exceptions are three proper names that are so familiar to Western readers in their older or nonstandard transcriptions that to write them any other way would merely cause confusion. These exceptions are Yangtze (instead of Changjiang). Chiang Kai-shek (instead of Jiang Jieshi), and Hong Kong (instead of Xianggang).

Occasionally, Honda quotes his interviewees in the original Chinese. In such cases, I have given the *pinyin* transcription and a translation of each Chinese quotation.

At times, Honda's writing style produces transitions that would strike an English-speaking reader as being non sequiturs. I have, therefore, taken the liberty of rearranging certain sentences and paragraphs to create a narrative flow more in line with what Western readers expect. Otherwise, I have translated everything except for one page and a few footnotes in which Honda explains his preferences for certain options in Japanese orthography or usage. I have also augmented a few sentences and added a few extra footnotes to explain certain background material that would probably be obvious to a Japanese reader, but not to a Western reader.

I would like to extend my thanks to the Pacific Basin Institute for arranging for the publication of this book by M.E. Sharpe, to Jane Kurokawa for acting as *nakōdo* (go-between) in these dealings, and to my many translator colleagues on the Honyaku Internet mailing list, who unselfishly searched their brains and their reference materials for the answers to my linguistic and historical questions.

AUTHOR'S PREFACE TO THE U.S. EDITION

Japan and China had already fought the Sino-Japanese War in 1894-95, but in 1931, Japan invaded China's northeastern regions in the "Manchurian Incident" (referred to as the "9—18 Incident" in China) and launched into a full-scale war with the Marco Polo Bridge Incident (called the "7—7 Incident" in China) in July 1937. The phrase "Nanjing Massacre" describes the atrocities that occurred after the initiation of all-out war from the first Japanese advances to the time of the occupation of Nanjing, a three-month period of atrocities that included massacres, arson, rape, looting, and indiscriminate bombing.

Japan invaded China and Korea on the noble-sounding pretexts of reacting against the incursions and colonialism of the Western powers in Asia and of liberating the colonies, but in fact, it was merely joining the Western attack on Asia. This invasion eventually turned into a direct assault on the Western powers, and the December 7, 1941, attack on Pearl Harbor served as a declaration of war on the United States and Britain. Along with Nazi Germany's aggression in Europe, this attack set off World War II.

In Europe, World War II was a clearly delineated struggle between fascism and antifascism, but the fact that the war in Asia took place in the colonies and semicolonies that had been invaded by the West adds a complication to the picture of a struggle against fascism. Although this is not the place to elaborate upon the topic, my view of the situation could probably be summarized as "Japan invaded the Asian countries, but it was as part of a struggle with the Western powers for supremacy in their colonies and semi-colonies."

At the time of the Nanjing Massacre, which took place between November 1937 and February of the next year, I was still a child of four or five, so of course I didn't know anything about it, and I don't bear any responsibility; but due to the censorship that prevailed during that period, Japanese adults were never told about it either. Yet Japan and Germany behaved differently after the end of the war. In Germany, events at Auschwitz and other war crimes were revealed by the German people themselves. They have expressed remorse for these acts and described them in detail in their school textbooks. In contrast, the Japanese people were not told about such incidents as the Nanjing Massacre for decades after the war. Although a small part of the story was revealed at the Tokyo War Crimes Trials, many people regarded these proceedings as nothing but a "kangaroo court set up by the victors," and they were not widely reported in the mass media. We could almost say that there were no investigations of these incidents at all by the Japanese, if it were not for such exceptions as the archival research of Professor Hora Tomio.

Given these circumstances, my 1971 book of reportage, *Chugoku no tabi* (Journey to China), in which I traced the path of the Japanese Army through China, caused a nationwide uproar when it was published in *Asahi Shimbun,* Japan's most influential daily newspaper. One chapter described the Nanjing Massacre in raw, vivid detail. As a result, I was targeted by Japan's extreme right-wing forces and received a number of threats, which prompted me to move out of my home and keep my address and telephone number secret, a policy that I have continued to this day. *Bungei shunjū* and other magazines put out by conservative publishers have continued their attacks on me for more than twenty years, and I have not only fought back but also taken three more trips to China for research focusing on the Nanjing Massacre. This book is a compilation of the material I gathered on these visits.

One may ask why someone who was a small child at the time of the Nanjing Massacre is so caught up in investigating it. My motivation is the experiences I had while covering the Vietnam War. When I was in Vietnam, I not only followed the U.S. forces and reported from their front lines any number of times but also reported from the other side, going behind the National Liberation Front lines and into North Vietnam. All this gave me an in-depth experience of the true face of the war. I therefore witnessed the cruelty of the U.S. forces to the common people of Vietnam, and it raised questions in my mind. I began to wonder how the Japanese Army had acted during World War II.

This was my motive for starting to investigate the truth about the Japanese army's behavior in China. Thus I wrote this book not as a means of apologizing to China but as a means of revealing the truth to the Japanese people. Having been a child at the time, I bear no responsibility for the actual massacre, but as a Japanese journalist, I bear some responsibility for leaving the story unreported for such a long time. Expressing remorse to China is the task of the Japanese government. It is not just that Japanese history textbooks have failed to take up the question of the Nanjing Massacre. Passages written by a group of scholars in an attempt to include the incident in the textbooks were actually deleted by the Textbook Certification Committee, and this led to years of legal wrangling between the Japanese government and one of the authors, Professor Ienaga Saburo. Even though Professor Ienaga was largely vindicated, it still cannot be said that the Japanese government completely lost the case.

The publication of the U.S. edition is meant to do more than simply inform the American people about the Nanjing Massacre. It is an unfortunate fact that, throughout Japan's history, it has never been possible for the people to alter the nation's power structure on their own: all the important transformations have come about through *gaiatsu,* or "outside pressure." Even the sketchy descriptions of the Nanjing Massacre in Japanese textbooks came about through external pressure from China and the government's grudging acknowledgment, not from the kind of heartfelt remorse that was seen in Germany. Thus I hope that the mere fact of my reportage being widely read overseas will serve as *gaiatsu* and will bring about a change in the disgraceful anti-internationalist behavior of the Japanese government and the conservative forces. In this sense, I could even be considered an ardent Japanese patriot, even though the extreme right-wing forces may intensify their attacks on me.

H.K.
November 5, 1998
The 61st anniversary of the Japanese landing at Hangzhou Bay

The NANJING MASSACRE

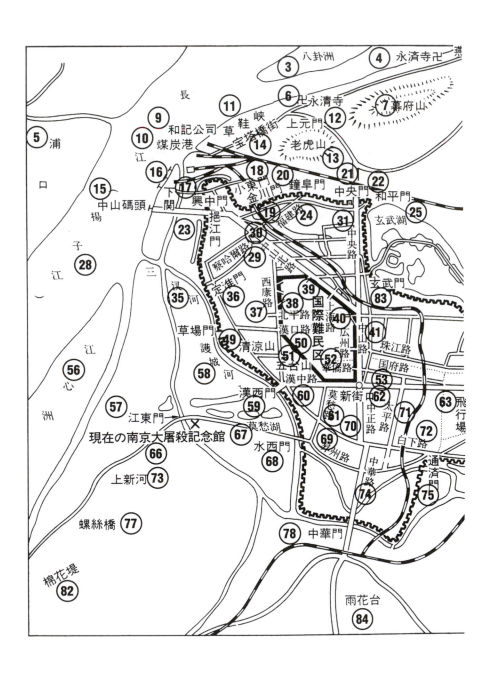

Nanjing City and surrounding area.

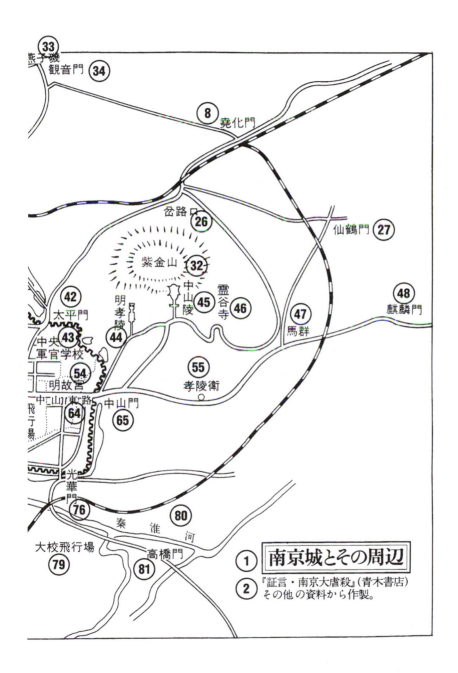

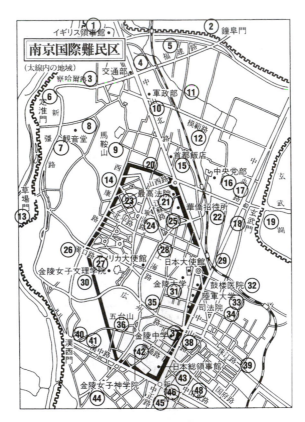

The Nanjing International Refugee Zone (within the bold lines). *Created from materials in the United States Library of Congress (provided by Kasahara Tokushi and from maps in* Testimony: The Nanjing Massacre *(Aoki Shoten)*

1. British consulte
2. Zhongfu Gate
3. Chahe'er Road
4. Ministry of Communications
5. Fujian Road
6. Dinghuai Gate
7. Xinjiang Road
8. Guanyingtang
9. Ma'anshan
10. North Zhongshan Road
11. Department of Military Affairs
12. Mofan Road
13. Caochang Gate
14. Xikang Road
15. Capital Hotel
16. Central Party Headquarters
17. Zhongyang Road
18. Xuanwu Gate
19. Xuanwu Lake
20. Shanxi Road
21. Supreme Court
22. Overseas Chinese Reception Center
23. Beiping Road
24. Ninghai Road
25. Jiangsu Road
26. Hankou Road
27. American Embassy
28. Shanghai Road
29. Japanese Embassy
30. Jinling Women's Literary Institute
31. Jinling University
32. Drum Tower Hospital
33. Infantry College
34. Court of Justice
35. Guangzhou Road
36. Wutaishan
37. Jinling Middle School
38. Zhongshan Road
39. Zhujiang Road
40. Hanxi Gate
41. Hanzhong Road
42. Huaqiao Road
43. Japnaese Consulate General
44. Jinling Women's Theological Institute
45. Zhongzheng Road
46. Xinjiekou
47. East Zhongshan Road
48. Guofu Road

CHAPTER 1

"ONE MILLION JAPANESE TROOPS LAND NORTH OF HANGZHOU BAY"

The evening edition of *Yomiuri Shimbun*, giving further reports of the landing at Hangzhou Bay. An article about the balloons advertising the "million person landing" can also be seen.

Before dawn on November 5, 1937, Japan's 10th Army, made up of the 6th (Kumamoto) Division, the 18th (Kurume) Division, and the 114th (Utsunomiya) Division, landed under opposing fire on one arm of Hangzhou Bay near Jinshanwei. A secret operation carried out under the escort of approximately 100 ships of the Japanese Navy's Fourth Fleet, it was the beginning of a large-scale invasion that would culminate more than thirty days later in the fall of Nanjing, then China's capital.

The five divisions of the Shanghai Expeditionary Force (the 3d Division from Nagoya, the 11th Division from Zentsūji, the 9th Division from Kanazawa, the 13th Division from Sendai, and the 101st Division from To-

The evening edition of the *Tōkyō Nichinichi Shimbun* (predecessor of the *Mainichi Shimbun*), announcing the landing at Hangzhou Bay.

kyo), which had been facing strong resistance from the Nationalist Chinese Army of Chiang Kai-shek, shifted their efforts to moving toward Nanjing, chasing the retreating Nationalist forces ahead of them. Later, they were joined by the 16th Division from Kyoto. The China Theater Headquarters was established under the command of General Matsui Iwane in order to direct the 10th Army and the Shanghai Expeditionary Force.

The *Asahi Shimbun* covered the landing at Hangzhou Bay as follows:

[Official announcement from the War Office, noon, November 6] Part of our army, with close and appropriate cooperation from our navy, executed a difficult landing under enemy fire on the north side of Hangzhou Bay before dawn on the 5th. The landing was a great success.

[Official announcement from the Navy Department, noon, November 6] At the behest of the Commander-in-Chief of the China Fleet, part of our forces under the direction of the Commander-in-Chief of the –th [*sic*] Fleet, escorted the troop transport ships under utmost secrecy and entered Hangzhou Bay before first light on the 5th. Riding on rough seas and fighting the thick fog that assailed them, they did their utmost to cover the military party's landing, successfully achieving the expected objectives.

[Special telegram from Shanghai, November 6] Announcement from the Military Information Office, noon, November 6: Before dawn on the 5th, a fairly large military party under close and appropriate cooperation from the navy, made a decisive landing under enemy fire in a district on the north side of Hangzhou Bay, successfully surprising and crushing the enemy in the vicinity. They are currently making great military gains.

(Evening edition of November 7, 1937; published on the 6th[1])

Although the Japan-China War had actually begun with the Marco Polo Bridge Incident (called the 7/7 Incident in China) on July 7, 1937, and con-

From a special extra issue of *Asahi Graph*: "Our fleet presses on splendidly toward Hangzhou Bay."

---

1. At that time, the evening editions of newspapers carried the following day's date.

1. China
2. Nanjing
3. Taihu Lake
4. Changjiang
   (Yangtze River)
5. Shanghai
6. Jinshanwei
7. Hangzhou Bay
8. East China
   Sea

tinued with the second Shanghai Incident, the offensive against Nanjing was a turning point. With these victories, the Japanese military lost its ability to turn back and eventually found itself caught up in a quagmire. Even if we take the long view, following Japan's trail through China for half a century from the Sino-Japanese War through World War II and then to defeat, the Nanjing offensive was a major milestone.

It is widely known that after the landing at Hangzhou Bay, balloons were launched in Shanghai and elsewhere proclaiming, "One million Japanese troops land north of Hangzhou." There may well have been one million troops, but the balloons were largely a strategy designed to crush the morale of the Nationalist troops offering resistance in the vicinity. Here is a dispatch from a special correspondent in Shanghai, which appeared in the evening edition of the *Yomiuri Shimbun* on November 8, 1937:

> At noon on the 6th, a large advertising balloon unfolded and floated high in the skies over the north bank of the Suzhou River, and at the same time a great war cry suddenly arose from our troops. Look! Can you not clearly read what is written on the balloon floating lazily in the low rain clouds south of the Yangtze River? "One million Japanese troops land north of Hangzhou Bay."

The Nanjing offensive was a massive event, both in its scale and in its historical significance, so quite a few newspaper reporters and novelists followed the troops. In addition to their records, announcements, and reports, a number of memoirs from the officers and enlisted men themselves remain. Even though they operated under the limits of both military censorship and self-censorship, the works of such writers as Ishikawa Tatsuzō and Hino Ashihei also contain things that deserve reexamination. Hino participated in the Hangzhou Bay landing as a noncommissioned officer, and he published an account of his experiences under the title of *Earth and Soldiers*.

Either of Hino's heartfelt memoirs, *Earth and Soldiers* or *Barley and Soldiers*, probably could have been used as an antiwar tract, but the author did not intend them that way. Rather, they are filled from beginning to end with deep affection for the fellow soldiers who suffered with him. In it, for example, he describes what happened when his unit captured a pillbox. (Excerpted from the edition published by Shinchō Bunko.)

From a special extra edition of *Asahi Graph* reporting on the Japanese military landing at Hangzhou Bay. This is the landing of the rear guard units following the landing of the advance units on November 5.

The Chinese soldiers piled out of the pillbox. All of them looked very much like Japanese people. They seemed to have been hit by a hand grenade, and they appeared one after another: one gasping for breath, one with his face scorched black, one with his chin blown away, one with his left cheek in shreds. They bowed obsequiously, their hands together, with expressions that seemed to plea for help. . . . We thought there weren't any more of them, but then I heard voices moaning loudly in the darkness. Straining my eyes, I saw some dark people squirming on the dirt floor of the middle room. I moved closer, my pistol at hand. . . . However, they weren't moaning; they were crying. I got down on the floor and touched those two soldiers who were making such a pitiful noise. "*Lai, lai,*" I said. "Come, come." They finally stood up. The faces that came into view out of the darkness by the light that seeped in through the gunsight were so young and beautiful that I was startled. Both of them were about the same age, almost boys, and so beautiful that they could have been mistaken for girls. Their faces were streaked with tears, and they leaned on my shoulders. They began to say something, but of course, I didn't understand them. One of them took a notebook out of his pocket and showed me a photograph, which I assumed was a picture of his mother. I could easily imagine what they were saying, and I thought they must be brothers. I briefly considered leaving the two of them behind when we withdrew. However, with the two of them leaning on either shoulder, I led them out front. They urgently put their hands to their necks, as if begging me not to kill them. I nodded my agreement. I thought I saw a touch of joy pass across the dejected faces of these young soldiers. . . . When I returned to the village where the main battalion was already camped, there were prisoners lined up in a row. Private Yoshida came up to me. "Sir," he said, "chow is ready." I went into the house, and then to a creek out back to wash my face and hands. I seemed to have injured one ear a bit. My first rice in a long time tasted wonderful, as you can imagine.

Yet, when this work was published, the following lines were deleted by the censor, although, of course, they have been restored in the currently published version. They describe the massacre of the prisoners:

I became drowsy as soon as I lay down, and I slept for a while. I woke up on account of the cold and stepped outside. There was no sign of the prisoners who had previously been tied together with electrical wire. When I asked a nearby soldier what had happened to them, he said, "We killed them all."

I saw that the bodies of the Chinese soldiers had been thrown into a trench. The trench was narrow, so they lay on top of one another, some of them half submerged in muddy water. Had they really killed thirty-six people? I was at once sad, furious, and nauseated. I was about to turn away in my dejection when I noticed something strange: the bodies were moving. I looked closely and saw a blood-streaked, half-dead Chinese soldier moving around among the bottom layer of corpses. Perhaps he had heard my footsteps; in any case, he laboriously pulled himself up with every bit of strength and looked straight at me. His agonized expression horrified me. With a pleading look, he pointed first at me and then at his own chest. There wasn't the least doubt in my mind that he wanted me to kill him, so I didn't hesitate. I set my sight on the dying Chinese soldier and pulled the trigger. He stopped moving. Platoon leader Yamazaki came running. "Why did you waste a shot like that when we're surrounded by the enemy?" he said. I wanted to ask, "Why did you do such a horrible thing?" but I couldn't say it. I left with a heavy heart.

That the above account is fact, not fiction, was substantiated by the literary critic Kobayashi Hideo, who was in China as a special correspondent for the magazine *Bungei Shunjū* and wrote about the incident as follows, after hearing of it directly from Hino. The "x's" in the text are evidently parts deleted by the censors.

This is what happened. Hino led seven soldiers who, using the dead angle of the machine gun to approach the largest pillbox, scrambled up, and tossed seven hand grenades through the ventilation pipes. Then they went around to

From a special extra edition of *Asahi Graph* reporting on the landing at Hangzhou Bay. The caption of this photograph reads, "November 9: The Imperial Army passes through Jinshanwei as it presses urgently onward."

the back, broke down the doors, and jumped in. They cut down four men and tied up thirty-two regular troops with xxx. Hino said, " I just couldn't kill those guys once we had them tied up, but with the situation being what it was, well, I didn't know about it, but when I went out at night, there were xxxxxxxx in the trench. Among them there was a guy pointing to his chest and begging me to kill him, and I felt sorry for him, so I xxxxx him.

Despite the discrepancy of "thirty-six people" versus "thirty-two people," there is no doubt that this is the same incident.

Thus massacres occurred directly after the landing at Hangzhou Bay, but due to censorship, the Japanese people knew nothing about them. The acts of violence, mass murder, rape, and arson that Japanese officers and enlisted men perpetrated against ordinary civilians were expunged from the newspaper reports and literary works, and of course, the Chinese point of view was completely absent.

In November 1983, a full forty-six years later, I visited the spot on Hangzhou Bay where the Japanese troops had landed. From there, I followed the main path of the Japanese troops in the Chinese theater, gathering material and conducting interviews all the way from Hangzhou Bay and Shanghai to Nanjing.

This project was something I had first thought of ten years before, soon after

The landing point at Jinshanwei today. The embankment on the right did not exist at that time.

publishing my first account of China, *Journey to China*. However, due partly to the international situation, I was unable to realize this idea. One of the reasons I finally carried out my plan was the textbook controversy of 1982: the Japanese Ministry of Education authorized textbooks which, among other things, reinterpreted the invasion of China as an "advance." China, Korea, and the other countries of Asia reacted with rage, causing an international incident. Even so, this project is not something I did for China, but something I did for Japan.

The Japanese have been accused of lacking international consciousness, but contrary to popular belief, this is not simply a problem of language. Rather, the core of our problem is that we are an "unrepentant tribe."

By the time of the textbook controversy, both East and West Germany had gone to great lengths to deal with their legacy of war crimes from the World War II era, investigating the atrocities without regard for any statute of limitations, and reexamining their own roles. Italy had done the same. On the other hand, in the 1950s, Japan shamelessly chose a prime minister suspected of being a class A war criminal.[2] This is why I felt that my project was truly needed.

My motivations remained unchanged throughout those ten years. I adhered to my original idea of timing the trip for November and December, the

---

2. This was Prime Minister Kishi Nobusuke, who assumed the post in 1957.

Looking out from the landing point across the shoals to the open sea at low tide.

same season in which the events actually occurred.

My journey from Hangzhou Bay to Nanjing was an attempt to collect that missing half of the story after forty-six years and to ask survivors of the period about their experiences. The passage of forty-six years meant that even people who were boys and girls of ten then would be fifty-six, and people who were thirty years old then would be seventy-six, so the number of living witnesses was steadily declining. A young interpreter, Wang Zhaoxiang, of the International Liaison Office of the All-China Journalists' Association (similar to the Japan Newspaper Publishers' and Editors' Association) accompanied me from Beijing, but in this part of China, there were a lot of elderly people who did not understand the standard language, so in every region we benefited from the cooperation of local interpreters.

From Shanghai to Jinshanwei on Hangzhou Bay is about two hours by car. The first thing that surprised me, coming to China twelve years after *Journey to China*, was that political propaganda and slogans had disappeared from the streets. My previous visit had occurred at the end of the Cultural Revolution, just before the Lin Piao incident, and I felt then as if I had been ejected from a time capsule and into another era. The most noticeable change in the villages on my second visit was that the peasants' houses had become more substantial. I was told that the enthusiasm for rebuilding and expanding houses had begun a few years before and was still continuing. Everywhere we went we saw trucks and oxcarts hauling bricks. The agricultural

Memorial tablet commemorating the Japanese army's landing near the landing point along the shores of Hangzhou Bay outside Jinshanwei.

production system based on people's communes had already been disbanded in fact, if not in theory, and beginning in April of the next year (1984), the administrative units would revert to the old designation of *xiang* "township."

Part of the old Ming dynasty city wall remains in Jinshanwei. Originally, it was three *li* (about 1.5 km) square and two *zhang* two *chi* (about 6.6 meters) high. It was built of earth in the nineteenth year of Hongwu (1386) and faced with brick on the outside. Its purpose was to ward off raids by Japanese pirates. The vice-chairman of the commune told me that a provincial official, Fang Mingqian, had directed the local people in constructing the wall at their request after they had suffered at the hands of the pirates. Since only the imperial residence was allowed to have a square wall, Fang Mingqian incurred the Ming emperor's wrath and was sentenced to death. The people built a great mausoleum in memory of his virtue. However, this mausoleum was burned along with several other buildings during the Taiping Rebellion and later rebuilt. Part of it was again destroyed during the Japanese invasion, and later, it was completely burned during the Cultural Revolution as a symbol of "superstition."

We drove for several minutes along the seaside embankment and came to a T-shaped intersection, where a stone tablet commemorating the Japanese invasion had been set up. It was titled "Class Education Tablet," and it told how before dawn on the third day of the tenth month (according to the old peasant calendar[3]) of 1937, the Japanese militarists had invaded here and pursued the "three all" policy of burn all, kill all, loot all. In addition to the specific data, there was the statement, "The Japanese people also suffered during that war." It ended with, "We must keep this firmly in mind, so that we never allow such an invasion again."

The occasional truck or cultivator passed by the stone tablet, but in general, it was a peaceful rural scene. As I made my way through the tall grasses to the shore, I could see the island of Dajinshan far off in the open sea. Until the Yuan dynasty, the island was a peninsula connected to the mainland, and the sea there was shallow. At the time of the Japanese invasion, this stretch was a mud and sand beach, but now it is a concrete embankment. According to an excerpt from *Earth and Soldiers*, the Japanese landing took place as follows:

> Suddenly our boat stopped as if it had hit something. We had touched bottom. Looking around us, we saw a whole group of ships up on the shoals, and here we were in the middle of the sea. "Jump in," our platoon leader ordered. We jumped into the water. We were soaked up to our knees, and our feet got stuck in some sort of slime. The water was so cold that it seemed to pierce our kneecaps. Soldiers from all the boats were standing in the water. Some of the men from the accompanying vessels landed in up to their waists. Someone even fell over into the water. As far as the eye could see, there was nothing but the surface of the water, nothing that looked like land. Then I noticed the thick fog. As we walked about fifty meters, the water grew shallower and disappeared, replaced by a muddy beach. It was frequently difficult to walk. We were all wearing the traditional split-toed work boots instead of army boots, but our feet got stuck in the slime, and we couldn't pull them out. . . . It was already broad daylight, and the fog hadn't completely lifted, but suddenly an embankment stretching off to the side with trees and pylons appeared before our eyes as if out of nowhere. All at once something came whizzing past my ear with a whine. I threw myself down into the mud. . . . We attached bayonets to our rifles. The embankment appeared to be about 700 meters away. We began a fierce advance. I was in the leftmost flank of the front line, and I shouted to the soldiers to keep as far apart as possible. The bullets came at us in a constant hail, but we couldn't see any sign of the enemy soldiers. . . . Finally, we made it to the embankment. We intended to switch to hand-to-hand combat at that point, but we found no enemy there.
>
> The area was full of salterns and dry fields. Trenches had been dug all over the embankment, and beyond them were machine gun nests. These were secure positions, but the enemy seemed to have abandoned them and fled in the face of our attack. A goat and two or three chickens emerged from the two huts that were there. The chickens ignored us completely as they pecked for food. Private First Class Takahashi suddenly took off after them, caught a chicken, and brought it back. He wrung its neck and began plucking it with practiced hands.

---

3. The old lunar peasant calendar is in common use among the Chinese people even now. I quote whichever calendar a particular source happens to use.

"We've got something to go with our rice tonight," he laughed.

According to "The China Incident Army Campaign," the eighth volume of the *War History Library* put out by the War History Office of the Defense Agency's Defense Research Institute (Chōun Shimbunsha, 1975), the Hangzhou Bay landing took place at three locations.

> Dawn on the fifth. The army made a surprise landing: the 6th Division (augmented by the Kunisaki Detachment) in the area at the west side of the city of Jinshanwei, the main force of the 8th Division in the area at the east side of the city of Jinshanwei, the left detachment (the 35th Infantry Brigade under the command of Major General Tezuka Seizō) [with the exception of the 114th Regiment] and the Field Artillery 12th Regiment, a nucleus of the Third Battalion) at an area at the left of the 6th Division. Eliminating enemy resistance, they advanced northward together over difficult terrain along the Huangpu River. That is, the 6th Division and the Kunisaki Detachment captured the city of Jinshanwei

Looking across the moat to the former site of the main gate of Jinshanwei (approximately where the tree in the middle of the background now stands). A part of the old city wall still stands behind the house directly ahead.

after the landing, and the main force advanced northward on the 8th to an area on the left bank of the Huangpu River southwest of Songjiang. The 8th Division advanced to the vicinity of Lianglinzhen on the sixth, and the left detachment to the east of Fengjingzhen on the eighth.

Now here is an account of these events from the Chinese side, as told by the vice-chairman of the Jinshanwei Commune, Mr. He Fuming:

On the third day of the tenth month of 1937, according to the old peasant calendar, the invading army of the Japanese imperialists came into Hangzhou Bay off Jinshanwei and landed on the beach under the cover of bombardment from their warships. They poured into Jinshanwei from three directions: Jinshanzuizhen, Qijiadun, and from Baisha Bay. The Nationalist army was within the old earthen embankment, and the ordinary people were living inside and outside the city walls, but when they heard artillery and guns fire, most of them fled. The people who waited too long to flee, however,

Chen Fuxing

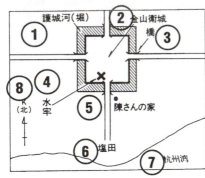

1. Moat
2. Town of Jinshanwei
3. Bridge
4. Water dungeon
5. Chen's home
6. Salt field
7. Hangzhou Bay
8. North

were raped and massacred by the Japanese forces. In particular, the people who lived near the city gates were bayoneted or else tied up inside their houses and burned to death. Within three days, 80 to 90 percent of the houses, amounting to 3,059 rooms,[4] were destroyed by fire. The number of people massacred was 1,015.

One of the survivors is Chen Fuxing (55), who became an orphan when his entire family was killed. Chen, who was nine years old at the time according to the traditional way of counting ages,[5] told me of his experiences:

At that time, Chen Fuxing's house was about thirty meters outside the gate of Jinshanwei (see map). It faced a road leading out of the city after crossing the protective moat surrounding the city wall. There were about twenty members of the extended family living in the eighteen rooms of the two adjoining houses, including the Chen household of nine people. Among them were Chen's father (age 29) and younger sister (3); his mother had died of illness about a year before. The family made its living by farming but also worked in the salt fields from time to time.

On November 3, two days before the Japanese landing, young Chen went to the home of his mother's family 3 kilometers outside the city in order to attend the funeral of his mother's older brother. Since the Japanese invasion

---

4. Most of the peasant houses in this area are built so that the main room faces onto the street and any other rooms are constructed straight back in a row, like railroad cars. The houses are separated from neighboring buildings by brick walls.

5. Most ages are quoted in the traditional East Asian system, called *kazoedoshi* in Japan, by which children are considered to be a year old when they are born and gain a year every New Year. Ages according to the traditional system are therefore one or two years older than under the Western system. The current ages given for the interviewees are their ages at the time of the interview.

occurred while he was at his grandparents' home, he stayed on for a while.

Seeing the black smoke rising in the skies over the burning town of Jinshanwei, Chen's youngest uncle suggested that it might be a good idea to go back and check on his family. Accordingly, about a week later, when things had quieted down a bit, Chen set out for home alone. He remembers that the sky that day was full of gloomy clouds.

As he approached the town, he saw corpses scattered everywhere alongside the road and in the river, as well as the remains of pigs and cattle. There were spots on the road where blood had coagulated and dried. Looking out to sea, he saw Japanese warships forming a solid line off the coast.

It was about two o'clock in the af-ternoon when he arrived at his house.

The former location of the water dungeon.

It had been almost completely burned, with just one blackened wall remaining. Since the rice bin had also burned, there was scorched rice scattered around. However, there was no sign of his family. Breathless with worry, he ran around looking for them. The city moat was near his house, and there was a pond built off it for bathing water buffalo. Bodies were piled up in this pond, and a little dirt had been thrown over them. As Chen ran toward it, he saw a man whose face and feet were sticking out of the dirt: it was his father. Chen gave a loud, forlorn cry, dug his father's body out of the dirt, and tried to pull it away, but it was too heavy. Overwhelmed by the situation, he cried bitterly but kept searching further, until he found the body of his father's youngest brother under a fallen shapeng *tree. He had been run through with a bayonet four times. Chen stayed there crying for about two more hours, but no family members or acquaintances showed up.*

It was during that time that he was found by some Japanese soldiers in the vicinity and taken prisoner. Near the gate was a water-filled dungeon that had been built by the Nationalists. It was a deep pit about one and a half meters wide and about three and a half meters long filled with water, and it functioned more as a torture chamber than as an ordinary jail: people placed there did not last very long. The Japanese soldiers threw Chen into the pit,

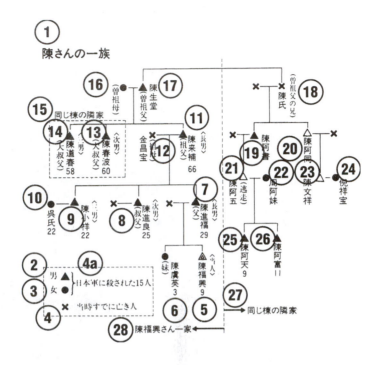

1. The Chen clan
2. Males
3. Females
4. People who were already dead at the time of the invasion
4a. The fifteen people killed by the Japanese
5. Chen Fuxing (witness), 9
6. Chen Yuying (younger sister), 3
7. Chen Jinfu (father), 29
8. Chen Jinliang (uncle), 25
9. Chen Xiaoxiang, 22
10. Wu Shi, 22
11. Chen Laibu (grandfather), 66
12. Jin Changbao (grandmother)
13. Chen Chunbo (great-uncle)
14. Chen Daochun (great-uncle)
15. People living in the adjoining house
16. Great-grandmother
17. Chen Shengtang (great-grandfather)
18. Chen Shi (elder brother of Chen Fuxing's great-grandfather)
19. Chen Ashu
20. Chen Atong
21. Chen Awu (fled)
22. Zhou Amei
23. Chen Wenxiang
24. Ni Xiangbao
25. Chen Atian
26. Chen Afu

where seven men were already confined. Since he was so small, the water came up to his chin, even when he was standing. He stood there for about seven hours, wedged among the other men, and gradually began to lose consciousness.

In the middle of the night, perhaps about one in the morning, two Japanese soldiers came to check on the water pit. They must have thought that Chen, who was practically unconscious, was dead, because they pulled him out of the pit, took him to a vacant lot about eighty meters away, and left him there.

The boy soon regained consciousness, and a bit of strength returned, so he went through the ruined town wall and fled toward the home of his mother's family. On the way, he encountered an elderly neighbor woman, a distant relative, who knew what had happened to his family. The Japanese army had entered the town from the west. Setting up machine guns on the south gate, the one facing the ocean, they had begun firing indiscriminately outward from the town. Almost all of Chen's family, living on the other side of the moat from the guns, was killed at this time, and the cattle and horses were also shot. However, his father's youngest brother and his three-year-old sister were still alive after this. The Japanese soldiers soon appeared with their bayonets ready and stabbed not only the uncle but also the little sister in the belly. The uncle was stabbed four times, but the sister died after one blow. The family tree of the fifteen people killed, both the eight people from Chen's immediate family and the seven people from the adjoining house, is shown opposite.

Ten days later, after the main Japanese forces had left and only a small guard unit remained, relatives claimed the bodies that were piled up in the pond. Chen lived with his mother's relatives until he was eleven, helping with the farm work. Then he was hired out as a farmhand, tending cattle until at the age of thirteen, he was adopted by a peasant family. Up until the end of the war, he was often commandeered as a coolie or forced into other labor under the control of the Japanese army or the turncoat government of Wang Jingwei.[6]

I was surprised at how many women I met in the course of my journey who had been raped by Japanese soldiers. Yet it was rare for the victims to talk of these humiliating experiences in any detail, even though they had happened in the distant past. This kind of reticence is not something unique to Chinese women, but the fact that I was a man and had also come from the same country as the Japanese soldiers made it all the more difficult for them to talk. Therefore, most of them spoke through commune officials and other third parties.

The seventy-two-year-old woman whose story I am about to tell had related to me her experiences of maltreatment at the hands of the Japanese soldiers forty-six years before, all except for the most important part of the account, the actual rape, which she told to the vice-chairman of the commune. He told it to me later. The woman did not ask me to conceal her real name, but I will use a pseudonym here:

---

6. Also known as Wang Zhaoming. He was originally part of Chiang Kai-shek's inner circle, but he went over to the Japanese side and helped establish a puppet government in Nanjing. He died of natural causes in Japan.

At the time of the Japanese landing, Liu Meiling was twenty-six years old. She and her husband, also twenty-six, had three children, the oldest of whom was a six-year-old boy, and her mother also lived with them in a house outside the walls of Jinshanwei.

It was two days after the landing, the afternoon of November 7, when three Japanese soldiers showed up at her house. The six family members hid in the cookhouse, in a space between the stove and the wall where firewood was kept. But the soldiers soon found them and the husband was immediately taken outside and shot. Then, a Japanese soldier knocked Liu Meiling over with his gun stock as she held onto her eight-month-old child. She bled from the ear and lost consciousness.

She was bedridden on account of her injuries for three years after that. Her mother begged in order to provide her with food.

Just before the end of the war, her oldest son, about fourteen or fifteen years old by that time, was commandeered to haul wood. She said that they were assigned to tear down a portion of Fang Mingqian's mausoleum for firewood. While he was working, some wood fell on him, and he was killed.

The preceding is what Liu Meiling told me directly. However, while I was listening to another survivor's story, she sat in a corner of the room, wiping tears from her eyes as she spoke to the vice-chairman of the commune. After she had left, the vice-chairman came to me and said: "This is what Liu Meiling told me to tell you. After being struck with the gun stock, she was raped, with the three Japanese soldiers taking turns. And that wasn't all: she was confined in her house, and just about every day, three or four Japanese soldiers at a time came and raped her, so she doesn't even know how many soldiers humiliated her day after day."

As the main force of the Japanese army proceeded northward after the landing, most of the inhabitants of the villages they passed through had already fled, but since the local people had no way of knowing how troop movements might change in response to conditions, there were quite a few people who were unable to flee in time. In Shanyang commune,[7] north of the coastal landing spot, a total of 351 inhabitants were killed, 1,146 buildings were burned (4,269 rooms = 829 houses), 470 pigs and 849 cows burned to death or stolen, and 120 women raped. Since an unknown number of the women were killed after being raped, they are included among the number killed.

These figures are based on a survey of the inhabitants of Shanyang com-

---

7. One of the so-called people's communes. Two years later, the people's communes were abolished and renamed "townships," a unit that corresponds to the town or village level.

mune. If you think about conditions in Japan's cities during the war, you can clearly see that in large cities such as Shanghai or Nanjing, it would be difficult to confirm the number of victims in all the confusion; indeed, it would be next to impossible. However, in villages and small towns, the inhabitants know one another well, and even long after the fact, they would know who had been killed. China is currently in the process of compiling local histories for every region, and the compilers are assiduously gathering figures about the victims of the Japanese army. As I understand it, one of the motivations for this effort is the 1982 textbook controversy.

Taking a further look at the numbers, we find that 137 of the 351 people killed in Shanyang were over the age of sixty, 21 of them were children of ten or less, and the remaining 193 were between the ages of eleven and fifty-nine. Of the 2,048 people who were drafted for coolie labor, 72 were never heard from again. Thirty-nine people were imprisoned. At the time, the total population of the commune was about 15,000. Nine hundred fifty-seven water-powered mills were burned. A total of 5,925 *mu* (1 *mu* = 6.67 ares) of rice ready for harvest was burned in the fields, and 57,400 *jin* (about 35 metric tons) of rice ready for husking was piled up and burned. An undetermined amount of cotton bolls and 2,335 piles of firewood were burned.

In Tingnan, one of the eight seaside villages that make up this commune, all 166 houses were burned. In Nijia, 123 of 130 houses were burned, and 49 people were killed. This includes twelve families that were completely wiped out.

Here are some actual examples:

Pei Yinbao was a woman living in Yangjia village. Her son Qi Zugen was bayoneted, and her three-year-old grandchild's head was split down the middle, after which Pei's breasts were cut off and she was then stabbed. Her son's wife survived only because she happened to be at her parents' house, so three out of four family members were killed.

In Jianguo village, Li Quanbao was shot to death as she stepped outside carrying her seven-month-old daughter, and she fell into a rice paddy. The baby was found sucking at her mother's breast. She was brought up by her older sister and is still alive.

Qi Jinyu, a peasant from Xiangyang village, hid in his house along with six people who had fled from neighboring houses, but Japanese soldiers found them and bayoneted them all. Five died instantly, but two survived with serious injuries.

Three men from Xiangyang, Zhu Jiahe, Shen Yougen, and Cheng Amei, hid in a rice paddy, but they were found and taken to the home of Hu Asi. The Japanese soldiers stripped them naked, cut off their arms and legs, hung them from a loom, and set the house on fire, burning it to the ground.

The elderly peasant Liu Dongsheng lived alone with his wife in Meiyuan village. Japanese soldiers showed up, stabbed Liu to death, and set the house on fire. His wife hid and avoided discovery, but after losing her husband and her house, she went mad and committed suicide by throwing herself into the river.

CHAPTER 2

"MORE OF OUR TROOPS LAND AT SHANGHAI"

The evening edition of the *Asahi Shimbun* reporting the landing at Shanghai.

As I mentioned before, the Nanjing offensive was initiated by the 10th Army that landed at Hangzhou Bay, and the Shanghai Expeditionary Force that had been fighting in Shanghai. I would like to relate some of the things I heard from survivors of the Shanghai campaign, that happened at approximately the same time as the Hangzhou Bay landing. But first, for the benefit of the generations that regard World War II as "something that happened long before they were born," I would like to review the events that led up to the Japanese army's landing at Shanghai.

After choosing imperialism and militarism as its paths to modernization after the Meiji Restoration, Japan developed in such a way that the fundamentals of its economic policies could be summed up in the slogan, "Enrich the nation and strengthen the military." For example, in order to collect the wealth of the population and divert it into the munitions industry, the government revised the land tax system and strictly enforced tax collection in cash from the agricultural and mountain villages, and they also took what had previously been natural areas owned in common and claimed them for the imperial family and the nation. The peasants impoverished by these measures provided a source of cheap industrial labor, and so the nation was able to undergo a forced, undemocratic modernization that dramatically benefited the military.

The Sino-Japanese war of 1894–95, fought over the question of who would dominate Korea, proved to be a great victory. Although the Japanese militarists' invasions of Asia were carried out in the name of the just cause of resisting the Western powers, they actually became a struggle for dominance against those powers. The Russo-Japanese war of 1904–05 resulted in the extension of Japanese domination from Korea to Manchuria, the northeast corner of China, and from then on, Japan's grip on China grew increasingly stronger. The Manchurian Incident (1931–32; the Chinese call it the Nine-Eighteen Incident) served as a prelude to the real Japan-China war.

The first Shanghai Incident occurred in January 1932, the year after the beginning of the Manchurian Incident but before the Japanese army (the Guandong Army) had occupied all of Manchuria. It involved a clash between a Japanese naval landing force and Chinese troops. In February, the Japanese army's 9th Division and 24th Mixed Brigade (12th Division) were dispatched as reinforcements to the area of Jiangwanzhen, north of Shanghai, but they were forced into an intense battle by China's 1st Route Army. On March 1, fighting broke out in earnest with the landing of the 11th Division at Qiliaokou on the southern bank of the Yangtze River, but eventually the situation calmed down and there was a ceasefire agreement.

Once Manchuria was under Japanese control, there was no stopping the expansion of Japan's dominance over China. Japan split the five northern

The August 23 issue of *Asahi Graph* reporting on the Shanghai offensive. A warship in the Yangtze is providing protective fire to the riverbank.

provinces off from the government of the Republic and moved toward strengthening control over them. Within Japan itself, the February 26 Incident of 1936 intensified the intrusion of the military into the political process. With the signing of the Anti-Comintern Pact at the end of the year, the fascist powers of the East and West joined hands, and the country's course through world history became clear. This is the background against which the Marco Polo Bridge Incident occurred on the outskirts of Beijing on July 7, 1937, and led to an all-out war between Japan and China. In an attempt to consolidate their control over northern China at one blow, Japanese occupation forces in China received reinforcement from the Japanese Guandong Army and the Korea Army, and at the beginning of August, they occupied Tianjin and Beiping (present-day Beijing).

During the Xian Incident of the previous year, a conference between Chiang Kai-shek and Zhou Enlai had effected a reconciliation between the Nationalist Army and the Red Army. Forming the Anti-Japanese People's United Front, they suspended their civil war and stopped compromising with Japan, but before they could respond to the unfavorable truce negotiations, the second Shanghai Incident occurred. As soon as the August 13 engagement between the Japanese naval landing force and the Chinese Nationalists began, the General Staff Headquarters first dispatched the 3d Division (Nagoya) and the 11th Division (Tsūzenji) as the Shanghai Expeditionary Force, and they landed under enemy fire on the south bank of the Yangtze north of Shanghai. According to the Defense Agency's "The China Incident Army Campaign" (Part 1, p. 27), the landings took place at the following two locations:

> Just after midnight on the 23d, the 11th Division entered the anchorage off the Chuansha estuary. Around 5 o'clock, they began a forced landing in an area north of Chuanshazhen, routed the enemy along the riverbank, and in the afternoon, took indisputable control of most of the vicinity of Chuanshazhen, whereupon they prepared to attack Luodianzhen.
>
> In the staging area of the 3d Division, the covering force for the landing (the first special landing party and the nucleus of the 1st Infantry Company) boarded separate ships at Shanghai before midnight on the 22d. Destroyers preceded them and put pressure on the enemy through naval bombardment. At about 3 o'clock on the 23d, they executed a forced landing in the vicinity of the Wusong railroad wharf (about 1 km south of Wusong garrison), destroyed the enemy who were on the riverbank, and advanced along the lines of the military-built road. Thereupon the main body of the division landed in their wake and achieved one victory after another. By the end of that same day, the first line of troops had advanced from the moat (about 24 meters wide and 4 meters deep) about 1,500 meters south of the Wusong railroad wharf to the lines stretching about 500 meters south of the wharf. Afterward this line became the covering position for the main force. The numerically superior Chinese army resisted for several days, but the division was able to repel them and secure their position.

The first reports of this event appeared in the evening edition of the *Asahi Shimbun* on the 24th under the headline "More of Our Troops Land at Shanghai."

> Special telegram from Shanghai, August 23: 10:40 A.M. August 23, the xx Press Section: With close cooperation from the Navy, the Imperial Army succeeded in landing in a certain area early this morning, the 23d, and they are currently heading toward the xxx area, mopping up the enemy they find along the way.

But the fighting techniques of Chinese Central Army were different from those the Japanese army had encountered in the northern provinces. The

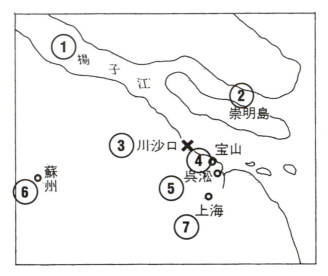

1. Yangtze River   5. Wusong
2. Chongming Island   6. Suzhou
3. Chuanshakou   7. Shanghai
4. Baoshan

Amadani Detachment, a part of the 11th Division, set out from the waters off Qingdao after the main party and landed at Wusong on September 3. A sergeant who had been summoned to join the Amadani Detachment related in a postwar memoir (Miyoshi Shōzō, Landing Under Fire at Shanghai, Tosho Shuppansha, 1979) what had happened to the 3d Division, which had landed ten days earlier:

> The sight that met my eyes when I crawled up onto the embankment at Wusong was nothing short of hellish. It was so brutal that the battlefield of the demons of Ashura couldn't have been worse. The top of the embankment was a mountain of corpses as far as the eye could see, and they lay in heaps so that you couldn't see the ground. The bodies of thousands of soldiers had fallen every which way, piled up like tuna in a marketplace. At the same time, a nauseating stench of death hit my nostrils.
> This was what had become of the officers and men of the 3d Nagoya Division. Whether or not they knew that the Chinese Central Army had been lying in wait for them here—they must have been mowed down as soon as they landed. They died without really knowing what was happening to them. . . .
> On top of that, all the bodies were swollen with putrefaction, due to the decay of the internal organs, and the soft parts of the bodies had burst through from the pressure. Even the eyeballs bulged six or seven centimeters out of their faces. Some of the bodies had become masses of maggots, and on top of these tens of thousands of squirming maggots were swarms of black flies.

When I saw all of this, I nearly passed out.

According to the postwar account of Lieutenant General Yamamuro Munetake who led the 11th Division, which landed at Chuanshakou on August 23, the same day as the 3d Division (Maru, March 1972), this landing at Wusong claimed up to 10,000 victims.

The second landing at Shanghai was on too large a scale to be called an "incident." Rather, it was a decisive battle in which nearly a million Japanese and Chinese soldiers fought desperately. Finding itself in a close contest, Japan sent in the 101st (Tokyo) Division, the 9th (Kanazawa) Division, and the 13th (Sendai) Division in quick succession between the latter part of September and the beginning of October. At the same time, the battle lines in the northern provinces expanded, but the main theater of war shifted to the Shanghai area.

In short, it was this fighting in the northern outskirts of Shanghai and along the banks of the Yangtze that led up to the Hangzhou Bay landing operation.

I took a short trip about 40 kilometers northwest of Shanghai to see the spot where the Japanese forces had landed. We drove past the Baoshan Iron Works at Yuepuzhen, where we could still see the ruins of the Nationalist army's pillboxes, before arriving at Chuanshakou, the landing point of the 11th Division. We followed a road that ran through rice paddies along an irrigation ditch to the bank of the Yangtze and ended up standing on an embankment that was built in 1956–57 and therefore had not existed during the war. On the opposite shore of the broad mouth of the Yangtze I could see Chongming Island, and I could not tell which way the cloudy gray water was flowing. A flock of ducks bobbed up and down among the waves stirred up by the cold wind.

"That's the remains of a Japanese gun battery," said Yu Fugen, assistant secretary of Baoshan County's Luojing commune, pointing to what looked like a concrete wedge poking above the surface of the water. He said that it was submerged at high tide. On the inner slope of the embankment was a commemorative tablet about 2½ meters high, larger than the one commemorating the Hangzhou Bay landing. On the back of the tablet was carved, "We will never forget." Then, under the heading "We will never forget the seas of blood and the deep enmity," there was a brief account of the August 1937 Japanese landing and the murder, arson, rape, and looting that followed. "The blood flowed together with the rivers and changed the colors of the sea," the plaque said. It told how 2,244 people in the Luojing area had been killed, beginning with the massacre of the nine members of Wen Aisheng's family, and how buildings numbering to 10,908 rooms had been burned. Under the leadership

A commemorative plaque marking the site of the Japanese landing at Chuanshakou on the northern outskirts of Shanghai.

of Mao Zedong and the Communist Party, the Chinese people had crushed Japanese militarism, but in a spirit of internationalism, they made a distinction between the Japanese militarists and the Japanese people, maintained their traditional ties of friendship, and so on. That is how it was explained on the tablet, which had been erected on August 13, 1973.

"Within an area about three kilometers wide and more than ten kilometers long, all the people's houses were burned to the ground," Yu Fugen told me. "Aside from the houses that were used for the Japanese troops to live in, they left behind only the houses used as stables or as interrogation rooms. They committed atrocities from the very beginning, killing off all the people who didn't flee in time."

Luojing commune is made up of five villages: Chenxing, Luojing, Xiaojing, Shuangcao, and Duchuan. One of the survivors of the war era, sixty-year-old Gu Qingzhen, who was in Shuangcao at the time, told me of his experiences:

When the Japanese troops invading Shuangcao occupied Hanjiazhai hamlet, they burned all the houses on one end so that they would have an unobstructed view. Gu, fourteen at the time (12, according to the Western system of counting ages), lived with his parents, who were peasants. Most of the people had already fled, and indeed, Gu's older brother had gone on ahead of the rest of the family, but the reason the other three stayed behind, sadly enough, was to protect their household goods. They were not the only impov-

The coast where the Japanese landed is once again the site of a peaceful rural village.

erished peasants who risked their lives in this way: there were many others who had painstakingly labored to acquire a house and possessions and were extremely attached to them. Of the 300 inhabitants of the hamlet, a little over thirty remained, mostly old people and children.

Gu's house was about five miles inland from the banks of the Yangtze. On the cloudy afternoon of the thirtieth day of the seventh month according to the old calendar (September 4), eight Japanese soldiers showed up and began burning down the houses in the area. The remaining villagers hid themselves in the rice paddies, which was possible because the rice plants were quite tall and only a month away from harvest.

However, as house after house burst into flames, Gu's neighbor Yin Kun, an old man in his fifties,[1] dashed forth out of the paddy field, because he could not stand to see his own house being burned. He was soon detected by the Japanese soldiers and felled with a single shot. Seeing this, his son Yin Baosheng also ran out, quickly hoisted his father over his shoulders, and carried him back into the paddy field. From where he was hiding, Gu was unable to see whether the older man was still alive or not.

Around noon, the Japanese soldiers withdrew, and Yin Baosheng carried his father back to their own house. The main building had been burned and only one room of the cookhouse remained. Eleven people from the neighbor-

---

1. When the interviewees refer to "old men" or "old women," they are referring to people over the age of fifty.

A tea shop built with scorched pillars and beams scavenged from buildings burned by the Japanese.

hood, including Gu and his parents, went to check up on the father.

But just as they were discussing what to do about their noon meal, the eight Japanese soldiers came back. Realizing that Gu and the others were there, they surrounded the building, leaving the thirteen people no chance to flee back into the rice paddies. One of the Japanese soldiers thrust his bayonet through the door. Yin Baosheng tried to keep the door closed, but the Japanese were able to push it open, and the first soldier entered. The door opened inward, and Yin Baosheng, who was standing behind it, took a cleaver and attacked the soldier. But the soldier dodged the attack and called out for the other seven. The thirteen people panicked and tried to hide in various places

When I went to see the tea shop built from the remains of burned buildings, I found three survivors of the Japanese invasion among the customers: Chan Guangbei (73, his older brother was killed), Liu Aba (72, his mother was killed), and Xu Agao (72, his grandmother was killed).

around the room, but there was really no place to hide except in the attic, under the bed, and behind the stove, where Gu, his parents, and an elderly neighbor woman hid.

When the eight Japanese soldiers charged in, Han Jintang, an elderly man who was unable to find a hiding place in time, threw himself down on the bed. He was immediately bayoneted and tumbled onto the floor. The people under the bed and in the attic were also bayoneted to death one after the other, but then Han Jintang, who was seriously injured, cried out, "Jiuming!" (Help!) The old woman hiding with Gu's family was Han's wife, and hearing his cries, she impulsively ran out from behind the stove. When the Japanese soldiers saw her, she tried to return to her hiding place, but they stabbed her in the back and she

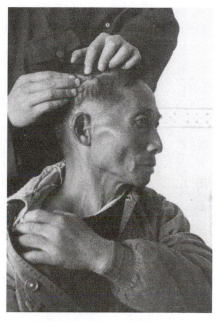

Gu Qingzhen showing where Japanese soldiers bayoneted him in the head and shoulders.

fell on top of Gu and his family. The soldiers then stabbed Gu's parents, who had thrown themselves over him. The bayonet passed through his mother's heart and also ran his father through. Only Gu's head was visible as he lay under his father, and the bayonet stabbed him in the head and also passed through his right shoulder. He lost consciousness.

(At this point in telling the story, Gu began to weep. "What did they have against those old people and children?" he asked, and for a while, he was unable to continue.)

When he regained consciousness, it was after midnight. His head, neck, and shoulders were sticky with his own blood and that of his parents, who lay on top of the lower half of his body and were already dead. The Japanese soldiers still seemed to be around; they were outside, talking in loud voices. Gu had no medicine or anything like that available, and as he waited for dawn, he rubbed ashes from the stove into his head and shoulders so that at least he could stop the bleeding. Fortunately, the bayonet had pierced him below the collarbone and missed all his vital organs, so there was not much blood loss.

As it grew light, there was no longer any sign of the Japanese soldiers. When Gu inspected the room, he saw that the other twelve people were dead.

These two photographs were provided by the Shanghai Municipal Archives and appeared in the *Liberation Daily* of August 6, 1982. They were published in connection with the international controversy generated by Japan's revision of its school history textbooks and were intended as examples of the arson, mass slaughter, rape, and looting perpetrated by soldiers of the Japanese military. The photographs were listed as belonging to the bureau of the director of the former French Concession, but the details of times and places they were taken are unknown.

Outside, too, he found that a lot of people had been killed. Bodies were scattered all around—near the river, near the grove of trees, near the fertilizer pit—and there were charred bodies inside the remains of the houses. He walked on until he met an old woman he knew from the same village, and she took him to the place where his brother had fled.

Over a month later, Gu, his brother, and other people from the village went back to the site to have a look. More than thirty bodies were all completely decomposed, and people went around weeping as they gathered up the remains of their relatives. There were no coffins available, so Gu and his brother rolled the bodies of their parents up in grass matting and buried them near the burned-out ruins of their house.

CHAPTER 3

"THE CITY OF SUZHOU HAS FINALLY FALLEN"

The *Tokyo Nichinichi Shimbun* announcing the capture of Suzhou.

With the 10th Army's landing at Hangzhou Bay, the Shanghai Expeditionary Force, which had been bogged down in a bitter struggle despite reinforcements, was able to switch to a war of pursuit, as the Chinese Nationalists weakened and began retreating. The situation at that time is described in Chinese military records as follows (from *A Brief History of the War of Resistance*, edited by the Republic of China National Defense Historical Affairs Department, 1952):

> As our main combined forces in the Wusong-Shanghai area were retreating to the lines at Qingpu and Baihe Harbor on the morning of the 9th, we were attacked by enemy planes, and before we were able to prepare ourselves fully, the enemy advancing from Songjiang quickly took Qingpu.
>
> On the 12th, the main force of our left flank retreated westward, and the right flank shifted its position to Sujia and points west. At this time, the enemy moving westward along the Nanjing-Shanghai road advanced to the southwest of Anding; at the same time, a corps of enemy that had landed at Hupu attempted to cut off our rear lines of communication. Based on previous plans, our forces withdrew to our main encampments at Zhapu, Pinghu, Jiashan, Suzhou, and Fushan (the Wufu encampments).
>
> From the 15th on, a fierce battle erupted at the Wufu encampment, and the enemy sustained a great number of casualties, but they continually added reinforcements. In order to avoid a showdown with the enemy, we had our main force fall back to the Wuxi-Jiangyin lines (Wanxi encampment), and at the same time, we shifted the 15th and 21st Combined Forces to the Anji, Xiaofeng, Ningguo, and Xuancheng areas southwest of Taihu Lake. Our relief units engaged in fierce combat everywhere from Wangliang on east.[1]

Thus on November 10, Japanese newspapers reported "the 89th day of supremacy in Shanghai since the incident," and on the 12th, Nanshi and Nanxiang were captured. On the 13th and 14th, the 16th Division (Kyoto) made a preemptive landing under fire at Baimaokou on the Yangtze. Ishikawa Tatsuzō's book *Living Soldiers*, which is based on the experiences of a military unit during those times, described the situation as follows (from the Shinchō Bunko edition)[2]:

> Before dawn the line of ships arrived at the spot where the Baimao flows into the Yangtze. Nearly 30 small battleships were lined in a row, and as the day began to dawn, they all at once opened fire in the direction of the right bank. It

---

1. This is how the passage was translated into Japanese for *The China Incident Infantry Campaign*, vol. I, published by the National Defense Agency's War Research Office.

2. Ishikawa Tatsuzō's *Living Soldiers* was published in the March 1938 issue of *Chūō Kōron*, but in a well-known censorship case, the sale of that issue was banned as soon as it appeared. The author was prosecuted in Tokyo District Court and sentenced to four months' imprisonment (suspended for three years).

The 16th Division lands at Baimaokou on the Yangtze (from a special edition of _Asahi Graph_).

was an indescribably grand manner of attacking. The riverbank was enshrouded in a sandstorm that obscured the early morning light. The enemy's attack came mostly in the form of machine gun fire, and the men could hear the bullets bouncing off the sides of the ships. In the end, a curtain of smoke arose near the shore, and in the weak morning breeze, a thick, flame-yellow smoke covered the surface of the water. . . .

All of a sudden, the enemy shore appeared 2 meters in front of their eyes, and the ship ran aground. In water up to their knees, the soldiers deployed at the edge of the riverbank, stuck grass into their helmets, and lay down. They did not come under attack. Some fighting appeared to have broken out on the right flank, but ahead of them, friendly forces had already advanced about 600 meters. . . .

There was a water buffalo tied up in a shed near a farmhouse that was a bit removed from the hamlet. The soldiers decided to take possession of it, so the interpreter looked into the house through the back door. A wrinkled old woman was quietly stoking the fire under the stove.

"Hey, Granny," the interpreter said, standing in the doorway. "We're Japanese soldiers, and we need your cow. It's too bad for you, but you're going to have to give it to us to take along. . . . We'll at least spare your life and when the war is over, we'll bring your cow back."

The cow began to walk down the dusty road. The soldiers were in a good mood. This continent had infinite riches, just there for the taking. They began to view the local people's rights of ownership and private property just as they viewed wild fruit—something to be taken at their pleasure.

On November 19, Changshu and Jiaxing were occupied. On the same

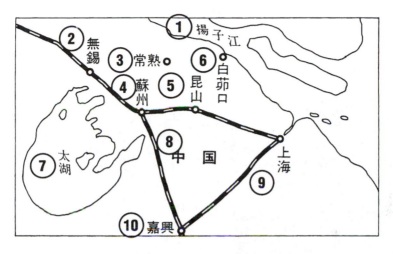

1. Yangtze River
2. Wuxi
3. Changshu
4. Suzhou
5. Kunshan
6. Baimaokou
7. Taihu Lake
8. China
9. Shanghai
10. Jiaxing

day, a separate unit charged into Suzhou, the city of canals, familiar to Japanese people as the capital of the kingdom of Wu in the Spring and Autumn period and the site of Hanshan Temple. The event was heralded in Japanese newspapers under the headline "The City of Suzhou Has Finally Fallen."

[Suzhou, the 20th, Newspaper Union] On the 18th, after occupying Sunjiabin, which had been under the control of a thousand enemy troops, the Fujii Unit began its advance at 10 o'clock that same evening, scattering the enemy before them, and before dawn on the 19th, its advance elements entered the eastern outskirts of Suzhou. Due to a long rainy spell, the clouds hung low, and the high tower of Bao'en Temple was visible only dimly in the mist. The enemy within the city included about 40,000 troops of the 15th and 53d Armies, but they were completely unable to withstand our onslaught and fled in a panic west toward Wuxi. Thus it was that the Iwazumi and Kanbara Units marched side by side into the city from the northwest in a grand fashion. The frantically fleeing stragglers within the city had lost the will to fight, and we took about 2,000 of them prisoner during mopping-up operations. The approximately 500 residents remaining in the city hoisted Rising Sun flags at every door and welcomed the arrival of the Imperial troops. Thereupon the Fujii Unit entered the city through the north gate, and staged a triumphal entry ceremony, raising three shouts of *Banzai!* Rising Sun flags fluttered over the Imperial consulate, the Bao'en temple, and every other building, and the shouts of *Banzai!* shook heaven and earth. Tears shone in the eyes of the officers and men standing in formation, and their voices trembled with excitement as they cheered. Thus

Suzhou was finally returned to the hands of our troops (evening edition of the *Asahi Shimbun*, November 21, 1937, published on November 20).

You will not find the Chinese point of view amid all this pompous press coverage. Either such articles were suppressed by the censors, or the writers exercised self-censorship, or the views of the Chinese people were absent in the first place. But here are the experiences of one peasant, Wu Shuijin (57), who was eleven years old at the time:

Wu Shuijin.

The hamlet of Meixiang in Loufeng village is in the outskirts of Suzhou on the northern side, a little clump of houses just north of the railroad linking Shanghai and Nanjing. The main road north to Changzhou runs along one side of the hamlet, and about 200 meters south of there at Yangjing Crossroad it joins with the road from Shanghai to Wuxi in a T-shaped intersection (see map on page 44).

Since there had been bombing attacks before the Japanese came, the nine members of Wu's family had fled 3 li (about 1.5 km) to an area in Lumu village called Beiduan. After a while, they started to worry about their house, so on the 18th day of the 10th month according to the old calendar (November 20), Wu's mother went ahead to check out the situation. Seeing no sign of Japanese troops in the area, she assumed that it was safe, but unfortunately, the Japanese showed up just after she had left to inform the others.

Unaware of this fact, five of the nine members of Wu's family returned to Meixiang along with two other residents of the hamlet, making a total of seven people. Besides Wu himself, there were his father and mother (both 37), his oldest brother (20), and his youngest brother (1). His oldest brother's wife, his older sisters (age 17 and 14 or 15), and his other younger brother (7) remained behind.

It was raining on and off that day. As they approached Meixiang along the main road from the north, a young man suddenly leapt over the wall that ran along the back of the houses and dashed across the field toward the riverbank, desperately looking for somewhere to hide. Two Japanese soldiers followed right behind him and shot him dead. This happened not more than 20 meters in front of Wu's party, and so of course, the Japanese saw them. Eleven-year-old Wu was terrified and begged his father, "Let's go back to Beiduan." But his father just assured him that they would be fine. After all, they had not done anything wrong, so they made no attempt to run away.

Just then the two soldiers came at them, pointing their rifles. They detained the group, searched their belongings, and then took Wu's older brother and the other two residents of Meixiang away. The remaining four members of the Wu family were taken to a house where thirty or forty other people were already locked up, all of them people who had been caught while passing by on the road. It was eight o'clock in the morning.

The people pressed their hands together in attitudes of supplication and begged the guards, "Please let us out. We aren't soldiers or anything like that." It did not do any good.

By eleven o'clock there were about sixty people in this unfurnished, 30-square-meter house, At that point, the Japanese soldiers began coming in every two or three minutes, taking one or two people at a time outside, including Wu's father. The process took over an hour. During this time, people began to hear gunshots, but they did not think it had anything to do with them. After all, this was just after the beginning of the invasion, and people couldn't imagine that ordinary civilians would be killed outright. They simply assumed that those who had been led away were being questioned and released. In fact, the gunshots they were hearing were the sounds of their fellow captives being killed, one after another.

Wu and his mother, who was holding his infant brother, were the last ones left in the room. To this day, he does not know why the three of them were saved for last. When the Japanese soldier who had been standing guard at the entrance went away for some reason, Wu's mother urged him to run away, but he was so terrified that he could not move. With her baby in her arms, his mother trotted over to the door, stepped outside, and gestured insistently for Wu to follow, all the while keeping a lookout. Their own house was on the opposite edge of the hamlet from the house where they were being held. Since there were Japanese soldiers in the hamlet itself, Wu and his mother took the long way around on the footpaths through the rice paddies.

Suddenly they spotted the body of a man in a kneeling position. It was Wu's father. They later learned that he had run away from the house where the massacre was taking place. He had been hunted down and shot to death some 300 meters from the cluster of houses.

Wu's mother nearly passed out from the shock, but it would have been dangerous to cry out, so she just urged Wu along, and they went and hid in their house. Then she broke down. She cried and cried and at times seemed close to fainting.

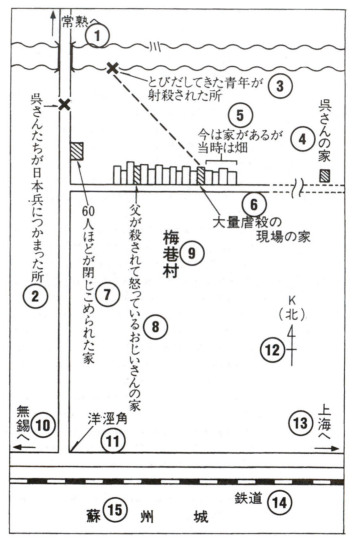

1. To Changzhou
2. Where Wu and the others were captured by the Japanese
3. Where the youth who came running out was shot
4. The Wu family home
5. Once an open field, this area is now built up
6. The house where the massacre occurred
7. The house where sixty people were imprisoned
8. The home of the angry old man whose father had been killed by the Japanese
9. Meixiang village
10. To Wuxi
11. Yangjing Crossroad
12. North
13. To Shanghai
14. Railroad
15. The city of of Suzhou

Japanese troops "crossing under enemy fire" after an engineering battalion built a temporary bridge across the Suzhou Canal. (From a special issue of *Asahi Graph*.)

By about eight in the evening the rain stopped, although it was still cloudy. The two of them retrieved the body of Wu's father with the help of two young neighbors. They dug a hole in the field behind the house, put the body into it, and covered it with door boards. This was the age-old custom of people too poor to buy a coffin.

At about three in the morning, before dawn, Wu, his mother, brother, and the two young men who had helped them, slipped away to Beiduan. It was still cloudy, but a bit of moonlight could be seen where the clouds were thin.

Wu's older brother and the two people who had been taken away with him were never heard from again. Long afterward, Wu heard from a neighbor that his older brother's headless body had been among those found when the villagers went to clean up the site of the massacre.

The place in Beiduan where the family had fled to was a stranger's house and cramped, so the seven remaining family members (Wu, his mother, his older sisters, his younger brothers, and his older brother's wife) left there to live in an old, run-down temple. Wu's mother had managed to suppress her tears during the time they were living with strangers, but around the time the family moved to the temple, she lost her mind. She no longer prepared meals and spent all her time either staring into space or crying.

About two months later, the children took their mother back home. The soldiers had left Meixiang, but they sometimes came out from Suzhou to loot,

The settlement at Meixiang village. The home of the angry old man whose father was killed by the Japanese is on the left.

so it was still dangerous. Even so, the children thought that their mother's mental state might improve if she could return to her own house. She did not recover, however, and became partially paralyzed, possibly because of some brain disorder. She died within a year. The older brother's wife remarried and left, and Wu's two older sisters were sold to other families as tongyangxi.[3] *The youngest brother, who had been an infant at the time of the massacre, died of illness at the age of six. Out of an original family of nine, only Wu and the older of his younger brothers remained.*

When I visited Meixiang, the house in which Wu and the others had been confined no longer existed, but one wall of the house where the massacre had occurred still stood about 50 meters off the main road. Most of the house had been torn down about two months previously to make way for a new two-story building.

I was told that an old house with the same layout as the "massacre house" was nearby, so I went to see it. Built in the style typical of the area, the houses in this little settlement were lined up with their front entrances facing the road and the rooms built straight back from the entrance, one after an-

---

3. *Tongyangxi* were young girls who were sold to another family with the idea that they would work as unpaid servants until they were old enough to marry one of the family's sons.

other. Each house was separated from its neighbor by a brick wall.

In another house, I was shown an old-fashioned bed. (Actually, this bed is connected with the story of another survivor, whose story is told below.) After I had taken a picture of the bed, I went out through the front door and found an elderly man of approximately seventy emphatically shouting about something. He had approached the Suzhou journalist and the hamlet official who were with me and begun addressing them in an agitated voice. I wondered what he was so angry about.

When I pressed for an explanation, the Suzhou journalist, Lang Qisheng, looked perturbed, as if he did not want to tell me what was going on, but he finally did. Upon finding out that a Japanese had come to see the massacre site, this old man had recalled the death of his own father. He could not understand my purpose in coming, and now, of all things, this *dongyang guizi* (Eastern devil)[4] was barging into his house, all the way to the bed. Did he have to put up with the Eastern devils coming here even now?

That was how I found out that there was someone else who had survived the massacre that killed Wu's father and older brother, someone who had been hit but had managed to escape danger by hiding under a bed just like this one.

Wang Mugen.

Wang Mugen (78) of the second production brigade of Lumu village in Wu County outside of Suzhou, was thirty-two years old at the time the Japanese occupied the city. Three or four days before the city fell, on the fourteenth day of the tenth month according to the old calendar (November 16), Wang was drafted along with six other peasants to serve as a coolie for the Nationalists during their retreat to Wuxi. However, he had a congenital malformation of his left knee, and the Nationalists, figuring that he would be of little use to them, let him go. He was on his way home, coming from the direction of Tiger Hill, on the western edge of the city, when he happened to pass by Yangjing Crossroad (see map). There was no sign of life in the town:

---

4. During the war, Chinese people routinely referred to the Japanese as *dongyang guizi* ("Eastern devils") or *Riben guizi* ("Japanese devils").

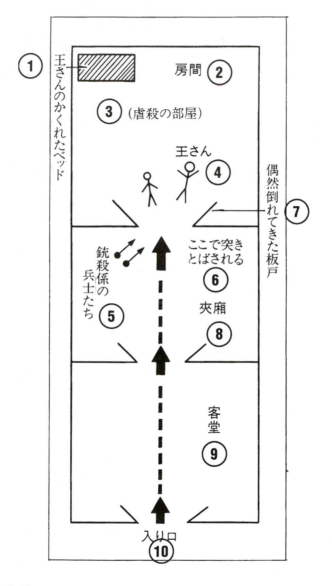

1. The room where Wang hid
2. Bedroom
3. The massacre room
4. Wang
5. The soldiers with bayonets
6. Where Wang was speared and tossed
7. The door that happened to fall on him

most of the residents seemed to have fled. By the side of the road was the body of a naked woman, her lower abdomen split open. Otherwise, he saw no one on the road.

About half a li *(250 meters) farther on, a line of about ten* Riben guizi *("Japanese devils," or soldiers) suddenly appeared, running from the opposite direction. There was no place to hide on the spur of the moment, and with his crippled leg, Wang was unable to run, so he just stood frozen with fear. The soldiers caught him and tied his hands, while one soldier made a deliberate throat-cutting gesture. They searched him and found two* yuan, *which they confiscated. Then they took him to Meixian, to a house belonging to Tao Xiaohe.*

It is thought that there were about 100 Japanese soldiers in the hamlet of Meixian. The house where Wang was taken faced the road, and three corpses lay scattered around the entrance. He was led through the parlor and into the spare room. When he came to the entrance of the innermost room, the bedroom, he and another person were shoved into it. At the same time, two shots rang out, and a bullet passed through Wang's shoulder. He fell on top of a pile of twenty or thirty corpses. The room had old, decrepit double doors, and one of them, perhaps loosened by the reverberation, fell on top of him. Wang did not know whether the person with him was dead and he did not move.

He realized that blood was steadily oozing out of the wound in his shoulder, but he bore with the pain and lay still. The Japanese soldiers brought someone else in and shot him dead also. Then, when there was a bit of a lull, Wang, his hands still tied, crept across the room and crawled under a bed that stood in one corner. The space between the bed and the floor was covered with boards, one of which was mounted as a flap so that Wang was able to push it open and crawl under. It was not actually built that way in order to allow people to hide, of course, but to facilitate cleaning. However, when Wang closed the flap, he could not be seen from the outside, particularly since the bed was in a dark corner.

Soon another victim was brought in and shot dead in the same way as the others. Wang suddenly felt the urge to cough, perhaps because of his wound, but he was able to control it by pressing his bound hands to his mouth. The round of killings continued until nightfall, with the two or three soldiers at the door shooting people as they were being shoved into the room.

As darkness deepened, the room grew quiet. Wang's shoulder wound had stopped bleeding. He quietly and tentatively crawled out from under the bed, his movement hampered by the pile of bodies. A lamp was lit in the next room, its flickering light creating a horrific effect as it reflected off the bloody faces and hands of the corpses. There did not appear to be any Japanese

The entry into Suzhou, November 19. (From the December 15 issue of *Asahi Graph*.)

soldiers inside the house, but Wang could sense that they were outside, so he crawled back under the bed.

There were more mass killings the next day. On the third day, the Japanese had some Chinese forced laborers move out the bodies. By evening, the Japanese appeared to have left, so Wang finally emerged from under the bed.

On the way back to his home village, about one li *(500 meters) from Meixian, he saw more bodies here and there along the road. He did not see another living person, and there was an especially large pile of bodies at the foot of the bridge.*

When Wang arrived home, he treated his shoulder wound by smearing it with lard. Only his sixty-year-old mother was in the house. The other four members of his family, including his wife, his daughter, his widowed brother, and his brother's son, had fled to another village about 5 kilometers to the northeast.

Several days later, the Meixian residents who had family members and relatives among the massacred victims gathered to look for the bodies. They soon found them, along with the remains of the Chinese forced laborers. Wang also returned to the site and heard the villagers' stories.

There had been eight forced laborers with the Japanese soldiers, of whom two were later shot to death and six were taken away to be used for other work. (When asked why those two laborers were killed, Wang said, "Just on a whim. I don't know.") The eight laborers had been made to dig a hole about 4 meters wide, 6 meters long, and 1 meter deep, with a meter-high earth border piled up around it, so the depth from the top of the border to the bottom of the hole was a little over 2 meters. The bodies of the massacred victims were taken there and buried. No one knows exactly how many there were, but people think the number was somewhere between 100 and 200.

The people who dug up the bodies duly took care of their family members and relatives, but there were also a few dozen victims whose identities were unknown. They had either been brought in from elsewhere or had simply been unlucky enough to be passing through at the time. They were reburied in what the villagers called the "hundred person pit."

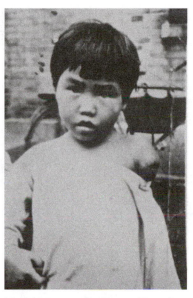

Liu Lulan as a five-year-old orphan who had lost her left arm.

During the occupation of Suzhou, there were places that the Japanese army was unable to enter at will, namely, the church-related hospitals managed by third-country nationals, such as the Americans. (These hospitals are now known as the Suzhou Number One Hospital and the Buoxi Clinic.)

In one of these hospitals was an orphan girl who had lost her left arm during the Japanese attack that killed her parents. One day, while this six-year-old girl (five years old according to the Western system) was in the hospital, a young Chinese man took

Liu Lulan today.

her picture. She grew up not knowing what had become of the photograph, and eventually, she became a teacher at an elementary school in Suzhou.

In the summer of 1982, when the controversy over the Japanese school history textbooks became a cause célèbre, the Shanghai newspaper *Liberation Daily* ran a variety of special features on the Japanese imperialist invasion. An article appearing in the August 6, 1982, issue contained a photograph of a *xiao guniang*—a little girl—who had lost her left arm at the shoulder. The girl's name was not mentioned, but Liu Lulan, a fifty-two-year-old teacher at the Fengqiao Village Central Elementary School, was startled to recognize herself when she read the article.

The young man who had taken the picture was at the time associated with the movement called "Youth Working to Resist Japan and Save the Nation." He had visited the hospital in order to capture on film the truth about the brutal, indiscriminate attack, and he had hoped to go to America and make an appeal to the world. His name was Liu Liangmo, and the article revealed that he was currently the vice-chairman of the Shanghai City Political Consultative Conference.

Liu Liangmo had submitted the photograph of the little girl with the missing left arm to the *Liberation Daily*, but he had no way of knowing whether she was still alive. But Liu Lulan then looked him up in Shanghai, resulting in an emotional reunion after forty-four years, and he gave her a copy of the old photograph as a memento to take home. This reunion was just one of the ripple effects of the textbook controversy, and because of it, I was able to hear more of Liu Lulan's story:

At the time of the invasion, Liu Lulan's parents were twenty-five or twenty-six years old. They earned their living as street vendors in the city of Suzhou, and she was their only child.

One day in August, after the Second Shanghai Incident, Liu Lulan was playing with a neighbor's child in a street a little more than 10 meters from her house, when suddenly the warning sirens sounded. At almost the same instant, a bomber formation appeared in the sky overhead, heralding the first bombing of Suzhou. Since it was the first attack, the little girl had no idea what the siren meant, but soon the bombs began to fall. A nearby hit turned a section of the narrow street into a scene of confusion: the earth trembling, people falling, rising clouds of dust, and deafening noise. She stood watching these horrific sights until a few seconds later, when another bomb fell and she lost consciousness.

Liu soon came to, but she did not truly understand what had happened. It was only after she had taken two or three steps that she realized that her left arm had been shattered below the elbow. Her arm hung limply out of her sleeve, seemingly held there only by skin. When she tried to lift up her blood-ied left arm with her right hand, the pain was so unbearable that she fainted again.

When she once again awoke, she was in a hospital bed in the Buoxi Clinic. The Red Cross had brought her there, and the doctors had removed most of her damaged arm, so that it now ended just below the shoulder joint. Or-phaned, she never saw her parents again, and their bodies were never found. ("They were taken from me so suddenly," she wept, as she recalled those days.)

All the people in the beds around her had been injured in the bomb attack. Nearby was a woman who was the mother of a girl and two boys, and she had suffered severe internal injuries when a wall of her house had collapsed on top of her. She died within a short time, and since the children's father had been killed instantly during the bombing, these children, too, became orphans.

After spending nearly two years in the hospital, Liu Lulan was taken in by an orphanage.

By the time the Japanese army invaded Suzhou, most of the residents of the city proper had fled. In the suburbs, some people ran away, while others did not. When the frontline troops moved on toward Wuxi, an occupying force remained behind in Suzhou. The soldiers of this unit occasionally ventured out into the suburbs with the express purpose of looting and raping, sometimes alone or in pairs, or even in platoons of twenty. This is what I heard from Cao Quangen, the mayor of Jinguang village in Huqiu township outside Suzhou:

> We often heard shots when they came to the village, but that was usually the soldiers killing pigs and other livestock. The old people formed a vigilante group and established lookouts. They'd give the warning when the troops showed up, letting the women know that they needed to hide right away.

Lu Jieduo (63) of the second squad in Jinguang village was seventeen years old at the time. Besides all the countless stories of rapes perpetrated by Japanese soldiers, she was one person who was able to tell me the story of a narrow escape.

Her sister, Xu Genbao, then twenty-seven years old, was married and liv-ing about 300 meters away at Caojia Bridge (Huqiu township). One day in late November or early December, a couple of weeks after the capture of Suzhou, one of the "Eastern devils" came to the area and began chasing after a young girl, who managed to escape. However, the soldier then caught sight of Xu Genbao, who just happened to step outside at that moment. Xu retreated back into the house, but the soldier took off after her.

Xu's two-room house stood at some distance from the rest of the houses in

Lu Meiduo.

the vicinity. The oldest of her three children, a nine-year-old girl, was outside, but her other children, a five-year-old girl and a one-year-old boy, were in the front room, the baby having been lain to sleep in a wooden tub. Xu fled into the back room, but the "Eastern devil" came right after her. He threw her down on the floor and was about to rape her, but she somehow struggled free and ran outside. She kept running for about a li *(500 meters), then turned and looked. Smoke was pouring out of the house where she had left her children: the soldier had set it on fire in spiteful retaliation. Horrified, she rushed back.*

The flames were already raging when Xu ran inside and picked up her son out of the wooden tub. Her five-year-old daughter had already escaped from the house barefoot. Even though the children were safe, the fire burned fiercely and spread to the roof. As Xu learned later, before setting the fire and running off, the soldier had bolted and closed the door of the inner room so that it would be impossible to remove any household articles. Distraught, Xu set her son down on the ground and watched the flames, stamping her feet and fretting, "What are we going to do? What are we going to do?" Her nine-year-old daughter rolled around on the ground, crying. The neighbors, along with Lu Jieduo and Xu's husband, who had been at a nearby teahouse, taking a break from work, came running and tried to put out the fire, but it was too late.

Afterward, Lu Jieduo, Xu Genbao, and their families fled to the nearby village of Huangtuqiao (now Huangqiao Township), about 3 or 4 li *away.*

Xu Genbao is already deceased, but I asked her second daughter, Xu Xiaomei, who was five years old at the time of the incident, what she remembered. "The flames leaping up and what the water looked like when they threw it on the fire," she said. "That's all I remember."

The morning edition of the *Yomiuri Shimbun* carried the following story on November 22, under the headline "The Fall of Wuxi Imminent."

Special telegram from the Shanghai Main Office (November 21): Without taking a break after their assaults on Changshu and Suzhou, our troops are continuing their hot pursuit of the enemy as they head straight toward Nanjing. Contending with muddy conditions, they are advancing forcefully from two directions, Changshu and Suzhou, as if passing through unguarded borders. According to aerial reconnaissance, the frontline troops are already closing in on the stronghold of Wuxi. They have taken their positions for the attack, and the fall of Wuxi is expected in a day or two.

Meanwhile, the Hangzhou Bay Landing Force, which has occupied Jiaxing and Nantaozhen, pushed forward along the rough road south of Lake Taihu and took Huzhou (Wuxing) on the twentieth. They immediately charged on with superhuman endurance and strength toward Nanjing.

CHAPTER 4

"THE IMPERIAL ARMY OCCUPIES WUXI"

The *Asahi Shimbun* reporting the fall of Wuxi. The page on the left displays a photograph of the signing of the accord among Japan, Germany, and Italy.

R oughly speaking, the various units of the Japanese army followed two routes in their assault on Nanjing. The Shanghai Expeditionary Force headed toward Nanjing from the north side of Taihu Lake, passing through Suzhou, Wuxi, Changzhou, Danyang, and Zhenjiang (or Jurong). The units of the Tenth Army (the Hangzhou Bay Landing Force) approached Nanjing from the south side of Taihu Lake, passing through Jiaxing, Huzhou, and Changxing (or Guangde).

For the troops following the northern route, Wuxi was the next major target after Suzhou. In November 1937, Nakayama Masao[1] was following the army in central China as a contract employee of the War Office. In *The Wakisaka Unit*, which the War Office published in 1938 in commemoration of the first anniversary of the fall of Nanjing, he describes the night before the assault on Wuxi as follows:

> Heedless of rain and snow or day and night, the unit struggled with cold and hunger as it moved forward. Thus the battle formation took shape in the frosty, moonlit fields of Jiangnan near Wuxi. The Wakisaka, Shimoeda, and Fujii units advanced along the Jinghu Railroad from the southeast, and from the northeast came the Ōno, Katagiri, Noda, and Sukegawa units, which had taken Changshu. The freshly formed Hanaya unit attacked head on from the east, so that Wuxi was attacked from three sides.
>
> The Wakisaka and Shimoeda units, fresh from having taken Wangting, battled a blizzard on the 22d, rain on the 23d, and a quagmire of mud on the 24th, finally arriving at Lixiangshang, about 3 kilometers from the south gate of Wuxi. A stream lay in front of them, and on the opposite bank were scattered pillboxes and skillfully constructed dugouts, where the enemy had installed themselves, desperate to hold off our fierce assault. The thoroughly prepared enemy attacked us fiercely with barrages of small arms fire and machine gun shells.
>
> Pyun! Pyun! Pyun!
>
> Shells from rifles and machine guns flew past our ears.
>
> Dokan! Dokan! Dokan!
>
> With a sound that seemed loud enough to knock the earth off its axis, the enemy attacked us with mortar fire at close range, with shells exploding to the front, to the side, and to the rear, raising up clouds of smoke and pillars of fire.
>
> Yet the Wakisaka unit succeeded in advancing under enemy fire.
>
> Sergeant Ōtani, Private Nagai, and Private Hosokawa from the Kishi company were able to capture a machine gun position on a grave mound about

---

1. Nakayama Masao (1911–1969) was from the town of Rubeshibe on the island of Hokkaidō. After joining the staff of the army's pictorial magazine, he became editor-in-chief. After the war, he used his father's experiences as the basis for the novel *Bakurō Ichidai* (The Life of a Horse Trader), which was made into a film starring Toshirō Mifune in 1951. He became president of the Japan Youth Hostel Association. He ran for the Diet for the Liberal Democratic Party but lost.

The entry into Wuxi on November 25. (From the December 15, 1937, issue of *Asahi Graph.*)

1 *ken* (6 feet) high at the right edge of a stand of willows on the opposite bank of the stream. Sergeant Ōtani became the triggerman, and under a hail of bullets, he took aim at some heavy artillery at the left edge of some woods about 150 meters ahead, where enemy trenches could be seen between the branches. Then he blew them away in a spray of bullets.

Nakayama Masao's reportage continues on in the same hero-worshipping vein, and it was published with a "recommended" label from the Information Division of the War Office. On the other hand, Ishikawa Tatsuzō's *Ikite iru heitai* (Living Soldiers) was suppressed by the military. It contains the following depiction of the night before the assault on Wuxi:

There was a flat-topped peasant house near where Second Lieutenant Kurada, Privates Hirao and Kondō, and Sergeant Kasahara of the machine gun squad had sat down in a row to smoke a cigarette. The roof had been blown off, the door had fallen onto the dirt floor, and the vegetable garden in back had been trampled into the ground. It appeared even more desolate in the deepening twilight. After the shooting had stopped, the men's ears were suddenly assailed by a sound coming from the house.

"Hey," said Sergeant Kasahara, who was somewhat of a lecher. "That's a woman crying. A *guniang* (young girl)."

"Wonder what she's doing here," mumbled Second Lieutenant Kurada, almost to himself.

Hirao was listening to this conversation from a distance, and he said, "I'm going to take a look." Then he leaped to the top of the trench and trotted off toward the house.

Supply convoy making its way through the smoldering ruins of Wuxi. (From the December 15, 1937, issue of *Asahi Graph*.)

"Hey, it's dangerous," Second Lieutenant Kurada warned, looking back over his shoulder. "Be careful!"

"I'm going, too!" Sergeant Kasahara scrambled out of the trench and looked back down, grinning.

As the other soldiers watched, Hirao and Kasahara went through the entrance where the door had fallen and disappeared into the darkness of the dirt-floored room. The crying stopped.

The soldiers waiting back in the trench grew edgy. They didn't have much contact with young women, and while on the battlefield, they had become strangely obsessed with them.

Finally, Kasahara and Hirao strolled leisurely out of the house through the same entrance. When they had jumped back into the trench, Hirao said, '' Her mother caught a bullet and is dying. It's a seventeen- or eighteen-year-old *guniang*, poor thing."

"Is she any good?" one soldier asked.

"Yeah, very good," Hirao replied in a somehow indignant tone. . . .

The stars reminded the men uncannily of home. When they looked up at the stars, they felt as if they were no longer in China. The slight mood of sentimentality in the air made the trench seem even quieter.

The silence was broken as the sound of the young girl's crying once more reached the soldiers.

"She's crying again," Hirao whispered.

As the night wore on, the crying took on a more agonized tone, disturbing the silence of the darkened battlefield. The girl gave out a wailing lamentation, which before long turned into quiet, choking sobs; then she suddenly burst into a long, drawn-out, animalistic groaning or howling and then into something resembling a scream. . . .

"This is getting on my nerves!"

As I turned to look, Hirao bounced up to the stop of the trench and stood there, a silhouette against the dark, starry sky.

"Where are you going?" Private Kondō asked from within the trench.

"I'm going to kill her," he said casually. With that, he drew his bayonet close and headed toward the house in a hunched-over run. Five or six other soldiers followed him over the edge of the trench, their rapid footsteps audible as they trotted along.

They ran into the dark house. The starlight streaming through the shattered window revealed the sobbing girl crouching there, just as before. Hirao grabbed her by the collar and pulled her up, but her arms were wrapped around the dead body of her mother, and she refused to let go until one of the soldiers twisted her arm and pulled the body away. Then the soldiers hauled the girl outside, her legs dragging on the ground. Screaming like a madman, Hirao raised his bayonet and stabbed the girl in the chest three times. The other soldiers, too, took their knives and began stabbing her indiscriminately. She was dead within ten seconds and collapsed like a pile of bedding onto the dark ground. The raw, warm smell of blood wafted up to the flushed, excited soldiers.

When the unit forced its way into the city of Wuxi, the *Tokyo Nichinichi Shimbun*, to give just one example, carried the following report in its evening edition of November 23 under the headline "Imperial Army Occupies Wuxi":

Suzhou, November 22, Dōmei: The advance guard of the ___ Unit occupied Wuxi at 11:30 A.M. on the morning of the 22d.

Shanghai, November 22, Dōmei: Our two units, the __ and the __ , which made a fierce attack on the city walls of Wuxi after arriving on the 21st, joined to launch an attack from both the north and south simultaneously on the early morning of the 22d. After fighting for several hours, the left flank ____ unit, forced its way through the railroad station at the southern gate of Wuxi, making a decisive military gain at one blow, and at 11:30 A.M., they raised the victory song to signal their occupation. The enemy's large units are fleeing en masse toward Changzhou (Mujin) by road and rail, and the air corps of both our army and our navy are bombing them relentlessly.

Shanghai, November 22, Dōmei: Thanks to the fall of Wuxi, the two lines of defensive positions for Nanjing, from the Jiangyin fortifications to Taihu Lake, will soon be breached, and the days of the Jiangyin battery are numbered.

Of the approximately 100,000 people living within the walls of Wuxi, almost all the ordinary civilians had fled, but some of them had sought refuge in the many houses that remained in the suburbs. One of the outlying peasant villages was Anzhen township, and it was attacked by a small unit of Japanese soldiers on November 22, the same day that the forward divisions captured Wuxi. Zhang Bingnan (58) is one of the survivors from Daizhaoxiang, a hamlet in that township, although the most important witness, Feng Jingliang (76), had died in

August, 1983, just three months before my visit. For this reason, I have incorporated Feng's experiences into Zhang's account:

Zhang Bingnan.

A cold rain was falling on that day, when over a hundred Japanese "devils" showed up in Anzhen township at about three in the afternoon. It was a small squad traveling separately from the main unit, which was moving west along the principal road from Changshu to Wuxi. When they crossed Furong Bridge and entered the first hamlet, Daizhaoxiang, two people who happened to be walking down the road were shot to death without warning. Zhang, who lived in the hamlet, was eleven at the time, and he saw all this from his hiding place in a thicket. Since the hamlet was close to the main road, most of the residents had fled, leaving behind only two elderly women, one of whom was Zhang's grandmother, and one elderly man.

The old people hurried to offer the Japanese soldiers chickens, salt, and other supplies. Zhang's grandmother led some soldiers into her kitchen and handed over some salt and all of her chickens, which may be why the old people were left alive. However, all the fifty or so chickens in the hamlet were taken, along with several pounds of salt.

Proceeding farther south to the hamlet of Qiangengshang, the soldiers killed the only remaining resident, a blind man named Qian Zengfa, who was evidently bayoneted to death in his bed. In the third hamlet, Nanqiantou, twelve households with a total of forty-nine people remained. When they became aware of the approach of the "devils," they tried to run away, but it was already too late for that, and only eleven people managed to break away. The remaining thirty-eight were captured.

The twelve houses of Nanqiantou stood in a row along Jiuli Creek, and there was a garden about two meters wide between the houses and the water. The hundred or more soldiers herded the thirty-eight people to that area and surrounded them. There were two young women in the group, one seventeen and unmarried, and the other pregnant. Both were taken off to separate houses and raped by one "devil" after another, an ordeal that left them too weak to stand.

Having raped the two women, the soldiers turned to arson and mass murder. Some soldiers dragged the two women back to the garden, while others

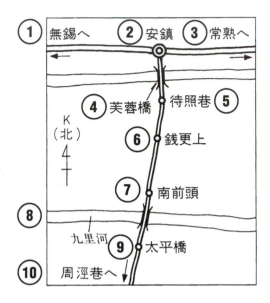

1. To Wuxi
2. Anzhen
3. To Changshu
4. Fuyong Bridge
5. Daichaoxiang
6. Qiangengshang
7. Nanqiantou
8. Jiuli Creek
9. Taiping Bridge
10. Zhoujingxiang

took on the job of setting fire to all the houses. The hellish events that followed occurred almost simultaneously, so Zhang was unable to tell them in chronological order, but here are some of the things that happened.

The soldiers rammed a broom into the vagina of the younger woman and then stabbed her with a bayonet. They cut open the belly of the pregnant woman and gouged out the fetus.

Three men, unable to bear the sight of the flames consuming their homes, desperately broke through the ring of soldiers and headed off in the direction of the houses. They encountered some other soldiers who were determined not to let them through and forced them into one of the furiously burning houses. Seconds after the soldiers had locked the door from the outside, the roof collapsed in flames on top of the men.

A two-year-old boy was bawling loudly in reaction to the noise and confusion. A soldier grabbed him from his mother's arms and threw him into the flames. They then bayoneted the hysterically sobbing mother and threw her into the creek. The remaining thirty-one people were made to kneel facing the creek. The soldiers stabbed them from behind with their bayonets, twisting the blades

The villagers were made to kneel at the edge of this creek before being bayoneted and tossed into the water.

to disembowel them, and threw them into the water. One of the peasant men was skilled in several of China's traditional martial arts, but he, too, was stabbed thirteen times and killed.

The reason that we know the details of these events is that one man, Feng Jingliang, miraculously survived. He was thirty years old at the time, and for some reason, perhaps because the soldier wielding the bayonet was inexperienced, the blade pierced only his right jaw when he was stabbed from behind. He was thus thrown into the water with only minor injuries. Because he was wearing padded cotton clothing, he was easily able to float, and he clung to a bamboo rod as he drifted among the bodies of his neighbors. About an hour after the "devils" had left, the residents who had fled previously came back and rescued him. It was at that same time that Zhang, who had been hiding in the thicket up in Daishangxiang, arrived on the scene. The two women who had been raped lay covered with blood in the garden, while corpses bobbed and floated in the creek, staining the water red.

Of the thirty-seven people who were killed, one was a resident of Wuxi who had taken refuge with relatives, so thirty-six were natives of Nanqiantou.

A currently existing house in Nanqiantou uses the burned remains of a house (blackened pillars) from the war era as its framework.

The names of the heads of households, the number of victims in each household, and the number of rooms lost to fire are listed below.

Head of household	Number of persons killed	Number of rooms burned
Feng Fengxian	1	5
Feng Shuqian	7	5
Feng Zengbao	4	5
Feng Abi		3
Feng Qiaogen	4	7
Feng Genxiang	1	6
Feng Genyuan	1	5
Feng Quangen	3	5
Feng Meigen	3	4
Feng Shaotang	6	4
Feng Jingxian		8
Feng Zongbao	4	7
Total	34	64

Four households from the above list were completely wiped out. Two hundred fifteen mu *(about 15 hectares) of freshly harvested rice that was waiting to be threshed was burned.*

Proceeding farther south, the Japanese soldiers burned the entire hamlet of Taipingqiao, over one hundred houses. The inhabitants had, of course, heard of the tragedy at Nanqiantou and had already fled. The soldiers headed southwest through Songshan and Meicun, evidently aiming toward the railroad station at Zhoujingxiang. ✳

In the vicinity of Taipingqiao is a hamlet called Beidaochang. On the day of the massacre at Nanqiantou (November 23) a different group of Japanese soldiers showed up and I heard about the ensuing events from a peasant woman named Yan Yingquan (age 62), whose parents and older brother were killed.

Yan Yingquan.

At about eight in the morning, the inhabitants heard gunfire from the direction of Beizhai, a hamlet that lay to the east. They also saw balloons, which, the old people say, the Japanese military often used to indicate targets for bombing.

Yan Yingquan was sixteen years old by the traditional method of counting ages, and she was living with her parents and older brother. Since they had to leave in a hurry, her father loaded rice and other daily necessities onto his shoulders, and they all set out along roads made muddy by recent rains. With them were her father's brother's wife and three neighbors, so that a group of eight people was trying to flee to the west. But it was too late, because an advance guard of Japanese soldiers closed in on them. The villagers were only about twenty meters away from their homes when they came under a hail of bullets. The eight people fell over onto either side of the road.

Of the eight, Yan Yingquan and her parents ended up on the north side of the road, and the other five people on the south side. Yan had not been hit, but she lay low in the rice paddy with the others. Her mother lay face down, with her head pointing to the west, and Yan lay with her head next to her mother's, but facing the other direction. Her father lay at his wife's feet, but with his head pointing west. Yan expected to be able to hear her mother breathing, but she had been killed instantly.

"It's all over for me!" her father called out to his wife. When Yan raised her head slightly, she saw her father lift one arm and stroke the gaping wound in his back. He kept calling weakly, despite the fact that *his wife did not answer. "Agen di niang, wo wu lai le. (Daughter of Agen, it's all over for me)."[2]*

Yan just lay there, silently listening to her father's voice. Soon a company of soldiers rushed past, holding their blood-smeared bayonets over their heads. There was no reaction from the five people on the other side of the road.

After a while, it became quiet, and the girl stood up, thinking that the soldiers had left. However, another company still remained in the hamlet, and when they noticed her, one soldier came chasing after her. She ran and hid in a mulberry orchard about 30 meters away, but soon other soldiers found her and began shooting, although the bullets did not hit her. About 400 meters away from the mulberry orchard was a pond, and near it was a cemetery surrounded by tall, thick bushes. As she fled to the thicket, she was shot at four times, but she again escaped without being hit.

After hiding in the thicket until evening, Yan went to the place where her parents had fallen. Her father was already dead, and his silver coins had been stolen off his corpse. The other five people were also dead, and Yan Yingquan was now an orphan.

In between Anzhen township and Wuxi is a peasant village called Dongliang township,[3] another refuge for evacuees from Wuxi. On November 24, the day after Yan Yingquan's family was killed, 222 people were killed in two hours at a small settlement within the township called Xuxiang. Only 94 of them were residents of the community; the other 128 were refugees from Wuxi. The victims were male and female, and ranged from nursing infants to eighty-year-olds. The account of the incident is based on the experiences of three survivors. Xu Quanchu (57) was eleven years old, and three of the seven members of his family were killed. Xu Yuanzu (49) was three years old at the time. He was held in his mother's arms when she was bayoneted to death; his lip was cut, and he lost the sight in his right eye. His childhood memories were supplemented by those of his grandparents and some neighbors who survived. Gai Hegen (62) was sixteen years old at the time and lost five out of the eight people in his family.

Since the community of Xuxiang was surrounded by a waterway, the inhabitants enjoyed the illusion of safety. There were a fair number of refugees from Wuxi, and the population of the community, originally 63 households containing 224

---

2. In the Wuxi area, wives are addressed as the "Daughter of [their father's name]."
3. Xuxiang has been renamed Chunluo. Townships are units comparable to Japanese villages, but there are smaller units as well. What I refer to as "small settlements" are very small, only about ten to twenty households. Settlements or communities, are larger, but there is no clear distinction.

individuals, increased to over 400. Unfortunately, some Chinese (Nationalist) soldiers had also arrived and taken up a position in one corner of the community.

That day, it rained heavily all morning and then gradually cleared up. Either a small contingent or the main force of the soldiers came down the creek in rubber boats from the northwest, the direction of Anzhen township. The Chinese soldiers, who were camped at the northeast edge near the creek, engaged the Japanese soldiers.

Of the Chinese forces, one squad on a small hill overlooking the creek was completely wiped out, and the others retreated. It was about four in the afternoon when the Japanese entered Xuxiang.

At that time, eleven-year-old Xu Quanchu lived with six other people: his father (56), his mother (52), his two older brothers (25 and 18), his oldest brother's wife, and a girl cousin. Their house consisted of rooms lined up front to back, and the large first room had been further divided twice, making a total of four rooms.

When the Japanese soldiers invaded the village, Xu Quanchu's older brothers went and hid in the toilet, and his cousin and sister-in-law hid behind some things in the front room. Xu Quanchu and his parents sat on the bed in the same room (see drawing at right).

Xu's mother was sitting on the bed holding him when the soldiers came in, and his father was lying down. Seeing the three people on the bed, one of the soldiers raised his pistol and fired, and yet—whether he had forgotten to load it or whether he had run out of bullets, no one knows—the shot was a blank. With that, the soldiers simply pro-

Xu Quancheng.

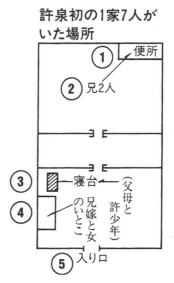

許泉初の1家7人が
いた場所

1. Toilet
2. Two older brothers
3. Bed
4. His older brother's wife and female cousin

ceeded into the inner rooms. (When asked why the soldiers did not bother them any further, Xu said he thought it was probably because his parents were "old people.")

However, the soldiers soon found the two brothers who had hidden in the toilet. They immediately dragged them out to the front yard and killed them. The twenty-five-year-old brother had his head split open with a Japanese sword, starting at the right ear, and the eighteen-year-old was stabbed in the belly with a bayonet.

Sensing that his sons were being killed, Xu's father felt compelled to do something, and he went to the front door. The soldiers spotted him immediately, dragged him outside, and killed him in the same place as his sons, slicing open the back of his head with a Japanese sword.

Xu Yuanzu showing the scar on his lip.

Three-year-old Xu Yuanzu (who was two years old by the Western method of counting ages) had not yet been weaned. His nine-year-old sister and his grandparents had already evacuated to the hinterlands, so the only people at home were Xu himself and his parents, who were both thirty-six years old.

When the Japanese came, they pounded on the door with the barrel of a gun. His father stood up to open the door, and was shot to death as soon he opened it. Hearing the shot, Xu's mother gathered up her son, whom she was nursing, and went to the door, where she was bayoneted to death on the spot. Since she was stabbed in the breast, Xu suffered a cut lip but was otherwise uninjured. Xu stayed by the bodies of his parents just inside the front door until morning, crying and completely covered with blood. By the time his grandparents heard what had happened and came running, Xu was nearly dead.

(Xu's story thus far was told to me by his neighbor, Xu Genmei, who was in his thirties at the time.) Xu Yuanzu's grandparents came and picked him up, washed the blood off him, and tended him until he recovered. However, they were unable to summon a doctor, and it soon became apparent that he had become blind in his right eye. The cause was unclear—whether it was because of being covered with his parents' blood, or crying too much, or having acquired some bacterial infection.

Gai Hegen showing the scars on his chest.

Gai Hegen, then sixteen, was from a family of eight people. In addition to his parents there were his grandparents, his older brother and sister-in-law, and his younger brother; his sister-in-law had already been evacuated to the home of some relatives who lived farther inland. His older brother had been working for a railroad company in Guangdong Province, but he had returned home to get married, and indeed, it was only twenty-nine days after the wedding.

When the Japanese soldiers knocked at the door, Gai's older brother first went to answer it and was shot dead. Hearing the shot, his mother went out, and she, too, was shot dead. Gai's father sneaked him out the back door, but there were also a lot of Japanese soldiers in the vacant field behind the house. Gai and his father ran only about 7 or 8 meters before being shot.

His father fell dead, shot in the heart and right thigh, and Gai himself was hit twice. One bullet passed through his right arm and into the left side of his chest, just missing his heart. The other blew off the tip of his left little finger.

Young Gai lost consciousness and lay motionless. The main force left for Wuxi, but a small group of soldiers remained to occupy the community. As it grew dark, Gai regained consciousness, but he remained lying on the ground. A soldier hit Gai's head with the barrel of his rifle to see if he was still alive, but the youth played dead, enduring the pain.

When it was completely dark, Gai got up and immediately encountered his eleven-year-old brother, who had been looking for him. The two of them went into Xu Genmei's house by the back door and hid there, along with his wife and children. Xu Genmei had hidden them in their own house and piled up rice straw around the entrance to make it look uninhabited. He then had hidden himself in the pig barn, but just before dawn, he came and breathlessly told them, "If we don't run away, the Japanese devils will set this place on fire, too." They all fled to the cemetery together.

At the eastern edge of Xuxiang were the two largest houses, belonging to Xu Shengxian and Xu Yaoxian. Xu Shengxian's second son, Xu Xinhe, had studied in Japan, and he thought that his family would be all right, even if the

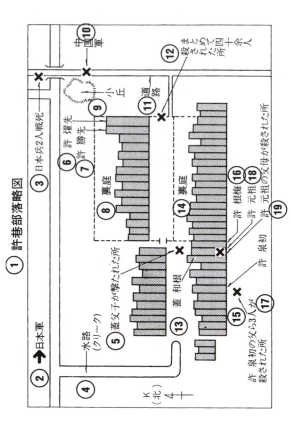

1. Simplified map of Xuxiang hamlet
2. Japanese troops
3. Two Japanese soldiers killed in battle
4. Canal
5. Where Gai's father and brothers were shot
6. Xu Yaoxian
7. Xu Shengxian
8. Backyard
9. Small hill
10. Chinese troops
11. Road
12. Where forty people were killed
13. Gai Hegen
14. Backyard
15. The place where Xu Quancheng's father and two other people were killed
16. Xu Genmei
17. Xu Quancheng
18. Xu Yuanzu
19. Where Xu Yuanzu's parents were killed

Japanese came, because he would be able to talk to the soldiers or find some personal connection with them. Reflecting this belief, there were over forty other people in the house, including refugees. They included Xinhe's older brother, who was a physician in Wuxi and several of his neighbors, all of them placing their hopes in the returned student.

But these hopes were in vain. The former exchange student provided himself with a white flag, surrendered when the Japanese forced their way in, and said something in Japanese, but the soldiers ignored him and summarily rousted everyone out of the house. The people were herded out the front door, taken to a circular depression near the entrance to the community, and shot to death en masse.

Those killed among the sixteen persons in Xu Shengxian's household, aside from Xu Shengxian himself, were his wife, his older brother, his oldest son, his second son, his third son and daughter-in-law, his oldest daughter and son-in-law, and three grandchildren, twelve people in all. His five-year-old grandson was not hit by the bullets, but he was smothered by bodies and blood in the course of the massacre. This was the largest number of victims from a single family.

In addition to Xu Yuanzu's parents and Gai Hegen's parents and grand-parents, the following three married couples were also killed:

The parents of Xu Kunxiang
Xu Ronggen and his wife
The aunt and uncle of Tao Jizhen

The arson following the massacre destroyed 93 rooms along with 150 mu (about 10 hectares) of rice plants. Among the inhabitants, six children were orphaned, and twenty-two women and thirteen men were widowed.

You Chunyi, a foreign affairs official of Xidong County, the location of both Anzhen and Dongliang townships, gave the following speech when I visited the area:

> It's regrettable that you couldn't have come just three months earlier and heard stories from that miraculous survivor, Old Man Feng. However, since we have heard his stories any number of times, we can tell them in detail. This is the first time a foreigner has come to gather material about these events, and I am truly grateful that the Japanese people will learn the facts after forty-six years. We, too, are currently in the process of editing a regional magazine, and if we don't record these stories for the education of the next generation now, all the elderly witnesses will have disappeared from the scene.
>
> "*Hantian chi shui, koukou zai xin tou*" (If you drink chilly water, you feel each mouthful in your chest) is a Chinese proverb. But in this case, we cannot forget that we are talking about bloody water, not chilly water. Not forgetting

Zhang Zhongrong.

the past is the basis of true Sino-Japanese friendship, and if we remain ignorant, we can never attain true friendship. General Secretary Hu Yaobang, too, has spoken of "moving toward a century of Sino-Japanese friendship," and your research will prove to be a great contribution. We admire you, and we would like once again to express our heartfelt thanks.

It was on November 22 that the advance forces of the Japanese army entered Wuxi, but most authorities say that the city was not completely occupied until the 25th, and some references say it was the 26th or 27th.

According to Zhang Zhongrong (67), twenty-one years old at the time of the incidents, the city of Wuxi had about 100,000 inhabitants before the Japanese invasion,[4] and it had prospered as one of China's four largest rice trading and distribution centers. Its main commercial streets, Beitang

Wuxi today: Beitang Avenue.

---

4. Zhang says that Wuxi had 100,000 inhabitants, but some reference books say that it had 150,000 or 200,000 inhabitants.

Avenue and Beida Street, flourished, stretching for 3 li (1.5 kilometers), lined with stores, more than 20,000 of them for a population of this size. It was the center of finance, with about ten banks and twenty smaller financial institutions, and about 3,000 grain transport vessels gathered and dispersed from the city.

The residents began to flee after the first Japanese bombing attack on October 6, when over 500 people were killed or wounded in the vicinity of Wuxi Station. The bombing raids grew in ferocity, and the evacuation of citizens to rural areas increased proportionally. However, there were more than a few people who fled too late or stayed behind to "guard" their homes. Most of the women who did so ended up being raped.

The regiment portrayed in Ishikawa Tatsuzō's *Living Soldiers* stopped in Wuxi for three days of rest. And then:

> It was under these kinds of circumstances that the surviving soldiers most lusted after women. Like dogs chasing rabbits, they roamed the streets, several men abreast, looking for women. This kind of lawless activity had been severely restricted along the battle lines in northern China, but by this point, it was difficult to restrain the men's behavior.
>
> The men adopted a haughty, self-satisfied air, as if each of them were an emperor or a tyrant. If they were unable to achieve their aims in the streets of Wuxi, they went out to the houses surrounding the city. It was quite a dangerous thing to do, because there were still stragglers from the Chinese army in hiding and some civilians had weapons, but the soldiers experienced no reluctance or hesitation. They felt as if no one in the world could be stronger than they. Given this attitude, it goes without saying that virtue, law, remorse, and human sympathy lost all power over the men.
>
> Thus some soldiers returned to Japan with silver rings on the little fingers of their left hands. When asked where they had gotten the rings, they would laugh and say, "It's a memento of my dead wife."

Sixty-year-old Zhang Xiyuan, then twenty-four, worked in the family business of sugar wholesaling. His father, Zhang Junlin, then sixty-two, was originally from Changzhou, Wujin County, but he had come to Wuxi and achieved success in his business. Three or four years before the **Zhang Xiyuan.**

Japanese invasion, he had built a new three-story house, which was located at number 7 Nanjian Street at the Chang'an Bridge in Tantoulong, somewhat removed from the commercial district. He stayed behind with his sixty-year-old wife, Zhang Xiyuan's mother, in order to prevent the house from being looted or destroyed.

The rest of the family, including Zhang Xiyuan and his wife, his older brother and his wife, and two children, had fled to the opposite shore of Lenghu Lake, outside the city. There was also a thirty-year-old sister, but she had a husband and a child, and they had fled to Nanjing by boat. Zhang Xiyuan's mother herself told him what happened when she and his father stayed behind in Wuxi.

On the day that the Japanese army invaded the city, some Japanese soldiers broke into the Zhang family's three-story house. Zhang's mother, thinking she was safe on account of her age, was caught off guard when the soldiers came after her. After they had trapped her on the third floor, they stripped her naked, raped her, and then molested her further with a stick.

With so many Japanese soldiers in the city, it was now impossible to flee, so toward dawn, the Zhangs left the house and hid in a place where the Japanese seemed unlikely to go. (All the women left in the city did something like this.) After three or four days, they went and hid in the interior of the Nanbei Commodities Office (a cooperative of business people who sold specialty products from many regions), which was across the street about 10 meters from where they had been. When Zhang's father went out into the street, some Japanese soldiers showed up, and he tried to run back into the Commodities Office, but the soldiers caught up with him right by the door. He was stabbed through the head and then shot. By the time his wife came to the door to see what was happening, he was already dead. The bayonet marks from when he was stabbed in the head could be seen on a post, 15 centimeters thick.

Meanwhile, the sister who had fled to Nanjing and her family were living as evacuees in their boat at Pukou, on the opposite shore of the Yangtze. Around the time of the fall of Nanjing, some Japanese soldiers found the family and made them disembark on the riverbank. Aiming to rape Zhang's sister, the soldiers poked at her shoulder with their bayonets in order to make her go along with them. She managed to push the bayonets away with her hands, and immediately the soldiers kicked her and sent her tumbling into the river, shooting at her as she fell. Her husband, Zhang's brother-in-law, jumped into the river and pulled her out, but she was already dead. She was buried on some nearby land without coffin or ceremony.

Li Shenzhi (61), fifteen at the time of the Massacre, at one time lived with his mother on a side street about 100 meters from Beida Street. He was at school

the first time Wuxi was bombed, and since neither the teachers nor the pupils had any experience or prior knowledge of bombings, the teacher directed the pupils not to move from their seats and to hide under their desks without talking. Li said that some of his classmates wet their pants in fear. He was eventually evacuated to a peasant village, but his mother stayed behind to guard the house.

Hearing that the Japanese had occupied the city, Li became worried and returned to his home just before the city was put under blockade on the 28th. He found that all the women, including his mother, had blackened their faces with charcoal and were trying to make themselves look as old as possible. They did not go out during the day, nor could they allow the smoke

Li Shenzhi

from their cooking fires to be seen, which meant that they could not even boil rice. Since the Japanese never showed up late at night or before six in the morning, everyone cooked the day's rice before six o'clock and waited until late at night to make any necessary trips outside.

Four days after young Li returned home, some Japanese soldiers came hunting for women in Zhoushilong near the house of his eleven-year-old cousin, Yuan Xigen. They spotted the boy's twenty-two-year-old sister, Yuan Juren, and began chasing her. When they had nearly caught up with her, Xigen jumped up to block their way. He was immediately shot dead, but his sister was able to get away. When Li came running, his cousin's body was lying in the doorway.

The headquarters of the Japanese army was in an area called Sheqiao. One day, not long after his cousin was killed, perhaps a week after the fall of Wuxi, Li was out on the street when two soldiers ordered him to come along with them. They arrived at a residential area called Caijalong, where the houses were laid out so that it was possible to pass from one rear gate to another, allowing escape in times of danger. The soldiers broke down the door of a locked-up house and made Li enter to see if any people were there. Once they knew that the house was uninhabited, the two soldiers forced their way in and began looting whatever caught their eye. They were particularly happy to find some high-quality bowls. They made Li carry the part of the loot that they could not carry by themselves, and they hauled it back to Sheqiao. Li recalls that on the way there, he saw the naked body of a woman who appeared to have been stabbed in the genital area, perhaps with a bayonet.

In the house next door to Li's, there was a fatherless young woman of nineteen named Zhang Eryuan, whose poor health made her incapable of running. One day, shortly after the fall of Wuxi, a unit of twenty or more Japanese soldiers appeared, and the people, including Zhang Eryuan, hid inside a large air-raid shelter. However, when it looked as if they were about to be discovered, the people fled from the air raid shelter, except for Zhang Eryuan, who could not run. She was captured inside the shelter and raped by all the soldiers, one after another. According to some eyewitnesses who were hiding nearby, the soldiers emerged from the shelter laughing as they fastened the belts of their trousers. When the men whom the city's rape victims had come to call the "animal soldiers"⁵ left, neighbors went into the air raid shelter to get Zhang Eryuan out. She was lying there unable to move. She managed to get back to her house, supported on all sides by the neighbors, but she died about a week later, her genital area swollen and infected.

The bustling commercial center of the city that ran along Beitang Avenue and Beida Street was laid waste by arson and looting. The area burned for five days. In the end, only half of a single building survived the flames. The Lianrong Bridge, an arched wooden bridge, also burned and collapsed into the river, later to be replaced by a concrete structure, and the Hongni Bridge still bears the marks of the fire. According to Zhang Zhongrong, the devastation allowed one to see a bell tower which had previously not been visible from the shopping area.

Here is how the arson is depicted in *Living Soldiers*:

> The morning the soldiers left Wuxi, they set fire to the houses where they had been billeted. Or rather, many of them left without dousing their outdoor bonfires, fully expecting that they would flare up and spread.
>
> It was a way of demonstrating to themselves that they were resolved not to retreat to this place, and there was also some notion of preventing stragglers from coming back here. Furthermore, it also seemed to them that burning this city confirmed their control of it.
>
> The procession of soldiers marched out of the city and came to a broad plain. When they turned to look back, the sky over Wuxi was filled with swirling clouds of black smoke that obscured the sun. The rising flames could be heard from far away, giving off a sound like a rushing wind. With the large units

---

5. The Chinese people called the Japanese soldiers "devils," but the women who were raped referred to their tormentors as "animal soldiers." (In reality, of course, most animals do not—cannot—commit rape, so it actually is a human activity.)

gone, the city of 100,000 people became an outpost for a small guard unit, and there was almost no trace of the residents. The flames leapt from intersection to intersection and from neighborhood to neighborhood until they burned themselves out.

According to the privately published *Memorial Record of Captain Watanabe Toshimasa* (Tokyo, 1939), this is what Captain Watanabe wrote in his field diary after passing through Wuxi on November 29:

> Left Suzhou in an engineering corps iron boat. Weather clear with frost. Continued upstream to Wuxi. Arrived 5:30 P.M. The city walls are about 4 *ken* (24 feet) or more, not inferior to those of Suzhou. They look fine stretched out against the evening sky. Stayed overnight at a school outside the city. The nearby flames overwhelm the night sky.

Nine days after this, on December 8, Sasaki Motokatsu, who was following the army as a field postmaster, wrote the following in his diary, which was published in 1973 as *The Field Postal Flag*:

> Three or four times in the 10 *li* from Changshu to Wuxi, the truck rolled over dirt-covered corpses that lay in the road. Since a long, drawn-out supply column moving in the opposite direction took up the other side of the rode, we could not avoid driving over the bodies. Near Wuxi we saw a pathetic sight, a pale girl of sixteen or seventeen standing by the side of the road holding a tiny baby. She must have just given birth. When we entered the city of Wuxi, we saw a lot of dead bodies, some of them naked. Groups of sneak-thieving poor people were nervously making their way among the abandoned houses. There was a dark-complected girl, her eyes shining with fear. She cowered to such an extent that I wondered if she was purposely putting on an air of exaggerated terror. The truck was resupplied with gasoline at a repair shop. I went on foot to the post office and came to the foot of a wide bridge, where I saw a charred body. The belly had been split open like a melon, maybe by dogs, with the guts spilling out bright red with blood.

Sasaki's diary further describes Wuxi as it was seven days later on December 15:

> The streets of Wuxi are as desolate as ever. The naked, charred body that was lying at the foot of the bridge has been eaten by dogs, and its legs have been reduced to bones. The driver ahead of us made a wrong turn and ended up going part of the way to Suzhou before turning back. On the way, we saw some soldiers employing Chinese laborers to burn a number of blackened bodies. Perhaps because the fighting was so fierce, the people in and outside of Wuxi are very timid. They often bow to us with a gesture that looks as if they are shielding their eyes from the sun. Many of the poor people come foraging for cooking utensils or clothing. Giving their children Japanese Rising

> Sun flags to hold, they return to the outskirts of the city, marching in rows with the foraged goods carried on poles balanced on their shoulders. You can see this kind of scene all over, but Wuxi seems to me to be the worst.

Zhang Zhongrong described conditions in Wuxi after the Japanese had occupied it: "After the fire, the smell of burning and the stench of rotting bodies hovered the air in the city, and there were a lot of bodies floating in the canal, too. Old bodies would come floating to the surface, and new ones would get thrown in. We kept seeing them until February of the next year. As far as the evacuees were concerned, the first ones made their way back in January, more than a month after the invasion, but it took about half a year for eighty or ninety percent of the population to return."

On November 26, the morning edition of the *Yomiuri Shimbun* reported the combat-related death of twenty-eight-year-old journalist Watanabe Mineo, who had been covering the attack on Wuxi. At the same time, it also carried the following article under the headline "Our Army Closes in on Changzhou":

> Shanghai, special telegram to Yomiuri: (November 25). Our army, which shattered stubborn resistance from the Chinese forces to completely occupy Wuxi on the morning of the 25th, is pursuing the retreating enemy without stopping to rest. The Noda, Sukegawa, and Ōno units have already passed through Dingxiangshang, and joining forces with the Hanaya and Adachi units, they have set out at once for Wujin (Changzhou) and are putting pressure on it. The Army Air Corps and the Taki and Nonaka units are giving their all in cooperating with the infantry units, carrying out repeated bombing attacks on the retreating enemy troops. One can see the abandoned corpses of the enemy piled up on the Wuxi-Danyuan road, a mighty demonstration of the effects of our bombing.

CHAPTER 5

"THE RISING SUN FLAG OVER THE CITY WALLS OF CHANGZHOU"

The *Yomiuri Shimbun* reporting the fall of Changzhou.

The first reports of the occupation of Changzhou appeared in the evening edition of the *Asahi Shimbun* for November 30, 1937, under the headline "The Rising Sun Flag over the City Walls of Changzhou."

> Special telegram from Shanghai, November 29: (released by the Shanghai military, 1:30 P.M.) At around noon on the 29th, our Ōno, Sukegawa, Noda, Katagiri, Mikuni, and Imanaka units took Changzhou and continued on to push the enemy in the direction of Nanjing.
>
> Shanghai, November 29, Dōmei: The Katagiri, Ōno, Noda, Sukegawa, Mikuni, Imanaka, and other units that poured into the city engaged in fierce street-to-street fighting all night, gradually pushing forward against stubborn resistance from the remaining enemy, but at dawn, they were able to switch to an all-out attack and expel them. By noon, they occupied the entire area within the city walls of Changzhou, and in addition, they are now pursuing the defeated enemy along the Jinghu Railroad. On the city walls, our inspiring Rising Sun flag flutters against a cloudless early winter sky.

Very few Japanese books or magazines describe the assault on Changzhou. Among the materials that I have looked at, even the ones that mention Changzhou devote only two or three lines to it. All that the soldiers portrayed in *Living Soldiers* did was pass through Changzhou and spend the night there as a rear guard unit, and the episode is described as follows:

> The majority of the unit arrived in the newly captured city of Changzhou during the morning that day (note: November 30). They camped here and there within the city and ate lunch. The houses outside the city wall were so thoroughly destroyed that it's safe to say that not one of them had its roof. On the bleak deserted wall, there was just a red Rising Sun flag fluttering, and the figures of the two guardsmen who stood on the wall with their bayonets looked small against the clear sky.
>
> Since they had been marching along without encountering any combat situations, the soldiers were in a relaxed mood when it came time to rest. They even seemed to be enjoying themselves, as if they had come together as a group for a sightseeing trip. The weather was unusually fine, with calm, clear springlike warmth following two or three days of cold. Sasanaqua bloomed in abundance in the garden of a devastated mansion, and in the ruins of a sandbagged position, a half-starved dog lay sunning itself.
>
> The soldiers commandeered a donkey from a house outside the city walls, and they took turns riding it up and down the deserted avenue. They also commandeered a pig, tied a rope around its neck, and led it back to their camp. Of course, it would end up as part of the evening meal.

Present-day Changzhou is an industrial city of 3,020,000 people, but it is better known to tourists as the center of the 1,500-year-old traditional craft of making combs. When I toured a factory that turns out eleven million combs per year, I learned that in 1915, some combs from Changzhou were displayed at the opening ceremony for the Panama Canal, and that they were also awarded a gold medal at the 1926 Philadelphia Exposition. Forty-five percent of the combs made here are exported.

I learned of the events surrounding the fall of Changzhou from Chen Bi of the Changzhou Journalists' Association.

The first bombardment by Japanese planes occurred on October 13, when over a hundred people were killed or injured in the vicinity of the railroad station. Among other horrors, bodies were found in trees, and shattered legs were found lying on the ground. The bombing continued for about forty days after that. Of the city's four districts, Guanghua was the most severely hit, turning into a virtual wasteland, and two streets, Mishihe and Doushihe of the Jinglou district, along with fifteen or sixteen streets of the Tianning district, were destroyed. The ships in the canal were also bombed.[1] Industrial plants bore the brunt of the devastating attacks, including the locomotive factory and the electrical generating plant at Qishuyan and the yarn and thread factory belonging to the Dacheng Company.

It was on November 27 that a Japanese infantry unit reached Qishuyan, which is about 10 kilometers outside Changzhou. First, they seized the locomotive factory and the electrical generating plant, and they sent up white balloons as a signal to their aircraft. This led to the worst bombing ever in the city proper, and most of the population fled.

As soon as the Japanese arrived in Qishuyan, the Nationalist Chinese army began retreating from Changzhou, fleeing west toward Jintan or southwest toward Piaoyang. Two days later, on November 29, the Japanese invaded the city not only from the direction of Qishuyan, but also from the direction of Wuyi Lake.

"The Japanese soldiers who occupied Changzhou went crazy with looting, arson, and raping any woman who hadn't managed to leave the city," Chen said, "and it went on for days. The smoke from the huge fires reached Caoqiao, sixty kilometers away, and ashes fell from the sky at Wuhuang, thirty kilometers away."

Of the 166 shops on Nanda Street, Changzhou's main commercial street, except for an undertaker's establishment and a drummaker's shop, all were completely burned. According to what Chen called "incomplete statistics," 9,000 *jian*[2] of houses, shops, temples, and factories were destroyed by fire in Changzhou, including Qishuyan.

---

1. The canal referred to here is the so-called Grand Canal, which flows 1700 kilometers from Beijing to Hangzhou, linking a series of rivers and lakes. It also flows through Changzhou, Wuxi, and Suzhou, and it has been a major thoroughfare since ancient times.

2. Although written with a character that can mean "room," a *jian* does not necessarily correspond to a literal room. According to Dr. Louis S.C. Smith and his assistants, whose book *War Damage in the Nanjing Region* was published in 1938, it usually refers to the

Xun Jian'an, who died in 1980, three years before my visit, was secretary of a collaborators' organization called the Society for the Maintenance of Order. According to his testimony, squads for disposing of and burying bodies were formed about one month after the fall of the city. The number of bodies buried by the squad members reached about four thousand, and there were many others that were disposed of by other people.

One person who remained in Changzhou was Guo Zhigeng, age sixty-six. He met up with the Japanese, was stabbed in six places, and lived to tell about it.

Guo was twenty years old then. His family made its living selling tea and kept a shop within the city. Since the retreat of the Nationalists and the onslaught of the Japanese occurred with unexpected speed, the city was thrown into confusion. Not being able to get hold of a boat that would allow them to flee to any place very far away, Guo's parents and some other members of his family first fled to Dong'an in the suburbs. Guo, his two younger brothers, and a cousin remained behind to watch over the shop.

The Japanese came and tried to push open the door of the shop. The four people inside, determined not to let them in, pushed back from the other side, but realizing that it was hopeless, they ran away from the door and out of the shop. There was a narrow crevice between the wall of their shop and the wall of the neighboring house, the kind of place that was hard to detect unless one knew where to look for it. The four young men went and hid there.

The following morning, they returned to the house, but they were caught when the Japanese showed up again and forced them to carry tea canisters on their shoulders. These tea canisters were tall rectangular wooden containers with round lids, about the size of a kerosene container, and they were kept in a glass case. The four youths were taken to a Japanese encampment about a kilometer away, and along the way, they saw bodies lying here and there in the streets.

The four of them did not walk to the encampment together. Rather, each of them was escorted by a different soldier, and Guo was the last to arrive. As he left the encampment, he saw the sixteen members of the family of Qian Lingshu, a Chinese industrialist, being escorted by Japanese soldiers. (He later learned that they were all bayoneted to death.)

The present-day Changzhou Zipper Factory on Huaide Road near the Huaide Bridge was at that time a machine tool factory, and near its gate was a large air-

---

distance between rafters. This usually means a space 10 to 12 feet wide, but the length varies from region to region. In the Changzhou region, the length is usually 15 to 18 feet, meaning that a *jian* is about 175 square feet of floor space. According to Hori Tomio, writing in *Materials Concerning the Nanjing Massacre in the Japan-China War*, the average dwelling in the area was 4.2 square *jian*, and the average peasant house was about 2 *jian*.

The site of the trench where residents of Changzhou were massacred. It was located in the space between the two men standing with outstretched arms.

raid shelter with doors. Although it was quite large, it was of simple construction: just a ditch like that used for sewers, only lined with bricks and then covered over. Guo had heard that this shelter contained the bodies of the victims of a massacre. According to stories told by residents, some people had hurriedly taken refuge there when the Japanese invaded; they had been discovered and had been mowed down with machine guns. The rumors were true, because when Guo looked through a crack, he could see bodies in a tangled pile that reached nearly to the inside of the door. Unnerved by the sight, Guo gave up on the idea of going home and instead went to the home of a peasant acquaintance named Zhou, who lived on the western outskirts of the city.

Yet, he was worried about his brothers and cousin, who should have gone on to the family home ahead of him, so he decided to go home anyway and left Zhou's house the next day. However, he got no farther than a place called Lanling before he was captured by Japanese soldiers. He was taken to a large house, where soldiers were burning desks, chairs, and other furniture to keep warm. Ten or more Chinese were there, evidently having been conscripted into service.

It was time for lunch, and the Japanese boiled up some rice and ate it. Of course, the captured Chinese were also hungry, and they tried to ask the soldiers for something to eat, but there was no interpreter, and none of them could speak Japanese. Of the entire group, all were illiterate except Guo, so he decided to try communicating with the Japanese in Chinese characters. He approached a man who appeared to be a platoon or company commander and wrote the character for "hungry" in the dirt in front of him. Talking among themselves, perhaps saying something such as, "It seems this guy can write," the soldiers wrote things like "Chinese soldier" and

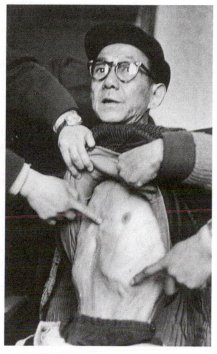

Guo Zhigeng showing two of the six places where he was bayoneted

"middle school student" in the dirt and made Guo copy them. They then forced Guo outside, made him shoulder a rifle, and inspected the palms of his hands. They suspected him of being a Chinese soldier, but as Guo himself told me, "They were probably easy on me, because I was still young."

Then, taking Guo back inside, the soldiers talked among themselves again and finally gestured at him as if to say, "Go home." He told the other conscripts, "I've been released, so I'm leaving before you," and then went outside. He had walked no more than 100 meters when two shouting Japanese soldiers came after him. One appeared to be a commissioned or non-commissioned officer and carried a pistol, and the other carried a bayonet.

They led Guo to a cemetery about 15 meters away. Its graves were of the mound type, and it was surrounded by an earthen wall, but there was plenty of extra room within the wall. First, the officer began pistol-whipping Guo, and when Guo took a defensive posture to avoid being hit again, he was knocked to the ground and beaten viciously. Then the second soldier ran him through with the bayonet. Guo recalls being stabbed three times in the back and chest as he writhed in agony, but then he lost consciousness.

An angry Cheng Biequan.

It was already dark, evidently around midnight, when he miraculously regained consciousness. He had trouble breathing, and his clothes were stuck to his body with dried blood, but he somehow managed to struggle to his feet and make a getaway.

When he had his injuries checked, it was found that he had been stabbed six times: three times in the back, twice in the chest, and once in the neck. Fortunately, none of the blows struck his heart, and he believes that the reason that none of his wounds were very deep is that he had been wearing thick clothing. The wound in his neck was particularly superficial, and Guo says that the bayonet must have hit one of his neck bones and slipped.

Before telling me the story of how his parents were killed, sixty-eight-year-old Cheng Biequan explained the meaning of his name. "Bie means 'catfish,' and the catfish that is under the feet of Guanyin, the goddess of mercy, is being held down so that it doesn't cause earthquakes, right? I wonder if the Japanese went wild because Guanyin didn't restrain them."

Cheng had been working in Shanghai, but because of the war, he returned to Changzhou, where his parents lived in a house near the main gate of the city, and where he had other relatives as well. When Changzhou, too, was threatened, he fled to his wife's parents' home in the country. This is why he did not witness the actual invasion of the city.

Soon he heard terrible news from his aunt: his parents' home had been burned, and his parents and his younger brother's wife had been killed. According to the aunt, who was the younger sister of Cheng's sixty-year-old father, the two rooms in the rear of the house had been completely destroyed by fire, and the three front rooms had been damaged. (At this point, Cheng paused to wipe tears from his eyes. "Whenever I remember this, the sadness just wells up inside of me," he said. As he continued speaking, his breathing became more labored, and the expression on his face became more one of extreme anger than of sorrow.)

As a result of discussing what to do about burying Cheng's murdered parents and sister-in-law, Cheng, two male relatives, and another aunt, this one the wife of his father's younger brother, went to the burned-out house.

As they approached the main gate of Changzhou, it was still light, and since it would be dangerous to be discovered by the Japanese, they hid in a sorghum field on the other side of the river and waited for nightfall. There were only two peasant houses nearby, and the four people were in the perfect position to see across the river to the back door of the Cheng house. Near the door lay the body of a woman, but being so far away, they could not tell whether it was Cheng's mother or his sister-in-law or some complete stranger.

However, two Japanese on patrol found Cheng and his three companions. Since Cheng looked like a young student, the Japanese made ready to kill him on the spot. They forced him to kneel, facing away from them. He could hear them loading their rifles. All at once, there came the sound of a young woman's voice. Immediately, the two soldiers took off in the direction where the sound had come from, leaving Cheng kneeling there. His relatives pulled him to his feet, and they all ran off.

He returned to his wife's family home, and he didn't have the courage to venture back into the city. Having gone through the terrifying experience of nearly being shot to death, he become a nervous wreck, jumping and trembling when even slightly startled.

After the coldest days of winter had passed and the weather turned warmer, there were fewer incidents of mass murder and violence, and Cheng's aunt began to worry that the bodies of her family members would rot in the open, so the four relatives set out together once again. The aunt in the city had told them that the bodies had been thrown into a trench about 20 meters from the house by a Red Cross burial squad. According to this aunt, Cheng's mother's leg had been severed, and she had died near the back gate. An eyewitness had said that Cheng's mother had not been killed instantly but had managed, despite her serious injuries, to crawl outside the house, where she had lain groaning for a couple of days before dying. ("It's heartbreaking," Cheng commented, and then he was unable to continue for a time. After he wiped his eyes and began speaking again, he looked up, the expression of anger on his face intensified.)

Entering the city, Cheng and his relatives went to the trench where the bodies were said to be. Several dozen bodies remained unclaimed, some buried in the mud, but most scattered above ground, and the powerful stench of decay was enough to make a person pass out. Unable to bear the stench, Cheng and his party drank some cheap liquor and set about the task half-drunk.

Decay had set in on all the bodies, so much so that it was difficult to recognize faces. They identified the body of Cheng's mother by the fact that it was *missing a leg, and they recognized his sister-in-law by her clothing. Cheng's father had a branch-like growth on his right thumb that resembled a sixth finger, which made him easy to recognize.*

They moved the three bodies to the family home and buried them in simple coffins that the aunt had provided. She never told him many more details about the deaths of his family members, because his nervous state had not returned to normal since his narrow escape from death.

After that, Cheng returned to his wife's family's home, but driven by the necessity of making a living, he returned to Shanghai, where things had calmed down.

CHAPTER 6

"SEIZING JURONG, WE CHARGE ONWARD"

The *Yomiuri Shimbun* reporting the fall of Jurong.

According to *Captain Watanabe Toshio's Reminiscences,* this is what Watanabe wrote in his field diary for November 30:

> Left Suzhou at 9:00 A.M., heading for Fuzhou. Collected more than ten Chinese and made them come with us.

The Ōno unit closing in on Jurong. (From the December 29, 1937, issue of *Asahi Graph.*)

The Japanese often seized men at random and drafted them as coolies or conscripts in order to carry not only their own baggage and equipment but also the goods they had looted. The men were not given a chance to notify their families—they simply went missing, and it was not unusual for even children to be taken in this way. The ever-increasing numbers of Chinese men who were forced to accompany the soldiers are described as follows in *Living Soldiers:*

> During the course of the march, we gradually lost many of our military horses and replaced them with Chinese horses and water buffalo. At the same time, we also rounded up an increasing number of Chinese coolies. It was a strange scene, Chinese men helping us attack Nanjing. Leading the water buffalo by their muzzles, the men walked briskly in bare feet, wearing baggy, black padded trousers. The soldiers walked along beside them, puffing on cigarettes. They poked them in the shoulder with the elbow of their right arm, the one with which they held their rifles.

Zhou Guisheng.

"Ni! Nanjing, hao guniang, duoduo you?" they would ask. ("Hey, you! Nanjing, good girls, many-many there are?")

If the conscripts understood this broken Chinese, a shadow would come across their dirt-streaked faces, and they would answer curtly, with a forlorn smile,*"You."* (There are).

Sixty-five-year-old Zhou Gui-sheng, who now lives on Changzhou's Nanda Street, came from an impoverished family of construction workers who had no acquaintances or relatives in the country. Since they would have had no money to provide food or heat for themselves, even if they had fled to the country, they were stuck in the city. Then nineteen years old (18 years old by Western reckoning), Zhou was captured by the Japanese during their invasion of the city, just as he was about to cross the Guanghua Bridge on the way home from viewing the bomb damage. Here is what happened to him when he was drafted to accompany the Japanese soldiers to Nanjing:

After capturing Zhou, the Japanese soldiers made him stand around while they rested, cooked, and ate their meal. They captured another Chinese at the same time, a man of about forty, but they simply searched him to see if he had anything of value, tossed him into the river, and shot him dead when he bobbed to the surface.

On the other side of the bridge was a general store, and of course, the door was closed, but it bore signs advertising cigarettes. One soldier, evidently thinking he could commandeer some smokes, rapped on the door, and a young woman answered. She was immediately taken to a small pier along the riverbank, where the soldiers tried to strip off her clothes. She put up a determined resistance, but the soldiers eventually succeeded in stripping her naked as their comrades eating lunch nearby looked on, cheering and applauding. She tried to cover herself with a handkerchief, and while resisting the soldiers' attempts to pull it out of her hands, she fell into the river. The soldiers aimed at her head and shot her.

A boat happened by, with one rower at either end and three or four passengers. As it approached the pier, the soldiers took aim and opened fire, killing everyone.

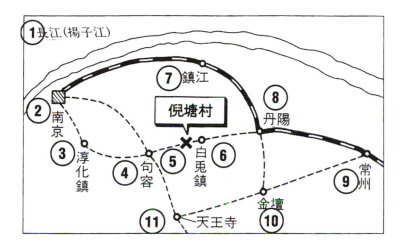

1. Yangtze River
2. Nanjing
3. Shunhuazhen
4. Jurong
5. Niyang village
6. Baituzhen
7. Zhenjiang
8. Tanyang
9. Changzhou
10. Jintan
11. Tianwang Temple

The unit finally left, and Zhou was forced to go along to carry baggage. When they came to the city's cultural center, they rounded up about twenty more Chinese men and pressed them into service as coolies. They were forced to take off their outer garments and their hands were tied until it was time to shoulder the baggage.

The unit headed for Nanjing, passing through Danyang and Jurong. On the way back from Nanjing, Zhou and his fellow coolies were shot en masse, but the story of how he miraculously survived will be told later.

The December 6 evening edition of the *Asahi Shimbun* (published on December 5) carried the news of the occupation of Jurong as the lead story on its front page, under the headline "Seizing Jurong, We Charge Onward."

Shanghai, December 5, Dōmei: At dawn on the fifth, the _____ Unit completely captured Jurong.

Wulipu, December 5, Dōmei: Our troops, which entered Jurong at eleven P.M., mopped up the enemy with repeated nighttime attacks, and reached the airport at the northwest edge of the city. As the sun rose, they gave three shouts of *Banzai!* as they raised the Rising Sun flag over the tallest building in the city and over the airport.

Wulipu, December 5, Dōmei: Our troops, which completely captured Jurong in the early morning of December 5, have left a small unit behind to guard the city, but the main force has moved on, concentrating their forces in preparation

Ni Nianke, witness to a large-scale massacre.

for the attack on Nanjing, which is only 40 kilometers away.

Wulipu, December 5, Dōmei: The enemy defeated in the fight for Jurong are fleeing in confusion toward Nanjing. Our forces have shifted to giving chase. The frontline troops will reach Jiegang Garrison by 8:00 A.M. at the earliest, and they are pushing onward.

According to Huang Hechao, the director of the Jurong county government office, the advancing troops of the Japanese army invaded the city from the direction of Danyang on December 4,[1] but since most of the city's residents had already left, the scale of the massacres was actually larger in places on the way to Jurong, such as Maoshan and Tianwangsi. The majority of the towns and villages along the way were burned, and what happened at Baituzhen was especially horrible.

At Niyong village in Guhuang township, Ni Nianke (56) not only witnessed a massacre but also lost his family. Here is what he experienced as a boy of ten:

At about 4:30 in the late afternoon of December 4, a day of comparatively fine weather, the Japanese approached a bridge at the eastern edge of the village. There were eighty-six households in this hamlet, which was strung out along the road. When the people heard the gunfire, they abandoned their homes and fled in all directions. At that time, Ni's family consisted of his grandmother, his father, his mother, his two older brothers, two younger sisters, and his oldest brother's wife and son, ten people in all. During the confusion, only his oldest brother, twenty-year-old Ni Lianke, stayed behind to guard the house. Ni Nianke fled with his grandmother and mother to a ditch along the Niyong River, about 1 li (500 hundred meters) away. The others hid wherever they could.

As it grew dark, flames could be seen in one corner of the hamlet. Ni Nianke, his mother, and his grandmother could only watch uncomprehendingly

---

1. The eighth volume of the Defense Agency's War History Research Office's *Library of War History*,"The China Incident Army Campaign," says, "The pursuit unit of the 16th Division broke through the enemy who occupied positions near Jurong on December 5," and other Japanese sources also specify the 5th. However, the entry in the field diary in *Captain Watanabe Toshio's Reminiscences* is hearsay, and it says "December 4."

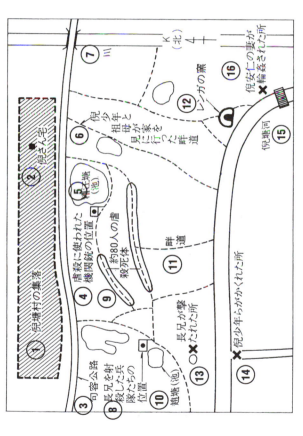

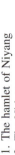

1. The hamlet of Niyang
2. The Ni home
3. Jurong Highway
4. The position of the machine guns used in the massacre
5. Zaowangyang pond
6. The path that Ni and his grandmother followed when going to check up on their house
7. River
8. The position of the soldiers who shot Ni's older brother
9. The bodies of approximately eighty massacre victims
10. Zhaoyang pond
11. Path
12. Brick kiln
13. Where Ni's oldest brother was killed
14. Where Ni and the others hid
15. Niyang Creek
16. Where Ni Anren's wife was raped

as the sounds of the flames mingled in a terrifying manner with the barking of dogs and screams of people. However, just before dawn, another resident, a peasant named Ni Anren, came running to their hiding place and told them what happened: some residents unable to flee, along with some refugees from elsewhere, forty people in all, had been captured and locked into Ni Anren's house, which was then set on fire. They were burned to death.

After dawn, perhaps about eight or nine o'clock, a procession of about eighty conscripted Chinese men came under guard from Xijing, the nearest village to the north. They marched with their hands tied behind their backs and linked to one another like beads on a Buddhist rosary. They were not captured Nationalist soldiers, just ordinary residents of the area around Xijing. As Ni Nianke and the others watched the procession from their hiding place, it left the Danyang-Jurong highway and walked along a path among the rice paddies in the direction of the Niyong River. At a point where the path split into two near a pond (Zaowangyong) close to the road, the men were made to sit down. There they were raked with machine gun fire until all were killed.

Now, Ni Nianke, his mother, and his grandmother became worried about the house and about the safety of the older brother who had remained behind. Hoping that no harm would come to an old woman and a child, young Ni and his grandmother returned to a village by a path that lay east of where the eighty men had been massacred. There was no sign of the oldest brother, but the house had not been burned. Rumor had it that houses that flew the Rising Sun flag would not be burned, so they took some cloth, hurriedly fashioned a flag, and hung it over their front door.

Then they saw a gruesome sight: a nearly fleshless skeleton hanging from a tree in the neighbors' yard. Strips of meat that had clearly been torn at by dogs that lay on the ground below. They later learned that the skeleton was that of a peasant youth in his twenties named Li Taidong, a large fellow 186 centimeters tall. The barking dogs that the people had heard the night before had been German shepherds used by the Japanese military, and the screams had come from Li Taidong. The screams had lasted for about thirty minutes, and the barking for about an hour. The villagers later surmised that Li had been strung up naked and that the soldiers had sliced off his flesh to feed to the dogs.

So as not to be discovered by the Japanese, Ni Nianke and his grandmother decided to return to their hiding place by the river, but as they passed in front of one house, the boy, who was walking on ahead, was seen by a soldier. Raising his bayonet, the soldier poked at him, but at that moment, the grandmother, who was following closely behind, picked up a large stone and made as if to throw it at the soldier. However, the soldier did not harm the boy and simply gestured at him to leave quickly. The grandmother hur-

ried toward the river, gripping her grandson's hand.

In order to return to their hiding place, Ni and his grandmother had to go along the path where the eighty men had been massacred. Among the piled mass of bodies, there was one man who was still alive. Thinking that perhaps he could be saved, they stopped to untie him, but while they were doing so, he died.

Soon after they returned to their hiding place, they saw eight Japanese soldiers corner a woman at the foot of a dam about 200 meters east of their hiding place. Crying and screaming, the woman was raped by each of the eight soldiers in succession. At some point, she evidently lost consciousness, and even after the soldiers left, she lay motionless. They later found out that the woman was Ni Anren's wife. She suf-

The younger sister of Li Taidong, the young man who was fed to Japanese military dogs, is still alive.

fered from amnesia for some time after the incident, and although she eventually recovered her memory, she died four or five years later.

In the afternoon, the group noticed Ni Nianke's oldest brother, Ni Lianke, coming from wherever he had been hiding and trotting toward the river, with soldiers chasing him into the area between the river and the highway. Two shots rang out, and he fell over near a small pond.

The group's hiding place was not along the Niyong River itself, but along a narrow ditch that flowed into it from the south. Since there was a small boat at the riverbank, Ni and his group crossed over to the opposite bank and retrieved Ni Lianke after the soldiers had left. He was still alive, but he had been shot in the chest and the left hip. Through his pain, he told his family what had happened.

Realizing that it was dangerous to remain at home, he had fled to the edge of the village but was captured by soldiers and taken to a house. He was hit on the head with a rock and lost consciousness. The soldiers threw water in his face to revive him, but this time a soldier came at him with a bayonet. Ni Lianke grabbed it with both hands, but since the soldier jerked it away, he suffered deep cuts on his fingers. At that, the other soldiers gestured for him to go away. Thinking that he had been released, he set off for the river, and that's when he was shot. . . .

Niyang village as seen from the spot to which Ni and two others fled.

Ni's eldest brother died at midnight. Weeping helplessly, his family buried him in one of their own fields, about 60 meters away. Knowing that it would be dangerous to stay around, they fled south to Lijia village. They later learned from the brickmaker whose kiln was near the dam that the grandfather's younger brother had fled to kiln on the night of December 4 and had been shot. On the fifth, the village was set on fire, and of the eighty-six households, only one three-room house remained.

Luo Daxing (55), of Huangmei township, Luojiazhuang village, just to the northwest of Jurong, was from a family of tenant farmers, who ranked lower than the ordinary peasants. He was nine years old when the Japanese invaded, and his family name at the time was Sun. The household consisted of eight people including him: his father (55), his mother (53), his two older brothers (28 and 25), his two younger sisters (6 and 3), and a thirteen-year-old *tongyangxi*, a girl who had been taken into the family as a prospective wife for one of the brothers. In addition, he had two older sisters, but they were already married, and his third older brother had drowned as a child. The family made their living tending the mulberry orchards of a landlord about 500 meters south of the village.

It was about a week after the Japanese advance guard's "charge onward" through the area on their way to Nanjing that Luo's family was attacked and he was orphaned. This is how he related the events of that day.

Luo Daxing.

Even after Jurong was occupied, not very many people came through this village, which lay five kilometers outside the city. Still, most of the people who lived in houses facing the road had fled. Luo's family's house, however, was in a mulberry orchard well away from the road, so only his two older brothers, who were in the age group likely to be conscripted by the Japanese, ran away. The other six family members remained behind.

On the afternoon of December 14, a unit of Japanese soldiers came to Liaoyongtou, the village immediately south of Luojiazhuang, and set it on fire. Its inhabitants scattered. Luo Daxing's house—which was so humble that it could more accurately be called a shed—was located halfway between the two villages, so that each one was about a li *away. Someone who had fled from Liaoyongtou ran up to the shed in the orchard, shouting, "The Japanese devils are here! Clear out fast!"*

"We've got to get out of here right away!" Luo's father was alarmed.

Yet, Luo's mother was strangely calm. "We're still fine," she replied. "But the men will be captured, so they should take off first." It was normal for the men, who might be conscripted or mistaken for Chinese soldiers, and young women, who were in danger of rape, to be the first to leave.

Luo's father took what he could carry and immediately headed west with the men from the neighboring village. The remaining five family members (young Luo, his mother, his younger sisters, and the tongyangxi*) left home soon afterward, heading southwest. Luo thinks that they did this because most of the Japanese troops were approaching from the east and south and advancing northwest to Nanjing, but since both his parents died, he does not really know.*

After they had fled a little more than a li, *they came to the home of a slightly more prosperous peasant named Liu Changhua. The house stood off by itself, and when Luo's family arrived, Liu Changhua himself had already gone, and only his wife and son remained. "If you're found out walking around,*

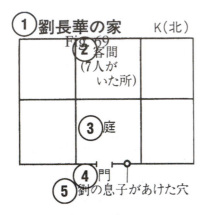

① 劉長華の家　　K(北)
② 客間
（7人が
いた所）

③ 庭

④ 門
⑤ 劉の息子があけた穴

1. Liu Changhua's house
2. The guest room where the seven
   people were
3. Yard
4. Gate
5. The hole that Liu's son punched in
   the wall

you'll be killed," Mrs. Liu told them, "so it would be better if you hid here." They agreed and stayed at the house.

The Liu's son was outside standing guard, and when he saw two Japanese coming from the direction of Liao-yongtou, he immediately informed the six people inside. "Let's get out of here!" Mrs. Liu urged.

"If we're seen fleeing, we'll be shot," Luo's mother argued, "and that would be even worse." But as they were arguing, the Japanese arrived at the gate of the house.

They came through the gate. One soldier stayed in the courtyard while the other entered the house, which was built around the courtyard in a U shape with a total of five rooms. The seven people huddled together in the parlor, the room directly across from the gate. As the soldier burst into the room, Mrs. Liu knelt before him, bringing her hands together in Chinese fashion, and began pleading desperately, "Xiansheng ya, women shi zhongtian de, dou shi hao ren. Qiuqiu ni rao ming a!" *(Sir, we're peasants. We're good people. We beg you to spare our lives!)*

The other six also knelt beside her, waiting for a response from the soldiers. But the soldier, probably unable to understand her variety of Chinese, simply ignored her pleas. He gripped his rifle with both hands and swung it from his hip to knock each of the seven people down, just as the men in devil costumes at village festivals push the visitors around with their staves. He went back outside, and he and the other soldier began pulling tufts of straw out of the thatched roof, using it as tinder to set fire to different parts of the house. Having done that, they left through the gate and locked it with the metal fittings that the family used when they were away, trapping the seven people inside.

At first the fire was weak, so the mud-walled room was not particularly hot, but within a few minutes, the flames had grown higher, and the seven people were in danger of burning to death. Liu's son grabbed a farm implement and chopped a hole in the wall. The soldiers were only about 200 or 300 meters away, watching the scene, but whether it was because of the flames and smoke or because their view was blocked by a toolshed, they did not notice the young man escaping. The other six also came out of the house

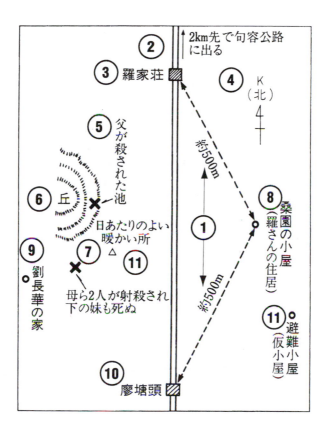

1. Approximately 500 meters
2. The road intersects with the Jurong Highway 2 kilometers farther on
3. Luojiazhuang
4. North
5. The pond where Luo's father was killed
6. Hill
7. Where Luo's mother and the *tongyangxi* were killed and Luo's youngest sister later died.
8. The hut in the peach orchard (the Luo family's home)
9. Liu Changhua's home
10. Liaoyangtou
11. The Luo family's hiding place (temporary hut)

one after another. But when Mrs. Liu saw her house going up in flames, she became hysterical and ran around screaming and crying, "Jiu ming! Jiu huo!" (Help! Fire!) The soldiers noticed her and immediately shot her dead.

Fortunately, young Luo and his family were able to escape from this frightful scene unharmed. It was already twilight. "Let's go to the shack," Luo's mother said. "Your father's probably there already." Like the other households in the village, the family had hurriedly built a hiding place after hearing that the Japanese were on the way, and theirs was in a patch of over-

grown weeds in the mulberry orchard about 200 meters from their house. Gunfire could be heard from the direction of Luojiazhuang, but they no longer perceived any sign of the Japanese soldiers in the vicinity of their shelter.

Unfortunately, they had misjudged the situation. As they were walking toward the shelter, two Japanese soldiers suddenly appeared in front of them. Overcome with shock, Luo's mother sank weakly to the ground, and Luo himself took off, running one 150 meters and jumping into a ditch to hide. The soldiers could not have missed seeing him run off, but perhaps because they saw that he was just a child, they didn't chase after him. As he watched from a ditch, his mother raised her hands to plead with the soldiers, and almost at that instant, two shots rang out. Both his mother and the thirteen-year-old tongyangxi *fell over.*

Afraid that he, too, would be killed, Luo lay flat in the ditch, which had no water in it at this time of year, but was still muddy. After ten or fifteen minutes, he cautiously raised his head to see the soldiers already far away, leaving for Luojiazhuang.

He ran to where his mother lay. She was still alive. The tongyangxi *was not moving and may have been killed instantly. His mother lay on her side, scratching at the earth with her right hand and reaching for the sky with her trembling left hand. She was silent, not screaming despite her evident pain. When she opened her eyes and saw her son, she moved her lips, but she could not even answer his cries. Then she rolled over onto her back, but although the boy saw no blood flowing so he did not know where she had been hit, there was some blood on her face. It was then that he realized that his mother would surely die.*

Next to his mother lay a glass bottle of cooking oil, a green kerchief, and a comb. These were important household possessions. Focusing his attention upon the items, he began gathering them up. Just then, his six-year-old sister, who had been standing to one side in a daze, suddenly let out a wail and threw her arms around him. She gripped his arms and refused to let go. Without fully understanding what had happened, she had come to sense the horror of the situation.

Their mother had stopped moving and appeared to have stopped breathing. The nine-year-old boy (seven years old by Western reckoning) took the hand of his six-year-old sister (who was actually four or five), and started to leave. The youngest sister, who was three by traditional Chinese reckoning but actually only a year old, could not talk yet, and she had been toddling aimlessly around her fallen mother. When she saw her brother and sister leave, she followed them.

(Beginning at this point in the story, Luo Daxing occasionally became choked with tears and had to stop speaking.)

"I was just a child, too. I couldn't do anything with two little sisters. If I had led the older sister and carried the younger sister, I wouldn't have been able to run when I needed to. There wasn't anything I could do."

He walked faster, in order to shake his youngest sister off his trail. She tottered after them for a few more steps, then gave up, stopped, turned around, and returned to where her mother's body lay.

It was already completely dark when they reached the shelter, and there was no sign of their father's having been there. The hut was stocked with uncooked rice and a pot, but since they had no matches and could not light a fire, they went to sleep without eating.

The next morning, before it was completely light, the two of them left the shelter and went to Liaoyongtou in search of their missing father. Bodies lay scattered around the burned-out settlement, and they saw no living person. At the edge of the village, a plump stray dog was gnawing on a human body. Not knowing where else to search, they began crying and calling for their father.

Suddenly his sister said, "Let's go back to where Mother is. Won't she be better after sleeping all night?" The little girl did not understand the concept of death, and even Luo harbored a faint hope that his mother might have come back to life. They headed back to the scene of the shooting.

No miracle had happened to their mother, but their little sister lay on top of the body. She had opened her mother's blouse and had her head buried there, apparently attempting to nurse. When she noticed her brother and older sister, she sat straight up and silently and desperately held out both arms, as if to plead, "Pick me up." Having spent the night out in the open in mid-December, the year-old infant was weak, seemingly too weak even to cry. Her brother and sister, too, were weak from not eating.

"There was nothing we could do. We were helpless. We abandoned our little sister once again and walked away."

(Luo Daxing gave a sob and had to stop talking, but after a while, he suddenly remembered something: "That's right. Today's December 14, isn't it? The day my mother was killed. It was exactly forty-six years ago today. I wonder if it's some sort of karma that we're talking about this on the anniversary of my mother's death.")

The two children had no recourse but to return to the shelter. After sunrise on the third day, they once again went to Liaoyongtou to look for their father. This time, there were no bodies lying around the village, but there were no living people, either. The villagers and the relatives of the dead had retrieved the bodies during the night and then gone back into hiding at dawn. "Let's go back to Mother," Daxing's sister insisted. "She may be all right this time."

The boy no longer held out even the faintest hope, but he said, "Yes, let's go see." As the two of them walked, he even began to take on some of his sister's optimism. "If she has come back to life by some chance," he thought, "that would really be something to be happy about." Besides, he thought his youngest sister might still be alive.

The baby was lying at her mother's breast, just as she had been the day before, but she was cold to the touch and did not move.

About 100 meters off in the direction of the shelter, there was a sunny area protected from the wind. The children stopped to rest there and dozed off. As the sun was beginning to set, two Chinese men, one about twenty and the other about thirty, happened to pass by. They were peasants from a nearby village who had been conscripted as coolies by Japanese troops heading for Nanjing. Having seized an opportunity to escape along the way, they were heading for home. Even though Daxing knew that these men were strangers, he asked them if they had seen his father. The men replied that they had seen nothing but corpses and had not spotted anyone who might be his father.

Not having eaten anything for three days, Luo asked them for food. They didn't have any, but when he told them that there was rice in his family's shelter, they said, "Well, we have matches," and so he led them there.

As the delicious-looking rice was cooking in the pot, the young men warned him against eating too much. "Sometimes if you eat too much at once, you can die. Eat a little bit now, and then more later." That night, the four of them slept in the shelter.

The next morning, as the young men were about to set out for their home village, Luo and his sister threw their arms around them and begged, "If you're going home, please take us with you!"

The men agreed, commenting, "Well, we could hire the boy to tend the cattle," but a shot rang out at the very moment they stepped outside the shelter. The young men ran off as fast as they could.

Not knowing what else to do, Daxing and his sister returned to the sunny hollow near where his mother's body lay. Their thought was that it was warm there, and besides, it was a place that villagers often passed by, so perhaps they would be able to learn some news of their father. At length, three men came by, carrying bodies on their shoulders. They were on burial detail, picking up the bodies that lay scattered around the village. One of the men was an acquaintance from Luojiazhuang. Luo jumped up at the man and begged him to take him and his sister to his house, since they had nowhere else to go. "Well," the man replied, "should I take you on after we finish the burials?" Afraid of being left behind again, Daxing and his sister stuck close to the men, following them around all day and watching the burials. The men had already buried Daxing's mother and little sister and the tongyangxi, although it was some time later that he learned this. According to Lu Jubao and Lu Caixing, who pointed out the burial mounds, his mother had been *buried near the place where she fell, and the sister and the* tongyangxi *had been buried in a nearby ditch. But there was no news of his father.*

About ten days later, the Japanese troops returned to Luojiazhang to "punish" the villagers, but they found out about it ahead of time and of course, everyone fled to the west, including young Luo. On their way, they came upon a small marshy pond on a slope by the side of the road. There was very little water in it, and a body lay at the water's edge. When they went to look, they found that it was Luo's father. He was bound hand and foot with gaiters, and there was what looked like a bayonet wound in his right temple. The body was already starting to decay.

The villagers guessed that Daxing's father must have run this far on the 14th. Being worried about his house and not wanting to run too far away, he apparently had hidden in the marsh and watched the goings-on from there. Caught in the act by Japanese soldiers, he would have been suspected of "spying," which usually meant being shot on the spot, but in this case, since he was tied up, it was assumed that he must have been killed after some kind of torture.

Luo and his sister were adopted by one of the men who had been on the burial crew. This was when their family name was changed from Sun to Luo. They never found any trace of their two oldest brothers.

According to records at Luojiazhuang, the three men buried fifty-five bodies. Thirty-six of them were residents of Luijiazhang and were identified. The remaining nineteen—young and old, male and female—were evidently refugees from elsewhere. It had been their tragic fate to be locked behind the sturdy doors of Kong Fangbai's well-built home and burned alive.

CHAPTER 7

"ZHENJIANG OCCUPIED"

The *Asahi Shimbun* announcing the fall of Zhenjiang.

The peasant Zhang Caili (fifty-seven when I interviewed him), was eleven years old in 1937, living in Houbenhu village, Guangli township, seven or eight kilometers northeast of Jurong, with his parents, older brother, and sister-in-law. At some time between eight and nine on the morning of December 5, a frantic, sweat-drenched straggler from the Nationalist army came running through the village. "The Eastern devils are coming!" he cried before hurrying on. "Clear out right away!" The village fell into an uproar, and Zhang's family, except for his father, ran away to a hillside about 1 *li* from the village.

After a time, Japanese troops burst into the village, and the refugees could see flames rising from one area. Since the hillside was fairly close to the village, it was still unsafe, so at about noon, the family fled about 10 *li* far-

Zhang Caili.

ther to the north, to some relatives who lived in the village of Jiexiang. The next day, Zhang's mother returned home alone to check up on her husband.

He was dead, due to the villagers' unrealistically optimistic ideas of how the Japanese would treat them. As the soldiers approached, a sort of village council made up of thirty people had prepared to welcome the troops peacefully.

They had lined up at the entrance to the village to greet the arriving troops. But all of them were quickly put under arrest and shut up inside a house. Conducting a search of the village, the Japanese rounded up an additional fourteen people, including Zhang's father and uncle (his father's younger brother), and imprisoned them in the same room as the first thirty. Then the soldiers surrounded the house and set it on fire, preparing to shoot anyone who escaped.

In the smoke and confusion, four or five people managed to get out of the house, but they were shot, one after another. Only one young man by the name of Wan Rensheng succeeded in evading the hail of bullets and escaping with his life. (I was told that he is still alive and living in Shanghai.)

Thus, forty-three villagers were either burned or shot to death, and 80 percent or more of the houses in the village were destroyed by fire. The son of another uncle (that is, Zhang's cousin) was forcibly conscripted by the Japanese troops and taken away, never to be seen again. Zhang said that he undoubtedly was killed in the early evening.

Gao Jiawen (55), a peasant in Guanglimiao, the next village over from

Gao Jiawen.

Houbenhu, was nine years old then. The Japanese had passed through Guanglimiao before the massacre at Houbenhu, but all the inhabitants had already fled.

After December 10, young Gao returned to his village, and when he heard of the massacre in the next village, he went to see what had happened. Some of the forty-three bodies had already been claimed by relatives, but there were still quite a few left, and they were charred beyond recognition. Since the building where the victims had been imprisoned was a distillery, there had been liquor jars standing around, and one of the victims had crawled into a jar to escape the flames. Only his body was not charred.

The next city after Jurong along the Shanghai Expeditionary Force's route was Zhenjiang, a city along the Yangtze, known to Japanese people as the place where the fifteenth-century painter Sesshū studied, and as the site of Jinshan Temple, which figures in the famous "Legend of the White Snake."

According to "The China Incident Army Campaign, Part 1," published by the Defense Agency Training Institute War History Office, "The Amatani Detachment of the Thirteenth Division advanced toward Zhenjiang via Danyang. Capturing a position south of Zhenjiang, they entered the city on the eighth and set up a battery in the vicinity.

The evening edition of the *Tōkyō Nichinichi Shimbun* (the forerunner of the *Mainichi Shimbun*) for December 9 reported the events as follows, under the headline, "Zhenjiang Occupied."

> Changzhou, December 8; Dōmei: With the force of flood waters, the Hanaya and Adachi Units, heading toward Zhenjiang, the fortress east of Nanjing, further continued their assault from Zhangguandu, and after passing through Xinfengzhen, they initiated their advance on the morning of the eighth. With the fierce support of the artillery, they finally rushed the city walls of Zhenjiang at 8:00 A.M. Clearing the walls, they charged into the city and routed the remaining enemy. The large unit finished their mopping-up operations at about 9:00 A.M. and raised the Rising Sun flag on the city wall.

Tang Rongfa (63) a retired senior employee of the Zhenjiang Office of the Yangtze Shipping Company, was seventeen years old at the time. He lived with his parents, two older brothers, and the first older brother's wife and son in the vicinity of Zhongshan Bridge near Jiangbian Park.

The Japanese bombing attacks began two weeks before the actual invasion. November 27 and 28 saw particularly severe bombing and strafing. Bombs even fell near Tang's house: in addition to two that fell in Jiangbian Park, one fell on a ditch where a large number of people had taken refuge, and another only about 10 feet further. Even now, Tang can clearly recall the sight of headless bodies and scattered limbs and internal organs.

Tang Rongfa.

The citizens of Zhenjiang began to evacuate the city, one after another, not only to the surrounding countryside, but in some cases, even to far-away Hong Kong. Yet, there were some residents who stayed behind to watch over their houses and property. In the case of Tang's family, his oldest brother fled to Baoying County with his wife and son, and his second oldest brother fled to Xiaojiabian. Tang and his parents stayed behind to guard not only the family's four-room house but also their sixteen pigs (two porkers, a brood sow, and thirteen piglets).

On December 8, when the Japanese infantry units came to Zhenjiang, bombs roared through the sky, and the Tang family spent the entire day in a bomb shelter. The next morning, when young Tang ventured outside the door of his house, he saw two Japanese soldiers who happened to be walking his way just at that moment. He panicked and ran back into the house, but the two soldiers came right after him with their swords and bayonets. They called out, "Xiaohai!" (Boy!) and a few words of broken Chinese and proceeded to search the house. Tang's father put his hands together and pleaded with them, repeating, "Yang xiansheng, yang xiansheng" (Foreign masters, foreign masters) Since there was nothing of obvious value, the soldiers left without further trouble, but within a short time, three or four more soldiers showed up. When they saw the pigs, they shot one of them and left after carving off the best parts. Then another group of three or four soldiers appeared, following so soon upon the previous group that they could have passed them on the way, and they, too, shot a pig. Groups of soldiers kept coming until all sixteen pigs had been taken. The reason that so *many soldiers showed up in such a short time was that a unit of cavalry was encamped at the nearby Zhenjiang Stadium.*

The neighborhood along the riverbank near Zhongshan where the Tang house stood consisted of over two hundred houses with thatched roofs, but most of the inhabitants had fled to the countryside, and only about ten houses remained occupied. Just before noon on December 9, the Japanese began to set fire to this neighborhood. The people remaining in the ten occupied houses came outside to plead with the soldiers, desperately begging them not to burn their homes. Some were ignored, but there were a few whose pleas were accepted. However, one old man, unable to bear the idea of his house burning, was shot as he tried to put out the flames.

When it was all over, only four houses were left, including the Tang family house. There were fires all over Zhenjiang. Only three of the city's thirty-eight districts were undamaged, and more than half of the rest were destroyed. Seventeen streets, including the main commercial street, Daxi Road, were laid waste.

Along the riverbank near Zhongshan Bridge, the twenty or more people from the ten remaining households, most of them old people or children, had no option but to live together in the four houses that were still standing. During the day, however, these houses were, in fact, abandoned. When the Japanese soldiers passed by, the people all had to kneel and say "Dongyang xiansheng" (Eastern masters), or else they would be beaten. If they were inside one of the houses when the Japanese came, they would be thought of as "hiding," and they did not know what would happen to them then. It was only after dark that they could finally go inside.

There were hardly any young women left in the city, but there were still many rapes. The wife of a blacksmith of Tang's acquaintance had not left town, having given birth only ten days before, but even she was raped. In the one of the four remaining houses that was closest to Tang's, there were two little girls, twelve and thirteen years old by traditional reckoning. The thirteen-year-old was the daughter of Wei Xiaobao, and the family name of the twelve-year-old was Xu. At about nine o'clock on the morning of the third day after the Japanese arrived (December 10), two soldiers appeared, grabbed the two girls, forced them into two of the empty houses, and raped them. The girls screamed and cried, and at one point, one of them ran out, naked from the waist down, clutching her trousers in one hand. People thought she had been driven mad. Soon after, the other girl also ran out in the same way. At about four o'clock on the afternoon of the same day, the same two soldiers returned, took the screaming, weeping girls, and raped them again. Not fifteen minutes later, four more soldiers came and took not only the two girls, but also the mother of twelve-year-old Xu, and the three of them were raped by the four soldiers.

That night, Wei Xiaobao shaved the girls' heads and gave them boys' clothes to wear, but the next morning, the 11th, when the first two soldiers showed up once again, they recognized the girls' faces and saw through the disguise. They were raped once more.

From then on, Wei Xiaobao hid his thirteen-year-old daughter under a crate in the interior of the house and piled things on top of it. After dark, twelve-year-old Xu, along with her entire family, slipped away to an unknown location.

On the morning of the 12th, the same two soldiers showed up once more. When they realized that both girls were gone, they forced all the people from the ten households to stand in a row, and they beat them one by one. Tang was not only beaten by hand but also kicked and hit with rods, while the soldiers kept screaming, "Hua guniang!" (The young girls!) The rest of what they yelled was in Japanese, but they seemed to be saying, in effect, "Bring out the young girls!" After beating everyone severely, the soldiers left.

The same day, three other Japanese soldiers appeared, one carrying a pistol, the other carrying only bayonets, although none of them had Japanese-style swords. This time they were after coolies, so seventeen-year-old Tang was led away.

Fires were still burning in scattered parts of the city, and corpses could be seen here and there. The group of conscripts, which consisted of Tang and ten or more other men, first came to Wangjia Gate. There they caught sight of an old man who was working in a vegetable field. When the three soldiers saw him, they said something among themselves, and the one with the pistol suddenly threw himself to the ground, aimed at the old man, and fired. The shot missed, but the old man started and ran off. As he reached the door of a ruined house, another soldier took hold of the same pistol, aimed, and fired. The old man fell flat on his back. Laughing loudly, the soldiers led their captives along to see the man they had shot. Blood was gushing out of his neck.

Soon afterward, when they reached a place called Majiashan, they met up with three passers-by coming around from behind a hill. One of them was carrying a load on his shoulders, another was pulling a wagon, and the other was pushing the wagon from behind. When the two groups were about 30 meters apart, one of the Japanese soldiers shot the man pulling the wagon. He silently fell to the ground, clutching his belly. Then the man pushing the wagon was shot, and fell with a loud cry and rolled around on the ground as blood flowed from his thigh, soon staining his trousers red. The man shouldering the load simply stood there, stunned.

Immediately after that, two more passers-by came from another direction, and they were felled by two shots. One apparently died instantly, but the other lay on the ground screaming. The soldiers approached and finished him off with a single shot. As a result, there were three corpses on the ground, one man stand-

ing frozen in place, and another in agony from his wound. The soldiers made the standing man load the wounded man onto his shoulders and then laughingly gave an order. Judging from their gestures, they were yelling, "Get out of here!"

Evidently, the three soldiers were having a killing contest to compare their marksmanship.

When the party arrived at Xiangjiawan, they found two vats of manure used for fertilizer next to a field. The bottom halves were buried in the ground, but the upper halves were above ground, and they were overflowing with human waste. The soldiers made Tang and the ten or more other Chinese men stand next to the vats while they shot at them. As the bullets struck, the men were hit with shards from the vats and splashes of excrement. The soldiers were in high spirits, and they laughed with amusement at the sight.

Next, all the Chinese, even the ones who hadn't been splashed with excrement, were driven into a nearby pond and made to stand in water up to their necks, When the wintry chill of the water became too much for them to bear, they came out shivering, to the renewed amusement of the three soldiers.

At that point, a man headed toward Zhuangquan village passed by wearing a long robe.[1] The soldier with the pistol crawled to a nearby grave mound, took aim at the approaching man, and shot. He missed, but the man took fright and ran, picking up the hem of his robe with one hand. The soldier who had fired the shot chased after him for a while but eventually gave up.

The party arrived at Zhuangquan village. Nearly all the houses were deserted, but an old man of about seventy and two women of about fifty and sixty were discovered hiding. The two women were dragged into an empty house and raped by two of the soldiers while the third one stood guard outside. Then the third soldier took his turn at raping the women. Afterward, the soldiers loaded Tang and the other Chinese with bundles of rice straw to take back for the cavalry horses.

As the party made its way over a railroad crossing near Wujiamen on the way back to the cavalry encampment, it met up with a man who appeared to be a cigarette peddler. The delighted soldiers seized all his cigarettes. Then they made one of the coolies unload his burden of rice straw and replace it with the cigarettes.

The cavalry horses were tethered in an area near the current site of the Zhenjiang bus station. Here Tang and the others unloaded their rice straw, and the man who had been carrying the cigarettes also unloaded his burden.

However, the soldiers found that one pack of cigarettes was missing. Conducting a body search of the man who had been carrying the cigarettes, they

---

1. There are two kinds of traditional long robes: the *daguazi* for summer and the *changpaozi* for winter. This man was wearing the latter.

found the missing pack. One of the soldiers slammed the man to the ground in a shoulder throw, cut off a piece of his clothing with a knife, and made it into a blindfold.

The blindfolded man was made to stand up, and Tang and the other coolies were made to stand around him. A soldier—not the one who had thrown the man to the ground—attached a bayonet to his rifle. With a shrill cry, he charged at the blindfolded man and stabbed him through the heart, killing him instantly. The other two soldiers dragged the body away and disposed of it nearby. Then they allowed Tang and the others to go home.

As Tang was passing by the stadium, he was hailed by one of the cavalrymen and ordered to carry water for the horses. He spent the rest of the day until dark hauling water, and then he went home.

Wang Xiang.

According to Wang Xiang, associate professor at Zhenjiang Pedagogical Training School, unpublished materials based on investigations and data collection carried out in 1951 put the number of civilians massacred at about ten thousand. I had heard about ten specific examples, but the areas that saw the most mass murder were Sanliupiao outside the east gate, Huangshan, and Qilidian. Chiang Kai-shek's army had been in those areas, but since they had retreated by the time the Japanese invaded, only civilians were killed. Incidents in which people were locked into houses and burned to death were particularly common.

Wang Xiang was able to tell about a number of rapes other than the ones that Tang Rongfa had witnessed.

At number 4 Caoxiang, there was a fifty-three-year-old housewife named Dai. Not only was she raped in her parlor in front of her family, but her house was set on fire. The entire family, nine people in all, committed suicide by jumping into a well.

At number 21 Hejialong lived Xue Shengquan and his wife, and they had four daughters. The oldest was married and lived elsewhere, but the second (age 17), third (age 15), and (not yet 10) were at home. Japanese soldiers went in and out of the house, one after another, taking turns raping the second and third daughters. Unable to bear the humiliation, the girls' mother ordered them to commit suicide, forcing them to drink a mixture of fuel oil and cheap liquor. The girls became feverish, collapsed, and rolled on the floor in agony.

At that moment, the next group of Japanese soldiers showed up, and the mother strangled her daughters with her own hands.

"A lot of pregnant women, sick women, and Buddhist nuns were raped, and what was really terrible was when they watched and laughed as they forced young Chinese men to rape elderly women. There were some Chinese who committed suicide out of anger at their own humiliation, because they saw this happen, and despite their mortification, they didn't have any weapons and were helpless." After telling me these things, Wang Xiang recited for me the following poem that he had written:

Gong Shanhua.

Dang nian zhan xue liu
Jinri heping youyi chou
Yi xiao min en chou

At that time, blood flowed in the war.
Now peace and friendship have flourished.
Once we smile, it smooths out the difference between kindness and hatred.

The daughters of Xue Shengquan were killed by their humiliated and angry mother, but when Gong Shanhua (60) tried to speak of the time his mother was raped in Zhenjiang, he said that the details "[were] hard for me as her son to bear, and I really can't talk about them." His father, meanwhile, was conscripted as a coolie and killed after he was no longer needed.

Before the Japanese arrived, Cai Zhuanbing (73), a peasant from Guantang village, Guantang township, in the southern outskirts of Zhenjiang, fled to Longwang Temple at the foot of Zhongshan, about 10 kilometers away. When he returned to check up on things on the morning of December 10, about half the 200 houses, with a total area of over 300 jian, had been burned.[2]

Most of the villagers had fled, but a sixty-year-old man named Jiang Guanxi told Cai that the wives of Hu Bangdong and Jiang Yiquan had been killed. Cai himself saw their bodies on the edge of town later.

There was only one unburned house that was still inhabited, that of Hu Zhaoming, and Cai stopped in there. In the house were four women, all of whom had fled from elsewhere. Two were elderly, and the two who were in their mid-

---

2. According to subsequent investigations, 126 *jian* were burned at that time. Cai tells me that when the Japanese attempted to build an airfield of 1,200 *mu* (80 hectares) in 1945, they tore down the remaining 100 or more *jian* of buildings.

twenties, the wives of Hu Liangge and Chen Xueyu, had hidden themselves in an interior room. About an hour after Cai's arrival, some Japanese soldiers showed up and demanded that the older women produce the hua guniang.

Hearing the soldiers' voices from the other room, the two younger women were chafing to run outside, but since the Japanese were in the front room, they could not. They hid in a space between the interior room and the wall, but the four Japanese still found them. Two of the soldiers guarded Cai and the two old women, while the others followed the young women into the space, which was about 2 meters wide.

After a short time, the two soldiers emerged from the space, smirking. They traded places with the two soldiers who had

Cai Zhuanbing.

been guarding the people in the front room. Again, after a short time, this second pair of soldiers also emerged from the space with smirks on the faces. It was thirty or forty minutes after their arrival that the four soldiers left.

The two older women immediately went to the space to see what had happened to the young women. Cai did not follow along, but the old women told him that the rape victims could manage nothing but wordless sobbing.

There are many and various accounts from Japanese soldiers themselves of how they committed rape, cut open the bellies of pregnant women, and participated in gang rape and mass murder. When my report was serialized in the *Asahi Journal*, some readers wrote in, saying things like, "The strictly disciplined officers and men of the Japanese military would never have done those kinds of things." It is for the sake of such people that I need to present some accounts from the Japanese side.

For example, the July 1971 issue of *Shio* was a special issue called "The Crimes of the Japanese in Mainland China: Testimonies and Reports from a Thousand People." It contained the following sorts of testimonies:

> There were people who did even crueler things. There was one who forced a pregnant woman to come along with him, stripped her naked, and drove a sword into her swollen belly. There was another who tied a woman hand and foot between two trees, stuffed a hand grenade up her vagina, and exploded it. . . . In short, they tormented any woman they found in any way they could. The soldiers amused themselves by talking about the horrible things they had done to women, and they spoke about it with pride. (Former Staff Sergeant T)

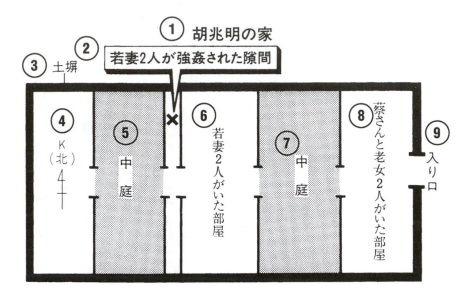

1. Hu Zhaoming's house
2. Where the two young women were raped
3. Earthen wall
4. North
5. Courtyard
6. The room where the two young women were
7. Courtyard
8. The room where Cai and the two older women were
9. Entrance

When the soldiers arrived at the hamlet, after the frontline troops had burned it to the ground, there was a girl—she may have waited too long to flee—who had blackened her face and put on men's clothes and had waded into the river to hide. The soldiers pulled her out of the river and made her rinse herself off.... The way it ended was that they tied her hands, shoved her into a shed that had straw piled up around it, and burned her to death. Then again, they were passing through a deserted village, when all of a sudden they heard voices from somewhere. They looked all around, but they could not see anyone. When they stomped on the ground, the voices stopped. "Aha!" they thought, and when they looked, there was an entrance to an underground cellar, and all the women in the hamlet were hiding inside. The soldiers practically fell over themselves rushing to gang rape them.... Afterward, they locked them up in a shed, nailed the door shut, and set it on fire. I heard these things from a soldier who was a friend of mine, but I couldn't help thinking that he had done some really brutal things. (Former Infantry Medical Corps Staff Sergeant A)

In a village near Suzhou, where I was, both the men and women were stripped naked and made to march single file. The Japanese soldiers assembled on either side of the road, applauding and having a great time as they watched. The men were driven into the river, and as each one's head broke through to the water's surface, he was shot and killed right there. It's not hard to imagine how the remaining women were treated. (Mrs. A, formerly in a pacification unit)

In *Sankō*, edited by the China Returnee's Liaison Committee (complete edition published by Banseisha), we find the following confession.

> Just because it was interfering with the satisfaction of my desires, I took a living human child, that is, an innocent baby that was just beginning to talk, and threw it into boiling water. When the mother, desperate to save her child, rushed over to the kettle, I sneered contemptuously and said, "If you take care of the brat, you'll be next, and I'll do it slowly." Then I kicked her in the abdomen so that she went flying, hit her head against the wall, and lay there on the heated brick floor. I sniffed and told her, "That's what you get for not behaving yourself." She was calling out her child's name and screaming pathetically for help, but I just said, "No matter how much you scream, you've had it," and tried to stop her mouth. She bit my hand and resisted with defiant, stubborn force, but the bestial part of my nature came to the surface, and I threw a quilt over her, sat astride her, and finally succeeded in raping her as she writhed on the floor. (Sergeant I of the 59th Division)

These things did not happen during the Nanjing campaign per se, but journalist Komata Yukio of the *Yomiuri Shimbun*, who followed the troops, wrote a book called *Aggression*, in which he reports about the types of things that happened in Nanjing.

> Women were the main victims, you know. Everyone from old women on down, they did them all. They'd come from Xiaguan in a charcoal truck and drive up to a hamlet and divide the women up among the soldiers, usually one woman for every fifteen or twenty soldiers. They'd choose some sunny place, like around a storehouse, then hang up leaves and make a place for their activities. They'd get a so-called red ticket, which had the company commander's seal on it, and then they'd take off their loincloths and wait their turn. There wasn't any soldier who didn't take part in the rapes. After that, they killed the women, for the most part. When they let the women go, they'd run off, and the soldiers would shoot them from behind. That's because the women would make a fuss afterward if they weren't killed, and if the military police found out, there'd be a court-martial. They didn't want to kill them, but they did. It is true that there were hardly any military police in Nanjing, but . . . (Private T of the 114th Division)

Given the countless incidents of rape and mass murder in China, we find an especially noteworthy example of testimony from the Japanese side coming from Kodaira Yoshio, who perpetrated the same kinds of crimes after his return to Japan. No one in Japan in the immediate postwar period will forget the name of this man, who was famous as a serial rapist and murderer and received the death penalty. This is what Kodaira said, according to the minutes of the preliminary examination (from the August 1971 issue of *Shinpyō*):

> At about the time of the Shanghai Incident, I committed a kind of terrific rape. Four or five of us went into a Chinese civilian house, tied up the father, and

stuffed him into a cupboard. We made them bring out the girls, and then we had our way with them. When you're talking about the Japanese military, thievery and rape just come with the territory. We stabbed them with bayonets, cut open pregnant women and took out the child. I killed five or six of them myself. I used to do some pretty brutal things.

CHAPTER 8

"THE CONTEST TO CUT DOWN A HUNDRED GOES OVER THE TOP"

The second report of the hundred-man killing contest.

The first report of the hundred-man killing contest.

Accounts of killing contests like the one that Tang Rongfa described in the previous chapter are also found in Japanese sources. One is a series of news reports about two second lieutenants from the Katagiri Unit of the Shanghai Expeditionary Force who embarked upon a "contest to cut down a hundred" with their swords as they left Wuxi to pass through Changzhou, Danyang, Jurong, and Zijin Mountain. The first reports appeared in the November 30, 1937, morning edition of the *Tōkyō Nichinichi Shimbun*:

CONTEST TO CUT DOWN A HUNDRED! TWO SECOND LIEUTENANTS ALREADY UP TO EIGHTY

Changzhou, November 29, Correspondents Asami, Mitsumoto, and Yasuda: The _____ unit, which covered the 40 kilometers between Changshu and Wuxi in six days, is moving so fast that it has smashed through from Wuxi to Changzhou, which is the same distance, in only three days. In the Katagiri Unit, which is preeminent in swiftness and rapid progress, there are two young commissioned officers who have undertaken a "contest to cut down a hundred" with their swords. It is said that since leaving Wuxi, one has already killed fifty-six men, and the other has succeeded in killing twenty-five. One is Second Lieutenant M (26)—originally from Yamaguchi prefecture—of the Toyama Unit, and the other is Second Lieutenant N (25)—originally from Kagoshima prefecture—of the same unit. As Second Lieutenant M, who has reached the third *dan* in bayonet training, rubs his fingers over the blade of "Seki-no-Magoroku," the sword at his side, Second Lieutenant N speaks of his treasured sword, which, although nameless, was inherited from his ancestors.

After leaving Wuxi, Second Lieutenant M has been making progress, shifting his course to move down 26 or 27 kilometers of the railroad tracks, while Second Lieutenant N has been advancing along a course parallel to the railroad tracks. On the day after their separate departures, Second Lieutenant N broke into an enemy pillbox in a nameless hamlet 8 kilometers from Wuxi, killed four enemy, and announced this to the advance guard. When Second Lieutenant M heard this, it made him determined to act, and that night, he invaded an enemy camp at Henglinzhen together with his men, and laid fifty-five enemy low with his sword.

After that, Second Lieutenant N killed nine at Henglinzhen, six at Weiguanzhen, and six at Changzhou Station on the twenty-ninth, for a total of twenty-five. Second Lieutenant M thereupon killed four in the vicinity of Changzhou Station, and when we reporters went to the station, we came upon the two of them conferring near there. Second Lieutenant M said, "With things going like this, I'll probably cut down a hundred by the time we reach Danyang, never mind Nanjing. You're going to lose. My sword has killed fifty-five, and it's only got one little nick on it." Second Lieutenant N responded, "Neither of us is killing people who run away. Since I'm serving as a _____ , I'm not winning any points, but by the time we're in Danyang, I'll show you what kind of a record I can rack up."

There was a second report on December 4, and the third report, which appeared on December 6, reads as follows:

IT'S 89–78 IN THE "CONTEST TO CUT DOWN A HUNDRED," A CLOSE RACE, HOW HEROIC! SECOND LIEUTENANTS M AND N

Jurong, December 5, Correspondents Asami and Mitsumoto: The two young commissioned officers, Second Lieutenants M and N of the Katagiri Unit, who are carrying out a "contest to cut down a hundred" as they head toward Nanjing, stood in the front lines at the invasion of Jurong. Just before the fierce battle to capture the city, Second Lieutenant M's score was eighty-nine, and Second Lieutenant N's score was seventy-eight, so they are locked in a close race.

Before quoting the fourth report, I would like to present some evidence that reveals the true story behind the "close race." After Second Lieutenant N returned to Japan, he spoke at the elementary school in his hometown and talked freely of the truth behind his supposed exploits. Shishime Akira, who actually heard the speech, wrote it up as follows in the February 1971 issue of the monthly magazine *Chūgoku* (China).

> That stuff in the newspapers about "the brave warrior from the provinces" and "the brave warrior of contest to cut down a hundred," that's about me. . . . Actually, I didn't kill more than four or five people in hand-to-hand combat. . . . We'd face an enemy trench that we'd captured, and when we called out, *"Ni, lai-lai!"* (You, come on!), the Chinese soldiers were so stupid, they'd rush toward us all at once. Then we'd line them up and cut them down, from one end of the line to the other. I was praised for having killed a hundred people, but actually, almost all of them were killed in this way. The two of us did have a contest, but afterward, I was often asked whether it was a big deal, and I said that it was no big deal. . . .

Thus, the hyped story of heroism was really a "contest to cut down a hundred" in name only. It was, in effect, nothing more than a "mass murder of prisoners contest." Looking at it realistically, it is hard to imagine that heroes of the caliber the seventeenth-century swordsmen Miyamoto Musashi and Sasaki Shōjirō were all that common among second lieutenants. It is unreasonable and flies in the face of common sense to say that someone could kill a hundred people in hand-to-hand combat without ever suffering a

---

1. Suzuki Akira's *The Illusion of the Nanjing Massacre* (published by Bungei Shunjū) is one of the pieces of "reportage" that holds that the reports of the "contest to cut down a hundred" are a complete fabrication, but in the end, he is unable to prove his point. Hori Tomio criticizes the problematic parts of this book in detail in the second volume of *The Nanjing Massacre* (published by Gendaishi Shuppansha). A book which takes the same views as Suzuki's, although more crudely, is Yamamoto Shichihei's *The Japanese Army Within Me*. *The Japanese Army Within Me* is apparently based on misapprehension

scratch. In any case, the conclusion of the "contest to cut down a hundred" was reported as follows in the morning edition of the *Tōkyō Nichinichi Shimbun* for December 13, 1937:[1]

CONTEST TO CUT DOWN A HUNDRED GOES OVER THE TOP, M 106, N 105, PAIR PLANS EXTENDED CONTEST

At the foot of Zijin Mountain, December 12, Correspondents Asami and Suzuki: The brave warriors of the well-known Katagiri Unit, Second Lieutenants M and N, who began a remarkable contest to see who could kill a hundred people with his sword by the time they reached Nanjing, made a record 106 versus 105 kills in the confusion of the assault on Zijin Mountain on the tenth. At noon, the two second lieutenants faced each other, each with his inevitably well-scarred sword in one hand.

N said, "Hey, I got a hundred and five. How about you, huh?" M said, "I got a hundred and six!" They both laughed and didn't bother to figure out which one of them had reached a hundred first. They quickly agreed to call it a draw and to extend the game, so that a "one hundred fifty person contest" began on the eleventh. It was at noon on the eleventh at Zhongshanling, which looks down upon Zijin Mountain, that Second Lieutenant M, who was in the midst of hunting down Chinese stragglers, told us about the conclusion of the "draw."

"I'm glad that we were both able to go over a hundred without knowing about each other. My sword Seki-no-Magoroku is marred because I sliced someone down the middle, together with his helmet, I've promised to give this sword to your company when I'm done fighting. At about three in the morning, some friendly forces flushed out some of the remaining enemy on Zijin Mountain, and I got caught up in the confusion. I stood straight up in that rain of bullets and thought, 'This is just fine,' as I shouldered my sword, and the fact that not one of the bullets hit me is due to Magoroku."

Then he showed us the sword Magoroku, which had shed the life blood of a hundred and six men under enemy fire.

About 50 kilometers southeast of Nanjing is a city called Lishui. The Japanese army captured it on December 4, but in the spring of the following year, Xi Jifu (62), then a student living in the Xiaoximen area within the city of Lishui, witnessed a "fourteen-person killing for show" carried out by a Japanese commissioned officer.

---

of the facts or distortions, as he attacks the journalists who reported on the "contest to cut down a hundred." The problem is not with Yamamoto himself, but with those who make use of his writings. Hori Tomio has exposed the falsehoods found in *The Japanese Army Within Me* in detail in "Was the Nanjing Massacre an Illusion?" (from *The Pen Conspiracy*, edited by Honda Katsuichi and published by Shio Shuppansha). In fact, after the war, the two second lieutenants who took part in the "contest to cut down a hundred" were condemned to death under Chiang Kai-shek's regime by the court in Nanjing, although the transcripts of the trial have not yet been made public. At any rate, behead-

Xi Jifu.

Xi himself had fled to the countryside (on December 1) three days before the Japanese invasion, so he did not see what went on then, and it was April of the next year when he returned to the city.

One day about a month after that, two units of the Japanese army encircled Tongji Street outside the city walls, which in those days included an area larger than the present-day Tongji Street. The approximately two hundred people in the area were rounded up by the Japanese and taken to Miaoshangou, one of the three execution grounds in the city, along with Daiximen and the Xiaoximen Stadium. Since Xi had a stall at an open-air market in the area, he was taken along with the others.

When they arrived at the Miaoshangou execution ground, fourteen Chinese men were tied up and made to kneel. Their hands tied behind them, they were strung together like beads in groups of three or four and blindfolded with blue or black pieces of cloth. The area was at the base of a small hill, and the men knelt facing it, with about a meter between each man and the next. An interpreter named Liang gave a speech that first spoke in glowing terms of "Sino-Japanese friendship" and "East Asian coprosperity," but then he said, "These fourteen are bad people. You must not be like them," although he did not explain specifically what they had done. Obviously, the neighborhood people had been brought to this place so that the men's punishment could serve as a warning to them. The "spectators" stood behind the line of men, and they were surrounded by about a hundred Japanese soldiers as a precaution. To one side, a heavy machine gun set up on another hill loomed over the watchers.

---

ing of prisoners without trial was clearly nothing more than "an everyday occurrence" (according to Uno Shintaro) among officers at that time. In fact, it was the rare officer who went to China with a sword and *did not* use it. These two officers were unfortunate in that they were condemned to death because their exploits happened to be given huge play in newspaper articles. This is why I have concealed their real names in the paperback edition of this book and used only the first letters of their family names. (Translator's note: Honda has also blanked out their names in the photographs of the actual newspaper articles.)

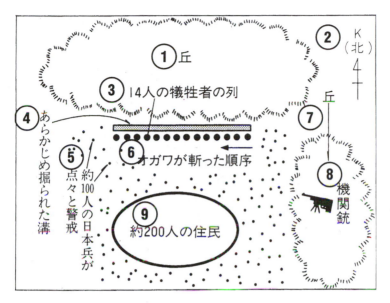

1. Hill
2. North
3. The row of 14 victims
4. The trench that had already been dug
5. 100 Japanese soldiers scattered about standing guard
6. The order in which Ogawa walked down the line beheading people
7. Hill
8. Machine guns
9. About 200 villagers

The man who carried out the cautionary executions with his sword was a commissioned officer named Ogawa, whom the local people referred to privately as "the Mowang of Lishui." (Mowang is the ruler of the Chinese Buddhist hell.) Since being stationed in Lishui, Ogawa had gained notoriety for beating or killing Chinese civilians for the most trivial offenses.

Ogawa had complete confidence in his own skills as a swordsman. He began cutting heads at the right end, that is, the east end of the line of victims, which stretched east to west, First, he splashed cold water from a large teakettle on the sword. Then he swung it and gave a loud cry as he let the blade fall on the victim. At that moment, the victim's head flew off, and the neck seemed to contract for an instant before beginning to spurt forth blood. The head rolled forward into a ditch that had been dug in advance. Ogawa worked his way down the line, never missing a stroke. Even though the men were blindfolded, they could sense when their turn was coming, and some of them hunched their shoulders in an effort to protect themselves. In such cases, Ogawa would hit the base of the person's neck with his sword. Thinking he had been cut, the victim would act startled and raise his head. At just that moment, Ogawa would strike. It took him thirty or forty minutes to finish off all fourteen men, and he used only one sword.

The house that Ogawa lived in has been preserved in its uninhabited state, and there are plans to turn it into some sort of memorial hall for "class education." It's ironic when you consider that Ogawa is said to have been fond of acting.

Evidently, a lot of officers and enlisted men perpetrated these sorts of set-up killings, and one personal account comes from Uno Shintarō,[2] who writes about such an incident from 1943, when he was a first lieutenant. The following is taken from his memoirs, *Record of the Enmities of a Japanese Sword.*

> I took my usual Sadamitsu sword and paused before spinning around and lightly touching the back of the blade to the mayor's neck to judge the distance. Then I checked the position of my legs, turned the blade back to the front, and let it fall.
> As the blade cut through the flesh with a sharp hiss, two or three streams of blood shot forth like a fountain. The mayor's head fell to the ground slightly before his body. The face was grimacing in agony, and the teeth chattered against the sand. It was stark and horrible. The smell of blood hung in the air. . . . Next, I went around behind the next forty or so village officials.
> (It's started out well, but what about the rivet? Has the sword gotten bent?)
> No abnormality in the rivet, but the blade appears to be slightly bent.
> (That's all right. I'll just continue as long as I can.)
> I touched the back of the blade to the next neck, and then returned to strike my blow. Then I went on to the third and fourth man, all without stopping for breath.
> But when I struck at the fourth man, the blade didn't go all the way through, and his head flopped forward onto his chest.
> (I've failed! Calm yourself!)
> I tried to force a smile, but I found myself in tears.
> "Hey, Guard! Bring that water bucket!"
> After roughly wiping the coagulating blood off with the water from the bucket, I wrapped a towel around the blade, laid it across my knee so that about 40 centimeters of the tip stuck out. It was bent by about five degrees, and I used both hands to force it back into shape. But it was still slightly warped.
> (Well, I've got to kill another five.)
> Just then, the five men began a horrible song that I'd heard before, "The Song of Resistance to Japan." They sang together through their tears.
> My angry determination returned.
> "Stop it! Why don't you stop? I'm going to kill you!"
> But doubts crossed my mind.
> (The rivets of the Sadamitsu are kind of loose. If they get any looser, I won't

---

2. With more than a thousand men confined in China's Fushun War Crimes Prison, Uno Shintarō was the only one of the eight hundred below the rank of captain to receive a severe sentence. He was an information officer for the infantry, and he wrote *The Chrysanthemum and the Samurai Sword* (published by Tanizawa Shoten).

be able to use it. But I shouldn't exchange it for Father's Sukesada sword and use that. Of course, it has tasted blood at Guoliu Bay, but I've been determined to let the Sukesada, which carries the spirit of my father, rest quietly until the time of some desperate, decisive battle. This Sadamitsu, which is my mother's spirit, was newly made during the reign of the present Emperor, but I never thought that even a strictly ornamental sword would bend like this. But if I exchange Mother's Sadamitsu for Father's Sukesada, that's like polluting it. . . . Yes! No matter what, I'll keep on using the Sadamitsu for my mother's sake.)

By then, the five men had stopped their singing, but they were weeping bitterly. I swung the sword even more ferociously and cut. The rivet curved some more and loosened, and the sword guard began to rattle. On top of that, a spot about 40 centimeters from the tip was once again curved about five degrees to the right. This is why I cut off two heads, stopped to repair my sword, cut off two more heads, stopped to repair my sword, until I lopped off the head of the ninth and last man. I was able to behead only the first and ninth man with one stroke.

The smell of blood lingered in the air. The assembled prisoners inside the iron-fenced enclosure stood stock still, not even wiping away their tears. (From *The Pen Conspiracy*, edited by Honda Katsuichi, compiled and published by Shio Shuppansha, 1977)

After this confession, Uno writes about the hundred-person killing contest between the two second lieutenants:

In November and December of 1937, the Japanese newspapers were overflowing with news of the assault on Nanjing every day. I was especially interested in the hundred-person killing contest between the two second lieutenants, M and N. The articles about how many they had killed up to a particular point were more wonderful than anything else, and at the age of eighteen, I became increasingly confident of the invincibility of the Empire. At that time, I had a blind faith in the *Legends of the Japanese Fighting Spirit and Valor Invincible in All the World*, so I believed that the hundred killings had all taken place in "hand-to-hand heroic battles that even the demons would flee," as a favorite phrase of the reporters covering the story had it. Yet, I have inferred from my own experiences I have previously described that it is indeed possible to kill that many people. Or rather, it must have been easy to do. Furthermore, when beheadings occurred in the so-called guarded areas, you did have the hassle of digging holes and burying the victims, and even then stray dogs might dig them up and eat them, but in the combat areas during the assault, we certainly had blanket permission to kill anyone we pleased, like the samurai of old, and I can easily believe that the two second lieutenants committed their full share of self-indulgent murder. All they had to watch out for were loosened rivets and warped blades on their swords, and those were not such a big deal. And about the fellows who were talked about so much in connection with the "contest to cut down a hundred," you can figure that during the assault, as the army was on the road, the units in the vicinity freely offered them as many prisoners as they wanted. In short, it would be more correct to call it the "fake contest to cut down a hundred." You know, it's clear from the fact that one of them, during his triumphant return to his hometown, said something on the order of, "I only cut down three in the heat of battle, and the

Chen Guangxu.

others were all people we had captured." It's even extremely doubtful that those three killed in battle were cut down in hand-to-hand combat. Whatever you say, it's silly to argue about whether it happened this way or that way when the situation is so clear. There were hundreds and thousands of M's and N's, including me, during those fifty years of war between Japan and China. At any rate, it was nothing more than a commonplace occurrence during the so-called Chinese Disturbance.

And so, the Japanese army moved closer to Nanjing, but atrocities followed one upon another in the peasant villages on the outskirts of the city. The following account exemplifies the sorts of tragedies that occurred when the Japanese army first entered a village:

Chen Guangxu, then twenty years old, lived in Xuxiang village (now called Xixiang), about a half hour east of Nanjing by bus. Her nine-person household consisted of her fifty-five or fifty-six-year-old father, her mother, her grandfather, herself, a sixteen-year-old brother, a younger sister, an older brother and his wife, and their seven- or eight-year-old daughter. There was an older sister as well, but she had been married off into a nearby household and had lived there as a tongyangxi *since childhood. According to the traditional calendar,[3] it was at dawn on the eight day of the eleventh month (December 10, by the Western calendar) that the Japanese first arrived in the village. Chen Guangxu was still in bed when a young relative came running, calling out, "Ershen! Ershu gei da si le!" (Auntie! Uncle has been killed!)*

Chen Guangxu hid under the bed as her mother dashed out. Her father had gone out to the work areas before dawn to bring in feed for the cattle, and her older brother was away somewhere. Since Chen Guangxu stayed hidden the whole time, she did not see what happened, but this is what she heard from her mother.

The work area where her father went to bring in hay was located a few houses away, near where the young relative lived, and it was used mainly for harvest-related activities, such as threshing. Just as her father was setting out for home with a bundle of hay under each arm, a Japanese soldier appeared, leading a young Chinese man of about twenty-four or twenty-five,

---

3. This is the peasant calendar described in a footnote 3 in Chapter 1.

who had been conscripted from some nearby village. The soldier was evidently the signal corpsman, tending the telephone lines.

The soldier said something to Chen's father in Japanese.

Since Chen's father did not understand, he did not answer, but the soldier shot at him with a pistol. The bullet entered in the upper part of the left side of his chest and traveled downward. Chen's father staggered two or three steps and then fell, landing on his buttocks. At that moment, another Japanese came along and stabbed him in the chest, killing him instantly. Then the two soldiers simply left. This is what Chen's mother heard about her husband's death from the young man who had come with the Japanese as a conscript.

By the time Chen Guangxu was told that it was safe to come out and went to the work area, her father was already in his coffin.

Since the family was no longer safe in the village, it was decided to send at least the young women to a refuge in the mountains. Chen Guangxu, her younger sister, and her older brother's pregnant wife, along with her married older sister, joined the group. It was a panicked evacuation, one which gave Chen Guangxu time only for a hurried glance at her father in his coffin. From the village to the mountain refuge was a two-hour journey on foot.

However, the next morning, Chen's pregnant sister-in-law went into labor. The village midwife had come along with the fleeing group, so she joined Chen, her sister-in-law, and her younger sister at a place about five hundred meters away from the rest. There the sister-in-law gave birth, but the newborn baby cried loudly, as might be expected. The four feared that if the Japanese heard the crying they would follow the group into the mountains and all the young women would be raped and murdered. (At this point in the narrative, Chen Guangxu's head dropped to a low level, and the way the words stuck in her throat indicated what a painful confession this was for her.) With great sorrow and regret, they decided to kill the infant, feeling that there was no other way to save the whole group. Chen Guangxu took the baby and smothered it by pushing it face down and head first under a large rock ("Larger than that table," Chen said, indicating the small table where a tea set stood). After piling up small rocks over the body to cover it thoroughly, she rejoined the fleeing group.

It was December 14, the day after the capture of Nanjing that the women came back to their village from the mountains. Chen learned that during her absence, around December 12, her older brother had been conscripted by the Japanese and taken away somewhere.

This village was eventually subjected to mass murder and rape when the Japanese reappeared after the fall of Nanjing, but I will describe that later.

Beginning with the next chapter, I will begin describing what I found out at our final destination of Nanjing. For reasons of space, I have been able to present the experiences of only about a third of the survivors I interviewed, and someday, I hope to tell about the other people's experiences as well.

As can be clearly seen from the preceding chapters, the mass murders, acts of violence, and rapes to which the Japanese military subjected Chinese civilians were not something that suddenly erupted with the capture of Nanjing. They began immediately after the landing at Hangzhou Bay. However, when people discuss the atrocities[4] that are commonly referred to as the "Nanjing Massacre," they sometimes limit the *time* of their accounts to the five days between December 12, when the Japanese first occupied the city, and December 17, when they held their victory celebration. In such cases, they naturally limit the *place* to the streets of Nanjing.

Yet, there were refugees who had fled into Nanjing from cities farther to the south (such as the family of Zhang Xifan's sister), and at the same time, there were civilians who had fled from Nanjing to the outskirts. A number of the cases I present in the subsequent chapters fall into either of these categories. It should also be clear from the preceding accounts that it was not uncommon for people who had evacuated to nearby peasant villages to be slaughtered there.

Thus, I would like it to be understood that limiting descriptions of the massacres, acts of violence, and rapes just to those five days in December or just to the city limits of Nanjing is meaningless. It is impossible to draw such boundaries. The "Nanjing Incident" was nothing more than a local aspect of the drive toward Nanjing, and it is not pushing things—indeed, it is the most logical view—to see the landing at Hangzhou Bay in late November as the beginning of the campaign. Of course, if we look at the big picture, it was simply a part of a sequence that began with the initial invasion of China, but

---

4. Since the term "Nanjing Massacre" tends to focus attention on the mass murders to the exclusion of the rapes, gang rapes, thievery, and pillaging that occurred, some scholars, including Hori Tomio, prefer the term "Nanjing Atrocities." Others prefer the term "Nanjing Incident," but the problem is that there are then two Nanjing Incidents in history. The first one occurred in March 1927, when Western gunboats fired on the city from the Yangtze. The pretext was that the Northern Expeditionary Army had ransacked Western and Japanese consulates when it was forced out of Nanjing by the National Revolutionary Army. Chiang Kai-shek took this opportunity to reach an accord with the Western and Japanese powers and he subsequently moved to suppress the Communists. The second Nanjing Incident, of course, refers to the atrocities that the Japanese visited upon the city in December 1937. When I asked for a Chinese opinion on the proper terminology at the Nanjing City Historical Society, the answer was,"If you just say 'Nanjing Incident,' it's not clear which one you mean, since Nanjing has such a long history and there have been so many incidents. In the end, we've settled on 'Nanjing Massacre.'"

looking at things on a smaller scale, we have to see the landing at Hangzhou Bay as the starting point.

Hiraoka Masaaki expressed a similar point of view in his book *What Did the Japanese Do in China?* (published by Shio Shuppansha):

> The Nanjing Massacre does not stand alone as an act of barbarism occurring within the city limits of Nanjing. We have to speak in terms of the cycle of offense against and defense of the major cities and the capital occurring in the approximately four months between the Shanghai Incident of August 13 and the occupation of Nanjing on December 13.

If the starting point is the landing at Hangzhou Bay or, as Hiraoka prefers, the Shanghai Incident, where is the end point? Speaking in broad terms, it's probably Japan's surrender on August 15, 1945, but the testimonies in the following chapters will make it clear that the December 17, 1937, victory ceremony in Nanjing was not the end point.

CHAPTER 9

"THE IMPERIAL FORCES MAKE AN ALL-OUT CHARGE ON NANJING"

A special feature section of the *Tokyo Nichinichi Shinbun*, December 8, 1937, anticipating the fall of Nanjing.

The excerpts I have taken from the *Library of War History* from the National Defense Agency's National Defense College War History Office (published by Chōun Shimbunsha) make no mention of—just to name one example—campaigns where large quantities of poison gas were used, and they conceal facts unfavorable to the Japanese military as much as possible. The fundamental reason for these omissions is that Japan, unlike Germany and Italy, has not followed up on the war crimes committed by its own people. The present-day Self Defense Force has thus inherited the crimes of the prewar Japanese military without repenting them, so of course, it has not described its own (the old Japanese military's) criminal acts during the Nanjing Massacre. By not acknowledging these crimes, we fail to grasp the complete picture of our own national character. Lacking this understanding, we keep appealing to the world, talking about Hiroshima and Nagasaki and the nuclear situation. We, therefore, gain a reputation for emphasizing our role as victims without ever reflecting upon our own violent aspect. This harms our credibility when we speak of peace, and we also give neighboring countries every reason to be wary and to wonder whether we will repeat our war crimes.

Even so, despite this characteristic, the *Library of War History* is often a first-class source for accounts of the day-to-day operations of the war. According to "The China Incident Army Campaign (1)," the final stage of the assault on Nanjing proceeded as follows:

December 1: The order of combat for the Central China Theater Force was dictated (made up of Central China Theater Command, Shanghai Expeditionary Force, Eleventh Army) according to Continental Decree Number 7. The Commander of the Central China Theater is General Matsui Iwane. On the same day, an Imperial command was issued with Continental Decree Number 8, "The Central China Theater Commander is to cooperate with the navy and attack Nanjing, the capital of the enemy nation" . . .

The advance guard of the 114th Division entered Lishui on the 4th, occupied Moluguan on the 7th, and immediately headed toward Nanjing.

The 6th Division, moving westward from Huzhou, received the command to attack Nanjing on the 2nd, and, accordingly, they set out on a forced march and caught up with the 114th Division on the 7th. Beginning on the 8th, they followed along the left flank of the 114th Division, and took part in the front line position assault on Nanjing.

The 18th Division . . . Kunisaki Detachment left Guangde on the 2nd, and reached Liangxi on the 3d, where they prepared for marine warfare. On the 6th they left Liangxi, mainly making use of the waterways, and on the 9th they occupied Taiping. On the 11th, they crossed the Yangtze near Cihuzhen, north of Taiping, and moved to the left bank.

Around December 5, contemporary newspaper reports on the war began proclaiming that the fall of Nanjing was only a matter of time. For example,

The Fukuda tank battalion during the assault on Nanjing. (Photographed December 8 at Tangshuizhen by Special Correspondent Kakuno for the *Asahi Shinbun*.)

when we look at the headlines of the morning editions of the three major newspapers, we see phrases such as "Nanjing Completely Surrounded, Imperial Army Morale High, Will Attack at One Stroke" (*Asahi Shimbun*), "When Will Nanjing Fall?" (*Yomiuri*), and "Nationalist Government Recognition Withdrawn, Declaration at the Same Time as the Fall of Nanjing" (*Tōkyō Nichinichi Shimbun*). Then the *Yomiuri Shimbun* reported the following in its evening edition for December 8, under headlines reading, "Imperial Forces to Make an All-Out Charge on Nanjing," and "The Fall Is Imminent."

> Yangshan: special correspondent Sasaki, December 7, urgent dispatch: The advance units, which pressed in on Gaoqiaomen, about one *li* from Nanjing on the evening of the 6th, are broadening the final hand-to-hand struggle. On the morning of the 7th, they made an all-out charge on one corner of the walls of Nanjing.
>
> (Zijin Mountain: special correspondent Kojima, December 7, urgent dispatch): After looking out over Nanjing from hailing distance, the Wakisaka, Hitomi, Isa, and Fujii Units spent the whole night in a headlong rush and the advance units have already arrived at Zijin Mountain. Before dawn on the 7th, they broke through the morning haze and waved the Rising Sun flag on the peak of Zijin Mountain. Looking down from the mountain peak, they saw Nanjing spread out before them, and they knew that in reality, it was in their hands.
>
> (_____Base, Special Correspondent Kosaka, December 7, urgent dispatch): Our _____aircraft flew in a formation of silver wings to carry out air raids,

delivering the final blow to Nanjing, which is clearly in its death throes. They soared over the defensive lines and through the skies directly above the city and returned home at about 10 A.M. According to reports from aerial reconnaissance, the anti-aircraft guns have fallen completely silent, and there is hardly any sign of human presence within the city. Our advance troops are mopping up stragglers without encountering any significant resistance. They are rushing through the foothills of Zijin Mountain, heading toward Nanjing, and they are approaching the vicinity of Zhongshanlu.

(Imperial Headquarters, Department of the Army, December 7, noon): On the morning of December 7, our frontline troops, advancing toward Nanjing, took the enemy defensive lines at Qixia Mountain (18 kilometers northeast of Nanjing), Qinglong Mountain (8 kilometers east of Nanjing), and Fang Mountain (15 kilometers southeast of Nanjing). They have finalized their positions for the assault on the city.

From this point, the number of personal accounts and military records increases dramatically. These may be broadly divided into accounts written by journalists or novelists and personal accounts of frontline officers, enlisted men, and military employees. One representative of the first group is the reportage of Ōyake Sōichi. However, his writings do not go as far as those of Hino Ashihei and Ishikawa Tatsuzō in depicting the Japanese troops, and they contain almost nothing about the Chinese people. Instead, he goes into great detail about the other journalists and cultural figures who were with him and about the soldiers who saw to their needs. Since he did no investigative reporting and never ventured to the front lines, there is no sense of tension except on those rare instances when a stray shell happened to land way back behind Japanese lines. Even when we are talking about accounts of life behind the front lines, Sasaki Genshō's *Field Postal Flag* (mentioned in Chapter 4), which was not written to be published in a magazine, is clearly superior. Let us just look at an excerpt from Ōyake Sōichi's reportage:

On the 12th, we had been hearing continuous gunfire and shellfire since the previous evening, and I was still awake at four in the morning. Unable to sleep due to cold and excitement, I got up and sat by the fire. Kosaka, followed shortly thereafter by Nakagawa, joined me, both of them saying that they couldn't sleep.

Evidently, the enemy were offering stubborn resistance at the end. At this rate, we feared that it would be impossible to take the city that day.

As the day dawned, Shimura, who had been out with the cavalry near Zhongshan Road returned and suggested that we go there, too. We'd be able to understand the war situation better, he said, and even though shells came in from time to time, we'd be all right if we were careful.

As we followed him timidly, we could hear those lightweight Czech-made machine guns firing nearby. Shells from trench mortars also seemed to be exploding in the vicinity. I lost my nerve and couldn't go on any farther, and when I held back, Shimura, who had been exposed to incoming shells since Shanghai, went on alone.

On the way back to the camp, I stopped to talk with four or five soldiers who were eating. As I was asking them now the fighting was going, I heard the familiar *hyururu* sound, and a shell exploded with a deafening roar only about sixty feet away from us. The soldiers merely stopped their chopsticks in mid-air for a moment, but I broke into a cold sweat, and undoubtedly, my face turned pale as well.

"No matter how much you get used to them, they're still frightening," one of the soldiers said soothingly.

I fled back to the camp in a panic.

About an hour later, Kosaka also came back, looking pale. He told me that he had been standing around talking with a soldier. The soldier left to relieve himself, and at that moment, a stray bullet landed right behind him. (From *Gaichi no Miwaku* [The Fascination of the Overseas Territories] Banrikaku, 1940.)

An example of memoirs from frontline soldiers is Sakaguchi Ichirō's *Dokuritsu kikanjūtai imad mōshachū nari* (The Independent Machine Gun Corps Is Still Firing Away) (Hihankaku, 1941.) Here is a part of his description of the fighting on the 12th:

Suddenly, some enemy came out of a house in a disorderly rush.

Da-da-da-da-da-da! went the machine gun bullets as the enemy began falling this way and that.

The rear half of the group panicked and fled back into the house.

The infantry began shelling these enemy troops. A shell came flying and landed to the right of the house. The second shell was right on target. It penetrated the roof and exploded inside the house, so we didn't see much smoke.

"Bull's eye!" Second Lieutenant Ōtomo cried out delightedly.

The gunners immediately aimed their machine guns at the door in order to shoot down the guys who would be running out. As soon as the next shell broke the windows, the enemy ran out.

Da-da-da-da-da-da!

The gunners all fired at once. Only about two or three of the enemy managed to flee beyond the mountain ridge, while the others fell down one after another.

"Prepare to advance!" the company commander ordered suddenly. "The company is to go through that hollow and advance to Yuguang Gate!"

The command squad's message was transmitted to each platoon. There was a concrete pillbox to the right of the hill where the house had been. However, these enemy soon fell silent, thanks to concentrated fire from our side. That's why the Shirai Unit was able to advance through the hollow. There were still some enemy left in the trenches around the pillbox, They panicked and tried to run away, so our gunners mowed them down.

Now we come to the 13th, the fall of Nanjing. Let's see what the official history, "The China Incident Army Campaign (1)" from the *Library of War History* has to say:

On December 8, we captured the enemy frontline positions in every area. On the 9th, the theater commander advised the enemy forces to capitulate, demanding that they reply by military envoy by noon on the 10th. They did not respond, so at 13:00 hours on the 10th, the theater commander gave the order to continue the assault and clean up the city.

In the Shanghai Expeditionary Force, the 16th Division broke through the enemy frontline positions on the 8th. On the 9th, they advanced to the vicinity of Xiaqilinmen and Cangbomen. Beginning on the 10th, they attacked Zijin Mountain and the districts on either side of it. On the 12th, they captured the lines that run north and south between the peaks of Zijin Mountain. . . .

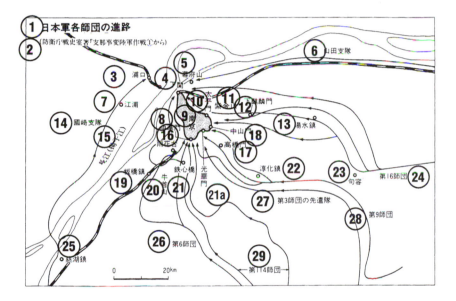

1. The routes taken by the Japanese divisions
2. (from *The China Incident Army Campaign*, edited by the War History Office of the National Defense Agency)
3. Hukou
4. Xiaguan
5. Wufu Mountain
6. Yamada Detachment
7. Jiangpu
8. Zhonghua Gate
9. Nanjing
10. Taiping Gate
11. Zijin Mountain
12. Xiaqilinmen
13. Tangshuizhen
14. Kunisaki Detachment
15. Yangtze River
16. Yuhuatai
17. Gaoqiaomen
18. Zhongshan Gate
19. Banqiaozhen
20. Niushou Mountain
21a. Guanghuamen
21. Tiexinqiao
22. Chunhuazhen
23. Jurong
24. 16th Division
25. Cihuzhen
26. 6th Division
27. Advance Guard of the 3rd Division
28. 9th Division
29. 114th Division

Before dawn on the 9th, the 9th Division stormed Guanghua Gate. The right flank attacked the enemy in the eastern suburbs of Nanjing, and on the 12th, they approached the city walls, but they encountered a moat about 200 meters wide and prepared to ford it. On the 10th, the left flank attacked the enemy on the eastern edge of Yuhuatai and captured Guanghua Gate, but after that, they made no further progress. Meanwhile, the unit that attacked the eastern edge of Yuhuatai broke through successive lines of stubbornly resisting enemy, but on the morning of the 12th, under orders from the division command, they temporarily halted the attack in order to regroup.

On December 2, after arriving at Suzhou, the 3rd Division advanced mainly along the route of the 9th Division as second line troops, but on the 11th, they were ordered to send an advance party to the 9th Division, and on the 13th, they joined in the attack on Nanjing.

In the 10th Army, the 114th and 6th Divisions attacked jointly in the direction of Yuhuatai, and on the 8th, they captured the enemy's forward positions. On the 9th, they broke through the second line positions, and beginning on the 10th, they attacked the third line positions at Yuhuatai and the retrenchment positions. Breaking through stubborn enemy resistance, they captured one position after another, and on the 12th, the two divisions occupied part of the city walls. . . .

On the 10th, the 6th Division sent part of its forces ahead from the banks of the Yangtze, but they encountered a large column of retreating enemy soldiers and wiped them out. On the 14th, they arrived at Xiaguan, a docking area north of Nanjing.

The Kunisaki Detachment eliminated enemy resistance and captured Pukou, cutting off the enemy's escape route.

In the early morning hours of the 13th, it was determined that the enemy within Nanjing had retreated.

Based on the summary of the attack plans that had been set forth ahead of time, each division sent skeleton companies of infantry into the city, where they carried out mopping up operations. Part of the 16th Division advanced to Xiaguan and fired upon enemy who were trying to escape up the river on ships. They inflicted a great deal of damage.

The news that the Japanese forces had entered Nanjing in the early morning hours of December 13 was first reported in the evening edition of the *Asahi Shimbun* on the same day:

> Zhongshan Gate, *Asahi* frontline communications headquarters, December 13: At 3:20 A.M. on the 13th, part of our Ōno unit charged Zhongshan Gate in the walls of Nanjing, captured it, raised the Rising Sun flag high on the walls, and gave a loud *Banzai!* At midnight, part of the Katagiri Unit occupied Zhongshan Road, and their shouts of *Banzai!* made Zijin Mountain tremble. Thus after an all-out attack from the eastern side of Nanjing, Zhongshan Gate and Zhongshan Road have fallen into our hands in quick succession.
>
> Daxiaochang, December 13, Dōmei: Anticipating the dawn of the 13th, the Fujii and Isa units crossed a moat a hundred meters wide on steel pontoons with the assistance of the engineering corps, burst into the city through two breaks in the wall, repulsed the stubbornly resisting enemy, occupied a position inside of Zhongshan Gate, and raised the Rising Sun flag.

Several units of the Imperial Army during the assault on Zhonghua Gate, Nanjing (taken by Special Correspondent Hayashi for the *Asahi Shinbun*, December 12)

The Imperial Army heading for Zhongshanling (*Asahi Graph*, December 29, 1937)

Daxiaochang, December 13, Dōmei: The Ōno, Katagiri, Isa, and Fujii units, which broke through into the city of Nanjing through two openings on either side of Zhongshan Gate. Taking off in hot pursuit after the remaining enemy along Zhongshan Road in the direction of the Ming Palace, they found the heart of the enemy position, and charged. Fierce house-to-house fighting ensued. Gunfire loud enough to shake heaven and earth is roaring across the eastern part of Nanjing. The enemy are stubbornly resisting and trying to ward off the advance of our troops, who are concentrating their fire on their frontline urban positions near the Ming Palace.

Daxiaochang, December 13, Dōmei: At 6:00 A.M. on December 13, the Isa, Fujii, Wakisaka, and Hitomi units captured the entire southeast side of the walls from Zhongshan Gate to Guanghua Gate, and they raised the Rising Sun flag.

Ma Mingfu

Ma Mingfu (53) is employed in the accounting department of the Nanjing Cigarette Company, and at the time of the Japanese invasion, he was living in a house near Shuixi Gate. His father (38) made his living working in a store that sold ducks. The rest of his family was made up of Ma Mingfu, his mother (30), two younger sisters (9 and 4), and one younger brother (1).

As the Japanese approached, the family fled to the home of Ma's maternal grandmother in Shazhouyu on the outskirts of the city. The family of Ma's maternal aunt, who had a husband, an eight-year-old daughter, and a five-year-old son, also fled to the same village.

"I was only seven years old then, but I can still clearly conjure up my memories of what happened when we fled. My father shouldered a yoke and put my sister and me in two baskets. My mother carried the baby, and since we thought it was just a temporary evacuation, we were all in a cheerful mood. My aunt's family also came in the same manner, with my uncle carrying his two children with a carrying pole. That evening my grandmother was extremely happy, because everyone was together for the first time in a long time, and being surrounded by her grandchildren put her into high spirits. And yet, the sad events that began happening the next day are something that I can never forget as long as I live."

After these words of introduction, Ma Mingfu went on to tell me about the "sad events," beginning with his own experiences and then adding what he heard later as an adult:

By the next day, the other villagers were moving furniture out of their houses and running around frantically. "The Eastern devils are going to come and burn our houses!" they said. This area was full of ponds and waterways, and a pond stood between this village and the road, connected only by an earthen dike. Ma's grandfather broke down the dike at the halfway point so that the Japanese would not be able to enter the village easily.

That afternoon, when the sun was already low in the sky, the Japanese showed up. As soon as they learned of the approach of the Japanese, the seventy or eighty people who were in the village left their houses and hid in a hollow about one li away. The soldiers took door panels and other furniture that they had taken from other villages and laid them across the gap in the dike, creating a temporary bridge. Then they stormed into the village. They set fire to all the houses, and then, when the village was completely engulfed in flames, they withdrew.

Not having any idea of the Japanese troop movements, the people hiding in the hollow decided to wait to see what would happen. After it grew dark, they got together and dug a trench about two meters wide, five or six meters long, and as deep as young Ma was tall, or a little over a meter. Then they spread boards and grass over it for camouflage. All there was to eat was some parched rice brought from home.

At about ten o'clock the next morning, the Japanese began firing upon them. They had taken a position on the hills that rose to the east of the hollow where the trench was, and so they had spotted it easily. Ma has no idea whether these were the same soldiers who had burned the village or a different group. At this time, about fifty people were hiding in the hastily constructed trench. Another twenty or thirty were at various places in the hollow. When the Japanese began firing, the people outside rushed madly toward the trench, but a number of them were killed before they could reach it. The trench soon was so full that people were lying on top of one another. Ma and his family were in the southeast corner of the trench near the entrance, leaning against the wall closest toward the direction that the Japanese were shooting from, and he was looking out between the boards that covered the top.

The hollow was taken up by a nearly square rice paddy, and the trench was on its northwest end. On the opposite side, that is, the side closest to the Japanese position, was a small hut, and that is where Ma's grandmother and her two sons, Ma's uncles, were hiding. When the shooting started, Ma's grandfather began to worry about his wife's safety, especially because she had poor eyesight. He may have thought that she would be safer in the trench than in the hut, but whatever the reason, he waited for the right moment and ran out toward the hut. He was a strong man, capable of shouldering 200 jin

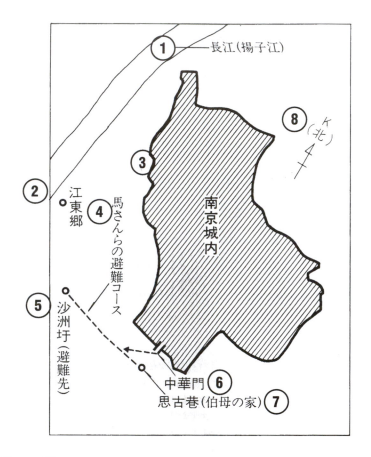

1. Yangtze River
2. Jiangdong Township
3. the city of Nanjing
4. the route by which the Ma family fled

5. Shazhouyu (their intended refuge)
6. Zhonghua Gate
7. Siguxiang (grandmother's house)
8. north

(120 kilograms), but as soon as he started running, the Japanese felled him with one shot.

Alarmed at her father's having been shot, Ma's mother grabbed her youngest son, Ma's one-year-old brother, and without any thought for her own safety, ran to her father's side. Everyone watched transfixed, except for Ma's four-year-old sister, who suddenly ran out after her mother. At that instant, a bullet whizzed past the baby's face and pierced his mother's chest. The four-year-old threw her arms around her fallen mother, and she was soon covered with blood. Suddenly she cried out, "I've been shot, too!" Right after that, two shots rang out and hit the little girl, tearing her open so that her innards burst out. Seeing this, Ma's father gave a loud sob and ran out into the rain of bullets. Ma was sure that his

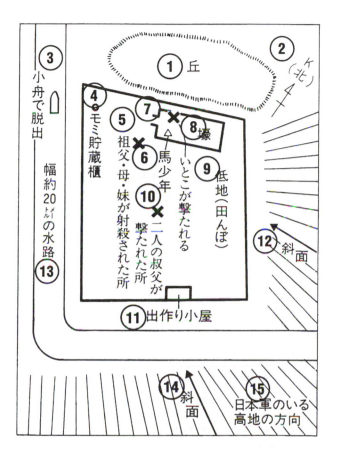

1. Hill
2. North
3. Slipping away in a small boat
4. Storehouse for unhusked rice
5. Where Ma's grandfather, mother, and younger sister were killed
6. Young Ma
7. Where his cousin was shot
8. Trench
9. Hollow
10. Where his two uncles were shot
11. Storage hut
12. Slope
13. Waterway about twenty meters wide
14. Slope
15. The high ground where the Japanese troops were

little brother was dead, but his father took the baby from his mother's arms and ran back to the trench. The baby was alive and uninjured, but his mother had stopped moving. Ma and his young girl cousin were crying loudly, and Ma tried to run out to his mother's side, but his father forcibly held him back.

Ma's grandmother and the two youngest of his three uncles were watching the commotion from inside the hut. (His oldest uncle was in the trench.) It was only 20 meters from the hut to the trench. Ma's grandmother could do nothing but fret hysterically, but the two uncles made an attempt to run toward the trench. The second oldest uncle, who ran out first, was felled with one shot. The third uncle seemed to leap into the air when the first shot hit him, and after he fell, two more shots hit him and killed him.

Three or four minutes later, Ma's cousin was hit. She had been leaning against the wall of the trench opposite Ma, and even though she made no attempt to go out, she was hit by a low-flying bullet. Badly wounded, she was soon soaked with blood.

Ma's second uncle, the first one to be shot, dragged himself along the ground, despite his serious wound, and managed to reach the trench.

After a while, the gunfire stopped. Ma's oldest uncle, long known for his courage and resourcefulness, made a suggestion. "If we just stick together in this place, we'll all be killed. We may be better off leaving here and scattering in all directions."

Some—not all—of the people warily emerged from the trench. "First Uncle" hid up against the embankment of the rice paddy, and he took young Ma, hid him inside a large woven reed container that was used for storing unhulled rice, and laid grass over the top.

The adults conferred among themselves and decided that it was essential for them to get away. The paddy was surrounded by water on two sides, including the southwest side, which was the side opposite from where the Japanese were. If they climbed over the embankment there, they would find two boats that were used for fishing. The people decided to wait until dark and then slip away in the boats. Ma left on the first boat. That is why he did not see what happened after that, but he found out later.

As the second boat was about to leave, someone either jumped in a little too energetically or stumbled and got his or her foot caught, but in any case, there was a loud thump. The Japanese heard this, and they may have been nervous about the possibility of a night attack, because they began firing intensively and randomly with their machine guns and rifles. Ten people died.

Ma Mingfu was separated from his surviving family members, and he rode through the darkness in the first boat with a group of complete strangers. After a while they got out of the boat and walked to Jiangtongmen Locks (present-day Jiangtong township), where Ma was put in the care of some strangers.

He later learned that his cousin had died from loss of blood shortly before the boats left. His injured second uncle was left behind in the trench. Although he conferred with everyone else, the other survivors were all caught up in spiriting themselves away and were unable to transport him. He evidently dragged himself back to the village, but he died a day later.

According to the caption in the *Asahi Graph*: "Aiming for Zhonghua Gate in the all-out assault on Nanjing, the Hasegawa unit broke through the walls. The south gate had been blown up by the advance demolition team of the Yamada Engineering Unit at 12:10 P.M. on December 12. All our fearless fighting units poured into the city and raised the rising sun flag on the 70-*shaku* walls of Nanjing." The photograph shows the moment at which the south gate was demolished. (December 12, 1937. Photograph by Special Correspondent Ueno.)

I will leave the rest of Ma Mingfu's story for later, when I discuss the aftermath of the assault on Nanjing.

Yang Yushi (77), who worked in a tea stall outside the southwest wall of Nanjing, once had seven children, ranging in age from ten to younger than one, but six of them were killed during the Japanese invasion, her husband was also killed, and her remaining daughter later died of illness.

The life of an angry, grieving mother who lost seven children and a husband is impossible to describe adequately in words, so I did not question her in detail. Before talking to her, I heard from two other witnesses, and the old woman just sat there staring at me and not moving. Or rather, it would be more accurate to say that she glared at me. Then, when it was her turn to speak, her eyes filled with tears as soon as she blurted out the first words.

Yang Yushi speaking tearfully.

Her words were disjointed, and the order of events was confused. The following is a direct translation of her story exactly as it was transcribed from the tape recording:

"The Japanese came and set up a machine gun at the exit of the air raid shelter and killed the seven children. I crawled out of the shelter and watched for a while, but my throat was really sore. . . . (At this point, she was overcome with tears and wiped her eyes.) Then they set the place on fire and burned up my six children. My oldest child was also in there. (Short pause.) My husband came to the air raid shelter to look for us. Then he was killed with a sword by the Japanese at the entrance to the shelter. I later heard that some old person had told my husband, 'You'd better not go. There's no use going. They've all been killed. They've been sprayed with machine gun fire.' They machine-gunned seven of them at once. Six of the seven were my children, and a neighbor girl was also with us in the air raid-shelter and got shot. (Another pause in which she is unable to speak.)

"When I came to the pond, I crossed the pond, and when I came to the river, I crossed the river, looking for my husband. I assumed that my second daughter was safe in the northern part of the city. When I came to the river, I crossed it, and it was about this deep. When I ran, I would slip and fall. It was winter, so it was cold. I thought, "What should I do?" but there wasn't anything I could do, so I became all nervous and cried. (Here there was a long pause.)

"Almost my whole family had been killed by them.

(Another long pause.)

"I looked around in the area of the air-raid shelter, but there was no sign of anyone. I went to look after a few days, but I couldn't find anybody or anything. My children were all burned up inside the air-raid shelter. There wasn't anything I could do. (Tears, and another pause.) The oldest child was ten, and after that, I had a baby every year: nine, eight, seven, the youngest one wasn't even a year old. . . ."

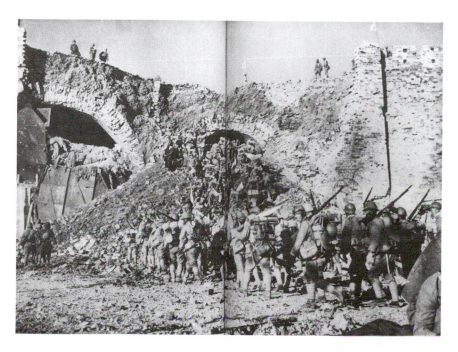

Japanese troops entering Nanjing through Zhongshan Gate. This photo, taken by Special Correspondent Kumazaki, appeared in an extra edition of *Asahi Shinbun* published on December 13, 1937.

The old woman, who had been able to get her story out up to this point, smothered her sobs in a towel and was unable to continue. There was no way I could ask her about the details, but the people who had brought her to me filled me in. According to them, Yang Yushi, six of her children, and a fifteen-year-old neighbor girl were in the air-raid shelter, but after shooting at them with machine guns, the Japanese set a fire at the exit to smoke them out. Only Yang Yushi herself survived, and when night fell, she took a quilt and crossed ponds and rivers to Weizi Street to her younger brother's house, where her she had left her surviving second daughter. When the Japanese came, Yang's husband was not at home, so when he came back to look for his family, the Japanese killed him with a sword. Of the six children killed, three were boys, and three were girls. The remaining daughter later died of illness.[1]

The Japanese soldiers who came into the city of Nanjing did not change their behavior, and rapes began occurring almost immediately. Even girls of

---

1. When I revisited Nanjing a year later, in 1984, I learned that Yang Yushi had since died.

Xia Shujin

eleven or twelve were gang raped and murdered. The following incident was particularly pathetic:

Xia Shujin (57) was seven years old at the time, one of five daughters. She lived in a nine-person household with her father (40), who was a laborer; her mother (40); two older sisters (15 and 13); two younger sisters (one four years old and the other just a few months), and her maternal grandparents (both 60). They lived near Xinlukou with six or seven other families in a compound surrounded by a wall, as pictured in the diagram. Inside the common entrance gate was a T-shaped courtyard, with rooms rented by the various families lined up on either side.

However, by the time the Japanese arrived in Nanjing, only the Xia family and one other family of four persons remained in the compound. An uncle and his wife had been living with the family, but by that time, they, too had left. Xia Shujin, who was only seven years old then, does not know why her family failed to evacuate, but she imagines that they found it awkward to move with old people and so many children.

At about nine o'clock on the morning of December 12, 1937, the Xia family had just finished breakfast and were starting on their household chores. Xia Shujin had nothing in particular to do, so she went out into the central courtyard.

Suddenly she heard someone pounding vigorously at the main gate. The old man who lived next door ran toward it, and he tried to undo the bolt. Xia's father also came running and headed toward the gate. The next instant, the bolt came undone, the door swung open, and some Japanese soldiers burst in, saying something in Japanese, Not understanding what they wanted, the old man simply stood there flustered, and the soldiers shot him down. Seeing this, Xia's father panicked, but as he turned to flee, the soldiers killed him with a shot in the back.

Horrified, Xia ran into the innermost of the family's rooms, and she and all her sisters, except the baby, crawled into a bed and covered themselves

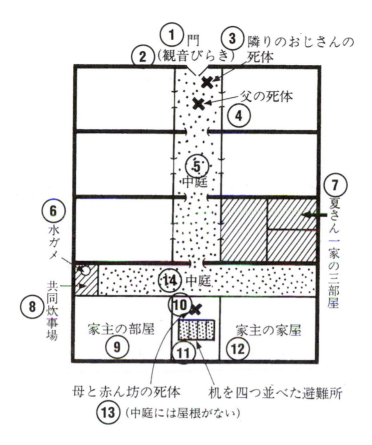

1. gate
2. (double doors)
3. the body of the elderly man next door
4. the body of Xia's father
5. central courtyard
6. water barrel
7. the three rooms rented by the Xia family
8. common kitchen
9. landlord's room
10. the bodies of Xia's mother and infant sister
11. hiding place made up of four desks
12. landlord's living quarters
13. the courtyard had no roof
14. central courtyard

with a quilt and the mosquito net that the family typically kept hanging from the ceiling even during the winter.

Soon, they were aware of a large mob of soldiers rushing into the house—in her excitement, Xia had forgotten to shut the door. They heard the sound of boots tramping on the floor and a murmur of voices, and then, almost at the same time, gunshots. Being under the quilt, they could not see what was happening, but their grandfather, who was near the door, was being killed.

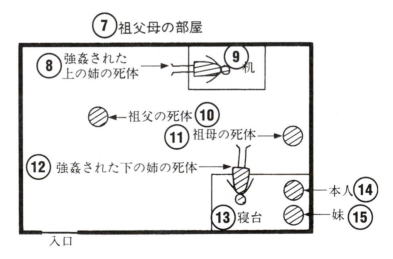

（1）夏一家の住居

（3）机

（4）祖父母の部屋

（2）
入り口
父母と子ども5人の部屋

寝台（5）

（6）伯父夫婦の部屋
（避難ずみ）

（7）祖父母の部屋

（8）強姦された
上の姉の死体

（9）机

（10）祖父の死体

（11）祖母の死体

（12）強姦された下の姉の死体

本人（14）

（13）寝台   妹（15）

入口

1. the Xia family's living quarters
2. entry the room occupied by the parents and five children
3. desk
4. the grandparent's room
5. bed
6. the uncle and aunt's room (hiding place)
7. the grandparent's room
8. the body of the raped and murdered oldest sister
9. desk
10. the body of Xia's grandfather
11. the body of Xia's grandmother
12. the body of Xia's raped and murdered second sister
13. bed
14. Xia Shujin
15. younger sister

Just after that, the quilt was torn away from them with the tip of a soldier's bayonet. The large room was packed with Japanese soldiers. Xia's grandmother stood in front of the bed, trying to protect the four girls huddled there, but someone shot her with a pistol, and whitish bits of her brains flew through the air.

Then the soldiers grabbed the two older sisters to take them away. Terrified, Xia Shujin began screaming, and at that instant, she was stabbed with a bayonet and lost consciousness, so she did not see what happened after that. She did not realize it at the time, but she had been stabbed in three places: the left shoulder, the left side, and the back.

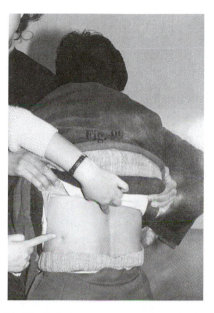

Xia Shujin's bayonet scars in the middle of her back, left side, and left shoulder

She does not know how long she was unconscious, but she became aware of her four-year-old sister, who lay uninjured but crying, under the quilt, which was wadded up against the wall. When the Japanese had ripped the quilt and mosquito net off the bed, they had evidently thrown them on top of her. At this point, there was no sign of the Japanese, and all was strangely quiet, but the room was filled with an eerie light. Their thirteen-year-old sister lay dead at the other end of the bed, naked below the waist, her legs trailing on the floor. In front of the bed, was their grandmother's body. Just inside the door was their grandfather's body. Against the opposite wall was a desk, and their fifteen-year-old sister lay dead on top of it, also naked from the waist down and with her legs trailing on the floor. Xia could not tell whether her sisters had been stabbed or shot to death. There was no sign of their mother or the baby.

She crept out into the courtyard with her younger sister walking beside her. She was so stunned that she hardly felt any pain, despite her serious wounds. The two of them made their way into the makeshift air-raid shelter in their landlord's inner court. This was not the typical air-raid shelter dug into the ground. Rather, four sturdy desks had been lined up together, with door panels on top and straw spread beneath. Because of the indiscriminate bombing attacks, the children had learned to take refuge there whenever they heard the buzzing roar of the Japanese planes.

The bodies of their mother and baby sister were right in front of the shel-

ter. Their mother lay stretched out, her trousers pulled off, and the baby lay at her side. The two little girls crawled into the straw in the shelter, covered themselves with a quilt that they had brought from the house to protect themselves from the cold, and there they stayed for nearly two weeks.

Since they were afraid to go out during the day, they hardly ever left the shelter, but at night, they went back to the house to look for food. In their grandparents' room was a large iron pot containing a thick layer of burned rice. This rice had been deliberately overcooked to make a type of food known as guoba, *which remains edible for a long time and is therefore useful for refugees or during emergencies. (Judging from the fact that they had cooked up some* guoba, *the family may have been preparing to leave.) The two children brought the pot to their shelter and ate from it. There was water in a large jar in the common cookhouse, but since they were too small to reach the water's surface, they took a box and used it as a step.*

After about two weeks, an old woman from the neighborhood found them. She was a stranger, but she took the children to the old people's home in Jianxiaoxiang. Several days later, the uncle who had fled the city came to the old people's home looking for them, and he took them back with him to the evacuation zone.

"I don't know what happened to the bodies of my family members. My parents don't even have graves, so I can't pay my respects, and when I think about that, I feel very bereft, even now." Xia Shujin also told me that the four people who lived next door, the parents and two children, were all killed.

Cui Jingui.

"Ordinary" rapes, if not pitiful incidents like Xia Shujin's story, came to be no more than everyday occurrences. Let us take as an example the story told by Cui Jingui, a seventy-four-year-old man who was twenty-four at the time and living at Hongwu Road, Number 224 Renyutang. He earned his living as a gatekeeper at Qingzhensi, a Moslem mosque, and his household consisted of eight people: Cui and his wife, his parents, his younger brother, and three younger sisters.

On December 14, the morning after the Japanese entered the city, the household split into two groups and headed toward the International Refugee Zone. His par-

ents, younger brother, and two of his sisters went to Guanjia Bridge (near the Hanzhong Gate at Xinjiekou, now the Zhaoshang marketplace.) Cui, his wife, his third younger sister, and a female cousin went to the Gaojia Inn near Taoyuan, near an arsenal.

The building that they fled to looked as if it had two stories when viewed from the outside, but actually, there was an attic that amounted to a third story. The women went up to the third floor, and Cui stayed on the second floor, which was divided into four rooms and linked to the ground floor by a wooden stairway, that ended in his room. The third-floor attic was usually used only for storage, so there were no stairs leading up to it. Anyone who wanted to go up there had to either use some kind of a step stool or climb up on someone's shoulders. When the door to the attic was closed, it became part of the ceiling, and it was cut off from the second floor. It could, therefore, serve as a hiding place for young women when the Japanese came on a "hua guniang hunt." All together, about ten women were hiding in the attic.

The second floor held about seventy or eighty people, including women and old people. Not all the women could hide on the third floor, because it was not very sturdily built. The ten women who were on the second floor were older than the ones on the third floor, and fearing rape, they had begun on the previous day (December 13) to cut their hair short like men and to smear their faces with soot from the cooking pots. The young men, too, were afraid of being conscripted for labor by the Japanese, so the first floor mostly held old men.

That afternoon, Cui suddenly heard cries from the first floor—evidently, the Japanese had come. Since he was young, he was worried about being conscripted, so someone threw a quilt over him. As the uproar downstairs continued, he heard a stampede of footsteps on the stairs. The second floor, too, was soon filled with cries and screams. Cui was in a corner near the top of the stairs, and he peeked out from under a slight gap between the quilt and the floor, but all he could see was the area of the stairs. The cries continued: it seemed as if women were being raped. There were about twenty people in the room, but the soldiers did not bother to take their victims into the next room. Instead, they simply raped them in full view of everyone. After perhaps thirty minutes, the soldiers had achieved their purpose, and Cui saw two of them go down the stairs. He recalls that their gaiters were in a criss-cross pattern instead of being wrapped around their legs, their yellowish uniforms had gray lines on the legs, and there were also thin yellow and gray lines around their caps . . .

He learned later that two soldiers had come to the first floor as well, making a total of four who came scouting for women. The two raped on the

1. Yijiang Gate
2. north
3. Nanjing
4. International Safety Zone (Refugee Zone)
5. Military Engineering Agency
6. Taoyuan
7. Guanjia Bridge

8. Central Market
9. the Cui family home
10. Renyintang
11. Zhongshan Gate
12. Yangpi Lane
13. Zhongzheng Road
14. Zhonghua Gate

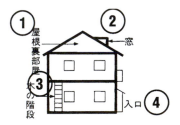

1. attic room
2. window

3. wooden staircase
4. entrance

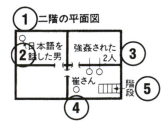

1. layout of the second floor
2. the man who could speak Japanese

3. the two women who were raped
4. Cui
5. staircase

second floor were the wife of a man named Wu and the wife of his younger brother.

Wu himself was fairly old, so he had been on the first floor. He had a canteen with him, and when the departing Japanese saw it, they mistook it for a military-issue canteen. They took him outside to shoot him, but the first shot missed. A man in hsi thirties who spoke some Japanese came down from a back room on the second floor to plead that Wu was not a soldier, and eventually he convinced them to release him.

Cui Jingui later joined up with a charitable organization called Chongshantang and became involved in disposing of and burying corpses.

Although the "contest to cut down a hundred" described in the previous chapter was a fraud, the days immediately after the Japanese capture of Nanjing saw some genuine killing contests.

Tang Junshan (78) was born in a peas-ant village in Jiangsu Province in 1909, and at the age of fifteen, he was appren-ticed to a shoemaker on Pingshi Street in Nanjing. At the age of twenty, he became a full-fledged shoemaker, but instead of going out on his own, he stayed on at the same shop. At the time of the Japanese in-vasion, he was twenty-eight.

Tang Junshan

As the Japanese began to move toward the city, Tang's boss asked him to watch over the shop and then fled. When the Japa-nese gradually moved closer, and the gun-fire became more fierce, Tang fled north to an acquaintance's house in Sanbeilou, closer to Yijiang Gate. His family home was in Liuhe County, about 35 li (17.5 ki-lometers) from the city, but he felt that it would be safer to stay in the Nanjing than to venture off in that direction.

Beginning on the night of December 12, the night before the fall of the city, Tang hid in the basement of his acquaintance's house, but when the Japanese appeared on the afternoon of the 13th, he became extremely curi-ous and wanted to see them, so he slipped out onto the street. Just then, he saw a group of what appeared to be Chinese soldiers who had surrendered coming from the direction of Shanxi Road, surrounded by Japanese soldiers. Tang noted that the uniforms of the Japanese soldiers were shorter than those of the Chinese soldiers and that they wore stained trousers and leather shoes.

Tang was watching the procession from about one hundred or two hundred meters away with a neighborhood youth, but as the soldiers drew closer, Tang and the youth hid themselves in a trash bin that leaned against a house by the road. The bin had no lid, so they took some straw that was inside it and covered their heads, but they could still see out. The Chinese soldiers who passed in front of them had their hands bound, some of them with wire that passed through holes in the palms of their hands. There also appeared to be civilians mixed in with the soldiers.

Seeing the horrible scene in front of him, the neighborhood youth who was hiding in the trash bin with Tang began to tremble, and his trembling caused the trash bin to rattle against the wall of the house. This attracted the attention of the Japanese who pulled the youth out of the bin by his long hair and beheaded him with a sword on the spot. Weak with terror, Tang crouched down into the trash bin, but a Chinese collaborator[2] who was with the Japanese pulled him out. The collaborator interpreted the soldiers' questions: "Are you a Chinese soldier?"

"I'm not a soldier," Tang answered. "I'm a city resident from a peasant background." After the collaborator had interpreted his reply, the Japanese began examining his hands. "I'm a shoemaker now," he explained," and that's why I have calluses on my hands." The collaborator also relayed this answer to the Japanese.

Just then, more Japanese soldiers came leading about a hundred more Chinese from the direction of Xiaomenkou, and Tang was perfunctorily handed over to them.

This group was escorted by six Japanese soldiers and two Chinese collaborators, who were also wearing Japanese military uniforms. They also had army dogs, German shepherds, along with them. The group, which consisted entirely of civilians, including a few women, was taken to the grounds of a clothing factory about five hundred meters away, where a pit had been dug. Only some of the prisoners had their hands bound, but what plunged them into despair was the sight of one or two hundred corpses already in the pit. Some Japanese soldiers were already on the scene, machine guns ready.

Anticipating a massacre, some of the people began to cry or to shout "Jiu ming! Help!" Amidst all the noise and confusion, they were divided into four groups of equal size that were made to stand on four sides of the pit, and each

---

2. The collaborators served as instruments of the Japanese during the occupation, and lived very comfortably. Typical of the collaborators were the Chinese who served on the Committees to Maintain Order. In this case, however, Tang simply assumed that his interrogator was a collaborator because "his Chinese was excellent." We cannot discount the possibility that he and the other supposed collaborator mentioned later were simply Japanese who spoke Chinese well.

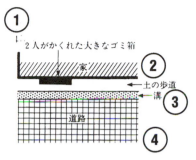

1. The trash bin where the two young   3. Ditch
   men hid   4. Street
2. Dirt sidewalk   5. House

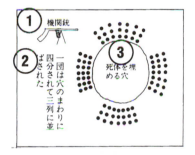

1. Machine guns   3. The pit where the bodies were buried
2. The people were divided into four
   groups and made to line up in three
   rows around the pit

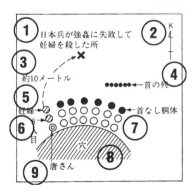

1. Where the Japanese soldiers killed   5. Pregnant woman
   the woman they were unable to rape   6. Eighth person
2. North   7. Headless bodies
3. About 10 meters   8. Pit
4. Row of severed heads   9. Tang Junshan

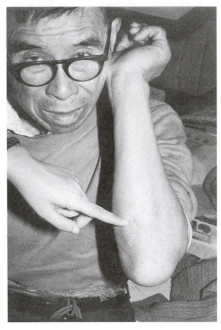

Tang Junshan showing where he was bayoneted after losing consciousness.

group was then divided into three rows, as the drawing shows. The eight captors, six Japanese and two Chinese collaborators, split up into two-person teams, one team for each group of prisoners. Then the head cutting began. Four of the soldiers went around slicing off the heads of the people in their assigned group while the other four, including the collaborators, picked up the severed heads and lined them up. In other words, the four teams were having a head cutting contest.

The three rows of victims were made to kneel facing away from the pit. Tang was at the end of the last row of his group, the row closest to the pit. The soldier began cutting heads on the east end of the front row. Some of the people were crying and screaming, while others were too frightened to move. As each head was cut off, blood spurted up and the body fell over. The heads were lined up in back.

The seventh and last person in the first row was a pregnant woman. The soldier thought he might as well rape her before killing her, so he pulled her out of the group to a spot about ten meters away. As he was trying to rape her, the woman resisted fiercely, shouting "Dadao Riben diguozhuyi!" (*Down with Japanese imperialism!*) The soldier abruptly stabbed her in the belly with a bayonet. She gave a final scream as her intestines spilled out. Then the soldier stabbed the fetus, with its umbilical cord clearly visible, and tossed it aside.

The eighth person was a man on the west end of the second row, or directly in front of Tang. The minute his head was cut off, his body fell backwards, knocking Tang into the pit like a domino. He has vague memories of his head being covered by the clothing of headless bodies, but he lost consciousness at that point. He now thinks that he must have passed out from sheer terror.

When he came to, he was in an air-raid shelter, being tended by a friend. This friend had been watching the entire horrific scene from inside a house on the grounds of the clothing factory, and he explained that after the massacre was over, the Japanese had thrown the bodies into the pit, all the while *walking around and bayoneting any bodies they thought were showing some signs of life. While unconscious, Tang was stabbed in five places—his back, his left arm, two places in his left leg, and in his left thigh—but he did not feel a thing. After the Japanese had left, the friend went to take a look. It was at that point that Tang moved slightly. He was covered with blood when he was dragged out of the pit, and his friend did not recognize him until he had washed the blood off.*

The friend took Tang to the large air-raid shelter in his home, about two or three hundred meters away. There the two of them lived for three months. However, Tang's wounds failed to heal completely, and his leg in particular festered and swelled. Since conditions in the city had stabilized, his friend took him to the Drum Tower Hospital, where his wounds still failed to heal, even after two months. He was then moved to the charity hospital run by the army of Wang Jingwei, where he was operated on. After spending nearly half a year there, he finally recovered. This hospital was in the Refugee Zone, and it was only upon entering the hospital that he discovered that there was such a thing as a Refugee Zone.

After his release from the hospital, he was forced to make shoes for the Japanese military at the clothing factory. During that time, he happened to hear his fellow workers talking about the pit where the head-cutting contest had taken place. It had been dug by about sixty Chinese conscripts, all of whom were killed and shoved into the pit after finishing the job.

Tang was at the factory for about two months, but during that time, there were two notable incidents.

In the first one, a female worker about twenty-two or twenty-three years old was discovered in the toilet area, tearing up cloth meant for Japanese uniforms into rags for use during menstruation. She was killed on the spot.

In the second incident, a male worker came to work in sweat clothes. Suspected of having stolen them from the Japanese military, he was tied to a utility pole, where four soldiers stoned him to death with bricks. Then they fed his body to their dogs.

Unable to feel safe living under such conditions, Tang slipped away to his family's home in the country and then on to Xuzhou, on the far northern edge of Jiangsu Province. He worked as a shoemaker and opened his own shop in 1941. It was 1955 before he returned to Nanjing.

To celebrate the fall of Nanjing on December 13, the *Asahi Shimbun* printed an extra edition consisting mostly of photographs. The *Yomiuri Shimbun* put out a "second evening edition" on the same day, with headlines such as,

Japanese troops entering the city through Zhongshan Gate. (*Asahi Graph*, December 29, 1937.)

"Complete Power of Life and Death over Nanjing" and "War of Annihilation Spreads Throughout the City." The accompanying article read as follows:

> On the walls of Nanjing, December 13, special dispatch from Correspondent Ukishima: Thanks to the left flank units' crossing of the Yangtze and occupation of Pukou and to the main units' capture of all the gates in the walls of Nanjing, fifty thousand enemy soldiers, everyone from the enemy General Tang Shengzhi on down, are now completely surrounded by our forces. Valiant street-to-street fighting crowns the end of the coming offensive on Nanjing, and a war of annihilation has developed. The Guangxi and Guangdong armies, under the command of Bai Zhongxi in the eastern part of the city, and the 88th Army, directly under the command of Chiang Kai-shek, in all the southern areas of the city, are continuing their frenzied defense, but our troops, who have begun an all-out offensive, secured the greater part of the city by 11:00 A.M., and they have occupied every important facility. All that remains is the northern part of the city. In every part of the city flames rise to the heavens, Our troops are showing the utmost bravery amidst random shots and random attacks, and the sound is providing the most incomparably thrilling score for the fall of a city ever known in the Far East since the dawn of history is being played. The fate of Nanjing is completely within the hands of our troops, and this is deemed to be a major turning point in the course of the war.

CHAPTER 10

"A WAR OF ANNIHILATION UNFOLDS"

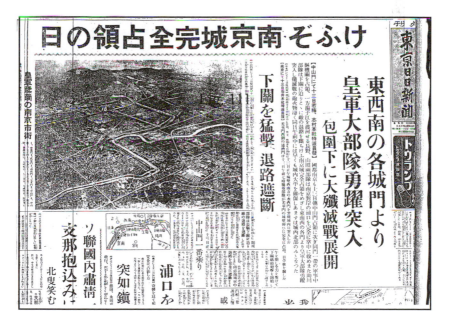

けふぞ南京城完全占領の日

東西南の各城門より
皇軍大部隊勇躍突入
包囲下に大殲滅戦展開

下關を猛撃、退路遮断

交那抱込み
ソ聯國内肅清

突如鎮
浦口を

北叟笑む

東京日日新聞

トリ ランプ

The evening edition of the *Tokyo Nichinichi Shimbun* for the day when the Japanese
entered Nanjing.

Of course, the "war of annihilation [that unfolded] in every part of the city" upon the fall of Nanjing was not centered on any single area, so no individual had an overall view of the situation. For this reason, it is extremely difficult to sort things out and obtain an accurate picture of the mass confusion and free-for-all fighting, but it is certain that the greatest disorder was centered on Xiaguan, in the northwestern part of the city along the Yangtze River. The hellish experiences of the multitudes in this area were horrible beyond imagination.

In his autobiography, *The Last Lord* (Kōdansha, 1973), Tokugawa Yoshichika writes about the staff officers who ordered the indiscriminate machine gunning of masses of people:

> Several days after I finished my inquiries and returned to Japan, the Japanese military carried out a huge slaughter in Nanjing. When I say "slaughter," I'm not talking about cutting down ten people or even a hundred people. These days, I'm sometimes asked whether the Nanjing Massacre was a fabrication, but I heard at the time that tens of thousands of Chinese civilians had been killed or injured. Fujita Isamu told me that the ringleader of the massacres was Lieutenant Colonel Chō Isamu,[1] a member of Commander Matsui Iwane's inner circle. I was also well acquainted with him.
>
> He is supposed to have told Fujita this:
>
> A crowd of fleeing civilians that included women and children was surging along the banks of the Yangtze, and there were a lot of Chinese soldiers mixed in among them. If the Chinese soldiers were allowed to get away, they could later influence the course of the war. This is why Lt. Colonel Chō ordered the soldiers who had set up machine guns along the front line to shoot them. The soldiers hesitated, because even if there were some Chinese troops mixed in, it was a largely civilian crowd, but Chō lost his temper, roared "This is how you kill people!" drew his sword, and killed the some of the soldiers with blows through the shoulder. Shocked, the other soldiers opened fire, and that's how the slaughter took place.
>
> When Lt. Col. Chō bragged about this incident, Fujita was shocked and imposed silence on him, saying, "Whatever you do, don't tell anyone about this."

One of the tens of thousands of Nationalist Chinese troops[2] who were routed was Liu Sihai, a private in the 87th Army of the Nationalist Chinese

---

1. Lieutenant Colonel Chō, who was promoted to Colonel the following year, was an information staff officer with the Shanghai Expeditionary Force, and he was assigned to the general headquarters of the China theater beginning in November 1937. Chō's orders to slaughter prisoners of war are discussed in Hora Tomio's *The Great Nanjing Massacre* (Gendaishi Shuppansha, 1982).

2. We find conflicting information about the actual troop strength of the Nanjing defense force, but *Yomiuri Shimbun*'s report of "fifty thousand" appears to be on the low side. In its December 27, 1937, report on Commander Tang Shengzhi's sentence to death by firing squad before a military tribunal after being blamed for having abandoned Nanjing, *Asahi Shimbun* gave the largest estimate, 210,000 troops. The latest Chinese research estimates the number at somewhere between 180,000 and 200,000, but because

Liu Sihai.

military, led by Major General Wang Lingjiu. Then twenty-six (seventy-two at the time of the interview), Liu was the older of two sons of a poor peasant family near Hefei in Anhui Province. When he was six years old, his father disappeared and was never heard from again, so he was sent out to work as a cowherd.

At the age of twenty-five, he went to visit some relatives in Changzhou, Suzhou Province, hoping for some clues to his father's whereabouts, but he was unable to find their house. Hungry and frantic, he told his story to the squad leader of a Nationalist army unit. "Why don't you join my unit?" the squad leader asked as he gave Liu some food. In fact, Liu had no particular interest in joining the army, but circumstances didn't allow him to go home, so he just drifted into the military.

I intend to tell you about Liu Sihai's experiences after he surrendered at Nanjing, but first I would like to show you the chapter entitled "Treatment of Prisoners" from the textbook used at the Army's Infantry School. *Studies in Methods of Fighting the Chinese Army* was published in January 1933 as a "secret" book. It starts with the following preface from the head of the education department, Katsuki Kiyoshi:

> This book comprises the research of Colonel Nagami, an instructor. Even though it cannot be said to be perfect, we are distributing it as a resource for education in methods of fighting against China for students and the assembled field officers.
>
> December, 1932
> Head of the Education Department at the Army Infantry School
> Katsuki Kiyoshi

In the introduction we find such statements such as "Most Chinese soldiers are in private armies and have no connection with their nation. A hun-

---

the attrition since the fighting in Shanghai had not been fully compensated for, the true figure is probably around 150,000. (See Kasahara Tokushi, "The Nanjing Defense Force: from Collapse to Massacre" in *To the Site of the Nanjing Massacre,* edited by Hora Tomio, published by Asahi Shimbunsha.)

dred different systems exist depending on circumstances in the country, and
no one has control. It is just as if we were to borrow trees from all over Japan
and bring them together."

The entire book consists of three volumes and an appendix, and the last
chapter in the first volume of *Studies in Methods of Fighting the Regular
Army* is called "Treatment of Prisoners." The first part of the chapter teaches
the reader how to disarm captives, and the second part, "Dealing with Prisoners" contains passages like the following:

> Unlike citizens of the other powers, prisoners of war do not necessarily have
> to be confined at the rear and wait for the war to be settled. Except in special
> cases, it is permissible to release them on the spot or in some other area.
> The Chinese do not have a full-fledged family registration system, and in
> addition, the military ranks also include many drifters, so those whose existence
> can be confirmed are few. Because of this, if you kill them for the sake of
> convenience or release them in another area, there will be no repercussions.

That is to say, according to this passage, it is all right to "release them on
the spot," but "there will be no repercussions" if you kill them. Many of the
people I talked to witnessed the second approach (killing), but we have not
yet heard from anyone who experienced the first approach (release). Here is
one such story:

*As the Japanese approached, the 87th Army was camped on Yuhuatai, an
upland abutting the southern edge of the city. Private Liu had fought for two
or three days with two rifles as his weapons, but all his officers had either
died in battle or fled. The unit had lost fire power and fallen into chaos, and
the retreat was beginning.[3]*

*Liu and his comrades cut across the city south to north, heading toward
the Yangtze until they arrived at Xiaguan just before noon. They tried to
cross over to the other shore, but there were no boats or other vessels. Many
of the panicked soldiers even grabbed hold of scraps of wood or oil drums
and set out to swim across the river.*

*The first sign of the Japanese was two or three tanks. They made the rounds
of the riverbank area and then left. About an hour later, a unit a few dozen
tanks came and sprayed the area with machine gun fire. Then an interpreter
who seemed to be Chinese called out in a loud voice, "Surrender! If you
surrender, we won't kill you!"*

---

3. Chiang Kai-shek ordered Commander Tang Shengzhi to withdraw on the evening
of December 11, but he did not pass the order along until five o'clock the next afternoon. (See "The Nanjing Defense Force and Tang Shengzhi," by Sun Zhai, translated by
Kasahara Tokushi and published in *Thinking about the Nanjing Massacre,* edited by
Hora Tomio, Fujiwara Akira, et al., published by Asahi Shimbunsha.)

Japanese troops shouting *"Banzai!"* after capturing Guanghua Gate. (*Asahi Shimbun,* photo by special correspondent Kojima.)

A large number of Nationalist Chinese soldiers, including Private Liu, turned their caps backward and surrendered. The number was probably fewer than ten thousand, but there may have been several thousand, at least.

Once they were all assembled in one place, someone who seemed to hold a high position in the Japanese military rode up on horseback. He had a beard about 3 or 4 centimeters long that stretched from ear to ear. He began giving some sort of a speech in Japanese. Liu doesn't know the details of what he said, but according to the interpreter, the gist of it was, "You're peasants. We're going to release you. Go straight home."

A Japanese-produced leaflet promising "If you surrender we absolutely will not kill you."

They were told to make white flags, using whatever cloth was at hand. Liu used his own handkerchief and tied it to a tree branch about 30 centimeters long. A lot of baggage and clothing left behind by refugees lay scattered along the riverbank, and he took off his military uniform and put on some of the abandoned clothing.

Raising their flags, the released prisoners took off in a disorderly mass for their various hometowns. Liu joined with forty or fifty other people who were headed for Anhui Province. They walked along the Sancha River to Jiangdongmen, intending to go to Wuhu. All along the way, they saw a tremendous number of corpses, not only of soldiers, but also old people and children. At one point, they saw seven bodies, including two women, tied together with wire that pierced their collarbones, and one body had an unused bullet stuffed in each nostril. All of them appeared to have been bayoneted.

When they reached Jiangdongmen, they met some Japanese soldiers in front of the minimum security prison. Liu and the rest of the released prisoners showed their white flags, as they had been instructed back at Xiaguan, and said, "We are soldiers who surrendered and were let go."

But these Japanese soldiers unceremoniously arrested everyone and immediately led them to a vegetable field just east of the prison. The prisoners were made to stand—not kneel—in a single line and were surrounded by fifty or sixty Japanese. Ten or more of these had swords, and the rest had bayonets. Liu does not remember hearing anything that sounded like a command,

Sword-cut scars on Liu's neck.

but suddenly, the soldiers rushed in all at once, their swords and bayonets at the ready. The last thing Liu remembers is the terrifying sight of a Japanese soldier running toward him with his sword in both hands, raised to strike.

It was dark when he came to. Two dead bodies lay heaped on top of him, and as he pushed them aside to get up, he saw the stars in the sky. He recalled the old saying, "In the next world, you can't see the stars," and he thought, "Somehow, I'm alive." He had been cut on the back of the neck, but fortunately, not very deeply, and the bleeding had nearly stopped. Deciding to leave the area while it was still dark, he walked about half a li until he found an air-raid shelter. Two dead Chinese soldiers lay near the entrance; their damaged rifles at their sides. Liu went inside and hid.

At dawn, some Japanese came to the entrance of the shelter and shouted something in their own language, most likely "Come on out!" If they had come inside, all would have been lost, but the soldiers just left, perhaps because they could not see Liu in the dark recesses of the shelter.

The story that comes next after Liu's in chronological order is that of Zhao Shifa (71), who was in the Chinese army and was taken prisoner. In this case, there was no mass release, just a mass murder.

Twenty-five years old at the time, Zhao was born and raised in Nanjing, the second of the three sons of a man who sold teacups and other drinking vessels from an open-air stall.

When the Japanese landing at Shanghai made it clear that war was imminent, Zhao, who had been helping with his father's business, was drafted as a laborer with the Nationalist 88th army stationed at Nanjing. The laborers ranked below even the lowliest private, and although they carried rifles, their main duties were limited to miscellaneous errands, such as carrying ammunition. When it came time for battle, the privates devoted themselves to fighting, but the laborers' main job remained the same, and fighting was of secondary importance. After three months, Zhao was promoted to private, thanks, he says, to personal connections.

It was just after his promotion that the Japanese army began pressing on

Nanjing. Zhao doesn't know where the headquarters of the 88th Army was, but his unit was on Shanxi Road in the city. On the evening of the Japanese onslaught, he was assigned to guard Guanghua Gate, and he stood on top of the city walls, returning enemy fire. The Japanese fire, however, was relentlessly fierce, and since a large force was attacking, Zhao's unit was unable to hold out for long. As they were being driven back, fighting all the way, a formal order to retreat was issued. That night, Private Zhao and some others rode through the city on a truck to Xiaguan. The troops who had retreated before them had crossed the river in boats, but by this time, there were no boats left.

Zhao Shifa.

Since there was nothing else to do, they walked downstream along the river until they came to Baota Bridge Road, adjacent to Meitan Harbor, where they crawled into a house. It was still dark, and they could not see much of their surroundings, but in fact, it was a neighborhood of mud brick houses with thatched roofs packed closely together, and these were not abandoned houses: most of the inhabitants had remained behind. The two-room house that Zhao and his seven companions entered belonged to a family named Ying. The family stayed in one room, and the soldiers in another. The dirt-floored room was so small that when the soldiers lay down, they took up all the space.

The Japanese soldiers came by when it was dawn, so in order not to be shot, Zhao and his companions changed out of their military uniforms and into civilian clothes. Zhao put on something he had picked up along the way, but others in his group got clothing from the Yings. At a loss about what to do with their discarded uniforms, they threw them into a pond.

At eight or nine o'clock, they heard a loud shout outside: "You'd better come out quickly and greet the army of the Great Japanese Empire!"

Both soldiers and civilians decided that instead of hiding, it would be safer to come out, surrender, and beg for their lives.

The building of the Red Swastika Society, a Buddhist charitable organization, faced the street, and as they sat at its entrance, they saw Japanese troops coming from the direction of Meitan Harbor. Most of them had beards, and they marched in ranks, shouldering their rifles. They simply marched past, as the civilians and disguised soldiers knelt on either side of the road

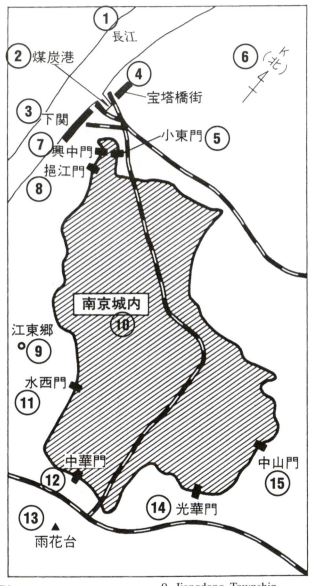

1. Yangtze River
2. Meitan Harbor
3. Xiaguan
4. Baota Bridge Avenue
5. Xiaodong Gate
6. North
7. Xingzhong Gate
8. Yijiang Gate
9. Jiangdong Township
10. Nanjing
11. Shuixi Gate
12. Zhonghua Gate
13. Yuhuatai
14. Guanghua Gate
15. Zhongshan Gate

in a worshipful attitude. However, when some of the Japanese came by again, the spectators had to resume their pose. It was noon by the time they returned to the Ying house, but in the afternoon, they had to come out once again and "greet" the troops. Since someone from the Red Swastika Society advised them that it would be best to show up the next morning as well, they spent another night with the Yings.

The next morning, they followed the advice of the Red Swastika Society and stepped outside again. A large number of Japanese were already there. All the people who showed up, whether soldiers or civilians, were made to kneel on either side of the street. Then seven or eight Japanese soldiers started circulating among the crowd, picking out men who appeared to be in their twenties. They picked them out simply by sight, since they had no interpreter with them, but one of the Japanese spoke a little Chinese, and he asked each man, "Are you a soldier?" Almost all of them answered "No," as did Zhao, but he was selected anyway.

The young men singled out were made to stand in the middle of the street in a four-line column. When the selection process was over, there were perhaps five hundred of them standing there, with Zhao almost exactly in the middle. Eventually, armed Japanese soldiers stood at intervals alongside the columns, and even though Zhao doesn't remember any order being given, they began heading toward the river. The procession was nearly a li *in length, and as it set out, Zhao thought, "They picked only men in their twenties, and they asked if I was a soldier, and even though I threw away my uniform, there's probably no getting around the fact that they suspect me because of my haircut, so I'm wondering if we're all going to be killed. If that's the way it is, if I'm going to die anyway—I'll try to break away."*

The distance between the Japanese soldiers who were guarding either side of the procession was about 30 meters. Zhao's position was in the second from the left of the four columns marching toward the river. Not more than a hundred paces beyond their starting point, Zhao caught sight of the entrance to a narrow alley to his left, and he leaped into it in a single jump. Somehow, none of the Japanese saw him do it, and of course, none of the other captives told on him. He made an additional leap into the garden of one of the houses that faced onto the alley, and then he hid himself in an adjoining abandoned house.

He crawled under a bed, but one wall of the room he was in just happened to face the main street, because the configuration of the houses around the garden was like a table lying on its side. Besides, the wall was no more than a framework of woven reeds covered with earth, and the earth had fallen away at the bottom, so he was able to look out from his hiding place and see what was happening on the street.

The bodies of Chinese people shot by the Japanese. (China News Agency.)

It was about 400 meters from his hiding place to the riverbank, About five minutes after the last of the procession had passed out of sight, Zhao began to hear fire from heavy machine guns. He was unable to judge just how many guns there were, but for ten minutes there was hardly any break in the sound of shooting.

Even after the shooting stopped, Zhao was too frightened to go out, so he stayed hidden until dark. Figuring that the people at the Red Swastika Society would take pity on him, he sneaked into their building under the cover of darkness.

The next morning, when the people from the Red Swastika Society came, they hired Zhao to work for them burying the bodies of massacre victims. He found that the riverbank where the procession had gone was overflowing with corpses. On the shore of the downstream inlet lay the bodies of the approximately five hundred victims of the machine guns. The piles of bodies extended down to the water's edge, and some of the bodies were already washed away. Putting together the scene before him with what he had heard of the machine guns, he surmised that a separate unit of Japanese soldiers must have been waiting there with their heavy machine guns ready and must have shot the first Chinese as soon as they arrived. He wondered whether the victims who had come along behind had been pursued with bayonets into the place where the people in front had fallen.

There were air-raid shelters here and there near the site of the massacre, shelters that were actually dugouts built by local residents, and these, too, were full of corpses, both adults and children, but they had been killed with bayonets, not with machine guns. In some cases, boards or earth had been thrown on top of them.

Zhao and the ten or more people who made up the temporary burial squad decided to dig a trench and bury all the bodies in it. The trench was about a meter wide and 1.5 meters deep, and it stretched for about 100 meters parallel to the river. Burying everyone took an entire day.

The next day, too, Zhao and three others continued picking up scattered bodies in the vicinity of the massacre site and hauling them off to be buried. During that time, some Japanese soldiers with swords showed up and summoned the four men to work as coolies for the army. The next day, they were made to carry loads of beef to Xishan Bridge, and then the day after that, they were released. After that experience, Zhao went to the International Refugee Zone in central Nanjing and stayed there.

Whether we are talking about the prisoners of war who had surrendered or the people who had thrown away their military uniforms and were hiding among the populace, these were not battlefield killings, but outright massacres contrary to international law. Particularly in the latter case, where the distinction between defeated soldiers (deserters) and civilians was not clear, the principles tended to be "If in doubt, punish one and all" and "Indiscriminate slaughter within the midst of slaughter." Beginning with Xiaguan along the Yangtze, mass murders were carried out all over within and outside the city, with the victims counted in tens or hundreds or even thousands, as in the so-called assembly-line massacres.

Professor Hora Tomio's book *The Great Nanjing Massacre* (Gendaishi Shuppan, 1982)[4] is an exhaustive collection of accounts from the diaries of some of the participants. Here are excerpts from just a few of them:

> December 13: At around two o'clock in the afternoon, we completed general mopping-up operations and secured the rear. We reformed our unit as we moved forward and arrived at Heping Gate.

---

4. The first time that Hora Tomio took up the topic of the Nanjing Massacre was in his 1967 book *The Riddle of Early Modern War History,* published by Jinbutsu Ōraisha, although this book also discussed other incidents. Later, in 1972, he amended and published the section on the Nanjing Massacre separately. In response to the insistence of certain right-wing journalists that the Nanjing Massacre had never happened, he published *A Critique of the Construction of an Alleged Hoax: The Great Nanjing Massacre* (Gendaishi Shuppansha, 1975). The revised edition of this became *The Great Nanjing Massacre,* which I have referred to before. In 1986, *The Proof of the Great Nanjing Massacre,* a sequel with verification of the earlier book, was published by Asahi Shimbunsha.

After that, prisoners surrendered one after the other until the number reached several thousand. Although the overly excited soldiers heard the officers' attempts at restraining them, they slaughtered all the prisoners. (Sasaki Tōichi, *A Certain Soldier's Autobiography*)

December 15: Instead of going through the city on the way, we went around the outskirts, and we came out at Taiping Gate by way of a side street at Heping Gate and entered the city. At the entrance to Taiping Gate the bodies of about 500 Chinese soldiers were piled up. It seems we had killed them all. . . .

January 24: Xiaguan was truly a beautiful harbor. As soon as we had left a certain part of Nanjing, we saw thousands of Chinese lying dead on both sides of the street. The wind brought the smell of death, and it was tough on the marching soldiers. (Gaiga Kanji's diary of following the troops; *Mainichi Shimbun*, September 21, 1981)

For 2,000 meters, or maybe it was even more, there were more bodies floating in that wide river than I could count. As far as I could see, nothing but bodies. On the riverbank and in the river. These weren't soldiers, but civilians. Adults and children, men and women. It was as if they filled the whole river. They flowed along slowly, like rafts. When I looked upstream, I saw a mountain of bodies that seemed to continue on forever.

From what I saw, I'd say that there must have been fifty thousand bodies, and almost all of them were civilians. It was as if the Yangtze had become a river of corpses. (Excerpted from *The Yangtze River Is Weeping*, an account of the dispatch of the 6th Kumamoto Division to China, edited by the Sōka Gakkai Youth Division Antiwar Publishing Committee)

In the firing trenches that stretched along the road passing through Guanghua Gate were countless burned and blistered bodies, and there were other bodies spread out under the wooden beams that littered the road. Seeing the arms and legs sticking out from underneath was like a picture of hell on earth.

Seeing the tanks roll mercilessly over them, hearing the sound of the treads, smelling the stench of death and the odor of gunpowder smoke, I thought I was standing in a burning hell or in the hell of the lake of blood. (Suzuki Jirō, "I Witnessed the Tragedy at Nanjing," *Maru*, February 1971)

There are also documents supporting these accounts. On page 19 of "Observing the Situation in Central and Northern China" (Kokusei Ishinkai, 1938), the Vice-Minister of Overseas Affairs and Political Affairs, Vice Admiral Yasumi Saburō writes, "When we left the city of Nanjing and went to Guanghua Gate, I was told that until a few days ago, cars had been driving over bodies." Yasumi was writing on or around December 19, sixteen days after the fall of Nanjing. Here is another account:

The next morning I went out driving with two or three comrades. The bodies at Bajiangmen had all been cleared away, and there was no more of the horror of

According to the *Asahi Graph* for January 5, 1938, this photograph was taken on December 17 and shows "stragglers who have infiltrated the Refugee Zone." Some people say, however, that the individuals shown are wearing police uniforms. Whatever the case, it is assumed that they were all killed.

passing through the gates of hell. As we passed Xiaguan, of course, just as Fukazawa had said, there was an incredible pile of bodies of Chinese soldiers along the Yangtze River side of the road. In some places, the bodies were charred, having been doused with gasoline and set on fire.

"It seems they machine gunned them," said Haraigawa. "Even so, there sure are a lot of them, aren't there?"

There were over a thousand. There may even have been two thousand. (Maeda Yūicihi, *Amidst the Flow of the War, from China to French Indochina*)

Along the riverbank, the bodies of the defeated soldiers that had been swept up lay in piles on the roads and under the quay. Nothing could be more pathetic than this. Who knows how many people have been swallowed and flushed away by the muddy waters of the Yangtze? During the great Kantō earthquake [of 1923], I saw many people piled up along the riverbank in Tokyo's Honjo ward, Midori-chō, but their number was nothing compared to this. (Sasaki Genshō, *The Field Postal Flag*, vol. 1)

Triumphal entry into Nanjing through Zhongshan Gate. At the head of the procession is Commander in Chief Matsui Iwane. At his right is Prince Asaka. (*Asahi Graph*, January 5, 1938.)

Units equipped with poison gas participated in the assault on Nanjing:[5] the Shanghai Expeditionary Force had Field Operations 1st and 2d Gas Company (A) and Field Operations 7th Gas Platoon, and the 10th Army had Field Operations 6th Gas Company (B) and Field Operations 8th Gas Platoon. This massive violation of international law, later activated on a large scale along the battle lines in China, had been planned since the beginning of the war. It is mentioned in the field diaries of some of the soldiers during the Nanjing campaign, and it is possible that it was used during the massacre, as the following example suggests.

> I saw with my own eyes the bodies of thousands of Chinese regulars gathered in one place. I never saw the bodies of so many soldiers before or since. There was something odd about the manner of their deaths. First of all, they had no visible wounds, and they seemed to have fallen under the Xiaguan embankment. Their appearance gave me the impression that they had crawled down there, come to the end of their strength, and breathed their last. . . .
>
> Rumors began to spread among us: "I wonder if they were killed with gas." (*Everyone Knows [the Hardships Suffered by the Women of China at the Hand of Million Man China Expeditionary Force], ed. Fujiwara Shinji)

---

5. This is according to a supplementary chart in *The China Incident Army Campaign,* 1, published by the War History Research Office of the National Defense Agency. Takasaki Ryūji, in his book *War Literature and Correspondence* (Ōbaisha, 1975), presents Okamoto Yoshio's *Yamahida/Sanpeki* (1943) as one of the rare works of wartime literature to depict a gas-equipped company.

Moriyama Yoshio, a front-line correspondent for *Asahi Shimbun,* is one person who witnessed these things. Having occupied Nanjing, the Japanese troops herded more than thirty thousand Chinese, most of them old people, women, and children, into the area surrounded by the city walls. After that, I'm told that they threw hand grenades down on them and shot them with machine guns from the top of the walls, killing everyone. The area within the walls was literally a mountain of corpses at that time, and it is said that the sea of blood was enough to soak one's boots. (Shinobara Seiei, "Nazism in the West, Imperialism in the East," *Nitchū Bunka Kōryū,* Number 157)

The excerpts above are just a small part of Professor Hora Tomio's *The Great Nanjing Massacre.* A colleague of *Asahi Shimbun* correspondent Moriyama Yoshio, special correspondent Imai Masatake, reported on the ceremony celebrating the army's entrance into Nanjing at the time as follows:

Nanjing, special correspondent Imai, December 17: On this day of shouting and excitement, the cheers of one hundred million countrymen resound. Today, the deafening cries of *banzai* rising to the top of the city wall are the marvel of the century. Jubilation is breaking out here, in a bold, splendid ceremony to celebrate our entrance in the city. It has been four months since this army assembled its troops for the holy war in central China, and as the magnificent result of our fighting, we have captured the enemy capital and gained ascendancy in all of China. Here, we have established the foundation of peace in East Asia. Can anyone look at the Rising Sun flag waving so magnificently over the headquarters of the Nationalist government without tears of emotion?

As he tries to convey to his homeland the actuality of the extremely majestic and soul-stirring grand ceremony, the pen of this reporter trembles with emotion and excitement. Over Nanjing are clear skies like those of Japan, deep blue with clear air and not a single cloud. . . . (*Asahi Shimbun,* December 18, 1937, evening edition [published on the 17th])

After the war, however, Imai regretted having written this kind of reportage, and he left us descriptions of the scenes of indiscriminate slaughter that he witnessed.

Even though there isn't a soul on the main street, this area is somehow full of Chinese people. They are all either women or old people, and they are clustered at every window, their eyes nervous and fearful. These are the faces of the people, the people that we see for the first time in several days. . . .

A private was pulling off a man's knit wool cap. If the man's forehead was pale, he would be assumed to be a soldier.

"Hmm, not pale. Well, all right, come over here."

The soldier poked at the man's shoulder. "That's no soldier."

"Still, plain-clothes soldiers are hiding in the streets. Take him away for now."

Privates with bayonets led the man away, and then they reappeared in a noisy throng.

The *Tokyo Nichinichi Shimbun* reporting on the triumphal entry into Nanjing.

When we went into the former [*Asahi*] branch office, it, too, was packed with twenty or thirty refugees. Some of them gave a welcoming cry when they saw us and rushed forward. They were the nursemaid and the houseboys who had been employed at the office.

"Oh, so you're all right?"

I went upstairs and flopped down on the sofa. I dozed off into a pleasant sleep, feeling as if I were taking a nap at home for the first time in a long time.

"Master! Something terrible is happening! Please come!"

I was shaken awake by the pale, frantic nursemaid, and she told me that the Japanese had assembled some Chinese in a vacant lot nearby and were killing them. Among them were a father and son, the Yangs, who ran a clothing store in the neighborhood. If I didn't hurry, they would be killed. These two were not soldiers, so could I please come out and rescue them? Behind the nursemaid stood Yang's frantic wife, her pockmarked face streaked with tears. Special correspondent Nakamura Seigo and I were alarmed and confused, and we ran out.

The lot was on Xiyang Hill near the branch office. Four or five hundred Chinese men squatted there, practically filling the whole lot. One side of the lot was made up of a half-destroyed, blackened brick wall. Six Chinese at a time stood and faced that wall. From twenty or thirty paces away, Japanese soldiers fired their rifles all at once into the backs of these men. Running to the fallen men, they then administered the death blow with a single bayonet thrust to the back. Their last cries rang out across the hillside. Then six more men stood up.

They were killed, one group after another. The four or five hundred Chinese squatted there in the lot, watching with blank expressions as the others were run through. This abstracted state, this nothingness, what was it?

Completely surrounding this scene was a crowd of women and children, watching in a daze. If I looked at their faces one by one, I could see that they were unmistakably filled with fear and hatred as their fathers, husbands, brothers, and children were being killed before their very eyes. They may have been crying out and weeping, but none of that reached my ears. All I could hear were the crack of the rifles and the cries of the victims, and all I could see were the rays of the sun low in the sky, staining the brick wall red.

Panting for breath, we approached a staff sergeant who was standing to one side. "There are some people here who aren't soldiers. Please spare them."

The stout sergeant simply sneered at us.

"They're a father and son who run a clothing store," I continued. "We'll vouch for them."

"Do you know which ones they are?"

"We do. The wife's here. If she calls, they'll come out." Without waiting for an answer, we pushed Yang's wife forward. She called out to them in a loud voice.

The wrinkled father and a young man of about twenty ran out of the crowd.

"It's these two. No way are they soldiers. They're clothing store owners who often come to the *Asahi* branch office. Well, you two, run along home."

Immediately the people in the vacant lot stood up all at once. The thought that they would be spared if they just appealed to these masters freed the crowd from their blank and dazed states of mind. They rushed toward us and clung to the hems of our coats. Turning our backs on the silent, stiff-faced sergeant, we left the vacant lot, all the time hearing countless gunshots behind us. (Special issue of *Bungei Shunjū*, "I Was There: The Testimony of Eyewitnesses," December 1956)

Corroboration of Imai's personal account comes from a fellow correspon-

"Our Imperial Supreme Commander favoring the Imperial Headquarters with his august presence." (*Asahi Graph*, January 19, 1938, "on loan from the Department of the Imperial Household.")

dent for *Asahi Shimbun* named Adachi Kazuo, who wrote about a mass murder that he witnessed together with Moriyama near *Asahi*'s Nanjing branch office. It appeared in a collection of Moriyama Yoshio's own writings and other people's memorial tributes in a commemorative volume published after Moriyama's death:

> On December 12, 1937, the Japanese main force ferociously attacked Nanjing from all sides. In conjunction with that, a large number of correspondents who were following the troops assembled in Nanjing, including Moriyama and myself.
>
> Near the *Asahi Shimbun* branch office was an open space where burned rubble had been cleared away. In the open space was a long line of Chinese standing under the watchful eyes of Japanese troops. Almost all the Chinese men who stayed in Nanjing had been rounded up and branded "plain-clothes soldiers." We managed to save one of them by testifying that he had worked for us in the days before the war. After that, the *Asahi* office was besieged by women and children begging us for help, but we did not have it within our power to save any others. The "plain-clothes soldiers" were shot one by one, right in front of their weeping and screaming wives and children.
>
> "It's sad, isn't it," I said to Moriyama.
>
> He looked as if he were about to cry. "With this, Japan has lost the right to win the war," he mumbled.
>
> At the same time that Japan was probably bubbling over with events celebrating the assault on Nanjing, our hearts were shaken with anger and

sorrow. (*Asahi Shimbun* contributing editor Adachi Kazuo, "The Great Nanjing Massacre," in *Collected Writings of Moriyama Yoshio,* 1975)

Adachi Kazuo is still alive, and when I asked him whether the scene described in this passage was the same as the one that Imai witnessed, he replied that it was a different occasion. He was together with Moriyama, but Imai and Nakamura were otherwise occupied at the time. Evidently the vacant lot near the *Asahi* branch office saw this kind of mass slaughter many times.

Continuing with Imai's accounts of the events that he personally witnessed, here is what he wrote about an extraordinarily large-scale massacre that apparently occurred that same night:[6]

> Dark night fell on the defeated capital, which had lost its electric power. The shadows cast by the oil lamps that we had managed to scrape together provided an appropriate background for talking freely about the events of the evening.
>
> Suddenly, we became aware of a sound coming from the wide asphalt street outside our building. It was the sound of light but firm footsteps, and it seemed to go on forever, as if hundreds of people, maybe thousands of people, were walking past. Every once in a while, we heard the tread of military boots.
>
> Throwing on our overcoats, we dashed out into the icy street. It was a long, long procession. I wondered where they had found them all, this endless line of Chinese people. I could see at once that this was a funeral procession being led to the slaughter.
>
> "Where are they going?"
>
> "To Xiaguan. It's a wharf along the banks of the Yangtze."
>
> "Let's go," I said, struggling to put on a jacket underneath my overcoat. We followed after them. . . .
>
> "Where are you going?" asked the soldier.
>
> "To the riverbank,"
>
> "It's forbidden. Take some other route."
>
> "But there is no other route, is there?"
>
> "Then go tomorrow morning."
>
> "Just now a lot of Chinese passed by here, right?"

---

6. Tanaka Masaaki's *The Fabrication of the Nanjing Massacre* (published by Nihon Kyōbunsha, 1984) is enough to make one laugh out loud, or rather, it is an excellent example of a work that is so convoluted that one would almost think it was a hoax in itself. For example, he treats Imai's personal account as "an alleged eyewitness account" and claims that Imai writes of having witnessed the massacre of 20,000 prisoners at Xiaguan. Yet, Imai does not say that he actually saw the massacre taking place. Furthermore, Tanaka makes no mention of the massacre that took place near the *Asahi* branch office, which Imai really did witness. Tanaka's method of argument, based on these kinds of selective excerpts, is completely lacking in persuasiveness. In addition, his handling of the diaries of General Matsui Iwane, which he revised on a large scale and to which he arbitrarily added his own words, was exposed in the morning edition of *Asahi Shimbun,* November 25, 1985.

The soldier did not answer.

"Where did they go?"

"I don't know.". . .

Then we heard the sound of machine gun fire so close that it felt as if the bullets were going to land at our feet. As the roaring tide of gunfire continued, we heard raking gunfire from the opposite direction for a time.

"They're killing them off."

"Killing them off? Those Chinese people?"

"Yes, sir. I think so. They're stragglers, so many that they can't finish them off all at once."

"I'm going."

"You can't, sir. It's dangerous. The bullets are ricocheting."

As a matter of fact, the shadow of the building was occasionally lit up with a popping sound, as if fireworks were going off, and we sometimes heard a whining sound as the bullets bounced off the zinc-plated walls.

I don't know how many tens of thousands of people there were. Probably only a certain percentage of them were stragglers, and it is not hard to imagine that the majority were residents of Nanjing. . . .

"I want to write about this."

"We will some day. For the time being, we can't, you know. But we *have* seen it."

"No, let's see it again. With our own eyes."

With that, the two of us got up, because the gunfire had suddenly stopped.

We went out to the riverbank. The muddy Yangtze, as brown as *miso* soup, flowed like a dark sash through the city, and milk-colored morning fog hovered above it, as if crawling on the water's surface. It would soon be morning.

We noticed that the surface of the wharf had become a dark, tangled mountain of bodies. Anywhere from fifty to a hundred human shapes wandered in a daze among the corpses, dragging them laboriously out and throwing them into the river. Groans, flowing blood, twitching arms and legs. And yet, the scene was as silent as a mime's show.

We could see the opposite bank faintly. On the wharf something was glimmering dully, like mud in the moonlight. It was blood.

Eventually, the job was finished. The coolies were made to line up along the riverbank, and then we heard the rattling of machine gun fire.

Throwing their heads back, tumbling backward, looking almost as if they were dancing, the group fell into the water.

It was all over.

More machine-gun shots raked the river's surface from a steamboat that was moored slightly downstream. Lines of spray rose and fell.

"There were about twenty thousand of them," one officer said.

Most of them were probably gathered up from here and there, crying out and staggering amid the rain of machine gun bullets, they fell into the Yangtze that frosty night. The Japanese even shot up the surface of the water, but there may have been a few who caught on to something and crawled out or who were rescued. Even so, this was a complete annihilation.

The ceremony to celebrate the fall of Nanjing took place on a stage that had been swept clean. . . . (Special issue of *Bungei Shunjū,* "I Was There: The Testimony of Witnesses," December 1956)

All the accounts I have presented so far have been from those who either witnessed the events or heard about them from eyewitnesses, but the following accounts were written by the actual perpetrators of the systematic slaughter. Most significantly, these are not postwar memoirs but field diaries written on the very days that the events occurred. The following excerpt comes from the field diary of someone who was later killed in battle, and there are reasons I cannot divulge his real name, so I will call him Yamamoto Gorō.[7] Born in Kyoto, he participated in the assault on Nanjing as a private first class in the Shanghai Expeditionary Force. Here are the entries from the two volumes of his pocket diary that cover the period from December 13 through the formal celebration of entry into the city, which took place on December 17. (Note that I have left blanks where the names and numbers of his units are mentioned, but otherwise, his diary is reproduced verbatim, including mistakes in Japanese orthography.)

A report on the large number of prisoners of war.

December 13, sunny.

Perhaps because they had learned their lesson from the shells of our valiant troops, the enemy retreated beginning at 3:00 A.M., but not without a last, ferocious volley of shells and rifle fire.

At 7:30, the battalion withdrew from its position and reassembled on the road, and with the mighty _____ regiment of the _____ battalion leading, we entered Nanjing at 2:30 P.M. The city was more beautiful than I had expected, and it seemed not to have been bombed very much. Many Chinese are gathered in the Refugee Zone. The _____ battalion is leading the tanks in mopping-up operations within the city, and they have secured part of the city without incident. We camped just outside the Refugee Zone. Under cover of our _____ battalion, the first to arrive in Nanjing, the commissioned officers and scouts raised the Rising Sun flag within the city at 2:10 P.M.

Upon entering the city, the main force of the _____ battalion lost two men

---

7. This field diary was brought to light by the members of the organizing committee of the exhibition "Kyoto's War Exhibit for Peace," which was held at the Kyoto Industrial Exhibition Hall from August 2 to 10, 1984. However, it was withheld from the exhibition at the request of the diarist's family.

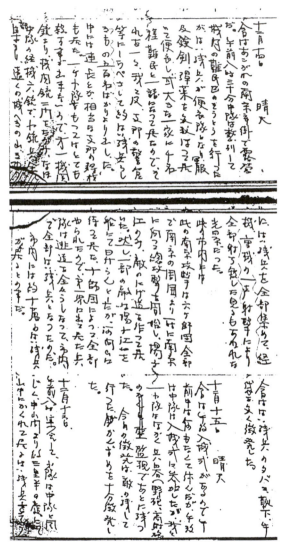

The entry from Private First Class Yamamoto Gorō's diary for December 14, in which he writes of having killed "about five hundred" prisoners.

and the _____ company lost nine due to a landmine that was on the road about two hundred meters from the gates. Furthermore, outside the city walls there was a large moat, and we encircled it with barbed wire and constructed a complete encampment. There were three gates leading into the city, but they had sandbags piled up against them and we couldn't open them, so the gates were. _____ with aerial bombardments.

There are a lot of stragglers within the city, and mopping-up operations are a real bother.

After entering the city, the _____ battalion carried out mopping-up operations led by tanks.

December 14, sunny.

Today we camped in the long-awaited streets of Nanjing. At 8:30 A.M., the company went into formation and carried out mopping-up operations in the Refugee Zone, but the stragglers have became plain-clothes soldiers, putting aside their uniforms, bayonets, and ammunition and changing clothes, or else they get together in one building with a thousand refugees, so we and some Chinese policemen examined them, and we selected about five hundred. Among them were regimental commanders and ranking commissioned officers. Since just one platoon couldn't kill all of them, we ordered two machine guns from the first machine gun unit and six light guns from the company, assembled all the rifle corpsmen, and we gathered all the stragglers in one place near a hill far away by the city walls. We killed them all, firing the light and heavy guns at the same time, and it was really a pathetic sight to see. In this Nanjing offensive, six divisions all together mounted an all-out offensive from the surrounding area, and the only escape route for the enemy was the Yangtze River. Some of the enemy tried to escape down the Yangtze in boats, but all of them were killed by the 10th Division, which was waiting for them, so the frontline soldiers completely lost their escape route and were in the city as stragglers. There are said to be a hundred thousand stragglers in the city. Today we commandeered the stragglers' cigarettes, stockings, and gloves.

December 15, sunny.

Today there was a ceremony celebrating our entry into the city, so there was nothing to do all morning, and I rested. In the afternoon, the company participated in the ceremony, but our platoon remained behind to guard the captured weapons (field artillery, antiaircraft guns). In the course of today's requisitioning we requisitioned the canned goods that the enemy had left behind.

December 16

We assembled at 8:00 A.M., and the platoon, like the company, assumed a position to mop up stragglers hiding in the mountains about 3.5 *li* from Zhongshan Gate, but our orders were changed, and we spent the whole night [illegible]. We are supposed to return to the city tomorrow.

The _____ regiment's mopping up operations resulted in rounding up four thousand men outside the city.

December 17, sunny.

Assembling at 6:00 A.M., the platoon became a foraging party for the battalion and returned to the city. When we returned, the other units had taken all the good stuff, and there was no good stuff for us. Even though Nanjing is large, you have to expect that the good stuff will disappear with ten divisions in the city. At 3:00 P.M. we arrived at our quarters within the city.

"Requisitioning" really means "looting," and it appears frequently in this diary. If other writings in this genre are any indication, the approximately four thousand men who were rounded up on the 16th by the _____ regiment were killed.

The ceremony to celebrate entering the city, mentioned in the entry for the 15th, is not the formal triumphal entry held by General Iwane on the 17th, but the morning edition of *Asahi Shimbun* for December 16 reports that "the triumphal entry of the front line units was set for 3:00 P.M. on December 15 under sunny skies."

Even judging only by the preceding diaries of direct participants and the experiences of eyewitness journalists, it is obvious that systematic mass slaughter took place in and around Nanjing, but we might ask ourselves how the upper echelons of the military were connected with these illegal massacres. Leaving aside the fact that the textbook for the Infantry School permits the killing of prisoners, it is also clear that orders expressed in the words "Dispose of them" were issued.[8] The following is an example of a full report of fighting from the third volume of Kojima Noboru's *The Japan-China War:*[9]

> At 2:00 P.M. today, we received the following orders from the regimental commander:
> 1. According to brigade orders, all prisoners of war are to be killed.
> As far as the method is concerned, how about taking eight or more of them and shooting them in quick succession? . . .
> At 3:30 P.M. all the company commanders gathered and exchanged opinions on the disposal of prisoners, and as a result, we distributed them among the companies (1st, 3d, and 4th companies): the first company in a valley south of our encampment, the third company in a hollow southwest of the encampment, and the fourth company in a valley southeast of the encampment, who each took about fifty prisoners out of the detention room and stabbed them to death.
> However, we placed heavy guards around the detention room and made sure that the prisoners being led away didn't suspect anything.
> Each unit finished its preparations by 5:00 P.M., began the executions, and finished by 7:30.
> The first company changed its original plans and tried to burn them all together but failed.
> Among the prisoners, there were those who were resigned and fearlessly extended their necks for the sword, those who stood up calmly before the bayonets, and some who wept and screamed and pleaded for their lives, particularly raising their voices when the commander was observing. (pp. 193–94)

Thus, it was common knowledge from the upper ranks to the lowest ranks that the prisoners, whether they had been routed out or whether they were "plain-clothes troops," were to be "disposed of." This was the standard pro-

---

8. See Hora Tomio, *The Great Nanjing Massacre* (Gendai Shuppankai, 1982); and Kojima Noboru, *The Japan-China War,* vol. 3 (Bungei Shunjū, 1984).

9. According to a telephone conversation I had with Kojima, he was unable to quote the full text of the original, because he had promised the owner of this detailed military information not to reveal specific names or places.

cedure from the time of the landing at Hangzhou Bay, but since Nanjing was so large, only the scale of the killings expanded. And it is also true, based on the reports of the eyewitnesses, that large numbers of civilians were included among the "plain-clothes soldiers." Furthermore, this common practice of "disposal" continued as a tactic even after the fall of Nanjing.

The next excerpt is from the diary of a soldier in the Nakano Unit, which was published the year after the fall of Nanjing. However, this particular section tells of what happened after the unit had advanced upstream to Taiping and Wuhu:

ヒ總統・皇軍を絶讃

"果敢！寡兵よく衆敵を撃破"

日本の戰術 十分研究

Hitler praises the Japanese army. (Evening edition of the *Asahi Shimbun*, December 17, 1937.)

> The streets were full of endless numbers of defeated enemy units who had lost their escape route. We didn't even have to fire a single shell at them. We caught groups of two hundred or three hundred with our bare hands. Then we were at a loss. We ourselves weren't getting our provisions replenished. We would have enough to do just advancing on Wuhu. How would we be able to feed and handle these more than a thousand defeated enemy troops? The untold tens of thousands of enemy who had resisted us in Nanjing had become mountains of corpses in an instant. Even so, we were confused about what to do.
>
> The creek became full of the reeking bodies of the enemy, and we no longer had water even to wash our dirty hands.
>
> We arrived in Taiping and stayed up all night as snow fell. (Taniguchi Katsu, *Zhengye, One Thousand Li,* Shinchōsha, 1938)

The reader should pay special attention to the part right after "we were confused about what to do," which begins a new paragraph with "The creek became full of reeking bodies." The "more than a thousand" prisoners suddenly become "reeking bodies." There is definitely something left out between these two paragraphs. The sentence, "The untold tens of thousands of enemy who had resisted us in Nanjing had become mountains of corpses in an instant," hints at a previous instance of "disposal." Takazaki Ryūji, who is well known as a scholar of wartime literature, sees this as a clear example of censorship. In other words, these "more than a thousand" prisoners also "became mountains of corpses" in the creek "in an instant." In the preface to the book, Major General Sakurai Tadaatsu wrote:

> What is laid out in this book, bit by bit, without any elaboration, is the true shape of the war.

Surrounded by onlookers, a Japanese soldier beheads a Chinese. (From the Historical Materials Editorial Department of the Second Historical Archives of China in Nanjing.)

The massacres that unfolded everywhere were systematic acts based on policies of the upper echelons of the Japanese military. A first-class source for demonstrating this is *Division Commander Nakajima's Diary,* which has only recently been made public. We have already seen how the Army Infantry School's textbook *Studies in Methods of Fighting the Chinese Army* stated that "there [would] be no repercussions" for killing prisoners, but this diary tells us that during the Nanjing offensive, the killing was a specifically stated policy of the commanding officers above the rank of division commander.

After spending the years beginning with the onset of the China war fighting all over the country, the commander of the 16th Division of the Shanghai Expeditionary Force, Lieutenant General Nakajima Kesago, died of illness in October 1945, at the place where he had been evacuated. His division had landed under enemy fire at Baimaokou as a support unit to the backup forces within the Shanghai Expeditionary Force, and it attacked from the north. Ishikawa Tatsuzō, author of *Living Soldiers,* was a part of this division. With the permission of his family,[10] Lieutenant General Nakajima's

10. According to Kimura, Lieutenant General Nakajima's oldest son, Nakajima Tomoyuki expressed the following opinion in reference to the publication of his father's diary: "If we omit part of it or add things, we will inadvertently invite unexpected

diary was made public as part of an extra issue of *Rekishi to Jinbutsu* called "The Secret History of the Pacific War," by Kimura Kujitsune. Kimura describes the diary as five notebooks about 16 x 11 centimeters in size, with a hundred pages per volume, covering the period from August 2, 1937, to August 5, 1938. The part published in the special issue dealt with a twenty-day period beginning with December 11, just before the fall of Nanjing. This is what Nakajima writes about the problematic policy toward prisoners:

> For the most part, it is our policy not to take prisoners, so we have decided to tidy up. If we capture a group of one thousand, five thousand, or ten thousand, we can't even divest them of their weapons. It's just that they completely lose the will to fight and come after us in big groups, and even though they are safe, once they do make a disturbance, finishing them off is a problem, so I get reinforcements with trucks, and make them responsible for guarding and guidance. On the evening of the 13th, we need the trucks for large-scale operations. Even so, since it is just after our victory, we are quite unable to implement things very quickly. From the beginning, I never imagined that we would have to deal with it in this way, so the staff officers are extremely busy. (December 13)

The diary continues on what a huge task it is to kill such a large number of prisoners and even includes a description of the methods.

> According to what I learned later, the Sasaki Unit alone dealt with fifteen thousand; the one company commander assigned to guard Taiping Gate dealt with thirteen hundred; seven or eight thousand gathered in the vicinity of Xianhao Gate; and they still keep coming to surrender.
>
> In order to dispose of seven or eight thousand people, quite a large trench is needed. So as not to be seen in the act, one plan is to divide them into groups of two hundred, lead them to a suitable place, and deal with them there.
>
> This final disposition of the defeated enemy in general has fallen to the 16th Division, and we have no time to enter the city or arrange for lodgings. We are really in a rush. (December 13)

Furthermore, he also describes the Japanese army's pillaging:

> We are inside the captured Nationalist government buildings. The 16th Division already sent in soldiers on the 13th, and they began mopping-up operations. Beginning early in the morning of the 14th, we reconnoitered in the Administrative Department, made plans for allotment of quarters, and put up a nameplate that said "Division Commander." Even so, when I went in to look, they had been rummaging in everything in the government chairman's office, and they had walked off with even some of the old things.

---

misinterpretations. I want to have the published excerpt to appear exactly as it is." This impartial attitude expressed by the family is a huge contribution to the correct interpretation of a historical incident. I wish that other people who have vital primary sources secreted away would make the same type of contribution to history that Nakajima's son has.

> After the entry ceremony on the 15th, I gathered up what was left, put it into a cupboard, and sealed it, but it was no use. When I went to look two days later, everything I expected to find there was gone. It's no use trying to keep something unless you put it into a safe.
>
> The enlisted men swipe whatever they see, and appealing to their commanding officers gets one nowhere. To my surprise, I have found that they act as thieves for the eminent officers.
>
> Seeking out things within your own territory and taking them is certainly a manifestation of the battlefield mentality, and it doesn't have to be thought of as a moral lapse, but when it comes to entering someone else's territory—and into a building designated for the commander, no less!—and blithely swiping things, I have to view that as really bad form.
>
> It's said that Chiang Kai-shek was in the quarters of the commandant of the military academy, so I should have had exclusive possession of it. Although I even sent out the 9th Regiment to take it for me, the commander of the Uchiyama Brigade (the 5th Heavy Field Artillery Brigade), who were not even in their own billeting area, broke in and completely wrecked it.

He also records that many men took stolen Chinese paper money, exchanged it for Japanese yen in Shanghai, and sent it home. In addition, he writes on December 31: "The electricity and running water in Nanjing were in operation until the morning of the 13th, during the mopping-up operations. The engineers and workmen were evidently disposed of, too, so there is no one to operate the systems." This seems to indicate that ordinary civilians were "disposed of" together with the prisoners of war. Furthermore, it was an everyday occurrence for soldiers who owned swords to "test" them during mass murders. We find the following scene in the diary:

> When Swordsman Takayama arrived at noon today, there were fortunately seven prisoners, I let him test his sword on them.

On the same day, Nakajima laments that a soldier took it upon himself to behead a major in a construction brigade, someone whom he himself had attempted to question. "I can't stand these lower-ranking soldiers," he complains.

And so the systematic slaughter went on inside and outside the city. The scope of of the massacres ranged from a few at a time, to tens at a time, to hundreds at a time, to thousands at a time, and here are some examples, starting with the small-scale killings and moving up to the large-scale killings.

Zuo Runde (63) was seventeen at the time, living with his father (45), mother (44), and two younger sisters (14 and 11). His father pulled a rickshaw, and young Zuo Runde was a junk dealer, who scavenged trash and coal cinders.

At the time of the Japanese invasion, Zuo Runde lived in Wangfu Lane in the Zhahu District. It was at eight o'clock in the morning that a Japanese army unit showed up. Hearing gunfire, Zuo ran out of the house to see a man of about thirty lying dead face down by the side of the road. He was wearing ordinary civilian clothes.

Around noon, Zuo happened to be outside just as Old Man Yang, a neighbor, came staggering home from somewhere, covered with blood. He got as far as the air-raid shelter before collapsing. Zuo helped Old Man Yang's family move him inside, but although they tended to him the best they could, he died about two hours later. He had been stabbed several times, evidently with a bayonet.

Zuo Runde.

In the afternoon, a group of twenty or thirty Japanese soldiers passed through the neighborhood, but Zuo hid in a far corner of his house.

The following morning at around eight or nine o'clock, some Japanese soldiers tramped through the neighborhood and hunted out Zuo, twenty-nine-year-old Zhu Kisheng (it's not clear what character "Ki" was written with.), and two fifty-year-olds named Zhang Si and Li, and took them away to the grounds of the Mofang flour mill about 50 meters away in Xiaowangfu Lane. Near the entrance were two or three Muslims who had also been brought there. They lived near Zuo, and he knew them by sight.

Surrounding the seven or eight Chinese were seven Japanese soldiers, one with a gun, one armed with an ax, and the rest with bayonets. The Chinese were forced to take off their cotton-padded outer garments and strip down to their underwear. Then they were driven out into the garden on the grounds. During that time, the soldier with the ax took a swing at the neck of the Muslim man who was two or three positions behind Zuo. Zuo turned to look, but neither the attacker nor the victim had said anything. Even though blood gushed from the Muslim man's neck, he did not fall over, perhaps because his wound was not life-threatening, but it was not clear why he had been attacked like that. Even so, Zuo, who had assumed that he was being taken away to work as a coolie, suddenly became more uneasy.

Once in the garden, the seven or eight Chinese were made to kneel in a line facing west, with Zuo in the northernmost position. Right next to him was a fellow resident of the neighborhood named Gan Shengzhi, who was *about two or three years older, and the Muslims were at the south end. Just then, one of the Muslims said, "I have a horse. I have a horse." One of the Japanese soldiers appeared to understand Chinese, and four or five of them went off with the Muslim man to look for the horse.*

Anyway, the number of Japanese soldiers was down to two, and there were six or seven kneeling Chinese. The soldier with the ax stood in front of the gate, and the soldier with the rifle attached to it a bayonet. Then he started stabbing the men, beginning with the south end of the line, where the other Muslims were.

Just as the soldier pulled his bayonet out of the back of the first man and was about to stab the second, Zuo silently touched Gan Shengzhi's arm, and after exchanging a nod, they rose together. The Japanese soldier, who first noticed them after he had pulled his bayonet out of the second man, came after them, stabbing at them diagonally. Gan Shengzhi adroitly made his way under the bayonet and ran toward the back gate. The bayonet pierced the skin of Zuo's left arm, but at that same time, he grabbed the handle of the bayonet and pulled at it with all his might. Determined not to have it taken away, the soldier resisted with too much force and ended up falling on his backside. Zuo took that opportunity to run out the back gate. A shot was fired, but it did not hit him. By the time the second shot was fired, Zuo had already passed out through the gate and made a turn outside the walls. The soldiers came out after him, but Zuo, who knew the streets and alleys of the neighborhood well, quickly threw them off the trail.

Zuo soon returned home, but that evening, the Nationalist government's public hospital on Fengfu Road, the Nanjing City Health Center, caught fire. Fearful that the fire would spread, more than twenty people from Wangfu Lane ran to help put it out, but Zuo, who was still unnerved by the day's events, stayed hidden. Almost none of the people who went to put out the fire ever returned home.

Shortly afterward, Japanese soldiers came in full force to Zhahu District, attacking from four sides. They began slaughtering residents on sight, with bayonets, swords, and clubs. Wangfu Lane, with its shacks and shanties, was thrown into massive confusion, and people fled in all directions.

Later, Zuo heard that the Japanese had either killed the people who went to fight the fire or thrown them alive into the flames. Some time afterward, when Zuo was working on a burial detail for the Red Swastika Society, he was sent to the burned-out ruins of the Health Center where he saw about a hundred charred bodies piled up.

Perhaps because it was dark, and perhaps because they were unable to guess how many people there were, the Japanese troops who surrounded Wangfu Lane missed some victims. Of the members of Zuo's family, his mother

Tangfang Alley, an old style street within the city limits near Zhonghua Gate with houses tightly packed along a narrow walkway. This was outside the International Refugee Zone. (Photographed December 23, 1983.)

and two sisters hid in the woodpile of a nearby house, and Zuo and his father fled to the home of one Zhuang Er, who lived behind them. This house had mud walls, and from the outside, it looked as if the walls had only one layer, but actually there were two layers, creating a hiding place. The walls had been built this way to provide a secret place for selling opium, and Zuo and his father and three or four other people were able to hide there.

It snowed lightly that evening, but the flakes melted as soon as they hit the ground. By dawn, there was a light dusting on the ground, but it, too, soon melted. Zuo and his father found his mother and sisters, and together they fled to the Refugee Zone. They learned that during the "encircling operation," nearly half the people remaining in Wangfu Lane had been killed.

Roughly speaking, the Refugee Zone was bounded on the east by Zhongshan Road, on the north by Xishan Road, on the south by Hanzhong Road, and on the west by Xitang Road. It was the location of many foreign institutions, and many foreigners also lived there. (See map on page 200.) It was overflowing with people who had fled there just before the Japanese entered the city, and by the time the Zuo family arrived, there was no shelter for latecomers. Even the large buildings of the universities were full to capacity. Left with no other recourse, the Zuo family built a hut of sticks and straw matting in a vegetable plot near Doucai Bridge. Since they had left their home almost empty-handed,

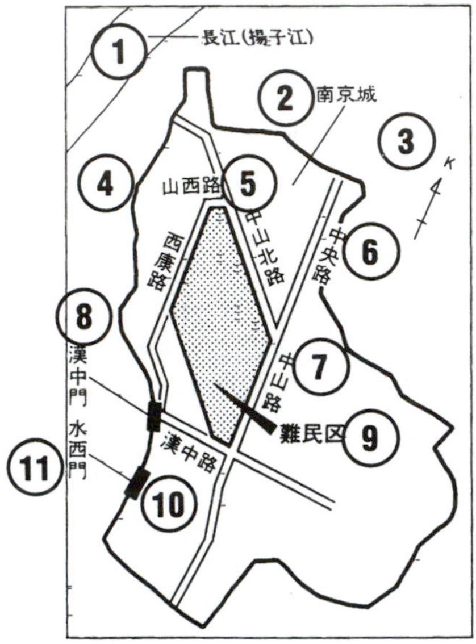

1. Yangtze River
2. Nanjing
3. North
4. Shanxi Road
5. North Zhongshan Road
6. Zhongyang Road
7. Zhongshan Road
8. Hanzhong Gate
9. International Refugee Zone
10. Hanzhong Road
11. Shuixi Gate

they had no food or anything, so they went to eat the rice gruel provided by the charitable institutions in the Refugee Zone along Shanghai Road, but they were not allowed to take any gruel away with them.

Zuo Runde will appear again later in this account, but the next story comes from Chen Guangxu, whose heartbreaking account of killing a newborn baby appeared in Chapter 8.

The women who had fled to the mountains at the approach of the Japanese returned home on December 14, but the next day, the villagers gathered and discussed means of dealing with further appearances of Japanese troops. They had heard rumors that if they greeted the troops with a banner that said "Welcome, Japan," their houses would not be burned, and they would not be killed, so they made preparations to do so.

Xuxiang village consisted of about two hundred households, most of them stretched out along the east-to-west road that ran through the community. On December 16, an uncle of Chen Guangxu, who had been sent out to stand watch, called out to inform the villagers that the Japanese were on their way. Just as they had planned, the men of the village hoisted several flags that

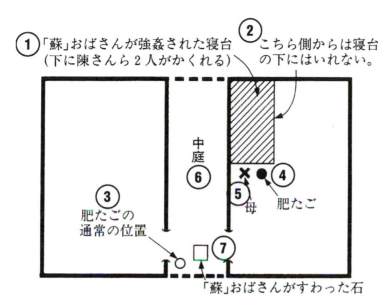

1. The bed where Aunt Su was raped (while Chen and the *tongyangxi* hid underneath)
2. This side of the bed was closed off
3. The usual position of the night soil bucket
4. Night soil bucket
5. Chen's mother
6. Central courtyard
7. The rock where Aunt Su was sitting

read "Welcome, Japan" and lined up on either side of the road to greet the troops. Chen Guangfu hid under the bed along with a tongyangxi named Shi from the house two doors down, and she placed a night-soil bucket in front of the bed. The large bucket was used as a chamber pot during the night, and the accumulated wastes were carried out to be spread on the fields as fertilizer. Chen assumed that the presence of the bucket would make the soldiers avoid the area of the bed.

There was a huge commotion outside, but being hidden, Chen Guangxu could not see what was going on. After a while, a woman of about forty, the wife of Su Renfa from three houses away, whom everyone called Su Laotai, or "Old Lady Su," was forced into the room by a Japanese soldier. ("In those days," Chen told me," a forty-year-old was considered elderly, and it was expected that you would die by fifty, so she thought she was safe, and that's why she was caught off guard.")

The Japanese soldier pushed Su Laotai down on the bed where Chen Guangxu and the tongyangxi were hiding. They could see his legs and boots as he raped her. Su Laotai was apparently too frightened to make a sound, because all the two girls could hear was the creaking of the bed. Chen's

Chen Guangxiu telling of her tragic experiences.

mother was crouched next to the end of the bed up against the wall and behind the night-soil bucket, so the rape took place right in front of her, but since she was suffering from cataracts at the age of forty-three or forty-four, she did not see much.

After the soldier had left, the girls were still afraid to come out, and they stayed hidden, even sleeping under the bed that night. It was the morning of December 17 when an uncle told them that it was all right to come out, and that was when they heard about the tragic events in the village from the people who had miraculously survived.

As the villagers met them with the welcoming banners, the arriving Japanese soldiers appeared to respond to the welcome, but then they appeared to be conducting some sort of investigation. What they finally did was to select about a hundred youths, most of whom were from the western end of the village, evidently having decided that they were the right age to be soldiers. One of them was Chen's sixteen-year-old brother, Chen Guangdong.

These approximately one hundred youths were led away to an 0.8-mu (50-square-meter) rice paddy belonging to the Chen family a little way down the road. Worrying that the young men would be killed, the older people followed along after them, but the Japanese simply chased them back home, as if this were no more serious than stealing pigs or chickens.

Because the paddy was so small, parts of the rows angled around the corner of the dirt ridge in an L shape. The youths were made to kneel in two rows facing each other. The soldiers surrounded them and all at once began killing them with bayonets. Some of the youths were not killed instantly and were stabbed several times as they cried for help.

Only one young man came through this mass murder completely unharmed, a coal-mine worker named Cui Yicai. The soldiers just happened not to stab him, but he fell over along with the others and played dead as the blood of the other victims splashed over him, and no one noticed. Two other young men, Liu Qingzhi and Shi Xian, received wounds that missed all their vital organs, and they were later treated and saved. Of the approximately one

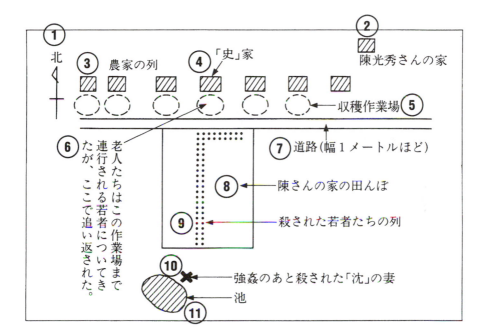

1. North
2. Chen Guanxiu's house
3. Row of peasant houses
4. The Shi family home
5. The harvest workshop
6. The old people followed along when the young men were taken away, but they turned back at this point.
7. Road (about 1 meter wide)
8. The Chen family's rice paddy
9. The row of dead young people
10. Shen's raped and murdered wife
11. Pond

hundred youths, only these three survived. However, by the time I conducted these interviews in China, all of them, being old, had died.

The massacre took place at about four in the afternoon. During this time, the women were hiding under beds or wherever they could, but at about five o'clock, a woman of thirty-five or thirty-six named Shen became worried about her husband and went to the home of the Shi family, which was near the site of the massacre. Upon being told of the mass murder, which had claimed both her husband and her younger brother, she gave a loud cry and ran outside weeping. Some Japanese who were still in the area found her, took her to the edge of a pond near the massacre site, raped her, and killed her.

In the home of Su Laotai, the woman who had been raped on top of the bed where Chen Guangxu lay hidden, was a tongyangxi *of fifteen or sixteen.*

She was captured by three Japanese soldiers, taken to the home of Chen's maternal uncle Shi Weiguan, and gang-raped. She was left too weak to stand, her genital area swollen and bloody.

The wife of Chen Guangxu's older brother, the one who had given birth in the mountains, had returned home, but she had suffered severe complications, and was ill and bedridden. The soldiers were about to rape her, but when they saw the condition she was in, they gave up on the idea. However, she died about a week later.

Chen Guangxu's mother had given birth to nine children, but four of her five sons were dead. The only one left was Guangdong, and for this reason she particularly treasured him. After both her husband and Guangdong were killed, she went mad with grief. She would go outside in the middle of the night and cry out in a loud voice, and then, when she was exhausted, she would lie down by the side of the road. Eventually she developed a tumor in her head, and she died the following year.

With the village of Xuxiang turning into a kind of hell by all the murders and rapes, no one had any idea what would happen next. The young women all decided to run away. On the following day, December 17, Chen Guangxu took her younger sister and went with about thirty other women to Qixia, a refuge run by some Americans. That day was Chen Guangxu's birthday, the day she turned nineteen.

The next living witness is a former Japanese soldier, someone from what we might call the "slaughtering side." He was a private first class in the Ōno Unit of the same 16th Division that Lieutenant General Nakajima, author of the previously excerpted diary, commanded. At the age of seventy-seven, he has carried out a thorough soul-searching concerning his direct role in the massacres, and he has spoken of them in detail, offering his own diary from that period. "Since I don't have much longer to live," he says, " I want to atone for my sins by leaving a description of the facts as they happened." Any number of wartime diaries proving that the Nanjing Incident really happened have been made public, but courageous confessions by living witnesses from the Japanese side are extremely rare.

The Committee to Implement a War Exhibit for a Peaceful Kyoto[11] has been working to dig up materials from the side of both the victims and the aggressors (invaders), and Itamoto Shirō (a pseudonym),[12] a sev-

---

11. The committee's headquarters are in the Marutamachi district of Kyoto, and the representative of the board of directors is Jugaku Akiko.

12. I have respected this man's wish that his real name and address be concealed, because some of the people who have previously offered these kinds of confessions and testimony have been innundated with threatening letters and telephone calls.

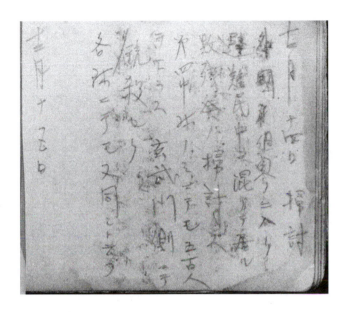

Itamoto Shirō's diary for December 14, 1937.

enty-seven-year-old farmer, the author of the diary that the committee found in the Tango region near Kyoto, is still alive and well, but for years, his conscience has tormented him about the massacres that he directly participated in. Itamoto, who is critical of the military unit histories and nostalgic accounts that have appeared in recent years, has used his old memo-type field diary as the basis for a detailed, tell-all memoir written in a university notebook. The following testimony concerning the part of the memoir dealing with the massacre was noted in the fall of 1986 during a detailed interview.

Itamoto, from Tango, in Takeno County, Kyoto prefecture, was a private first class in the Ōno Unit at the time of the assault on Nanjing. More precisely, he belonged to the 16th Division (Division Commander Lieutenant General Nakajima), 20th Regiment (Regimental Commander Colonel Ōno), 1st Battalion (Battalion Commander Major Nishizaki), 4th Company (Company Commander First Lieutenant Saka). The page in the small notebook notebook diary dealing with December 14, the day after the fall of Nanjing, reads as follows:

> December 14, mopping up.
> We went into the foreign concession and rooted out the defeated soldiers who were mixed in with the refugees. The 4th Company alone got no fewer than five hundred, and we shot them dead near Xuanwu Gate. The other companies are said to have done the same.

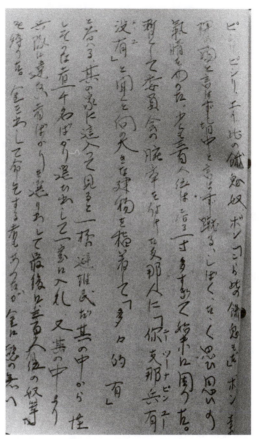

Itamoto Shirō's diary account of taking "about three hundred prisoners."

This happens to be the same killing of "about five hundred apparent stragglers" described in the field diary of the late Private First Class Yamamoto earlier in this chapter.[13]

Beginning on December 11, fierce fighting developed in the Xishan Highlands, which overlook the city of Nanjing, but somewhere between the evening of the 12th and the morning of the 13th, torches were waved on Zijin Mountain, and signal whistles were heard as the forces of Chiang Kai-shek went into full retreat. Itamoto proposed to his platoon commander that they give chase, but he was told to wait for orders from the

13. The particulars of the ways in which Yamamoto's field diary and Itamoto's testimony correspond to each other are laid out in Shimozato Masaki's *Hidden Regimental History* (Aoki Shoten).

company commander. At this point, they were about 1 kilometer from the city walls.

In the morning, Japanese troops marched in formation near Zhongshan Gate along the main road that Itamoto could see below to his left. Itamoto's platoon also came down from the highlands and cooked with their mess kits. A car owned by a Japanese newspaper drove up, and the reporters in it interviewed the soldiers and took their pictures.

It was at about two in the afternoon that the regiment sent the 1st Battalion on ahead with the regimental colors and advanced into the city. A large hospital, an in-patient facility for wounded Chinese soldiers, stood just a few hundred meters inside the gate. When they went inside, they found that all the patients who could walk had already fled, leaving behind only the most gravely wounded, the ones who could not move at all. The street, which emptied into Zhongshanbei Road, was littered with discarded weapons and uniforms, and even horses and vehicles had been abandoned, but there was no sign of human presence. After wandering around and looking at things for three or four hours, fifty members of Itamoto's platoon were assigned to spend the night at the electric company. The rest of the 4th Company stayed in various places within two hundred meters of them.

The storage area of the electric company contained a large amount of canned goods and other food, and even some aged spirits and red-colored liquor. After setting up an altar to their comrades who had died in battle, the soldiers held an impromptu victory celebration. They heated up the aged spirits in pots and drank and sang with abandon, embracing one another and breaking down into tears. Itamoto, who had left Japan four months before, thought, "The China Incident is over. In no time I'll be able to go home to Japan and to Tango." Overjoyed, he caroused until one or two in the morning. Yet when he went outside and started yelling, a battalion adjutant came by and warned him, "That's enough of that. The fight will continue. Go to bed right away."

When they gathered after breakfast the next morning, December 14, the company commander announced that 150 of the 200 men in the company had been assigned to mop up the Refugee Zone in the foreign concession. It took them about an hour to walk through the city to their destination. They saw almost no one about on their way there, only an occasional elderly woman.

When they entered the foreign concession, they saw a few—but not very many—of the remaining nationals of third countries such as France and the United States standing warily in front of their legations with their flags unfurled. The soldiers searched these buildings after an interpreter attached to the battalion command had negotiated permission.

A Tokyo department store's advertisement celebrating the fall of Nanjing.

Shortly afterward, on New Year's Day, 1938, Itamoto wrote the following account of what happened next:[14]

At dawn on the 14th, we were told that we were to go to the Refugee Zone that the International Committee has set up and conducted mopping-up operations. The tens of thousands of stragglers, who had been resisting fiercely until the day before, were surrounded on all sides, and not one had been able to flee. In the end, they had fled into this Refugee Zone. This day, we set about the task enthusiastically, aiming to avenge our dead comrades, intending to leave no blade of grass unturned and to comb the enemy out like lice. The platoons split up, searched those complex Chinese buildings one by one, and brought in all the men for questioning.

Second Platoon Liaison Sergeant Maehara and some others came upon a big room in one of those large buildings where several hundred stragglers were in the process of changing from military uniforms into civilian clothes. They were startled, and when they ran in to check upon the situation, they saw that these were prominent officers. And what do you know, all around them were huge piles of rifles, pistols, and Green Dragon swords. Some of them were in their military uniforms, some had changed into Chinese clothes earlier, some wore uniform trousers with Chinese clothes on top, but all of them were out of style or else they were wearing things that didn't match, so we could see at a glance that they had just thrown these clothes on. We took them out one by one, had them strip naked, and searched their belongings. We tied them together like a string of beads with electrical wires that hung loose in the street. Starting with Sergeant Ōnishi and Sergeant Imoto, the guys who were the most worked up took tree branches and electrical wire and came at them with all their might. "Look at all the trouble you bastards are putting us to!" Bang! "Do you know

---

14. This entry was written as part of *The 24th Infantry Regiment 4th Company's Memoirs of Our Comrades at the Front During the China Incident.* The members of the company wrote it when their commander, Sakanaka, was sent back to Japan to recuperate after being wounded. Itamoto's contribution was titled, "Mopping Up in Nanjing." The account was never published, but copies of it are said to exist in two or three public institutions.

how many of our comrades sacrificed themselves, all because of you?" Whoosh! Crack! "Don't you know how many of our people are crying because of you?" Whip! Whip!

"You devils!" Crack! "Hey, you devils!" Crack! On their bare heads, on their backs, we kicked, whipped, and beat them, avenging ourselves any way we wanted. There were a little more than three hundred of them, just a bit too many, and we had trouble disposing of them.

According to the battle report of the 4th Company, that incident yielded the following results:[15]

This morning, beginning at 10:00 A.M., we carried out a sweep of the second mopping-up zone. We shot and buried 318 stragglers.
The weapons captured were as follows:

Item	Number
Rifles	180
Bayonets	110
Rifle bullets	4,000
Pistol bullets	5,000
Pistols	60
Eyeglasses	2
Hand grenades	20

In other words, the more than three hundred men were all killed, but other "mopping-up" operations continued after that. These are written about in Itamoto's memoirs:[16]

After a while, we asked a Chinese who was wearing the International Committee armband, "*Ni Zhina bing you meiyou?*" (Do you have any Chinese soldiers?) He pointed to a large building a ways off and said, "*Duoduo de you.*" (There are a lot of them.) When we entered the building, we saw that it was packed with refugees. We picked out about a thousand suspicious-looking persons and put them all into one room. We selected the ones who were certainly soldiers, and finally tied up about three hundred of those guys. Some of them pulled out money and pleaded for their lives, but we didn't want their money. We took their ten-*yuan* notes or a pile of three five-*yuan* notes, tore them up,

15. A former corporal from the same company, although not the same platoon, as Itamoto showed me this report when I was at Itamoto's house for an interview.

16. When I first spoke with Itamoto, he said that he had not written this passage. and he made no mention of these 328 stragglers, but he finally acknowledged it after being confronted with Shimozato Masaki's *Hidden Regimental History.* (The details are on pp. 115–18 of Shimozato's book.) He had been denying authorship because memoirs had been published elsewhere, revealing his real name, and exposing him to threats from the fanatic right wing for being a traitor. He was also constrained by both ties and disagreements with the many former "comrades" from his unit who live in the area.

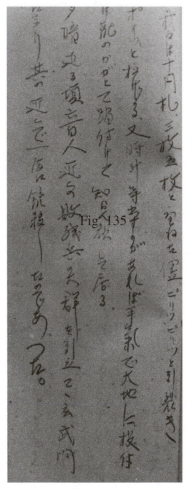

Fig. 135

The section of Itamoto's diary that tells of "bayoneting nearly six hundred people at once."

and threw the scraps into the air. When some of them offered watches and things, we calmly threw them on the ground and crushed them with our boot heels, keeping our faces perfectly expressionless.

At about six o'clock, when it was dark, we marched a large group of about six hundred stragglers to the area near Xuanwu Gate, where we shot them all at once.

Here are the details of the incident described above, as Itamoto told me during our interview.

Three large two-story buildings resembling Japanese elementary schools were located along the main avenue some distance into the Refugee Zone. They were connected by a hallway, with a cooking area in the central courtyard. Two or three hundred people were packed into each room, clustered in family groups. Itamoto's company went into these buildings in search of soldiers.

The company split up, with each platoon searching one building. Itamoto's platoon turned two rooms on the second floor of their building into interrogation rooms, took all the young men who were of the right age to be soldiers, and interrogated them one by one. The first room was a sort of "preselection" area, where the Chinese underwent a superficial preliminary screening without an interpreter present. Evidently, a Chinese-speaking interpreter was in the second room, but Itamoto was in the first room, so he really does not know if this was true. In any case, there were only two or three interpreters in the entire company. Three of the higher-ranking men in the platoon, such as the noncommissioned officers, conducted the interrogations, while the others undertook the task of moving the Chinese from one room to another. Private First Class Itamoto served as an interrogator.

As the young men were being dragged away from their families, both they and their family members would yell things like "Bu shi!" (I'm not!) or "Bu dui!" (You're wrong!), although Itamoto, being in the interrogation room, did not see much of this. Ten men were brought in at a time. In the entire course of the investigation, two or three thousand men were processed in quick succession, so the time spent on each man was extremely short. As the ten men were brought into the room, which was 5 by 7 jian—about 9 by 12 meters—in area, they were surrounded by Japanese soldiers and forced to strip naked so that the Japanese could search their clothes. As the interrogator said things like, "You're a soldier, aren't you?" in Japanese, the other soldiers would treat them quite roughly, kicking their legs out from under them or twisting their arms. Some soldiers even confiscated watches and other valuables. Usually three out of ten men from each group were detained after the "preselection" and sent on to the next room.

Of course, there were some actual soldiers among the young men interrogated, including some who wore underclothing with tags bearing the name of their regiment or company. However, the men who were definitely soldiers were no more than 10 percent of those detained as suspects. Most of the men were civilians who had fled from places like Shanghai or Suzhou, and only a few were from the city. Perhaps they were resigned to their fate; they accepted the interrogation meekly, and only a few offered any resistance. By the time the interrogations ended at about 1:00 P.M., about three hundred men had been detained as suspects, making a total of six hundred when they were combined with the stragglers previously picked up. The Japanese soldiers sent a message back to their battalion command, asking what to do with all them. After about an hour, during which they ate the rice that was in their mess tins, the answer came back: "Dispose of them appropriately." In specific terms, the men took it to be an order to take the prisoners to the Xuanwu Lake, kill them on the bank, and throw them into the water.

The six hundred men were made to line up in five or six columns outside. The men in the two outer columns were tied together like a string of beads, with pieces of downed electrical wire and telephone wire from the street tied around one thigh; the men in the three or four inner columns were not tied. This procession was surrounded on both sides by Japanese soldiers with bayonets ready, and then they headed to Xuanwu Gate, on the opposite side of the city from the Refugee Zone. Along with the company was a party dispatched from a machine gun company, which had brought along two heavy machine guns and six light ones.

It was a partly cloudy, chilly day. None of the prisoners tried to run off during the more than hour-long march across the city. However, Xuanwu Gate was blocked by a huge pile of sandbags, and there was no way to open it easily. Concluding that it would be too much trouble to clear the sandbags away, the soldiers decided to kill their prisoners on the spot.

At the foot of the wall on the right side of the gate was a broad pit that had resulted from digging up dirt to fill the sandbags. It was the perfect place for shooting and burying the prisoners.

The rows of captive young men were led to the area between the wall and the pit, and the front half of the group was moved down into the pit as the machine guns were being set up in a row. Since the prisoners were not blind-folded, they now realized their fate. A few—only about ten—tried to break out of the formation, but they were stabbed with bayonets.

As they descended into the execution pit, some of the prisoners turned to the Japanese soldiers and tossed them their watches or cigarettes. "We're getting an allowance from the Chinese," some of the soldiers joked, but when a man in one of the tied-together outer lines gave his watch to Itamoto, he was struck with an amazingly strong stab of pity. He grabbed the shoulders of a man who happened to be passing by—a man from the inner ranks, not from the outer ranks, which were tied up—and pulled him out of the proces-sion. Then he took the next man, too, saving two Chinese with an almost unconscious act, although he ended up saving not the man who had given him the watch, but two completely different ones.

Less than ten minutes after the prisoners had been assembled on the execu-tion ground, the order was given to fire. The eight machine guns simultaneously fired a round that lasted about a minute. Bits of flesh flew to land on the Japa-nese soldiers, who stood anywhere from 30 to 50 meters away. Itamoto, who was standing toward the front, found that his uniform was sticky with splashes of blood. Trying to escape the gunfire for even a little while, many of the prisoners piled up against the wall, but some looked straight at their executioners with heads held high. Any cries were drowned out by the thunderous rattling of the machine guns, but as soon as the order to cease fire was given, the soldiers' ears were assailed by an indescribable chorus of groans of aiyaa! and other cries. After two or three minutes, there was another order to fire. Again the loud report of the machine guns. A second pause. It took perhaps three rounds before the groans and cries were silenced.

Covering the bodies with dirt took about thirty minutes. The soldiers used a small shovel designed for digging trenches to dig up the earth around the pit and toss it in. Yet the resulting dirt layer was so shallow that the men in the pit could have easily poked their heads through. In fact, Itamoto wonders if there was anyone among the victims who received nonfatal wounds and was able to struggle out of the mass grave later on. Toward evening, while it was still light, the company withdrew from the area.

They walked for an hour in the direction of Xiaguan and the entire battal-ion assembled at the Nationalists' Department of the Navy building. On the way there, they saw the burned-out shell of a ferroconcrete building. This

was where another company in their battalion had taken about a hundred sus-
pected stragglers up to the roof and burned them to death with gasoline. It was
said that some of the victims had jumped off the roof, engulfed in flames.

For about a week, beginning on the 15th, Itamoto was assigned to guard
duty outside the city. During this time, he sometimes ate lunch near a build-
ing that was evidently the barracks of an artillery school. Japanese troops
seemed to be living in the barracks, but in the yard were about a thousand
men surrounded by barbed wire and being treated as prisoners. The location
was somewhere near Zhongshanling, but he does not know what regiment
they were from. According to the soldiers standing guard, the prisoners were
Chinese soldiers who had surrendered. When feeding the prisoners, the guards
would pack the rice into artillery shells and hand it over to them, saying that
the large shells were for three people and the small shells were for two people.
"It makes us mad that we have to feed our provisions to this bunch when
there isn't even enough for our troops," the guards grumbled. Itamoto later
heard that the prisoners were all killed at the Yangtze.

The two men whom Itamoto had rescued were used as cooks and general
laborers for a while. Neither was a soldier. The one named Wang was a magi-
cian, and the one named Chan was a watchmaker, and both of them came from
Shanghai. Itamoto learned a few magic tricks from Wang: how to make a bean-
bag appear in his mouth, how to cut and reattach a string, how to eat fire.

Even so, Itamoto still does not understand what was going on in the minds of
the victims on their way to the execution ground when they tossed things like
watches or cigarettes to the Japanese troops. "They've gone to the other world,
and they may be happy that we're having this conversation," he said tearfully.
Then he showed me some of the magic tricks he had learned from Wang.

Next we meet Wu Changde (75), the survivor of an assembly-line–style
mass murder of two thousand people.[17] In fact, he appeared as one of the
witnesses in the Tokyo War Crimes Trials (International Military Tribunal
for the Far East), but considering the circumstances, his testimony was con-
siderably abbreviated.[18] I took this opportunity to meet Wu directly and to
get a much more detailed account out of him, and this is what I heard in the
approximately half a day that I spent with him.

---

17. I also interviewed Chen Degui, who survived a different assembly-line–style
massacre in 1971, and wrote his story in *Journey to China* (Asahi Bunko).

18. The transcript of Wu's testimony may be found in Hora Tomio's *Collection of
Materials about the Great Nanjing Massacre*. During the Cultural Revolution, it was
reported that Wu had died, but this was a misunderstanding of the true situation: he was
in his home village battling a serious illness. However, he actually died in 1987 at the
age of seventy-nine.

Wu Changde.

Wu Changde, who had married into a family of tofu makers near Tangfang Bridge, was twenty-nine years old at the time. The household consisted of Wu, his wife (22), their son (3), his mother-in-law (50), and his mother-in-law's two younger brothers from Zhun'an, six people in all. Since his wife was an only child, he had been adopted into the family as an heir. Originally from Xuzhou in Jiangsu Province, he had been working as a traffic policeman in Nanjing for twelve years. Even after his marriage, he continued working as a traffic officer while helping out in the family's tofu business. He had never been in the military.

As the Japanese approached Nanjing, everyone except Wu, who stayed behind to watch the house, evacuated to his mother-in-law's family home in Zhun'an, Xinyi County. The Japanese entered the city two weeks later. A week before this, the Red Cross had said that a Refugee Zone (safety zone) would be set up, and anyone who fled there would not be killed.

Wu fled to the Judiciary Building along Zhongshan Road in the Refugee Zone. All the employees had left, and about three hundred people were staying in a large room that appeared to be a lecture hall. Among them were about twenty traffic officers of Wu's acquaintance, but all of them were in civilian clothes.

At eight o'clock on the morning of December 15, dozens of Japanese soldiers, some of them wearing the armbands of military police, suddenly burst in carrying bayonets. Startled, the refugees rose to their feet en masse, and without any explanation, the soldiers began forcing all the young, able-bodied men out at bayonet-point, yelling in Japanese the whole time. Only a few dozen old people, women, and children were left behind, none of them having any idea what all that shouting in Japanese had been about.

The main entrance of the Judiciary Building was closed, and when Wu and the others were taken out through a side entrance to Zhongshan Road, they saw other young, able-bodied men who had been herded out of other buildings, surrounded by Japanese soldiers. All were made to sit, and they did so silently, but nervously. Occasionally, the soldiers shouted something

Few traces of Hanzhong Gate remain nowadays. (Photographed December 1983.)

at them, but Wu did not understand what they were talking about. Eventually the number of Chinese men assembled in the street exceeded two thousand.

It was about 11:00 A.M. when the group set out on their way to Hanzhong Gate (near Hanxi Gate). Just as they were passing the Capital Cinema (now called the Victory Cinema), the procession suddenly halted, and everyone was made to sit. A soldier who happened to be near Wu took an interpreter and went into a fruit store, apparently to make a phone call.

Soon, several trucks pulled up behind the group. Soldiers piled out of the trucks, and Wu noticed that there were four heavy machine guns and ammunition in the back of one of the vehicles. Some soldiers were shouldering gun barrels that had been detached from their emplacements, and among them were members of the military police, who joined the encirclement. "I bet we're going to be slaughtered," Wu thought, but since he was not able to speak with any of the others, he had no idea what they were thinking. The trucks that had brought the machine guns moved up to the front, and the procession set out again, with the trucks leading the way.

They arrived at Hanzhong Gate at about 1:00 P.M. The more than two thousand men were halted just inside the gate and made to sit. The machine guns were unloaded from the trucks—first the gun barrels, then the emplacements—and moved outside the gate.

After twenty minutes or so, two of the Japanese at the front of the procession came around, each holding one end of a rope. They went into the crowd of Chinese and cut out a small group of about a hundred. Then the small

Hucheng River near Hanzhong Gate, the site of the "assembly-line massacre" that Wu Changde managed to escape.

group was led out through the gate, surrounded on all sides by Japanese soldiers. At this point, Wu thought that they would definitely be massacred, and the men around him also looked much more uneasy.

When twenty more minutes had passed, they heard the deafening sound of all the machine guns firing at once. Now the crowd, which had merely been uneasy up till that time, realized that a massacre was in store. A commotion arose, with some men crying and others shouting, but the soldiers who surrounded them closely with bayonets made escape impossible. Wu lost track of how long the firing continued, but the soldiers' bayonets were dripping with blood when they returned.

Thus, successive groups of one or two hundred were cut out of the crowd with ropes and led outside the gates. Occasionally, someone collapsed from fear and could not move, but such men were bayoneted on the spot.

When it came time for Wu's group, it was five o'clock. One hundred of them were cut out of the crowd by the two soldiers with ropes and prodded from behind with bayonets as they moved forward. Some walked silently, some wept, others cried out. Enough men were left behind to form two or three more groups.

The soldiers with the ropes pulled them along and led them to the embankment along the moat. Four machine guns in two groups of two stood on the embankment, and Wu and the others were driven down the embankment between the guns.

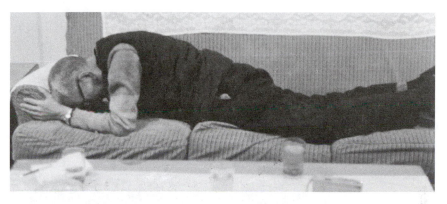

Wu Changde demonstrating the position in which he lay after falling among the corpses.

The instant he saw the bodies piled in front of him, Wu ran two or three steps and deliberately threw himself down in a flying leap forward. At almost that same moment, the guns began raking the area. He heard bodies falling with a thud. Cries. Screams. Voices calling "Mother!" or "Father!" Groans. Even a cry of "Dadao Riben diguozhuyi!" (Down with Japanese imperialism!)

The man who fell on top of Wu seemed to have been killed instantly. He did not move at all, and Wu could not feel him breathing. After the machine guns stopped firing, Wu heard rifle fire. He assumed that the soldiers were aiming at specific people.

After the rifle fire stopped, Wu sensed that someone was walking around on top of the bodies. Lying face down, with his arms wrapped around his head, he could feel the pressure through the body that was on top of him. Just when he thought that whoever it was had passed by, he felt a sudden sharp pain in his back. A soldier walking around with a bayonet to finish off any survivors had stabbed the man on top, and the bayonet had passed all the way through that body to pierce Wu.

As Wu tried desperately to bear the pain and lie still, the next wave of victims was killed in the same way, and then another, until all of the more than 2,000 men had been systematically slaughtered. It was just beginning to grow dark.

Soon afterward, Wu heard wood being tossed in his direction, and then he smelled gasoline. By the time he was able to form the thought, "I'll be burned to death," the fire had already been lit. The flames spread rapidly. As his clothes caught fire, he realized in a dazed way that he was on the cusp of life and death. He had a severe stab wound in his back, and he made a snap decision that it would be better to jump into the moat and die there than be burned to death. Tearing off his burning clothes, he scrambled frantically among the bodies and threw himself into the moat.

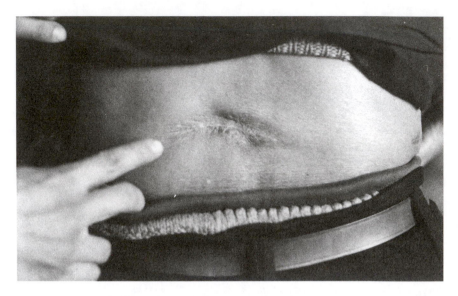

Bayonet scar on Wu Changde's back.

But since he knew how to swim, he did not drown. He came out of the water on the same bank that he had jumped off and crawled southward along the water's edge. After going about half a li *(250 meters) away, he came upon an empty small boat. There were some ragged clothes in it, and when he tried them on, he found that they were too small: the sleeves were too short, and he could not close the front. Even so, these clothes would help protect him from the cold. Continuing to drag himself southward along the edge of the moat, he arrived at the area around Shuixi Gate. All the houses in that area, the ninth block of Wachang Street, had been burned, but there was one house where the kitchen was still undamaged, even though the main house had been destroyed. The floor was covered with straw, and when Wu lay down on that straw, he fell into a deep, unconscious sleep.*

He just lay there, unable to get anything to eat or to tend his wound. On what he thinks was the tenth day, a Japanese soldier appeared in that kitchen. He was carrying a bayonet, but seeing Wu, who was in a severely weakened condition and covered with ash, he evidently assumed that he was just a beggar and left without doing anything to him.

"If I look like this, I may not be killed," Wu thought, feeling a small amount of hope. Besides, if he stayed, he would undoubtedly die by evening, so he made up his mind to return to the Refugee Zone. Fortunately, his wound had stopped bleeding, and the bayonet had not hit any vital organs. His face smeared with ash from the stove, an empty vegetable basket in his left hand,

Hanxi Gate, near Hanzhong Gate, has also largely been reduced to ruins. (Photographed in December 1983.)

and a crutch made from a stick in his right hand, he looked like a typical beggar as he walked unsteadily toward the Refugee Zone. Upon entering the city through Hanzhong Gate, he was challenged by a sentry. Pointing at his face and gesturing, he said, "I'm a sick beggar." Whether the sentry understood or not, he let Wu pass through unharmed.

When he arrived in the Refugee Zone, he went to the Refugee Hospital (now called the Drum Tower Hospital). It was run by the Red Swastika Society and he was able to receive free treatment. The bayonet wound in his back took over fifty days to heal.

The next witness is a man who survived an even larger massacre, one involving three or four thousand people.

Tang Guangpu was born in Funing County of Jiangsu Province in 1917 on the twentieth day of the eleventh month, according to the traditional calendar. When he was sixteen, according to the traditional way of counting ages, he joined Chiang Kai-shek's army, not as a soldier, but as a servant who did odd jobs. At the time of the attack on Nanjing, he was employed at the Army Officers' School Combined Instructional Unit Second Corps Third Barracks.[19] The City Defense Headquarters were located in the Jiaotong

---

19. The purpose of this unit was to provide "followers" for the students of the Army Officers' School during leadership training and battle drill.

Tang Guangpu.

Bank in the lively commercial area center on Xinjiekou, and the commander was Gui Yongqing. (The commanders of the Nanjing garrison as a whole were Li Zongren and Bai Chongxi, both of whom, Tang says, were then better known than Tang Shengzhi, who later collaborated with the Japanese.)

Tang Guangpu had been busy with tasks such as washing up tea cups and house-cleaning duties, but two or three days before the Japanese entered the city, he was sent outside of the city as a messenger, and this was the first time he saw a Japanese tank.

Somewhere around eight or nine in the evening on December 12,[20] twenty or thirty of the commissioned officers in the City Defense Command called the lower-ranking soldiers and orderlies together, and told them, "Remain behind, and resist to the very end." Then they themselves fled on horseback.

Since there was no longer anyone around to supervise or command, everything fell into disorder, and people left as they pleased. Tang left the Jiaotong Bank with five other employees at two or three in the morning. Mingling with the crowds, they made their way north along Zhongshan Road amid general confusion, attempting to leave the city through Yijiang Gate.

However, a disabled Nationalist tank had come to a standstill there, and bodies lay heaped around it. There were even some bodies on top of the tank itself. The pile was highest, 1 or 2 meters, right at the gate.[21] Even so, the crowds, a jumble of soldiers and civilians, were climbing over the corpses and squeezing through the small remaining opening. Tang had the impression that civilians were in the minority: he saw hardly any women, and most of the soldiers were still wearing their uniforms. Anyone who stumbled in this stampede was doomed to be trampled, so before trying to pass through the gate, Tang and his companions stopped in a nearby vacant lot, took off their gaiters, and used them to tie their arms together, so that if one fell, the others could support him on either side.

---

20. Tang himself admits that there may be some discrepancies in the times and dates in his narrative due to the great confusion and disorder.

21. The bodies at Yijiang Gate are said to have been those of soldiers in the Nationalist Chinese army. Evidently, fighting had broken out between the defensive troops who

Yijiang Gate. (Photographed in December 1983.)

In this way, they managed to pass safely through Yijiang Gate, and about a hundred meters beyond it they untied the gaiters and scattered in all directions. Tang teamed up with Kang Hecheng, who was about his age. It was around this time that Tang heard the story behind the stalled tank from someone else in the crowd. It seems that the tank had rolled over some people in its attempt to flee the city. A soldier had called out, "I'm not going to let you run away ahead of everyone without a fight!" and then thrown a hand grenade into the tank.

As they fled north from Yijiang Gate, they found a thick woolen blanket in a stalled car. It was deep blue and of high quality, probably something belonging to a wealthy person. Since the weather was cold, Tang wrapped it around himself over his uniform, but Kang wore only his uniform.

They came to the Yangtze and walked downstream (northward), looking for a boat or something that could substitute for one. It was dawn when they reached Yanziji. They had not found a single boat, or even a board or piece of wood that they could grab onto and float with. Every possible scrap, including the doors of people's houses, had been taken and used. Finally, they

were trying to flee and the guard units who were trying to stop them. Before Tang Shengzhi gave the order to withdraw on December 12 at 5:00 P.M., the guard units restrained troops who attempted to flee through Yijiang Gate or Sancha River. See the recently published *Materials Concerning the Great Nanjing Massacre* (Aoki Shoten).

found a kitchen table in one of the houses, carried it down to the riverbank, and tried to swim with it, but it was not buoyant enough and sank. Returning to the house, they found two wooden boxes, turned them upside down, and tied them to both sides of the table. They then climbed onto the table and rowed away, using a small military-issued shovel as a paddle. However, not only was this contrivance slower than a boat but also they were faced with a strong headwind from the open water. After a mere 10 li, about 5 kilometers, they returned to the shore.

As they came up on the riverbank, it was growing dark. Completely exhausted, they dropped down at the side of the road and immediately fell asleep.

The morning was already beginning to dawn when they were awakened by gunfire. They took off in the direction opposite the noise, but there was gunfire coming from there as well. They tried running in another direction, but there was gunfire there, too. Seemingly surrounded by Japanese, they got caught up in a crowd that was running in all directions, and through it all, they could hear light machine guns firing.

Suddenly some Japanese troops, probably cavalry, appeared on horseback and wearing khaki. One of them was carrying a light machine gun and was mounted on a tall, chestnut horse. Other soldiers were waving their swords or shooting and stabbing at people as they pushed them forward.

The crowd was driven into a vegetable field west of the street at Yanziji. When about three or four thousand people had been gathered, a large number of infantry showed up to join the cavalrymen, and they began searching everyone. Not a single person had any weapons, but if the soldiers happened to find anyone carrying valuables, they confiscated them. Even the blanket Tang was wearing was taken away.

Once the searches had been completed, the people were made to line up in four columns, and they were marched away under guard. Their destination was over 5 kilometers away, a collection of thatch-roofed barracks that the Nationalists had formerly used as temporary quarters during training. Each of several barracks was large enough to hold 2 or 3 tuan of troops,[22] or, in other words, two thousand people, and Tang and the others were stuffed inside the dirt-floored, unfurnished buildings like passengers on a rush-hour commuter train.

They would spend a week inside these buildings, but they were crowded in so tightly that there was no room to lie down and sleep, and there was nothing to spread on the floor. They had to sleep standing up, leaning on one

---

22. According to Professor Fujiwara Akira, formerly of Hitotsubashi University, a *tuan* was the unit below division in the Nationalist army. It corresponded to a regiment and consisted of roughly a thousand men.

another. Since they were not allowed outside for any reason, the people on the
outer edge of the building relieved themselves against the wall, but many of those
in the middle simply wet or soiled the
floor, creating wretched conditions. Since
they were given nothing to eat or drink
anyway, this became less of a problem as
time went on. They begged the soldiers
for water, if nothing else, saying that they
would starve to death, and they were finally given water on the fourth day. However, some of the older people died, and
when they died, they were simply tossed
out into a ditch. Occasionally, some of
the prisoners were led away to unknown
destinations and others were brought in.
Since they had no communication with
the other buildings, they knew absolutely
nothing about what was going on there.

The bus stop at Shangyuan Gate. (Photographed in December 1984.) This is in the valley between Wufu Mountain and Laohu Mountain, which the procession of prisoners passed through on the way to the mass execution.

On perhaps the seventh day after being brought to the barracks, that is, on
the morning of December 20, the Japanese soldiers announced, "There's no
food here, so we're moving you into the city, where you can get something to
eat." Before they set out, the prisoners' hands were tied behind their backs with
torn strips of new white cloth, a process that took until one in the afternoon.

Tang thinks that he and his friend Kang Hecheng were almost exactly in
the middle of the four-column procession of prisoners that left the barracks
surrounded by soldiers. He was disturbed to realize that they were marching
in the wrong direction if they were indeed headed for the city, Instead, they
were passing by the foot of Laohu Mountain,[23] between Shangyuan Gate
and Caoxie Ravine, headed toward the Yangtze. Since the prisoners had not
eaten in more than a week, their progress was slow and unsteady, but Tang
knows of no one who tried to run away. However, when people collapsed
from exhaustion, the Japanese untied their hands, dragged them to the side
of the road, and bayoneted them.

---

23. Laohu means "tiger," but this mountain, lying along the banks of the Yangtze,
does not much resemble a tiger when viewed from the river. When viewed from Xuanwu
Lake Park on the northeastern outskirts of Nanjing, however, it bears a certain resem-
blance to a tiger's head.

Laohu Mountain.

When the procession halted for a brief rest, a certain soldier cut Tang's hands free and led him out of the crowd. Just as Tang was thinking that he was about to be killed, he was ordered to kneel on the ground on all fours. Another soldier then sat down on his back to have his hair trimmed by someone who appeared to be a barber. When that was over, Tang was once again tied up and returned to the procession.

When they reached the banks of the Yangtze, the prisoners were made to sit in the order of their arrival. Some of them ended up having to sit in a reed-filled marsh. It was already growing dark, more so than usual because of the heavy cloud cover. Once they realized that this was their destination, Tang and the other prisoners began to think that they were destined to be massacred, especially since they could see two warships with machine guns on their decks. As the sky darkened, searchlights from the ships illuminated the area where the prisoners were.

Even after the entire group had arrived, there was no explanation in Chinese. Meanwhile, the prisoners in Tang's part of the group began furtively untying one another's hands. The first man untied the hands of the man in front of him with his teeth, and that man, in turn, untied someone else's hands, and so on, until many people, including Tang, had their hands free. Since he and the others were in the center of the crowd, it was hard for the Japanese soldiers to see what was happening.

Tang Guangpu standing at the site of the massacre. (Photographed in December 1984.) The area is a bog overgrown with reeds, and Tang says that he crawled along the water's edge for 50 meters.

After they had been there for about an hour, the soldiers for some reason began gathering dry grass and piling it up around the nearby trees. Then they suddenly ignited it, and Tang does not know whether they had poured some inflammable liquid on it, but the flames leapt up, illuminating the area. That was when the shooting started. Without knowing how many guns were shooting or where they were coming from, Tang and Kang reflexively crouched forward onto the ground, their shoulders touching.

The gunfire drowned out all other sounds, but someone fell on top of Tang's back, writhing in pain. More people fell on top of them.

The guns continued firing for what seemed like ten or fifteen minutes and then stopped. That was when they heard the cries that had been covered up by the noise of the guns, groans and sobs that now seemed to rise out of the earth itself. Tang could not look around to see what was happening. All he knew was that he was still alive. "Are you all right?" he whispered to Kang, who lay crouched next to him. "Yes," Kang replied. "Not a scratch. I'm fine."

After four or five minutes, the shooting started up again. At almost that instant, Tang was hit in the right shoulder. A bullet passed through him, but at first, he did not feel much pain. (Later, when he looked at the two holes in his shoulder, he determined from the angle that the bullets must have been fired from the deck of one of the warships in the river.)

After the second round of shooting ended, Tang could still hear cries arising from all over. He once again whispered to Kang Hecheng, but this time, there was no answer. He reached out his left hand and groped at Kang's body to find that his head was covered with blood. At the moment he realized that Kang was dead, he began feeling the pain in his shoulder. Just then, he also realized that the Japanese were walking around with bayonets killing the wounded. They came to the area where he was and stabbed him in the lower side, but since he was lying under dead bodies, the stab wound was so shallow that he barely noticed it. Anyway, he was more preoccupied with the severe pain in his shoulder.

Once the groaning could no longer be heard, the Japanese withdrew to the edge of the pile of bodies, and the searchlights from the ships were turned off. The area was now dark, and it seemed to Tang that the ships had left. The soldiers were still in a commotion out on the edges, however, and Tang could smell gasoline fumes coming from that direction. Yet it was not until flames leapt up all around him that he realized what the gasoline was for. The smoke was thick, and he found it hard to breathe. Realizing that he would be burned to death if he stayed where he was, he began crawling forward, but the pile of bodies in front of him was too high to get over, so he started crawling backward toward the river. The soldiers had not yet left, and they were stabbing any survivors who tried to escape the flames. In order not to be discovered, he crawled among and over the bodies that lay on the ground all the way to the riverbank until he reached the water's edge. Finally, having escaped the smoke and flames, he lay motionless with his legs up on the bodies and his head only a few centimeters from the water, almost in a handstand position.

The cloudy sky grew even darker, and there were occasionally snow flurries. Since it was cold, the soldiers had drawn close to the fire. Soon a siren sounded, the signal to assemble. The soldiers noisily went to assemble on the side of the fire away from the river. Tang thinks that this may have happened around midnight.

Reeds were growing along the riverbank, and using them as a cover, Tang slipped into the water. It was when the water hit his bayonet wound that he first felt pain there. He walked downstream in water that was anywhere from knee-deep to waist-deep for several hundred meters, but his hunger and pain made this too difficult, so he climbed out of the water at a reedy spot along the riverbank. He stumbled 4 or 5 li along the riverbank until he found a brick kiln[24] and went inside to hide. He intended just to doze for a while, but he was completely exhausted and fell into a deep sleep.

It was around ten the next morning when he awoke. Going down to the

---

24. This was a dome-shaped brick structure about 3 or 4 meters high.

riverbank to look for something to cross the river on, he spotted a small boat flying a Japanese flag and approaching from the open water. Fearing that the occupants were somehow connected with the Japanese, he scurried back to the kiln and hid. Peering out, he saw two men, one old and the other young, leaving the boat. He thought that he would get into trouble if he were found hiding in the kiln, so he lay down among the corpses that were scattered here and there even in that neighborhood and pretended to be dead. But when the two men passed by, Tang could hear them speaking the local dialect of Chinese, so he assumed that they were trustworthy. He got to his feet and begged them for help, bowing in front of the old man, telling him about the massacre, and showing him the wound in his shoulder.

The old man took pity on Tang and agreed to take him in his boat. He and the younger man were peasants from Baguazhou, which is south of Nanjing, but on the opposite bank of the river, and they had come here to gather rice straw for their cattle. Since Tang's wounds no longer seemed serious, he helped the men load rice straw, making four trips between the boat and a nearby pile of straw. Then they took him into their boat, making him lie down in the bottom and covering him with rice straw.

With this help, Tang Guangpu was able to flee to a place called Zhuzhen in Liuhe County, Jiangsu Province. For about six months, he survived there as a beggar, believing himself to be the only person who had been able to survive the massacre. However, in the summer of 1938, he was summoned by a shopkeeper of his acquaintance and asked to interpret for a Cantonese-speaking customer who did not speak the local dialect but had come from outside the city to buy provisions.

After interpreting for him, Tang became friendly with this Cantonese-speaking customer, whose name was Chu. At one point, when they were talking about their personal lives, Chu revealed that he, too, had escaped from the same massacre along the Yangtze. He had received a large burn on his back from the gasoline-fed fire before being able to run off, and he showed Tang the scar.

Within about a year, Chu decided to join the New Fourth Army (together with the Eighth Route Army, one of the precursors of the People's Liberation Army) and left Zhuzhen. Tang gave him pencils and a notebook as a farewell gift, but he never heard from him again. Half a year later, Tang himself joined the New Fourth Army.

The next witness survived an even larger massacre, one involving as many as seven or eight thousand people.

Luo Zhongyang (67), now a licensed practitioner of Chinese herbal medi-

Luo Zhongyang.

cine, joined the Nationalists' 64th Guangzhou (Canton) Army, 256th Division, at the age of sixteen.

The following year, that is, when Luo was seventeen, the Second Shanghai Incident occurred (August 13, 1937), and his unit was transferred from Guangzhou to Shanghai to face the invading army. After about two months of fighting, the unit withdrew, fighting all the way, to Nanjing to join the fight to protect the capital, and they took up a position at Qilin Gate, outside Zhongshan Gate. However, they were forced to withdraw into Nanjing from Qilin Gate about a week before the fall of the city. Since the leader of Luo's platoon had been killed in the fighting, he was promoted to private first class and put in charge of his platoon.

The order to withdraw from Nanjing came on the evening of December 12. Yijiang Gate was blocked, so they headed for the next gate, Xingzhong Gate, but it, too, was impassable. Even the city walls were covered with people trying to flee, but Luo and some of his men were able to climb over the wall on a hose from a firetruck. Some people fell off the wall or broke bones in their attempts to clamber over, but Luo held tightly to the hose with both hands and sometimes even with his teeth as he made his way down the outer side. He had to jump the last part of the way, and although he landed hard on the ground and rolled over, he was uninjured. By this time, his platoon had completely disintegrated, with members running off aimlessly in groups of two or three.

Luo and some of his men ducked into an abandoned house, discarded their military uniforms and exchanged them for some of the clothes that they found in the house. Luo put on a black padded civilian jacket and pants over a Nationalist Army sweatshirt which bore a tag reading "Overseas Chinese Committee to Save the Nation: Hong Kong Women's Donation Society." The only other thing he kept with him was a single hand grenade.

Of course, when they reached Xiaguan, they found nothing that could serve as a boat, so they walked along the river toward Baota Bridge. However, this area was full of desperately rushing mobs of people, and they were not getting anywhere, so they tried heading farther east to Yanziji, but no matter where they went, all they found were refugees and huge crowds. With no other recourse, they went back into the city, heading south and slightly *inland toward Jiangdongcun (now known as Jiangdongmen) and then east to Shuixi Gate. By this time, it was already dawn.*

That was when they saw a group of about a thousand men, apparently Chinese soldiers who had surrendered, kneeling in a cluster on the ground up ahead, surrounded by Japanese troops. Sensing danger, Luo suggested to his companions that they go back the other way, but they argued, "We don't have any weapons, so according to international law, they can't kill us." Luo could not bring himself to feel this optimistic, so he and three of the other more cautious members of his group left the others and slipped into an empty house a little way off to see what would happen.

Soon the owner of the house returned, just as the one thousand men were being led off somewhere. It did not appear that they were going to be killed, and the owner of the house, too, assured them that they would be all right. Luo and his companions, therefore, decided that they felt like surrendering, so they went outside and turned themselves in, although not before Luo had gotten rid of his hand grenade.

Luo and the others were made to kneel while more and more surrendering soldiers and other detainees were brought to join them, until the number reached seven or eight thousand. Japanese troops with machine guns stood around them, but Luo assumed that this was just a precaution.

Finally, they were given the order to move. They moved forward, surrounded by Japanese soldiers, but without being tied up or otherwise restrained. After a walk of between thirty and sixty minutes, they arrived at Sancha River, the name given to the part of the Qinhuai River that empties into the Yangtze. Because it was winter, there was not much water in the river, and although the Yangtze was 100 meters wide, the Sancha was less than half of that. Near the bank was a large vacant lot, with the river on one side and a row of mud brick houses on the other. As the prisoners assembled there, Luo could see a lot of Japanese soldiers and the flag of the Nakajima Unit.

Another thousand men were brought in from somewhere else, bringing the total number of prisoners to over ten thousand. By this time, it was eight or nine in the morning. A Japanese soldier began addressing the crowd through an interpreter. "Lianmen weishenme gong dikang dijun?" *(Why do all of you resist the Imperial Army?)*

Someone in the crowd called out, "Women shi weile baowei guojia, fengming er lai de." *(We were ordered to defend our country.) Others called out things like* "Women bu shi bing, shi laobaixing." *(We aren't soldiers; we're peasants.)*

Now another interpreter came forward—apparently a Japanese, judging from his strange way of speaking Chinese—and yelled at the crowd, "Lianmen bu xing, tongtong si la, si la!" *(You're no good. You're all going to die!)*

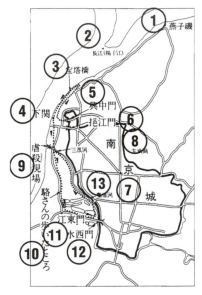

1. Yanziji Rock
2. Yangtze River
3. Baota Bridge
4. Xiaguan
5. Xingzhong Gate
6. Yijiang Gate
7. Nanjing
8. Xuanwu Lake
9. Site of the massacre
10. Where Luo Zhongyang walked
11. Jiangdong Gate
12. Shuixi Gate
13. Qinhai Waterway

Then he continued, *"How do you want to die? Incendiary shells? Gasoline? Machine guns? Bayonets?"*

Hearing this, some of the prisoners burst into tears of despair, but one of them shouted back, "If we're going to die no matter what, we'll take machine guns!"

Yet, the Japanese appeared to have decided to kill them with bayonets. Using the gaiters that were part of the Nationalist Army's uniform, they tied the prisoners' hands behind their backs and linked them together "bead style" in groups of ten. Since there were not enough Japanese soldiers to handle such a large crowd, the Chinese prisoners were forced to tie one another. Shouts of "Jiuming!" (Help!) along with sobbing and shouting could be heard. A few men tried to run away, but they were summarily shot.

The edge of the water and the row of mud-brick houses were about 200 meters apart. As shown in the drawing on page 231, the Japanese surrounded the tightly packed prisoners on two sides and set up machine guns. Luo's position was about twenty or thirty rows away from the river, relatively close compared to the positions of many other people in the

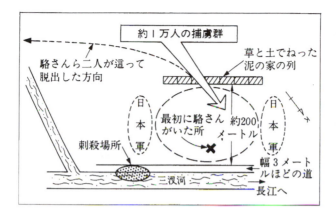

1. About 10,000 prisoners
2. Luo and his companion
3. The row of mud-straw brick
   houses
4–5. Japanese troops
6. North
7. Where Luo stood initially
8. About 200 meters
9. Where the stabbings
   occurred
10. A side channel of the river
12. Road (sic) about 3 meters
    wide
13. To the Yangtze

*crowd. The first ten men were brought forward and made to stand on the
embankment, still linked together. Suddenly, a line of Japanese soldiers
rushed forward and stabbed them in the back. Since the prisoners were
tied together, they fell forward all at once, and the soldiers stabbed them
again before throwing them into the water.*

*However, the Japanese had realized that tying up ten thousand men would be
too much of a chore, so only the first few groups were bound together, while the
others were simply led closer and closer to the water's edge. Ten groups of ten
each, or 100 men, were brought forward at a time, lined up on the bank, and
stabbed from behind in the vicinity of the heart by an equal number of Japanese
soldiers. Then they tumbled forward into the water.*

*Almost everyone in the crowd was sobbing or shouting, but Luo calmly
observed his surroundings, wondering if there was not some way to escape.
Since he was so close to the water's edge, his turn would come up soon, so
his first priority was to move backward, little by little. A few people at this
stage had tried to run out of the vacant lot or climb up onto the roof of one of
the houses, but they had all been shot.*

*This was indeed an "assembly-line murder," but it lasted a long time be-
cause of the huge number of people, and teams of Japanese soldiers took
turns with the bayonets. During this time, Luo managed to slip back to the
area near the row of mud-brick houses. Working together with two other
Chinese who happened to be near him, he made a hole in the wall of one of*

the houses, not a difficult task with walls made of reeds covered with dried mud. After widening the hole enough to barely allow a person to pass through, they crawled in one at a time, with Luo bringing up the rear. The other former soldiers around them were so distraught and confused, as well as so closely packed together, that evidently none of them noticed. It was now two or three in the afternoon.

The light inside the house was dim, but sufficient for seeing the inside of the room. The real entrance was on the side facing the next house, and as the three men huddled together in a corner on the opposite side, two Japanese soldiers came in with rifles. The three men thought it was all over and just sat there motionless. Three or four shots were fired, but whether it was a miracle or a coincidence, the bullets missed them completely. "I don't know what the significance is," Luo said thoughtfully, "but it wasn't just that the bullets missed us. It's that the soldiers simply left without doing anything else to us. Maybe their Buddha natures emerged and they ignored us on purpose."

By four or five in the afternoon, the sun was beginning to set, and still the killing was not over. Maybe a tenth of the prisoners, about a thousand, remained. Peeking through the hole in the wall, Luo saw that this last group was driven en masse to the water's edge and machine gunned to death all at once.

Even though it was dark, there were still Japanese soldiers around, so the three men stayed inside the house. The interior was divided into fourths by reed partitions, and they moved to one of the inner rooms. The distance between houses may have been 1 or 2 meters, but they did not have a chance to look, so they did not know whether a person could pass through there or whether Japanese soldiers would be there. The three of them made plans to wait until it was really dark, check their surroundings, and then flee down the river, avoiding the roads.

By around midnight, one of the men could not stand the tension any longer. He made a hole in the back wall and slipped out, never to be seen again. Luo and his remaining companion found an old, ragged discarded quilt top and crawled under it.

At about two in the morning, two Japanese soldiers suddenly came into the room. For some reason, they were carrying not rifles, but detached bayonets. As Luo and the other Chinese man held their breaths, the two Japanese whisked the quilt top off of them, took it to the opposite corner of the room, and lay down under it. Evidently exhausted, they fell asleep right away. Because of the darkness of the room, they had not noticed the two Chinese, but had merely thought that the quilt top was crumpled up in the corner.

Completely unnoticed by the soundly sleeping Japanese, Luo and his companion sneaked out through the hole in the back wall. They could see flames rising up on the site of the massacre and the forms of Japanese soldiers

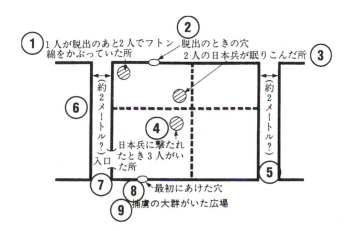

1. Where Luo and his companion hid under the quilt cover after the third man escaped
2. The hole through which they escaped
3. Where the two Japanese soldiers fell asleep
4. Where Luo and his two companions were when the Japanese soldiers shot at them

5–6. About 2 meters
7. Entrance
8. The first hole
9. The open space where the prisoners were

silhouetted in that light. They crawled along the ground, heading south to a branch of the Sancha River.

Walking south through the muddy water, they came upon a boat. After washing their feet, they boarded to find an old man sleeping, or so they thought. When they touched him, they realized that he was dead. They continued down the river, and within a distance of about 500 meters, they saw more than ten such small boats with dead passengers. Most were elderly men, but there were a few elderly women.

Each time they boarded a boat, they washed their feet. (The reason for this was that the Japanese considered dirty feet grounds for suspecting a person of being a straggler.) The boats were very small, no more than 5 or 6 meters long and 80 centimeters to 1 meter wide, and during the winter, they were usually hauled up onto shore. They were used only for fishing in the rivers and could not be expected to carry people across the Yangtze. In the confusion accompanying the fall of the city, the defeated soldiers and refugees had been desperate to cross the Yangtze by any means they could, and they must have tried to take these small boats, but since this stretch of river was far inland from the main channel of the Yangtze, it was obvious that the boats had not gotten the people very far.

Luo Zhongyang telling about the systematic massacre.

Suddenly, when it was close to dawn and they were near Fayun Temple, Luo and his companion heard a baby crying in one of the boats. When they went to investigate, they found a woman and a baby alone. The woman was a refugee from somewhere else, not a local resident. She let them on board, but when they begged to be allowed to sleep there, due to their overwhelming exhaustion, she pointed to another boat nearby and told them that it was empty and they should sleep there. Once they moved over to the other boat, they fell asleep immediately.

When it was fully light on the morning of December 14, the owner of the boat returned. He was about fifty years old, an old man by the standards of the time, and he demanded to know what Luo and the other man were doing on his boat. "We didn't have any other place to spend the night," Luo explained. "Couldn't you let us stay a little longer?"

"That's fine with me," the man replied, "but it's dangerous for you to be here without a refugee certificate. Wouldn't it be better for you to flee?"

Luo and his companion had to agree, so they went to Fayun Temple, the institution that gave its name to the area, and asked the priest, who went by the name of Xinjing, where they could get refugee certificates. "Try the Red Swastika Society," the priest suggested.

As they were walking around looking for the Red Swastika Society, they encountered a man who was wearing a Society armband and asked him about refugee certificates. "Where are you from?" the man asked.

When Luo replied that he was from Guangdong Province, the man told him, "In that case, forget it." As a rule, refugee certificates were available only to residents of Nanjing. However, Luo and his companion knew that they would be killed if they were found without certificates, so they stuck close to the man from the Red Swastika Society, feeling that he was their last hope. As long as they were with him, they thought, they would be safe.

They stuck to him like remoras to a shark as he moved through the city without saying a word. Then, suddenly, he stopped, pretended to pick something up off the street, and produced a refugee certificate, which he handed over. Luo and his companion struggled over the certificate for a while, and Luo lost out. With no other option, he kept following the man from the Society. Suddenly, he saw seven or eight Japanese soldiers 200 meters ahead. Again, he began desperately pleading with the man from the Red Swastika Society, who finally leaned over, pretended to pick something up off the street, and handed a certificate to Luo. By this time, the Japanese were only 100 meters away. The certificate was about as wide as a business card, only slightly longer, and it bore the inscription "Nanjing Refugee Certificate" along with an official seal. Ordinarily, one was supposed to attach it to one's clothing with a pin, but Luo did not have anything to attach it with, and he simply held it to his chest with his left hand.

Nevertheless, the Japanese were suspicious of him. After searching him, they said, "He's a Chinese soldier." But the man from the Red Swastika Society spoke up for him, "No, no, he's a law-abiding citizen," he replied. The Japanese accepted the assurance and said, "All right, move along," so Luo was spared. With that, he was able to get lost in the crowd in the Refugee Zone.

Once in the Refugee Zone, he was drafted as a coolie by the Japanese troops. First, he spent three days hauling provisions for them. Then, for the two remaining weeks in December, he was assigned to dispose of the bodies that lay along the river by throwing them into the water. One day, while he was at this task, the Japanese soldier who was supervising him noticed his sweatshirt. "You're Chinese Army, aren't you? If you're found out, you'll be killed."

Luo immediately started to take off his sweatshirt with the intention of throwing it away, but the soldier stopped him. "If anyone sees you do that, you'll be in trouble." He let him go off somewhere and dispose of the shirt in secret. ("Occasionally, there were Japanese soldiers who were like that," Luo told me.)

Even in the Refugee Zone, young men who did not have refugee certificates were continually being taken away and killed. About two months after the fall of the city, Luo was stopped and examined near Zhongshan Bridge. This time, the Japanese did not give any credence to his refugee certificate,

侵华日军南京大屠杀遇难同胞

挹江门丛葬地纪念碑

南京市人民政府
一九八五年八月

Commemorative plaques have been set up at all the principal massacre sites and at the main burial sites for massacre victims.

and they put him together with several hundred other people of dubious status. They set up a table in the square and made each person stand up on it as they asked the crowd, "Are there any family members or relatives of this person here?" It was a kind of identification parade, and of course, Luo, who was from Guangdong Province, had no relatives in Nanjing.

But when it was his turn to stand on the table, two men about sixty years old came forward. "He's a member of our household," they said. To have these two complete strangers speak up for him was like being rescued from hell by the Buddha.

"I am indebted to them for the rest of my life," Luo says. "Their names were Deng Baohe and Zu Zhengqing. Zu, in particular, didn't have any children of his own, and he became a sort of substitute father to me. Afterward, I frequently sent him money and food."

Later in the war, Luo's real father, his older brother, and his grandfather's younger brother were all killed by the Japanese in the family's hometown of Huizhou, Guangdong Province.

Some may be wondering how the Japanese newspapers dealt with these large-scale massacres. The morning edition of the *Asahi Shimbun* for December 17 carried the following article under the headline "With More Prisoners Than They Can Handle Stuffed into Twenty-Two Buildings, Food Is Becoming a Problem."

> Nanjing, December 16, special correspondent Yokota: The unprecedentedly large haul of 14,777 routed enemy soldiers taken prisoner by the Morozumi

Unit in the vicinities of Wulong Mountain and the Mufu Mountain Fort has the Unit reeling from the problem of how a comparatively small number of men can handle so many prisoners. As a result, the prisoners were first made to throw away their rifles and were put into nearby barracks. With more than a division's worth of soldiers taken prisoner, the holding area can't hold them all, not even after they have been packed like rush hour commuters into twenty-two large barracks. When Commanding Officer _____ displayed his superb magnanimity by saying, "The Imperial Army will not kill you," the prisoners raised their hands and reverenced him. Then they applauded and cheered, wild with joy. As a result, the undisciplined nature of the wildly inconsistent Chinese national character has been put to shame here by the Imperial Army.

The prisoners are members of Chiang Kai-shek's bodyguard, which has merged with the combined instructional unit and wears the same uniforms. The most perplexing matter is food, and even finding sufficient food locally for the Morozumi Unit itself is a huge problem. To begin with, since it was absolutely impossible to collect bowls for 15,000 men, we ended up not being able to feed them on the first night. As a result, the Unit is quickly rounding up all its pack horses and foraging for food. . . .

A photograph accompanies this article, and it shows the same scenes as photographs appearing on the photo page of the December 19 morning edition of the *Asahi Shimbun* and in the January 5, 1938, issue of *Asahi Graph*, but it was taken at a different moment. The caption for the photograph in the newspaper reads "Stragglers who had been hiding in the Nanjing Refugee Zone (December 17, Kawamura—Fukuoka Wirephoto)." The one in *Asahi Graph* reads, "Some of the prisoners picked up by the Morozumi Unit in the communities surrounding Nanjing (December 16, photography by special correspondent Ueno)." Judging from the contents of the two articles accompanying the photographs, it appears that the latter caption is the accurate one. Quite possibly, *Asahi* staff members back in Japan took it upon themselves to dream up the caption accompanying the newspaper article.

However, there is no further news on what became of that huge mass of 14,777 prisoners. Where could they have disappeared to?

As a matter of fact, there have long been indirect rumors to the effect that all the prisoners were killed.[25] Yet, because no one survived this particular

---

25. For example, Fujiwara Shinji's *Everyone Knows* (Shunyōdō, 1957) contains information that appears to be from a soldier who was assigned to get rid of the bodies after all the prisoners were "disposed of," but he seems to have confused Mufu Mountain and Wulong Mountain. Hora Tomio quotes Hata Kensuke 's "The White Tiger Unit, Stained with the Blood of Prisoners," from *Nihon Shūhō*, no. 298, but this is only inaccurate hearsay, since Hata was not following the troops at that time. He writes that the White Tiger Unit took a large group of prisoners into the city of Nanjing, but in fact, this unit did not enter the city at that time. On the other hand, a collection called *War Records of Local Military Units,* published by the *Fukushima Min'yū Shimbun* in 1965, mentions

A photo that appeared in *Asahi Graph* on January 5, 1938, taken by special correspondent Ueno. Evidently, all these men were later killed.

massacre, we have no direct testimony from victims on the Chinese side. The experiences of a certain noncommissioned officer in the Japanese Army may, therefore, shed some light on this situation. Just recently, a former non-commissioned officer in the Morozumi Unit, which actually disposed of the prisoners, has decided to tell the truth in detail. I will discuss his motives for telling the truth later, but because many of the previous veterans who have come forward with such accounts have been the targets of numerous igno-rant, mean-spirited anonymous crank calls and letters, I have respected his wishes in assigning him a pseudonym. The man I will call Tanaka Saburō, age seventy-three, was born in Fukushima Prefecture and is retired after a long career with the Metropolitan Police Headquarters. He has achieved the eighth *dan* in kendō, and he has also reached high rankings in jūdō, swords-manship, and other martial arts. Besides that, he is also an accomplished calligrapher, a regular Japanese renaissance man. His philosophical position is neither left wing nor particularly anti–left wing. One might say, rather, that he is a conservative, establishment type.

Tanaka has realized the necessity of leaving behind a truthful account of the fall of Nanjing now, forty-seven years after the fact, based on the traditional Japanese warriors' code, *bushidō*. He spoke after showing me the sketches he had drawn and the notations he had written in two notebooks during the war while he was in the hospital recovering from wounds received during the as-sault on Hankou in 1938. He tells what drove him to reveal the truth:

> It is a fact that after the fall of Nanjing we disposed of a huge number of nonresisting prisoners. No matter how much the Japanese deny it, this fact cannot be hidden, due to the existence of any number of living witnesses in China. I'd like us to acknowledge facts as facts, and at the same time, I would like the Chinese to stop making groundless claims about immense numbers of victims without any proof. I've heard that the Chinese are claiming that four hundred thousand people were massacred,[26] but in the end, what specific materials do they have to support that claim? In another twenty years, almost all the people in either country who have direct knowledge of the facts will be

the disposal of the prisoners, but since the incident reflects badly on the unit, the authors take pains to play it down, adding a lot of impossible details such as the idea that Chi-nese troops were firing from the opposite bank of the river or saying that the majority of the prisoners ran away, so that only about a thousand were killed. The account in *The China Incident Army Campaign,* published by the War Research Office of the National Defense Agency, relies almost entirely on *War Records of Local Military Units.*

26. "Four hundred thousand" is the figure appearing *in Testimony: The Great Nanjing Massacre,* produced by the Nanjing City Historical Materials Research Association, translated into Japanese by Kagami Mitsuyuki and Himeda Mitsuyoshi, and published by Aoki Shoten. An article about the book appeared in the July 22, 1984, edition of *Asahi Shimbun,* and Tanaka's comment seems to be based on having read the article.

gone. Shouldn't the people from both countries who really experienced these events leave behind an accurate record of the facts now, while they still can? I think that this kind of activity is important for bringing about true Sino-Japanese friendship.

Tanaka was in the Yamada Brigade, 65th Regiment (Aizu Wakamatsu—Morozumi Unit), 16th Battalion, 2d Company, belonging to the 13th Division (Sendai). He joined the army in time to take part in the Manchurian Incident (called the "9/18 Incident" in China), and when his unit was summoned to take part in the Nanjing offensive, he was a twenty-four-year-old noncommissioned officer.

On October 3, 1937, they landed at Wusong, near Shanghai. After walking inland only about 6 kilometers, they bivouacked for about a week near an estuary where the bodies of Chinese floated past. Due to the fact that they cooked with water from the estuary, about half the soldiers suffered from diarrhea. Meanwhile, they drilled and trained in platoons and squads, with Corporal Tanaka as a squad commander. On the 10th, the unit was shifted to the forward lines, and they came under attack on the 11th. Elite troops from the Nationalist Chinese Army surrounded them on three sides, coming in from Laoluzhai up ahead, Mengjiazhai on the left, and Sanjiacun on the right. Tanaka's unit fought desperately under opposing fire so fierce that it knocked down every stalk of bamboo in the grove that served as their attack position. During this time, 65 out of the 198 men in the company were killed, and even more were severely wounded and sent to the rear. Even though they received reinforcements as they fought, only 23 of the original members of the company came through the fighting completely unharmed. The company commander was wounded and evacuated, and out of six commissioned officers, three were killed.

"This is the kind of severe punishment we took. Of course, all of them died 'for their country.' I'd like to remind you that the assault on Nanjing took place as an extension of this fighting. It just wasn't the kind of atmosphere in which you'd immediately forgive and release your prisoners, merely because they had surrendered to you. The mood was one of avenging your dead comrades. I think we could expect the soldiers who fought on the Chinese side then to understand how we felt. Assuming that we killed ten thousand or twenty thousand, the way we treated them was a continuation of the battle. Given the mood of those times, we simply did not think of ourselves as 'committing massacres' We thought we were killing them 'for our country.'"

The 10th Army's landing at Hangzhou Bay turned the tide of the war. The news of the so-called Million Man Japanese Landing sent Chiang Kai-shek's army into a hasty retreat, with the Japanese army in hot pursuit. Tanaka's Morozumi Unit saw difficult fighting at Zhenjiang, but after that, they simply headed toward Nanjing along the Yangtze River without encountering any significant fighting. Along the way, they saw a lot of pillboxes under construction, and Tanaka remembers thinking, "We'd have been in a lot of trouble if they had finished building those." North of Nanjing, the Yangtze divides in two, with the wider channel curving around for 10 kilometers before rejoining the other channel near the Wulong Mountain battery position, but when Tanaka's unit reached this point, they encountered no significant resistance. When they followed the minor channel further, to a spot just short of Mufu Mountain, a huge mass of Chinese soldiers suddenly came to surrender to them. This was the group of prisoners featured in the newspaper article and the photograph. Each company worked feverishly to confiscate the Chinese soldiers' weapons. The prisoners were allowed to keep one blanket, aside from the clothes they were wearing. Then they were collected in the large buildings with mud walls and thatched roofs that the Chinese army used as barracks. As Tanaka recalls, these were located on the south side of a hill on Wufu Mountain; that is to say, they were on the opposite side of the mountain from the Yangtze. His sketches from that period also agree with that memory.

The prisoners' lives after they were detained were miserable. All they had to eat was a single small bowl of rice per day. Since no water was supplied, Tanaka saw prisoners drinking urine out of the drainage ditches that surrounded the barracks.

The orders to "finish off" the prisoners came on December 17, the day of the triumphal entry into Nanjing. In the morning, the prisoners were told, "We're transferring your detention camp to Changzhou (Chuanzhong Island)," but it took an entire battalion to get them ready for the move. With such a large-scale transfer, nothing could happen very quickly, and by the time all the prisoners had had their hands tied and everyone was ready to leave, it was afternoon. The long snaking procession of four columns first headed west and made a detour around to the side of the mountain that faced the river. Then they walked 4, 5, or no more than 6 kilometers. During that time, Tanaka saw two men dash out of the crowd of prisoners and threw themselves into the water, either because they had sensed what was coming or because they could no longer bear their thirst. As soon as they came to the surface, they were shot, and after seeing their heads torn open and their blood staining the water, no other prisoners tried to flee.

During this procession under guard, Tanaka spotted some suspicious human figures standing on the hillside. There were Japanese troops at the summit of the hill, but he was able to make out some people scattered about the hillside who seemed to be wearing civilian clothes. He became uneasy, wondering if they might they be from some international intelligence organization. At any rate, Tanaka thinks that there were witnesses to the ensuing events.

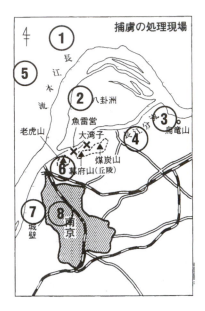

1. The main channel of the Yangtze River
2. Chuanzhong Island
3. Niaolong Mountain
4. Side channel of the Yangtze River
5. Where the prisoners were "dealt with"
6. Wufu Mountain (slope)
7. City wall
8. Nanjing

The crowd of prisoners was assembled on the banks of the Yangtze, on a flood plain dotted with willow trees. Chuanzhong Island could be seen across the channel, along with two small boats.

About three or four hours after the head of the procession had arrived at the riverbank, the prisoners began to notice the incongruity of their situation. They couldn't see any boats suitable for ferrying such a large quantity of prisoners over to Chuanzhong Island, and the day was drawing to a close without any sign of preparations to transport them. On the contrary, the oval-shaped mass of prisoners was surrounded on three sides, every side except the one facing the water, by a semicircle of Japanese soldiers and machine guns aimed inward. Tanaka was located near the extreme eastern end of the line of Japanese troops.

As it was beginning to grow dark, a second lieutenant on the opposite end of the line was killed by rebellious prisoners. The warning came down the line: "He was killed with his own sword. Be careful." Tanaka guesses that even though the prisoners had their hands tied behind their backs, they were not linked together, so it would have been possible for prisoners to undo one another's bonds with their teeth. Realizing the danger, some of them must have desperately attempted a last-ditch resistance, but the others in the crowd, who still had their hands tied, would have been unable to join them.

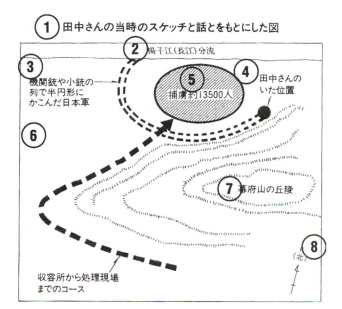

1. Diagram based on Tanaka's contemporary sketch and description
2. A branch of the Yangtze River
3. Semicircle of Japanese troops with machine guns and rifles
4. Tanaka's position
5. Approximately 13,500 prisoners of war
6. path followed from the detention camp to the execution site
7. hill on Wufu Mountain
8. North

It was soon after this that the order to fire was given.

The semicircle of heavy and light machine guns and rifles began spraying the crowd of prisoners with concentrated fire. Between the roar of all those guns firing at once and the death cries rising up from among the mass of prisoners, the scene along the riverbank was hellish. Tanaka kept firing his rifle, but in the midst of it all, he saw a sight that he can never forget: a giant "human pillar," created as the prisoners, who had nowhere to flee, scrambled up and over one another during their last struggles. Tanaka does not really know the real reason why this happened, but his guess is that the prisoners, with bullets pouring in at them horizontally from three sides, were of course unable to hide underground, so they instinctively tried to escape the shooting by climbing higher—even with their hands tied—over the bodies of those who were already dead. The "human pillar" grew and grew until it toppled over, and then the process started over, to be repeated three times during the shooting. The mass shooting continued for an hour, or at least until no one was left standing. By this time, it was almost completely dark.

Yet, there were undoubtedly some men still alive amid all that, some who were merely wounded and others who had fallen over and played dead. No one could be left alive. If anyone escaped, the wholesale massacre would become known to the outside world, causing an international incident. That is why Tanaka's battalion spent the whole night finishing off all the prisoners. Since the prisoners were piled up several men deep, taking all the piles apart and checking each body individually would be too much trouble, so they decided to set fires. The prisoners were all wearing winter clothing padded with cotton, and once that caught fire, it would not be easy to extinguish, and furthermore, the flames would provide light to work by. And of course, if a man was playing dead, he would certainly move if his clothes started burning.

The soldiers set fires at scattered spots among the piles of bodies. If they watched carefully, they could see supposed corpses reacting to the heat and reaching out to smother the approaching flames. Anyone who moved was immediately stabbed to death with a bayonet. Poking through the pile of bodies, the soldiers moved among the scattered, lapping flames, delivering final blows with their bayonets. Their boots and gaiters grew sticky with the blood and body fluids of their victims. Their cries of "The more enemy we kill, the sooner we'll win," "This is revenge for all our comrades from Shanghai on," and "This is a farewell gift to the surviving families" provided an indication of the mood they were in. There was no room for doubt. There was nothing in the backs of their minds as they stabbed the survivors except "Now our comrades will be able to rest in peace" and "We don't want to leave anyone who can run away and prove what happened." This, too, was part of the war strategy, and above all, they were acting in obedience to the order from the command headquarters in Nanjing: "All prisoners are to be swiftly dispatched."

During their night-long action, they moved beyond mere fatigue and entered an indescribable new dimension of exhaustion that had them carrying out their task in a trancelike state. When they returned to their quarters on the morning of the 18th, looking wretched, covered with body fluids, and smeared with charcoal, they immediately fell into a deep sleep.

Another unit was called in to help with disposing of the dead. If they simply shoved the stabbed or bullet-riddled bodies into the river, they might still be recognizable, so in order to erase their identity, they burned them, using drums of gasoline. However, they did not have enough fuel to reduce such a huge number of bodies to ashes, as happens during a cremation. Instead, they were left with a pile of charred corpses. Dumping all those bodies into the Yangtze was still a major task, and they were unable to complete it before the evening of the 18th. Making crooks from willow branches, they dragged the heavy bodies into the river, but it was noon of the 19th before they finished.

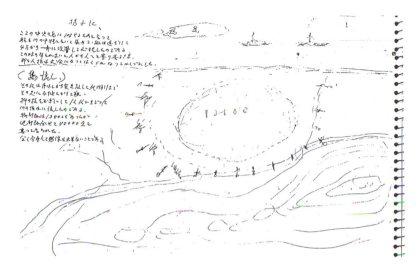

The original of the sketch that Tanaka drew while hospitalized the year after the massacre. The figure "13,500" is written in the area representing the clump of prisoners, and they are surrounded by machine guns. Two ships are in the side channel of the Yangtze, and Zhongyang Island is at the upper left. Tanaka's caption reads as follows:

"*Saying that we were going to send them to Zhongyang Island for the time being, we gathered them together after positioning ships in the middle of the river. After the ships had withdrawn, we attacked the prisoners from all sides at once and disposed of them. The way the men piled on top of one another so as not to be shot, that is, making a human pillar, which would reach the height of about 1 jō (10 feet) and then collapse, and then rise up and collapse.*

"*(Sending them to the island.)*

"*That night, we stabbed them to death, one after another, working until dawn. and after that we sprinkled gasoline over them. And then, using willow branches as hooks, we tossed them one by one into the river. My unit [disposed of] 13,500, but I've heard that all the units together [disposed of] 70,000. Thinking about it now, I find it quite unimaginable.*"

At the bottom of this sketch is a drawing of eight rows of long buildings labeled "thatched roof prisoner detention camp." The caption reads:

"*To tend the overwhelming number of 13,500 prisoners was beyond our capabilities. We couldn't even give them water. [Illegible] there were even some who drank their own urine.*"

"*I can state with absolute certainty that no one escaped the scene of that massacre alive,*" Tanaka says. "*Judging from what happened before and after, it would have been impossible.*"

After taking care of the prisoners, the Morozumi Unit crossed the Yangtze on the 20th and advanced to Pukou. Then they pursued the Chinese troops westward deep into the inlands for two weeks before returning to Pukou, where they were assigned to police the area.

Tanaka has a notation in his wartime writings in which he estimates that the total number of prisoners "finished off" and "taken care of" was seventy thousand. He heard that another large massacre, one not perpetrated by his

A memorial to "our compatriots who were caught up in the massacre" now stands along the Yangtze River on the west edge of Wufu Mountain near Shangyuan Gate. These kinds of memorials can be found at the principal massacre sites all over Nanjing.

unit, occurred in the foothills of Zijin Mountain. However, despite its massacres of prisoners, the Morozumi Unit did not indulge in random slaughter of civilians, and Tanaka says that they could not have, because they never entered the city of Nanjing.

One of the accounts from the Chinese side comes from *Return to the Secular Life* (published by Chungwai Library, Taipei, 1973), the autobiography of a commissioned officer of the Nanjing Defense Corps named Niu Xianming. It contains a description of what may be the same incident that Tanaka described. Here are the relevant passages:

> One or two kilometers along the riverbank downstream from Rongqing Temple (Note: a temple near Shangyuan Gate, where Niu was hiding) is a place called Dawanzi, a particularly shallow sandbar. The Yangtze flows north of Bagua Island, and the channel that flows south of Zhong Island is sluggish, allowing the formation of shallow sandbars.

About ten days after hearing the sound of gunfire, we finally learned that the devil soldiers had massacred over twenty thousand of our fellow soldiers there with machine guns.

The reader will remember that I and an elderly peasant were made to haul firewood to Shangyuan Gate. This was for the prisoners to cook with. At that time, all I could think about was my own safety, and I never even considered how the enemy would deal with their prisoners of war. They themselves should have considered it. Since they were already prisoners of war and had thrown away their weapons, they expected that at most, they would be detained and subjected to hard labor and that their lives would be spared.

Who would have thought they would be executed en masse at Dawanzi a mere two nights later?

The reason that the devil soldiers cut pomegranate branches in the neighborhood of Rongqing Temple that night was to use them as tools for piling the bodies into separate heaps. . . .

The bodies were finally disposed of one or two months later. I don't remember the exact date of the massacre, but since it was a moonlit night, it was around the fifteenth day of the eleventh month according to the peasant calendar, and if I remember correctly, it was about a month and a half before the new year. . . .

On my third research trip to Nanjing (fourth, if we count the 1971 trip that resulted in my book *Journey to China*), I was able to verify the location of Rongqing Temple. Until 1968, it stood at the foot of a mountain along the Yangtze River about 1 kilometer east of Shangyuan Gate, but I was told that it had fallen into disrepair and collapsed. Huang Shikun (age 53), who has been employed at the nearby quarry since 1963, told me that its popular name was Shiliusi ("Pomegranate Temple"), due to the large number of pomegranate trees in the area. This agrees with what is recorded in *Return to the Secular Life*, The temple's wall remained until quite recently, but it was buried under tailings from the quarry. In the picture, Huang is pointing to the former location of the temple.

One day around noon, a group of soldiers appeared, bringing with them some Chinese men wearing the armband of the Red Swastika Society. They came into the temple hall and designated a couple of us to join with them, demanding that we dispose of the bodies of the massacre victims. . . .

The distance between Rongqing Temple and Dawanzi was about a kilometer. . . .

When we were about halfway to Dawanzi, we were assailed by the odor of rotting bodies. The Japanese soldiers and the Chinese with them had come equipped with masks, but Ergong and I didn't even have handkerchiefs. It was already the coldest part of the year, and the air was very dry, so the corpses lying around in the neighborhood of our temple were in what amounted to a natural refrigerator, and they did not decompose. However, the bodies lying around here at Dawanzi were different. Some of them were partly submerged in the water, and the ones on the sandbar were also washed over by the tides, so they had decomposed. . . .

As we approached Dawanzi, it wasn't just the stench that was disconcerting. It was the amazing sight of a mountain of corpses piled up in one section of the grounds, their heads facing every which way. Since they were still partly covered by the remnants of their uniforms, I couldn't quite see the condition of their flesh, but looking at their faces, I could see that their noses were gone and that they had started to rot down to the bone in the area of the nose and mouth.

I couldn't imagine the actual massacre! No matter how many machine guns you used, you couldn't kill twenty thousand men at once in such a small area. They must have divided them into several groups. I wondered why we hadn't heard their cries. Perhaps they had been drowned out by the machine guns and had not reached me where I was, inside the temple.

That day, all the Red Swastika Society did was carry out a preliminary survey and investigate methods of burying the bodies. The actual clean-up began afterward and took place a little bit at a time over the course of a month. But I went only that first time. After that, I made Ergong go alone, saying that I was too busy. This is because I was posing as the chief priest of the temple, and it would have been easy for Chinese people to pick me out as an impostor, and also because I couldn't stand to look upon that distressing scene a second time . . . (Translated from Chinese into Japanese by Sugiura Haruka[?])

Hora Tomio assumes that this account refers to December 17, when there was a full moon, based on the passage that says, "it was around the fifteenth day of the eleventh month, according to the peasant calendar." Since this agrees with the Japanese records, he wonders if the massacre at Dawanzi corresponds to the one perpetrated by the Aizu-Wakamatsu Regiment at Mufu Mountain.[27]

The next witness, Shen Xiwen, is a Muslim. He is seventy-six years old, or seventy-seven to seventy-eight according to the old Chinese system. His most notable trait is his unusually detailed and accurate memory. Speaking quietly, he searched his memory for the answers to my questions, but he clearly distinguished the things he recalled from the things he did not know.

Shen's experiences make two important points very clear. The first is that mass round-ups and executions took place in the Refugee Zone even into January. The second is that the Muslims organized their own burial squad and were active in disposing of the bodies of the massacre victims.

Because of the importance of what Shen was telling me and the detailed manner in which he told it, along with the fact that he was old and could not talk for too long at a stretch, one day was not enough to take down his story. We came back two days later for interviews and visits to the actual scene of the events.

---

27. "A certain researcher of the Nanjing Incident" criticized the account in *Return to the Secular life* as "fabrication" and stated in the pages of the magazine *Bungei Shunjū* that our interpretation was "slanderous." Actually, it is the other way around: it is clear that this author himself is guilty of "fabrications." For details, see "Who Fabricated?" in *To the Site of the Great Nanjing Massacre* (edited by Hora, Fujiwara, and others) and "The Man Who Fabricates and Calls Other People Fabricators" in my own *Impoverished Spirits, Collection B.*

Shen Xiwen, who lived in Ji'exiang within the city walls of Nanjing, was an ahong *at a mosque. That is, he provided and prepared livestock for other Muslims to eat.*[28]

With the Japanese air raids becoming more intensive and increasing numbers of people falling victim to the indiscriminate bombing attacks, Shen moved with his family to Doucai Bridge in the Refugee Zone on the fifteenth day of the tenth lunar month (November 17). Only two men, a Muslim named Yi and a twenty-six-year-old non-Muslim gatekeeper named Zhang, remained at the mosque. The place they fled to, Number 28, Doucai Bridge, was overflowing with refugees. Their three-story building alone contained thirteen families with a total of over one hundred people. Shen's family at the time consisted of nine people: himself, his parents, his wife, and their five children, boys of eight, seven, and five, and girls of six and three. In addition to the nine members of the immediate family were Shen's cousin, who was in her twenties, and her mother, who was in her forties. They lived in a room adjoining Shen's room and joined the family for meals.

Even though the Japanese entered the city on December 13, they did not come to Doucai Bridge in the Refugee Zone until December 16. (We had this conversation on December 16, and Shen sighed, "It was forty-six years ago today. Just remembering those times makes me sad.") It was perhaps ten or eleven in the morning, and the Shen family and their two cousins, who were on the second floor, had just cooked some rice gruel and were about to eat. Suddenly, there was a commotion downstairs, and they heard crying and confused sounds. Shen hardly had time to think, "Have the Japanese soldiers come?" before two soldiers came up the stairs with their bayonets attached to their rifles.

The cousin was holding Shen's three-year-old daughter on her lap when the soldiers burst in. One of the soldiers grabbed the little girl by the collar and tried to pull her away. The cousin held on tightly and would not let her go, but in the end, she could not hang on. Holding his bayonet in one hand and taking the child in the other, he threw her into a corner of the brick-walled room. She gave just one brief cry and then lost consciousness, collapsing limply in the corner. With everyone stunned at what had happened, the soldiers forced the cousin and her mother into the back room and closed the door.

Shen picked up his younger daughter, who was gasping for breath, and the whole family made preparations to flee right away. Just then, things again became noisy downstairs, and one of the Japanese soldiers, hearing the commotion, opened the door to check the situation. Seeing that the family was

---

28. This job exists because Muslims not only avoid pork but also refuse to eat any kind of meat that has not been slaughtered and prepared by a fellow Muslim.

The house at Doucai Bridge in the International Refugee Zone where Shen (standing in the foreground) stayed. It has been slightly remodeled since then. The dormer is in the third-floor attic.

trying to escape, the soldier silently poked at Shen with his bayonet. In desperation, first Shen's mother and then the rest of his family knelt in front of the soldier, clasping their hands together as if praying. The soldier drew his bayonet back, returned to the back room, and shut the door.

This time, the Shen family got up silently and fled outside. When they tried to go left to Shanghai Road, they saw a veritable avalanche of people rushing toward them, yelling things like, "It's all over!" and "We'll be killed!" They tried going in the opposite direction toward Kuitouxiang, but again they were met by a mob of people crazy with fear. These people, too, were shouting things like, "As soon as the Eastern devils find you, they'll kill you." Directly in front of them was a vegetable field, and beyond that was Guangzhou Road. The Shen family ran toward the vegetable field, but they had small children with them, and they were also carrying the pot of rice gruel, so they could not run very fast. As they were crossing the field, yet another crowd came spilling in from Guangzhou Road. The thousands of screaming and weeping voices created a horrible effect. At one corner of the field on the Guangzhou Road side was a small hut that appeared to be a public toilet. The Shen family hurriedly went and stood under the eaves of the building on the side facing away from the road.

After a while, the Japanese seemed to have left, and the uproar quieted down a bit, so they quickly crossed Guangzhou Road and went to Jinling University (now Nanjing University). This had been designated as a refugee accommodation area, so they thought they would be safe. However, when they arrived at the main entrance of the university at about four in the after-noon, the iron-barred gate was shut, and the grounds were overflowing with refugees, right up to the edge of the gate itself. There were many people other than the Shen family pressing upon the gate and yelling, "Open up!" but no one came to open up for them. As it was growing dark, one of the refugees who was already inside told them, "It won't do you any good to stick around here. Go around back along the wall and come in the rear gate." They did not really understand the situation, but they went around to the back as di-rected, walking stealthily and sometimes crawling, so as not to be spotted by the Japanese. There were dozens of people waiting outside the rear gate, as well, but after a while, it opened, and everyone went inside.

The campus of Jinling University was flooded with refugees, and the build-ings in particular were all well over capacity. There was no room in the classrooms or any other rooms, so the Shen family found a spot on the stairs and sat down there. The inside of the building was filled with a mixture of shouts and weeping, and it was a dreadful situation.

That evening, the three-year-old girl who had been thrown against the wall died in the arms of her grandmother, who held onto her until the next morning. There was no place to bury her and no way to dig a hole, so they tried to sink the body in a pond in the yard, but it floated to the surface. With no other option, Shen added his daughter's remains to the row of bodies of infants and children that lay next to the pond. ("We threw her away," he said, wiping his eyes.) Much later, when the Muslim burial squad was organized and came to Jinling University, the bodies were in such a state that no one could tell one child from another.

At ten o'clock that morning (December 17), Japanese troops came to Jinling University as well. They searched the buildings from top to bottom and took all males from their teens and older—including Shen, of course—out to the athletic field. When I asked Shen how many soldiers came, he said that he and the other men were so frightened that they just trembled and looked at the ground, so he does not how many soldiers there were. He estimated at a glance that about a thousand men were lined up on the athletic field. Soldiers stood all around them, and there was also a line of machine guns.

The Japanese soldiers inspected the heads and hands of every man in the line. If a man was wearing a hat, the soldiers pulled it off and threw it aside. Shen had no idea why they were doing this, but as a result of these inspec-tions, the group was divided in two, and from the point of view of the people in line, who were facing north, the group on the right was larger, and the

Bodies left unburied along the banks of theYangtze River outside the city walls of Nanjing. (Photograph by Murase Moriyasu, then a member of the Meguro Supply Regiment 17th Motorized Quartermaster Corps, who also shot the photo on page 254.)

group on the left was small in comparison. Shen was sent to the right side. One man was sent to the left but tried to go over to the right side, and immediately a soldier bayoneted him. Seeing this, everyone was startled and realized that the situation was serious.

After everyone had been inspected and sent to one group or the other, the more than three hundred men on the left were led away, but just then, there was an uproar on the athletic field. The parents, wives, and children of the men who were being led away threw their arms around them, wept and shouted, and grabbed onto their trousers to pull them back. It was an indescribably pitiful scene, but as a result, several dozen men were suddenly released. Shen surmises that since the Nationalist Army, except for the commissioned officers, was made up almost entirely of unmarried men from poor peasant families, the Japanese saw the wives and children clinging to these men and decided that they were not soldiers.

In the end, about three hundred men ended up being taken away. Two Japanese led the procession, ten marched on the sides, and two brought up the rear, making a total of fourteen guards. The men never returned, and Shen later heard that they had been killed.

The men who had been sent to the right side returned to their families. During this time they exchanged information, and Shen learned that the checking of heads and hands was the haphazard Japanese method for determining whether someone was a soldier. The assumption was that if someone usually wore a cap with a visor, the effects would show up in the way his face was tanned, while hands were inspected for callouses. As the men came back into the building, there was more commotion and confusion: people coming down to look for their relatives, men fighting their way upstairs against the crowds in their eagerness to tell their families that they were safe, voices delirious with joy that their loved ones had survived unharmed, voices screaming at the news that their loved ones had been taken away. The noise continued well past midnight, and Shen got almost no sleep.

The next morning, December 18, rice gruel was distributed to the refugees based on the number of people in their household. Shen took a wash basin to get his family's rations.

The next two or three days were quiet, but after that, the Japanese showed up again from time to time. They came in small groups ranging from three to eight men, but their aim was always the same: they were hunting for women. They usually appeared during the day, but they sometimes came as late as nine in the evening. There was no way to resist armed soldiers, so some women were taken away knowing full well what would happen to them. However, the one woman who was able to resist effectively was a foreign woman in her thirties, whom the refugees called Ye Xiaojie, or "Miss Leaf." She was one of the managers of the Jinling University refugee center, and Shen thinks that she was American. At one time she energetically chased some Japanese soldiers away, and at another time, she talked some soldiers out of their plans to abduct women. Each time the Japanese showed up with rape in

Bodies left unburied along the Yangtze River at Xiaguan.

mind, the refugees called for "Miss Leaf" and begged her to help them.

Aside from these frequent and continual rapes, there were no major round-ups for the purposes of killing until January 3. On that day, a regular unit of the Japanese Army came to Jinling University and addressed the refugees through an interpreter. "We're going to be distributing residence permits, so

*everyone inside the buildings should come out. People with residence per-
mits will be free to leave the Refugee Zone and return to their own homes."*

*All the adults went out to the athletic field. A number of tables were set up
there, with two Japanese soldiers at each one, and the thousands of refugees
lined up in front of these tables. The people in line were made to kneel, and
they had to creep forward as the line moved. Before issuing the certificates,
the Japanese checked the heads and hands of all the young men, and those
who looked strong and muscular were made to take off their shirts and jackets so that the soldiers could check their shoulders. Those suspected of being
stragglers were separated out. There had been a certain turnover in the refugee population since the inspection on December 17, so some of the suspects
were newcomers, but others had already been checked and cleared in the
previous session. In the end, about two hundred men were separated out and
taken away somewhere. Again there were scenes of frantically crying families. One of Shen's cousins was taken, and the young man's mother cried for
several days. One of the men who had lived in a neighboring room in the
house at Doucai Bridge was also taken away, never to return.*

*Shen's parents were both over sixty, and they were having a hard time
tolerating the difficult life at the university, so they took the residence permits and went home. Shen and his immediate family stayed at the university,
and whenever they went anywhere else in the city, they made sure that they
were carrying a certificate stamped with the seal of the Nakajima Unit.*

*Shen's cousin and her mother—the women who had been shut up in the
back room with the Japanese soldiers—had also come to Jinling University.
He does not know when they came, but when they saw him, they just wept
uncontrollably and did not say a word. Shen thinks that because they had
been raped, they were ashamed to face their relatives, and he did not know
how to comfort them. Soon afterward, the two of them tried to commit suicide
by jumping into a pond on the university grounds, but they were rescued by
some bystanders.*

CHAPTER 11

"NANJING, WHERE PEACE HAS BEEN RESTORED"

Magazines vied with one another to carry articles glorifying the invasion and war. In addition to *Bungei Shunjū, Hanashi* and *Genchi Hōkoku* also published special issues and dispatched novelists and essayists to report from the front. Writers such as Kobayashi Hideo wrote many articles for *Bungei Shunjū* as special correspondents. These posters advertise a special extra issue of *Hanashi*.

Before continuing with the story of what happened after the capture of Nanjing, I would like to tie up a few loose ends from previous chapters.

As related in Chapter 9, young Ma Mingfu was handed over to strangers in Jiangdong County after several members of his family were killed in their intended refuge of Shazhouyu. It was twenty-four days later before his oldest uncle found him by walking around and making inquiries of those villagers in the area who seemed likely to have information about him. What Ma remembers most about his time in Jiangdong County is that although there was comparatively little killing, the villagers were made to kneel and listen to "admonitions" when the Japanese came through.

On the way back to his grandmother's home in Shazhouyu, Ma and his uncle saw a lot of corpses everywhere. Some lay scattered about, others were piled up, and some were even stacked up along the riverbank, with the victims' blood staining the river dark red. Decomposition was more advanced at the riverside locations, but the cold weather had retarded it somewhat.

When they reached Shazhouyu, they found that the survivors had performed makeshift repairs on their burned houses, and they were living in the ruins and in barracks. His father and younger brother were there to greet him. They set about the task of temporarily burying their relatives, because there were still about thirty bodies lying in the hollow where the Japanese had shot them, including six members of Ma's family: his grandfather, mother, two uncles, younger sister, and young girl cousin. Together with the friends and relatives of the other victims, they dug a large hole nearby and put all the bodies in it, creating a temporary cemetery. Their grief once again brought to the surface, the people wept as they buried the bodies, which had already begun to decompose. ("It makes me sad to remember this, too," Ma said, and for a while, he was unable to continue.) Two years later, the bodies were dug up and reburied in a real cemetery.

The Japanese troops came back to Shazhouyu once in a while, but their aim was always either to draft coolies or to rape women. For the duration, the young women of the village adopted the daily routine of fleeing to Taoshan, about 7 or 8 kilometers away, during the day and returning only after dark. One day young Ma Mingfu even went with them.

Once the family members had been buried, there was no particular reason to stay in Shazhouyu, and the word was that the mass confusion and indiscriminate murders that had occurred when Nanjing was first taken had subsided, so Ma's father decided to try returning to their home at Shuixi Gate, Qijiawan. He had left Nanjing with a lively family of six, cheerfully going to visit Grandmother. Now his wife and younger daughter were dead, and the walk back to Nanjing was a gloomy one. Weeping all the way, he took

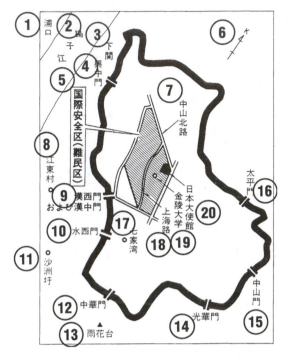

1. Pukou
2. Yangtze River
3. Xiaguan
4. Xingzhong Gate
5. International Safety Zone
   (Refugee Zone)
6. North
7. North Zhongshan Road
8. Jiangdongcun
9. Hanxi Gate and Hanzhong
   Gate
10. Shuixi Gate
11. Shazhouyu
12. Zhonghua Gate
13. Yuhuatai
14. Guanghua Gate
15. Zhongshan Gate
16. Taiping Gate
17. Qijiawan
18. Shanghai Road
19. Jinling University
20. Japanese Embassy

his two sons, leaving his oldest daughter with her grandmother. Clutching his infant son, who had not been weaned at the time of massacre, Ma's father was at a loss as how to feed the child. All he could do was chew some parched rice and transfer it to the baby's mouth.

Their house had been looted, and there was not a single piece of furniture left, not even a bed. Ma's grandmother was worried about the family, and she found a thirty-year-old widow whose husband had been drafted as a coolie and then killed. Ma's father and the widow were married at Chinese New Year. Their lives were as full of hardship as before, but they were able to get through somehow, due in part to the food that Ma's grandmother brought them from the village. Beginning the following year, young Ma was sent to his grandmother's home to help with the field work, and at the age of four-teen, he became a sort of apprentice on the railroad. This is what he was doing when Japan was finally defeated. After the Nationalist government collapsed, he worked at a food processing plant, and at the age of twenty-seven, he became plant manager.

Former Nationalist Army Private Liu Sihai, who had been wounded in the back of the neck (see Chapter 10), lay undiscovered deep in the air-raid shelter for perhaps a week. One morning, a light dusting of snow fell. When he peeked out through the shelter entrance, he saw people walking around on the street, so he sneaked into an abandoned house, filled two baskets with cooking utensils and dishes, shouldered them on a pole, and pretended to be a refugee.

About one li *down the road, he found a rundown, empty house, so he took shelter there. He later learned that it belonged to someone named Lin. An old man named Zhang, who lived next door, took pity on Liu and helped him any way he could. After two or three months, it became necessary for resi-dents of this area to obtain residence permits, even though it was outside the city, and to do so, they had to go to Wutaishan, inside the city. Liu was afraid to go alone, so he had Old Zhang go with him. At this time, the Japanese were requiring men who were the right age for military service to take off their shirts and be inspected, and some young men were taken away as a result. Private Liu also came under suspicion, but Old Zhang saved him by insisting, "He's no soldier. He's my son."*

At one point, three Japanese soldiers came to the Lin house and demanded something in Japanese. Liu tried offering a match, but they turned it down. After much gesturing, it became clear that they wanted him to give them his wife. When he said, "She's not here," and pointed in the direction of the city, they appeared to understand. Next, they indicated that they wanted to warm themselves by the fire, so they burned a chair and other furniture. During that time, one of the soldiers noticed the wound on Liu's neck, which was still festering a bit. One of the soldiers pulled at Liu's shirt and said something, but he somehow failed to grasp the implications of the wound.

Lin, the owner of the house, returned home around that time, and Liu earned his living working with him as a vegetable dealer. One day, when he was on his way to the city to sell vegetables, he saw three soldiers with bayonets at the city gate. Trembling with fear, he tried to pass through the gate, but one of the soldiers came running up to him, slapped him across both cheeks, and then slammed him to the ground in a judo throw over the shoulder. He did not understand what was going on, and he wondered whether he would be killed, but the interpreter told him, "You didn't bow, you know." This is when Liu first learned that he was expected to bow to Japanese soldiers.

The morning edition of the *Asahi Shimbun* for December 24 carried not only reports of the assault on Hangzhou but also a photograph titled "Nanjing, Where Peace Has Been Restored," with the further caption "Soldiers of the Imperial Army Distributing Candy to Refugees." On the same page, a headline reading "Self-Government Committee in Nanjing" led off the following article:

> Nanjing, Special Wire, December 23: At 11:00 A.M. on December 23, a mere ten days after its fall, the anti-Japanese capital of Nanjing saw the establishment of the Nanjing Regional Self-Government Committee. The names of the committee members were announced along with the establishment of the committee, and Tao Xisan, chairman of the Red Swastika Society, was nominated as committee chair. Immediately, on the afternoon of the 23d, in accordance with the agreement on Self-Government Committees, the committee members urged consultation and communication with the Self-Government Societies in every region and began their activities with the goal of establishing their new governing body within the year. They held the ceremony marking their initial meeting and the ensuing celebration in the buildings of the former Nationalist government. At present there are still stragglers lurking in the city, but since mopping-up operations are nearing completion, we anticipate that perfect order will be maintained with the cooperation of the Self-Government Committee's police officers and our military police. The sale of daily necessities has resumed in the Chinese parts of the city in the last day or two, thus stimulating the mood of recovery.
>
> Nanjing, Special Wire, December 23: On December 23, the newly established Nanjing Self-Government Committee made the following proclamations:
>
> • We anticipate the establishment of a governing body friendly to Japan.
> • Our goal is to cooperate with the new governing bodies established in every region in order to bring about the construction of true peace in East Asia.
> • We will get rid of anti-Japanese elements and those who resist Japan, and we anticipate the establishment of a new anti-Communist, pro-Japanese central governing body.

Nanjing would thus move to a new system of Japanese military occupation. There were still a huge number of dead bodies inside and outside the city, but as Shen Xiwen indicated, the new year saw fewer incidents in which groups of people were taken away never to be seen again. One of the organizations that undertook the task of burying the untended bodies was the Red Swastika Society mentioned in the newspaper article. Zuo Runde, whose experiences were described in Chapter 10, took part in this society's burial efforts. Here is some more of his story.

During the month he was in the Refugee Zone, Zuo Runde went to Shang-

hai Road every day to get his ration of rice gruel. One day, he heard from one of the men distributing the gruel that someone was looking for laborers. Since he was desperate to take on any available work, he said that he would like to apply.

"Do you have steady nerves?" the other man asked him. "You'd better, because the work involves picking up dead bodies." There would be no wages, but he would receive some uncooked rice and meals for the day, so he gladly signed on.

The burial activities were carried out by teams of three men who wore armbands and rode around in trucks flying the flag of the Red Swastika Society. One team member drove the truck and tallied the number of bodies, while the other two loaded, transported, and unloaded the bodies. Of course, young Zuo was stuck with the latter job. The tools that the team members used were hooked rods, ropes, and shoulder poles.

Upon arriving by truck at a site where there were bodies, they first laid two straw ropes on the ground, dragged a body out with the hooked rods, and laid it on top of the ropes. They tied the ropes around the corpse's chest and hips and then added another rope to tie the first two ropes together. Then they slipped a shoulder pole through the ropes and loaded the body onto the truck. Even though there were many places to bury them all together outside the city walls and in the surrounding communities, Zuo and his fellow workers usually transported the bodies they found either to two "ten thousand–person ditches" just east and west of Taiping Gate or to a "ten thousand–person ditch" on Meihua Mountain.[1]

As part of his duties, he had to search houses and yards, and he found bodies in horrific circumstances. In particular, the bodies of the women were in such bad shape that Zuo literally could not bear to look at them. ("Every time I remember, I start crying and can't talk," he said, and he was silent for a while.) For example, he found one dead woman tied spread-eagled to a bed with a soft drink bottle shoved deeply into her vagina. Since there were no indications of wounds on her body, Zuo guesses that she must have been killed by this kind of torture after an intensive gang rape. He saw both old women and little girls who had been raped and murdered.

About 300 or 400 hundred meters west of the Japanese Embassy (Zuo called it "the Japanese consulate"), which was behind Jinling University, the Japanese troops had had a large hole dug. It was shaped like a pot and was 7 or 8 meters across and 3 or 4 meters deep. One day, when Zuo and his

---

1. The "ten thousand–person ditches" were mass graves. They were especially common in the Manchurian mining districts, where miners who had been worked to death were thrown away like trash. They were also found at massacre sites, such as Pingding Mountain.

**Jiangdongmen (formerly Jiangdongcun), the former site of the "bridge of corpses."
The present bridge was built later.**

*fellow workers were having lunch in the Refugee Zone after a busy morning
of transporting bodies, they saw a large number of young men, numbering
perhaps in the thousands, being marched away in two distinct groups. The
next day someone from the Red Swastika Society told them, "There are bodies in that large pit, and the Japanese troops just threw a little bit of dirt on
top of them, so you should go pick them up." When they went to look, they
found a large number of fresh corpses, just as they had been told. Judging
from the appearance of the bodies, they had been bayoneted or killed with
swords, not shot. Asking around among the Chinese people in the area, they
learned that these were the victims of a massacre that had occurred on the
previous day, perhaps some of the same young men that Zuo had seen being
led away while he was eating his lunch.*

*However, the largest number of corpses that Zuo saw at once was in the
canal in Jiangdongcun (now Jiangdongmen), in the western suburbs outside
Shuixi Gate. It was the end of February. The 4- or 5-meter-wide bridge span-
ning the canal had been destroyed by the Nationalists before the fall of Nanjing. Swollen bodies had been thrown into the river at the place where the
bridge had been. Zuo guesses that they numbered in the tens of thousands, or
else they could not have made such a huge pile. Boards and doors had been
laid over the bodies, and they had become the foundations of a "corpse
bridge" that cars drove over. Zuo and his companions were dumbstruck with*

Zhonghua Gate, taken from outside the city walls. (Photographed December 23, 1983.)

horror at this incredible sight. Some time later, the bridge was rebuilt and named Zhongdao Bridge.[2]

There were also a lot of bodies outside Zhonghua Gate. In March, Zhousao Lane, which crossed the river and ran eastward, was so covered with bodies that one could hardly see the surface of the road, and Zuo's team cleaned it up in cooperation with other burial teams. They then went to Yuhuatai, to a pond that was below and slightly to the east of the present-day site of the memorial plaque. It was not particularly wide, perhaps only 20 meters in diameter, but it was very deep. Here, too, they found thousands of bodies, most of them Chinese soldiers. These bodies were buried on a hillside south of Putuo Temple.

---

2. This is connected with the fact that the 16th Division (Commander Nakajima's division) remained behind as an occupying force after the fall of Nanjing. There are several accounts of the "corpse bridge," although the stories differ from one another slightly. The testimony of Sun Dianyan, who lived near the bridge, was presented in the March 30, 1984, evening edition of *Asahi Shimbun*. In *Testimony: The Great Nanjing Massacre* (fn. p. 310), we read, "We approached the Zhongdao Bridge, which had been constructed on top of corpses. All these bodies were supposed to have been the nearly ten thousand prisoners of war (although about half of them were ordinary citizens) confined in the Nationalist Chinese Infantry Prison."

Furthermore, the same book says that Zhongdao Bridge was the name of the "corpse bridge" itself, but a Chinese journalist in Nanjing says that it is merely the name of the bridge that was built in that spot later.

Zhonghua Gate is made up of a series of free-standing walls. (Photographed December 23, 1983.)

Places with large numbers of bodies all together were taken care of with the cooperation of several burial teams, but places with fewer bodies were handled by only one or two teams. The laborers who dug the graves were organized separately from the three-person burial teams. Since Zuo was only a temporary worker, he does not know how many trucks were deployed, but his impression was that there were forty or fifty. Almost all the trucks were broken-down wrecks, some of them belonging to individuals and others belonging to organizations.

After taking care of the bodies at Yuhuatai, they continued farther east to Guanghua Gate, where they encountered another burial team coming from the opposite direction. Around that time, the beginning of April, the activities of Zuo's burial team came to an end. The burials that Zuo took part in were thus concentrated mainly in the southern and western parts of the city, and he did not see what happened in the north and east.

In addition to the Red Swastika Society and other charitable organizations, Nanjing's Muslims also organized their own burial squads. Shen Xiwen, whom we met in the previous chapter, went all over the area as a member of one of these squads. Here is some more of his story.

After the residence permits were issued, the streets of Nanjing became comparatively peaceful. By March, order had been more or less restored, and the refugees were able to go out shopping and to run errands. Occasionally, Shen's parents also came to Jinling University from the house near Doucai Bridge, bringing food. His father told of having gone to their old home near Ji'exiang, only to find it pillaged, with just the tables and chairs remaining. He also found out that Chen, the guard who had stayed behind at the Qingzhen Mosque, had been shot to death for trying to flee when the Japanese came. Shen's father was especially grieved over the death of Chen, his close friend for decades, and he cried when he told his wife the news.

It was about this time that the Muslim burial squads were organized[3] with the purpose of burying the bodies of Muslim victims of the Japanese with proper formality and reverence. Before the war, there had been about forty thousand Muslims in Nanjing, but since many had either evacuated to the rural areas or been killed, the population was sharply reduced. There was no way of finding the Muslims who had been taken away and massacred as part of larger groups, so the burial squads limited their activities to finding bodies that could somehow be identified as Muslim. The family members of most of these had already covered the bodies with cloth, thrown a bit of dirt on top so that the cloth would not be blown away by the wind, and placed an identifying marker on top of that. Most of the Muslims killed near the mosques throughout the city had been killed in connection with rapes. Since the Japanese would rape any female, regardless of age, many family members and imams and other mosque officials were killed trying to prevent these rapes.

The Muslim burial squad consisted of ten or more people. Since it was dangerous to operate alone, they went about in groups of four, supplied with boards and shovels and wearing armbands issued by the so-called Society for the Maintenance of Order.[4] They transported the bodies to the several cemeteries near the Refugee Zone that were used by the Muslims. Almost all the bodies had been either bayoneted, slashed or beheaded with swords, or shot.

---

3. The details of the establishment of the Muslim burial squads are described on page 72 of *Testimony: The Great Nanjing Massacre* (published by the Nanjing City Historical Materials Research Society and translated by Kagami Mitsuyuki and Himeda Mitsuyoshi, published by Aoki Shoten).

4. The Society for the Maintenance of Order was set up as a collaborative organization under the Japanese occupation. Those who cooperated with the Japanese were reviled as *hanjian*, "traitors to the Chinese people."

南京市悼念在侵华日军南京大屠杀中遇难同胞50周年仪
侵华日军南京大屠杀遇难同胞纪念馆

The city of Nanjing completed the Massacre Memorial Hall in 1985, and on December 13, 1987, a ceremony was held in the hall to commemorate the fiftieth anniversary of the massacre. The banners seen here were hung for that occasion.

Shen and the other members of the burial squad spent about a month between March and April looking for Muslim victims and burying them, but since they buried only those who could definitely identified as Muslims, the total number buried was only a little over a hundred. Their organization and activities were completely unrelated to those of the Red Swastika Society, the Red Cross, and the Chongshantang, the three organizations that cleaned up after the large-scale massacres. However, in the process of walking around in search of Muslims, they saw bodies resulting from large-scale massacres in various parts of the city. All of them were in places that had been designated as off-limits to civilians, so most people would have been unable to see them.

One example was at the foot of Jiuhua Mountain. Near the present-day site of the city gas works, they saw a semicircular pit, about 15 meters wide and 24 meters long, that seemed to surround the hill. Shen does not know how deep the pit was, but it was packed tightly with bodies. Most of them were either headless or missing some limbs, and since they had begun to decompose, the odor was overpowering. Shen is sure that these bodies numbered not in the hundreds, but in the thousands. The site was later cleaned up by some other organization, with most of the bodies being hauled away, although some were buried on the spot.

Another example was Wulong Pool in Tongchouli near Hanzhong Gate. At that time it was 20 meters by 30 meters, although it is now smaller and part of a park. This pool was completely filled with piles of bodies, and although there was almost no water, the bodies looked as if they had been pickled in some sort of red liquid. These bodies, too, were moved elsewhere by some organization, but a small number of them may have remained at the bottom of the pool.

Still another was the river at Jiangdongmen[5] outside of Shuixi Gate. This was such a huge number that Shen had no idea how many thousands there were, but according to the people in the area, most of bodies had already been taken away, and these were the remnants. Afterward, he saw another organization disposing of this mountain of bodies, a very small number of which were buried nearby.

Yet another place was along the banks of the Yangtze near Yizhang Gate. Here, too, an immense heap of bodies had lain along the river—or rather, had been piled up—for a long time. This particular massacre site was connected with one of Shen's personal experiences.

It was on December 16 that Shen fled with his family from the refuge at Number 28, Doucai Bridge, to Jinling University, and the events in question probably took place on the previous day, December 15. The three-story house where the Shen family was staying was several dozen meters up an alley that intersected Shanghai Road. At that point, although no actual Japanese troops had shown up near Doucai Bridge, they had already invaded the Refugee Zone in search of Nationalist army stragglers. At perhaps ten or eleven in the morning, Shen saw a large group walking along Shanghai Road. He and his family were on the second floor at the time, but they went up to the dormer in the third-floor attic, where they could get a good view looking down the alley to Shanghai Road.

The crowd on Shanghai Road was immense. Nowadays, this area is full of tall buildings, and the lines of sight are different, but at that time, there were hardly any tall buildings, and Shen had a long, if broken, view of Shanghai Road. The crowd stretched from the area of Mochou Road all the way to the area of Shanxi Road. It covered the whole street, leaving barely enough space on either side for one person to pass by, and in these spaces, Japanese soldiers walked along about 10 meters apart.

The crowd was made up entirely of men, most of them young. Almost all of them wore civilian clothes, but Shen thinks that some of them may have been Nationalist army soldiers who had changed into plain clothes. Every once in

---

5. The suffix *-men* typically refers to a gate, in this case, it is simply part of the place name. At that time it was called Jiangdongcun, and at present, it is part of Jiangdong Township. The large number of bodies that Shen saw here were apparently those in the "corpse bridge."

a while, another youth was rounded up and added to the procession. Shen, who was only thirty years old, realized that Japanese troops in search of stragglers might come to the house at Doucai Bridge, so he watched the goings-on for no more than five minutes, returned to the second floor, and hid under a bed. His family sat on the floor in front of the bed so that the Japanese soldiers would not see him if they happened to come in. Occasionally, he heard gunfire. He later learned that the Japanese had shot or bayoneted everyone who tried to escape.

Shen himself never actually saw what happened to the crowd, but he heard the whole story from an acquaintance of his, a thirty-year-old man named Chen, who managed a miraculous escape from the massacre. Chen had lived near Shen at number 23 Ji'e Bridge, and he had earned his living working in a soy sauce shop, but he had at first fled to Doucai Bridge, just as the Shen family had. According to Chen's account, the men were taken up from Yijiang Gate to the banks of the Yangtze, where they were raked with machine-gun fire until no one was left standing. Chen threw himself down directly after the gunfire started, and other bodies fell on top of him, so he played dead until dark and then slipped away. Shen told me that Chen was now dead, but he was not the only person to have survived that massacre. He thought that there might be other survivors and said that he would let me know if he was able to find any.

One day, during the time he was involved with the burial squad, he and two other squad members were on their way home after finishing the day's activities. As they passed by Yixin Bridge, they were summoned over by a Japanese soldier. He already had ten or more Chinese captives standing off to one side. Shen tried to show the soldier his burial squad armband, but he was ignored. All the men were taken directly to a large house with spacious rooms where some Japanese troops were billeted. As soon as they went inside, they were ordered to work at various household chores: washing dishes, polishing windows, cooking rice.

During that time, one of the Chinese was thought to be "slacking off" or "showing a defiant attitude." He was called outside and summarily bayoneted to death by the gate. At that, Shen and the others feared that they, too, might be killed afterward, but they also thought that if they worked hard and behaved themselves, they would probably be released in the evening, so everyone worked diligently, whether on laundry or housecleaning.

As it grew dark, the Japanese had fewer orders to give them, so Shen and the others knelt down in front of the "devils" and pleaded, "Your Excellencies, we have elderly parents and infant children waiting for us. Please find it within yourselves to let us go home."

One of the soldiers smiled slightly, handed each of the men a steamed bun, gave them pieces of paper to use as passes, and released them.

The figure "300,000 victims" is written at the entrance to the Nanjing Massacre Memorial Hall. (Photographed December 23, 1987.)[6]

It is commonly believed in Nanjing that a total of three hundred thousand prisoners of war and civilians were slaughtered by the Japanese troops. On December 3, 1983, the city of Nanjing dedicated a memorial plaque to commemorate the forty-sixth anniversary of the Nanjing Massacre, and Mayor Zhang Juhua used the phrase "our more than three hundred thousand compatriots who suffered" in his speech. However, when I asked Shen for his views on the widely quoted number, he replied, "My impression is that three hundred thousand is too small a number. I think there were more victims than that."[7]

Monks from Japan also joined in the efforts to dispose of the bodies. The North China edition of the *Osaka Asahi Shimbun* for April 16, 1938, carried a report written by special correspondent Hayashida, titled "News

---

6. There are some problems with the way exhibits are displayed at the Massacre Memorial Hall. One is the way the rows of skeletons are arranged. They do not look as if they are lying on the surface of the ground where they were discovered. Instead, they look as if they were dug up and then laid out on artificial (?) earth. Inevitably, they look as if they were brought in from somewhere else. The museum staff should have taken a cue from the displays at the sites of the mass graves in Manchuria. Furthermore, the photographs on display include many that cannot be clearly identified as being connected with Nanjing (or with the assault on Nanjing).

7. See page 285 for more detailed information concerning casualty estimates.

from Nanjing, Part 5: Sanitation." Here is what it said about the mass burial.[8]

> After the fighting was over, we first had to take care of the bodies of the enemy. Countless tens of thousands of them filled the ditches and are piled up along streams and rivers, and just leaving them there is harmful in many ways, not only to public health but also to the people's morale. . . . Thus the Red Swastika Society, the Self-Government Committee, and our own monks from Sanmyōhōji have joined forces to begin cleaning up the bodies. They load the decayed bodies onto trucks while reciting prayers and take them to designated places for burial, but this requires a considerable expenditure of money and manpower. The work continues from day to day amid the offensive stench of death, and the most recent figures list 1,793 bodies within the city and 30,311 outside the city. There have been about 11,000 yen[9] in expenses. The labor is continuing, with fifty or sixty thousand [sic] people at work, but since a considerable number of bodies remain outside the city around the mountains, the plans are to spend an additional 8,000 yen and finish disposing of them by midsummer.

The Red Swastika Society was active in disposing of the bodies, but the Chongshantang took over the main role in the early spring. One of the people who joined in this effort was Cui Jingui, whose account of an "ordinary rape" was featured in Chapter 9. Here is more of Cui's story.

Cui realized that being in the Refugee Zone would not spare him and his family from the danger of rapes and massacres, and so the next day, on December 15, they fled to a nearby arsenal, because it flew the American flag and therefore seemed safer. However, shortly after noon, a large number of Japanese soldiers showed up, forced several hundred young men outside, assembled them in a vacant lot, made them sit, and prepared to kill them with machine guns. Just then, an American drove up in a car. After he negotiated with the Japanese for a while, the men whose family members could point them out—"That's my husband" or "That's my older brother"— were released. This is how Cui was saved. The other men, however, were led away somewhere.

Since the family did not have any food, Cui went with his cousin Jin Xiaofu to get some at the place where his parents had fled, but on the way there, they were captured by the Japanese. For some unknown reason, the soldiers then and there cut a strip of cloth, wrote "Employee of the Higo Squad, Nakajima Unit" on it, and wrapped it around Cui's arm. The men picked up were assembled in the Central Marketplace (now known as the People's Marketplace) at Guanjia Bridge and then marched off in the direction of Zhonghua

---

8. Hora, Tomio, *The Japan-China War: Collected Materials about the Great Nanjing Massacre* (Aoki Shoten), vol. 1, p. 393.

9. For decades, the yen has been worth either a little more or little less than one U.S.

Gate, past countless burned-out ruins. The procession, consisting of several thousand men, stretched from the Central Marketplace to the crossroads with Yangpi Lane.

The Qinhuai River, which flows around the outer edge of Zhonghua Gate, is about 100 meters wide, but the width of the water actually flowing in it was only 30 or 40 meters. Since the bridge had been destroyed, a temporary bridge had been improvised out of cupboards and other furniture, and because of that, objects floating in the water were unable to pass through. The length of the bridge was thus clogged with 2 or 3 meters of bodies.

The procession had left the Central Marketplace at eleven o'clock in the morning, and they walked without any

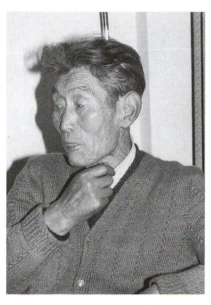

Cui Jingui showing the scar from when he was first stabbed in the neck.

rest. It was already sunset, about six in the evening, when they arrived at Jiangningzhen, a few dozen kilometers from the city. When they begged the Japanese soldiers to be allowed to go home because it was so late, the soldiers were unexpectedly willing to give them permission. Yet, because it was dark, Cui and Jin Xiaofu sat up all night on the embankment of a rice paddy.

The next morning, December 17, they joined six other people and began walking in the direction of Nanjing. When they came to a Japanese encampment at Youfang Bridge in the village of Xishanqiao, they were once again detained and taken to a small house. Here, they were told to undo the fasteners of their long padded jackets and taken back outside one by one. Cui was the fourth. As soon as he arrived at the edge of the river, he was bayoneted in the neck from the front, leaving a cut on the right side of his neck that fortunately bypassed all vital organs. He fell forward, whereupon he was again bayoneted from behind. The blade entered his head just behind his left ear. This is when he lost consciousness.

When he regained consciousness, it was around midnight and so dark that he could not even see the moon. Another man lay motionless next to him.

---

cent, but before and during World War II, it was worth several hundred times as much, so while 11,000 yen is now the price of one night in a moderately luxurious hotel, it was a substantial amount of money in 1938.—Trans.

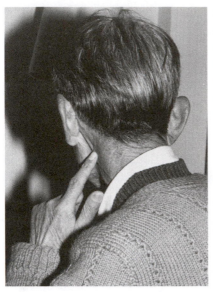

The scar from the wound Ciu Jingui received when he was stabbed a second time after falling over.

Some distance away, some Japanese soldiers were building a bonfire. Finally, it grew cold, and the soldiers went inside, so Cui crawled and rolled to the water's edge. The water came only up to his thighs, so, reeling from his wounds, he crossed the river.

He fled without any idea of the direction, and at dawn on December 16, he came to a house and knocked on the door, but no one would answer. A little farther on, he met an old woman who took him into her house and fed him a little thin rice gruel. Recovering his strength a little bit, he tore off a part of his jacket and made a cord to hold up his pants.

After being given directions, Cui set out for Nanjing, only to meet more Japanese soldiers at Maogongdu. They assumed that he was a Nationalist army straggler, and he was made to kneel in order to be beheaded. Fortunately, the Chinese interpreter showed up and said, "This man is an ordinary peasant. His collar is different from that of a soldier." The Japanese released him.

After passing through Saihongqiao and seeing many bodies along the way, he arrived at Nanjing. Just after he had entered the city by Shuixi Gate, he collapsed and lost consciousness, both from the effects of his wounds and because of relief at reaching his goal. When he awoke, he was in Shuangshigu. Miraculously, an acquaintance had come by and rescued him. That night, his father came and took him back to Guangjia Bridge. The area around there was nearly deserted, the inhabitants having fled to the Refugee Zone. Since there was no doctor available, they made a paste from burnt cotton ashes and oil. The bayonet had pierced his esophagus, so when he ate gruel, some of it came spilling out of the wound.

It was three months before Cui could be up and around. (His wife, sisters, and female cousins remained in the arsenal in the International Refugee Zone the whole time.) After a discussion with his father, he decided that they should go to the Refugee Zone, too. Everywhere they looked on the streets they saw signs reading "Anmin gaoshi" (Advance notice to the people), and posters bearing a photograph of a Japanese soldier holding a Chinese child who was carrying a Rising Sun flag. The posters were titled "Sino-Japanese Co-prosperity."

However, once they reached the Refugee Zone, they found that life there was difficult due to food shortages. A lot of refugees were still there, but Cui and his family decided to return to their original home on Hongwu Road.

At about this time, Tao Xisan created the Great People's Society, a sham self-governing body, and organized three charitable institutions, the Chongshantang, the Tongshantong, and the Tongrentang.[10] Cui, who was unemployed and desperate, joined up with the Chongshantang and ended up disposing of bodies. Each of the six burial teams consisted of ten people. Cui's "work uniform," which was a sleeveless vest, was stamped with the character chong (reverence) on the front and back, and the flag of the Chongshantang flew at the worksites.

The first day, they went to the riverbank outside Hanzhong Gate to take care of an immense mountain of bodies. He could not tell whether they had been burned to death or whether they had been set on fire after being killed, but almost all of them were charred. In most cases, it was impossible to identify their clothing, and the limbs of several of them were scattered about.[11] The team transported the bodies to a vacant lot, divided them into four piles, and threw dirt over them, creating burial mounds instead of laying them in pits.

However, even that first day's work left Cui physically and emotionally exhausted. When he pleaded that the work was impossible for him because his wounds had not completely healed, his supervisor offered to switch him to different work. He was transferred to the Jinhua Soy Sauce Factory (now the Nanjing Number Two Pharmaceutical Plant), located in Erdaogengzi, outside the city near Hanzhong Gate.

But this was not easy work either. Inside the factory were four or five huge, metal soy sauce brewing vats, each 6 to 7 meters wide and 4 meters high, and every one of them was filled to the brim with bodies. Most of the bodies were upside down in the vats, with their feet in the air, and they needed to be transported to the burial grounds. The vats were equipped with ramplike, slanting ladders, and two workers climbed these ladders to carry one body

---

10. The Great People's Society (*Daminhui*) was a puppet nongovernmental organizations corresponding to the puppet administrations, the so-called Societies to Maintain Order, set up by the Japanese military. "Great People's Society" was the name used in Nanjing, and in northern China, they were called "New People's Societies." There were approximately ten charitable organizations, all referred to as some sort of *-tang,* and the Chongshantang, the Tongshantang, and the Tongrentang seem to be the ones founded by the Great People's Society. (This is according to Inoue Hisashi.)

11. It is possible that this was the site of the massacre that Wu Changde, a witness at the Tokyo War Crimes Tribunal, survived.

White patch

Dark blue cloth

1. The metal vat where the bodies were stuffed
2. 6–7 meters
3. Slanting ladder
4. About 4 meters
5. Bunghole for soy sauce
6. The Chongshantang uniform
7. White patch
8. Dark blue cloth

at a time up and over the side. The bodies at the very bottoms of the vats were dragged up with fire hooks. Next to these large vats were about a hundred smaller bowl-shaped vats, each 1 meter deep and 1 meter across. There had also been bodies in these, but by the time Cui went to the factory, most of these had already been hauled away, and there were only a few left. Cui did not notice whether there was anyone counting and keeping track of the bodies.

He found himself unable to tolerate not only the hard labor of hauling bodies but also the strong stench of the death, the putrefaction, and the dirt. After only one day, he quit this job, too. Since the wage was 1 yuan per day, Cui received only 2 yuan for these two days of work.

In the meantime, Cui decided to lay in a stock of rice so that he could go into business for himself selling food. When he went to see if any rice had come into Xiaguan, he found that the railroad station had been burned, but someone he met there happened to tell him that there was supposed to be a shipment of rice arriving from Liuhe at Baota Bridge. Accordingly, he walked along the Yangtze to Baota Bridge, seeing masses of bodies on the way at Meitan Harbor. There was no rice at Baota Bridge, either, but along the river behind a meat processing plant was yet another immense heap of bodies. It was already March, the bodies had begun to decompose, and the stench followed Cui for nearly a kilometer. On the way home, he encountered four Japanese checkpoints, and at each one, he was forced to remove his cap and bow.

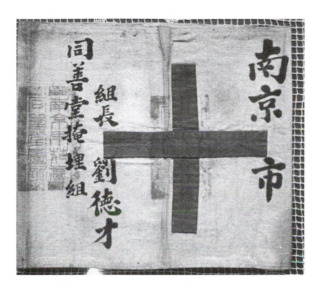

The Chongshantang, one of the organizations formed by the puppet government, also evidently organized a burial squad. (Photograph supplied by the Historical Materials Editorial Department of the Second Historical Archives of China in Nanjing.)

Here is an example of the kinds of articles we see when we look at the Japanese newspapers' coverage of Nanjing during that period. This is taken from the *Asahi Shimbun* for April 8, 1938:

NANJING'S RESURGENCE OF ACTIVITY

Nanjing, April 7, Dōmei: Since the birth of the restored government of the Republic of China, the number of refugees returning to Nanjing has risen to three or four thousand per day, and the population has suddenly jumped to four hundred thousand.

On the other hand, public facilities are gradually being restored in every area of the city. Repairs to the Xiaguan electrical generating plant, which has a power output of 30,000 kilowatts, have already been completed, and power is being supplied: points of electric light sparkle not only within the city walls but also in some places outside the city walls. Water is now being supplied to the entire city under the army's direct control, and before long, as more companies go back into operation, the economy will be completely functional. The Yangtze River Flour Mill is expected to begin operations as a joint venture, and its estimated output is four thousand bags per day, so this will solve part of Nanjing's food problems.

Since the twenty-fifth of last month, postal service has been established not only at the main administrative office, but also at five branch offices within the city. The telegraph system is already in service under the management of the Japan Radio Company, Ltd., and the telephones are being used provisionally by the military, although soon both Japanese and Chinese businesses and individuals will be able to subscribe, so we will have full-scale facilities. The city's recovery is truly remarkable.

This is how things were in the war-torn regions, particularly Nanjing, as they faced seven more years of Japanese occupation. These conditions may have seemed like "stability" compared to the period of the Nanjing offensive, but the life of the Chinese people under the control of a foreign military was far from "stable." Often, not only the perpetrators of anti-Japanese or antimilitary actions but uninvolved people as well were subject to retaliatory execution.

One large-scale example of an atrocity occurring after the fall of Nanjing was the massacre of the inhabitants of Mashan, one of the islands in Taihu Lake.[12] On March 12, the islanders, who had supplied Nationalist Chinese troops hidden in the highest part of the island with food and had cooperated with them until their retreat, were surrounded by Japanese troops. They were subjected to the threefold strategy of, "Kill all, burn all, loot all." About 1,500 people were killed, of whom 999 were native islanders. The rest were refugees from Wuxi and fishermen from other villages. One-fourth of the island's population of four thousand was slaughtered, and the others survived only because they fled to the mountainside and were not found. Everyone who was found was killed, including infants and old people. Eighty entire households were wiped out, and more than 3,000 *jian* worth of buildings were burned.

It often happened that one or two Japanese soldiers ventured into a village to hunt down women or to do a little looting, and there they fell into the hands of either guerillas or villagers exacting revenge for the invasion. Japanese troops would then pile into the area looking for the missing soldiers. As vengeance, they would burn the village and kill all the inhabitants.

The following events occurred in a peasant village just outside Jurong, about a month after the massacre on Mashan Island.

A company of Japanese soldiers was staying near Baiyang, a peasant village just southeast of Jurong. On April 22, 1938, five soldiers came to the village, where they abducted and raped a fourteen-year-old girl. Enraged, the more hot-blooded villagers tried to exact revenge, using their farm implements as weapons. Two soldiers who had wandered off from the main company were attacked and assassinated. Another was killed at Zhuxiang village, about 3 or 4 kilometers from Baiyang.

The Japanese began searching for the three soldiers who had disappeared.

---

12. After the war, the area between the island and the shore was filled in and turned into agricultural land. The island, therefore, became a peninsula.

Cai Dekun.

The bodies of the two who had been killed at Baiyang were found quickly, but the body of the third man remained undiscovered.

Another Japanese company was staying near Hetang village, 2 or 3 kilometers beyond Zhuxiang. One of the residents of Hetang, Cai Dekun (72), was then a twenty-six-year-old peasant living near the west edge of the village with his widowed mother, older brother and sister-in-law, and two younger brothers. There had recently been an incident on the eastern edge of the village, in which two soldiers had broken into the home of a peasant couple in their mid-twenties and raped the wife.

Cai told me about these incidents as background material, although he did not witness them himself. His own experiences began on April 24, two days after the three soldiers were killed.

It had been raining on and off all morning when two hundred Japanese troops came to Hetang. Thirty families fled in panic at the first report that the Japanese were headed their way, so only twenty-four people were left when the soldiers surrounded the village. Even they were hoping to find some opportunity to run away, but once it became clear that this would be impossible, Cai went to meet the Japanese along with two old men named Yuan and Chen, carrying a white flag. Their intention was to plea with the Japanese not to burn their houses.

However, as the three were on their way to meet the Japanese, a man named Zhu, whose house stood alone at the edge of the village, tried to break through the ring of soldiers and was shot dead. The three were shocked to see this, and Yuan said, "We'd better not run away." Despite this, they were arrested as soon as they reached the Japanese position. Since the twenty or so remaining villagers could not see exactly what was going on, they evidently assumed that Cai and the others were in the midst of negotiating with the Japanese to have their houses spared. They left their homes and began moving in a group toward where the three men were being detained. The Japanese arrested these twenty people as well, tied their hands behind their backs, and bound them together in pairs. Cai was tied up with a young man named Xiaolong.

The twenty-three residents of Hetang were taken to the foot of a hill called Machang, about 7 li to the south. On the way there, a man with a sword, who

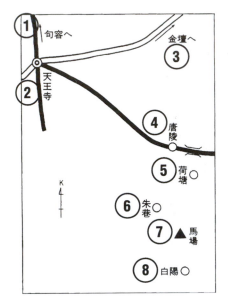

1. To Jurong
2. Tianwang Temple
3. To Jintan
4. Tangling

5. Hetang
6. Zhuxiang
7. Machang
8. Baiyang

seemed to be the company commander, asked in broken Chinese whether there was anyone who could read. When an old man volunteered, the soldier wrote out the following message in the ideographic characters common to China and Japan: "One of the Eastern masters is missing. Do you know where he is? He disappeared at Hetang." They were asking about the third missing soldier, the one whose body had not been found.

The old man conveyed the message to the other twenty-two villagers, but none of them knew anything. In fact, the news of Japanese soldiers being killed had not yet reached the village, and Cai himself had no reason to know about it.

At one of the small settlements along the way, they came upon a shed containing a single piglet. The soldiers decided to rest here, and they ordered Cai and Xiaolong to catch the piglet. The piglet was quick and nimble, and they could not catch it, so finally, a soldier shot it with a rifle and made Cai and Xiaolong carry the carcass to one of the eight trucks that had come along with them. During this time, the ropes that bound them together had naturally loosened and become undone, but even though the Japanese noticed this, they did not do anything about it. After all, Cai and Xiaolong were in no position to run away.

Shortly afterward, they saw the headless bodies of four Chinese lined up by the side of the road. All four bodies were sitting up with their legs sticking straight up and their heads in their laps. They had probably been beheaded to set an example.

When the prisoners arrived at Machang, they found that other Chinese people had also been brought there, about seventy of them all together. Almost all of them were from Baiyang, but some of them were from Zhuxiang and other nearby communities. Cai thinks that there may have been about five hundred Japanese soldiers as well, including some from Baiyang. He noticed that there was a machine gun set up by the stream with a cover thrown over it, but at this point, he had no idea that there would be a massacre, since he had not yet heard about the Japanese soldiers being killed. The people from Baiyang, however, had figured out what was going on. Unlike him, they knew that there was more than one machine gun.

Fearing retaliation, some villagers from Zhuxiang had reported that the missing soldier was buried in a shallow, muddy grave near their village. The recovered body was washed, dressed in a new uniform, and placed on the ground in front of the crowd of Chinese, after which the villagers from Baiyang were made to kneel in front of it as a sign of remorse. This is how Cai first learned that Japanese soldiers had been killed and how the soldiers who had brought the people from Hetang first learned that their missing comrade had been found.

Once he understood the significance of the soldier being killed, Cai realized all too late, "We'll be slaughtered for sure." The seventy villagers were lined up in three rows with their backs to the hill. Cai was in the center of the front row, and Xiaolong was almost directly behind him.

"Sit down!" the Japanese soldiers ordered.

Assuming that the firing would begin as soon as everyone sat down, Cai remained standing, covering his head with his arms and looking around.

Then he heard another order. "Si le!" (Evidently whoever gave the order thought this phrase meant "kill," though it really means "dead.") Sensing that they were facing the moment of death, the people began to cry and weep as if with one voice. All of a sudden, Xiaolong burst out of the line-up and took off in the direction of Machang Hill. He was immediately felled by a rifle shot.

Cai was also itching to find an opportunity to slip away, but the soldiers kept ordering everyone to sit. Just as he was about to sit, he heard a whistle, and suddenly the roar of machine guns and rifles joined the noise of the people's cries.

Cai himself does not remember exactly what happened then, but he knows that the machine guns and rifles were lined up facing the people and were aimed in the direction of the hill. Although the bullets missed him, he fell backward into a hollow place in the hillside, and not only did he land on top of a body but other people's bodies landed on top of him, including that of his father's older brother. His uncle had taken a bullet in the head, and blood bubbled out of the wound, dripping on top of Cai. Although Cai's uncle was still breathing, he did not say anything. Cai could hear the cries of people who had been hit but were not quite dead, and he was aware of the soldiers following the sounds of their voices so that they could stab them with bayonets.

He warily breathed as quietly and inconspicuously as possible until the cries of the wounded had stopped and everyone seemed to be dead. Then he heard one of the Japanese shout an order, which he assumes was "Fall in." Soon he could tell that the Japanese were leaving.

He could no longer hear his uncle breathing. Carefully, he slipped out from under the body and looked up at the sky. The sun was about to set, and its reddish light made the corpse-strewn slope stand out in sharp relief. Off in the distance, he could see the backs of the Japanese soldiers marching in the direction of Zhuxiang.

As he stood up, he saw that he was covered with other people's blood and even some bits of brain tissue. Just then, he heard a man's anguished voice calling to him from the edge of the crowd. The other survivor turned out to be Cai Dekun's cousin, Cai Deming. Gasping for breath, he explained, "I wasn't shot, but they bayoneted me three times." He was on the verge of losing consciousness, but he urged Cai Dekun to get away quickly.

Cai helped his cousin get up and supported him on his shoulder as they set out for home. However, his cousin was not very strong to begin with, and they were both shaking with fear, so that they kept stumbling and getting up and then stumbling again. They could not make any progress this way, and it was growing darker, so Cai felt that he had no option but to abandon his cousin and continue on alone.

Arriving at his home in Hetang in the dark of night, Cai threw his blood- and brain-spattered jacket into a pond, changed clothes, and ran off to the home of an acquaintance named Liu Guifan, who lived in an isolated house 5 li to the east. His neighbors, who had run off before the Japanese surrounded Hetang, had also fled in this same direction, and in effect, he was following them. The road was dark, and he was weak with terror, so he fell several times along the way, but he made it to Liu Guifan's house and spent the night there. The next morning, he left before dawn and headed over the hills to Wuxu, a village near Mao Mountain, where he had relatives. He hid there for two or three days until the excitement had died down and then returned home to Hetang.

His wounded cousin, Cai Deming, whom he had abandoned on the road, managed to crawl home in two or three days. Thanks to the ministrations of an herbal doctor, he recovered, but he died from an unrelated illness about three years later.

On March 24, about a month before the massacre at Machang, the Japanese government created *The Outline for Coordinating Relations between the Political Entities of Northern and Central China.* The idea behind it was to take the puppet government that they had already established in Beiping (Beijing), the so-called Provisional Government of the Republic of China, and coordinate it with their similarly constituted puppet government in Nanjing, the "Restored Government of the Republic of China." Their future aim was to combine the two regimes to establish a puppet central government at Beijing as one link in their "New East Asian Order."

Four days later, the ceremony marking the founding of the "Restored Government of the Republic of China" was held in Nanjing. The following excerpt from the concluding chapter of *The China Incident Army Campaign,* Vol. 1, published by the War History Office of the National Defense Research Institute of the National Defense Agency, conveys some of the attitudes of those times:

> The ceremony marking the establishment of the Restored Government of the Republic of China was held on March 28 in the ruins of the former Nationalist government's Great Ceremonial Hall under the five-colored flag. This government's aims included cooperation among Japan, Manchuria, and China and rejection of the Communist Party. They saw their mission as a restoration of their sovereignty to prewar conditions, stabilization of the people's morale, the raising of the people's standards of living, and the reappearance of peace in East Asia. The areas where this government held sovereignty at the time were the provinces of Jiangsu, Zhejiang, and Anhui, along with the special cities of Shanghai and Nanjing. They were determined to press toward the construction of a reborn China, and they dreamed of extending it to the areas of central and southern China where Chiang Kai-shek still held power.
>
> The Restored Government first carried out its functions from the Shanghai New Asia Hotel, but because of the vastness of the territory under its jurisdiction, the ministries and departments moved to Nanjing on June 22. However, since Shanghai was the center of commerce and foreign relations, some of the government functions set up [branch offices] in Shanghai, and the leaders had to travel back and forth between the two cities.
>
> The provincial governments were established later. The Jiangsu Provincial Government was set up in Suzhou on May 23, the Zhejiang Provincial Government was set up in Hangzhou on June 20, the Nanjing City Government Office was set up on April 24, the Shanghai City Government Office was set up on April 28, and finally the Anhui Provincial Government on July 24. Essential persons, from provincial governors on down, were appointed, and the preparations were made for setting up a government bit by bit.

The "Restored Government" thus constituted was seeded with Japanese advisers in every institution from top to bottom:

> The administrative institutions were set up so that they could not enforce anything without the consent of these advisers. The top administrators of the committees, departments, provinces, counties, and cities could carry their governmental duties only after consulting with the advisers and achieving their complete consent. (Shirai Katsumi, *The Japan-China War,* Chūkō Shinsho)

A report of Chinese resistance to the invasion. (*Asahi Shimbun*, December 25, 1937.)

Even after losing the fight for Nanjing and being driven to reestablish his capital inland, Chiang Kai-shek never completely surrendered. In pursuing Chiang first to Xuzhou and then to Hankou and beyond, the Japanese army overextended itself as the war spread into the vast Asian continent. But the decisive counterattack came from the Eighth Route Army and the New Fourth Army of Mao's People's Liberation Army.

In the end, the Japanese people shifted their attention from China to the United States, but even if the war had never expanded into the larger Pacific, Japan's defeat in China was certain.

I would like to leave you with the thoughts of Wu Changde, the man who miraculously escaped from one of the massacres described in Chapter 10 and lived to testify at the Tokyo War Crimes Trials:

> When I appeared before the International Tribunal, my attitude was different from what it is now. I wanted us Chinese people to get back everything that we had lost. By this I mean property, of course, but I also wanted to pay back the Japanese for the immense number of Chinese people who died during the invasion, or for those like me, who were badly injured. As one who had suffered a wrong, I wanted the ones who had inflicted the wrongs to undergo the same suffering that we had, or, in other words, I wanted them to pay for blood with blood.
>
> However, it's different now. My thinking changed after the Nationalists were defeated in the Revolution. (At this point, Wu lost control of his emotions for the first time, and tears began to roll down his cheeks.) The real cause of the suffering inflicted on the Chinese people was not the Japanese people themselves. It was the idea of Japanese imperialism that instigated the invasion and spurred the Japanese people on. Since equal numbers of Chinese and

Japanese people died in the war, we can't say that the Japanese were unscathed. In fact, imperialism was completely counterproductive for them. I learned this from the Communist Party under the leadership of Chairman Mao. We have to join hands with the Japanese people and fight imperialism. I am someone who saw and experienced the calamities that imperialism inflicted on us and our country from the time I was young, and I want to tell my experiences to future generations. We have to not only make them recognize the horrors of imperialism but also promote friendly relations between our children and grandchildren. That's what I think.

Wu Changde died the following year, in 1987, at the age of seventy-nine. One by one, the survivors of the Nanjing Massacre are dying off.

A Note Regarding Casualty Estimates

It is, of course, nearly impossible to calculate the number of surrendering, nonresisting soldiers or disguised soldiers who were slaughtered, along with the ordinary people who were caught up in the massacres or killed in the many acts of violence. The largest estimate comes from the Chinese side (the Nationalist government), which claims that a total of 430,000 people were killed, including 230,000 civilians and 110,000 military personnel. The extremes of the lower estimates are represented by Aida Yūji, who in a conversation with Yamamoto Shichihei, printed in the spring 1974 issue of *Kikan Rekishi to Bungaku,* claimed that about "one or two hundred people" were killed. Between these extremes, we find the 300,000 claimed by the city of Nanjing; or 200,000 soldiers and civilians, excluding battlefield deaths (Hora Tomio). Among the lower estimates are 38,000 to 42,000 (Hata Ikuhiko) or 3,000 to 6,000 (Unemoto Masami), but what the lower estimates have in common is that they do not include the killing of prisoners and surrendered soldiers as part of the massacre. Yoshida Hiroshi estimates that at least a hundred thousand soldiers and civilians were killed, excluding those who died on the battlefield. I have not made my own estimates or investigations of these figures, but to me the most problematic point is where to draw the geographical boundaries of the atrocities. Do we draw a line somewhere between Shanghai and Hangzhou Bay on one hand and the walls of Nanjing and Yangtze on the other and say, "From here on in, we count this as part of the Nanjing Massacre"? It is impossible. As I mentioned in Chapter 8, I think we need to take the approximately three months from November through January of the assault on Nanjing as a single phenomenon. If we think of it in those terms, we are dealing with too much time to say anything specific about the numbers of people killed, but no one can deny that the victims of the massacre numbered in the hundreds of thousands.

AFTERWORD TO
THE ORIGINAL EDITION

Between November 25 and December 27, 1983, I conducted the research for this book in China for the reasons outlined in the first chapter, and the results were published in the *Asahi Journal* over the course of about half a year, between April 12 and October 5, 1984. However, there are reasons for my not having published this series in book form until now.

I made a second research trip to China in November and December of 1984. While the first trip concentrated on the route of the Shanghai Expeditionary Force (the setting of this book), the second trip followed the route of the 10th Army from the landing at Hangzhou Bay. I did not make the results of this research public, because I wanted to make a third trip to gather material from within the city of Nanjing and also to conduct more research within Japan before putting all my results together in one volume of about 3,000 pages, along with material from the first trip that I had not before been able to include.

However, since this topic is not my journalistic specialty, I became preoccupied with other writing projects, and I was unable to pursue my research. At about that time, the *New Japanese History* textbook series, edited by the National Congress to Protect Japan (chaired by Kase Shun'ichi), became a sore point in relations with China and South Korea, giving rise to the so-called second textbook controversy of 1985. Shortly afterward, Prime Minister Nakasone paid an official visit to Yasukuni Shrine. Later, in the summer of 1986, we witnessed the dismissal of Education Minister Fumio after his speech expressing approval of Japan's imperialist policies, and the Nanjing Massacre became a topic of public discussion. At about that time, I began to receive inquiries as to whether my series of articles had appeared in book form.

Unlike the Germans and Italians, the Japanese have not made their own full accounting of their prewar actions. Inevitably, the subject of Nanjing kept surfacing in the public consciousness. If I were to wait until my entire 3,000-page manuscript was completed, I would not have been able to respond to this latest emergence of the problem, so I decided to publish this report of my first research trip. In addition to the portion that was serialized,

I have added only a few important materials, such as General Nakajima's diary. If I am able to live long enough, I hope someday to achieve my initial goal of completing a full-length manuscript.

As I mentioned in the main text, my efforts were greatly facilitated by Vice-Chairman Wang Yi, Manager Wang Fei, Assistant Manager Tu Peilin, Li Meizi, Wang Zhaoxiang, and other members of the International Liaison Department of the All-China Journalists' Association. In Nanjing, I received help from Mayor Zhang Yaohua, Assistant Secretary-General Zhang Yunran, journalists Ji Guangcheng and Xu Meiyuan, Professor Gao Xingzu of Nanjing University, Zou Mingde of the Second Municipal Archives of Nanjing, Zheng Liangwang (manager), Shen Caiyuan of the Jiangsu Province Office for Foreign Public Relations, and He Da, director of the Jiangsu Provincial Association of Journalists. Between Shanghai and Nanjing, I enjoyed the cooperation of Professor Wu Jie of Fudan University, journalists Xiao Mai and Fan Aiming, Assistant Manager He Fuming of the Jinshan County Jinwei Office of Public Relations, Xu Fugen of the Baoshan Country Luojing Party Secretariat, Cheng Wenhu of the Propaganda Department of Baoshan County, Assistant Manager Xu Gongming of Jiangwan (all of whom are in Shanghai), journalist Lang Qicheng (Suzhou), Assistant Section Head for Foreign Visitors Luo Lingen and employee Bi Jian of the Wuxi Office for Foreign Public Relations, journalist Zhu Deji, Manager Hua Shangzhi and employee Yang Qingsheng of the Mashan Office of Public Relations, Assistant Manager Zhu Azhu and employee Wang Zhangming of the Mashan Township Office of Public Relations (the above in Wuxi), Section Head Zhou Juncheng of the Changzhou Office for Foreign Public Relations, journalists Chen Bi and Sun Wei, Yuan Juncheng of the China Travel Service (in Changzhou), Representative Yao Jie of the Zhenjiang City Journalists' Association, journalists Feng Mingyi and Li Sicheng, Cheng Zhaoqun and Li Zhen of the Zhenjiang Office of Public Relations, Assistant Professor Wang Xiang of the Pedagogical Institute (in Zhenjiang), Jintan Party Committee Members Wang Shuanglin, Wang Yiming, and Shen Chengsong (in Jintan County), Manager Huang Hechao of the Jurong Office of Public Relations, and countless other individuals, more than I can list here. I want to express my heartfelt thanks to each of them. In Beijing, as always, I took advantage of the kindness of Tadokoro Takehiko, head of *Asahi Shimbun*'s Beijing bureau, and also received a great deal of cooperation from Yokobori Katsuyuki.

Furthermore, I received a great deal of help from Hora Tomio and Takasaki Ryūji in researching documents in Japan. In addition, the members of the Nanjing Incident Investigative Research Society (represented by Hora Tomio) and the investigative group (led by Fujiwara Akira) that the Society sent to Nanjing in December 1984 have helped me in various areas. I would like to express my deepest gratitude to all of them.

Honda Katsuichi
Nibutani, Hokkaidō
November 22, 1986

AFTERWORD TO THE ORIGINAL PAPERBACK EDITION

As I wrote in the afterword to the hardcover edition of this book, I have not yet published the material gathered on my second trip to China to research the Nanjing Massacre. Some results of my research have appeared in *Thinking about the Nanjing Incident* (written by Hora Tomio, Fujiwara Akira et al., published by Ōtsuki Shoten, 1987). This was a report of the first on-the-scene investigations carried out by the Nanjing Incident Investigative Research Society (represented by Hora Tomio, former professor at Waseda University), which included mostly historians, but also journalists and legal experts. I also participated to a certain extent, joining them in Nanjing in the course of my second research trip. When the Research Society sent out its second on-the-scene investigative group (led by Fujiwara Akira, formerly of Hitotsubashi University), I accompanied them, and this became my third research trip. The writings of all the participants in this trip were gathered together in *To the Site of the Nanjing Massacre* (Asahi Shimbunsha, 1988).

This paperback edition contains my reports from the two books mentioned above in addition to the text of the hardcover edition, along with a very small amount of additional material. Since I also gathered material on the Nanjing Incident in 1971, when I wrote *Journey to China* (Asahi Bunko), this makes four such trips for me. Even so, I would like to go to Nanjing at least once more, and then I will be able to write my 3,000-page report.

On reflection, it seems that the controversy over the Nanjing Massacre heated up in 1971, after my series *Journey to China* appeared first in the *Asahi Shimbun* and later, in paperback form. An account of the Nanjing Incident appeared in one chapter, and within that chapter, one single page described comments from the Chinese about the "contest to cut down a hundred" that occurred while Japanese troops were fighting their way from Shanghai to Nanjing. Since then, two magazines published by the Bungei Shunjū Corporation, namely *Shokun!* and *Bungei Shunjū*, have over the years used various unprincipled hacks,[1] to write features and commentary that try to disprove the existence of the contest, and, by extension, to try to deny the Nanjing Massacre itself. Several of these denials have been published in book form, but recently, the persistent attacks have relied heavily on such habitual misquoters and rewriters of materials as Tanaka Masaaki and Itakura Yoshiaki.

Yet these efforts to deny the Nanjing Massacre, found mainly in the pages of *Bungei Shunjū*, have paradoxically stirred up more controversy as increasing numbers of inside accounts from former soldiers appear. By now the fabrications and misquotations of the frauds-for-hire have been demolished from one end to the other, and they have quietly sunk out of sight. Of all the postwar controversies, few have been resolved so decisively.

The twenty or so members of the Nanjing Incident Investigative Research Society played a central role in completely defeating those who deny the Nanjing Massacre. They held regular bimonthly meetings, and on two occasions, December of 1984 and 1987, coinciding with the anniversaries of the events, they dispatched on-site investigative groups to Nanjing, enjoying the full cooperation of the Nanjing Municipal Historical Society. About ten people went on each trip, and their reports were published in the two collections mentioned previously, but some of the participants have reported their experiences in individual magazine articles or books. Here are the books, listed in chronological order.

Himeda, Mitsuyoshi, *et al.* translators: *Testimony: The Great Nanjing Massacre*, Aoki Shoten, 1984.

Ishijima, Tsurayuki: *The Chinese War of Resistance against Japan*, Aoki Shoten, 1984.

Fujiwara, Akira: *The Great Nanjing Massacre*, Iwanami Booklets, 1985 (second edition, 1988).

Yoshida, Hiroshi: *The Emperor's Army and the Nanjing Massacre*, Aoki Shoten, 1986.

Hora, Tomio: *Proof of the Great Nanjing Massacre*, Asahi Shimbunsha, 1986.

Takasaki, Ryūji: *War and War Literature*, Nihon Tosho Sentaa, 1986.

---

1. Some may object to the term "unprincipled hacks," but Tanaka Masaaki has really altered sources (cf. *Asahi Shimbun*, November 1984). Itakura Yoshiaki's rewritings are dealt with in "The Man Who Misused Sources and Accuses Others of It, " anthologized in my own *Impoverished Spirits, Collection B,* as well as in "Who Was the One Who Altered Sources?" anthologized in Hori Tomio's *To the Site of the Great Nanjing Massacre*.

Eguchi, Keiichi: *A Short History of the Fifteen-Year War*, Aoki Shoten, 1987.
Honda, Katsuichi: *The Road to Nanjing*, Asahi Shimbunsha, 1987.
Eguchi, Keiichi: *The Sino-Japanese Opium War*, Iwanami Shinsho, 1988.
Honda, Katuichi, editor: *The Great Nanjing Massacre Judged*, Banseisha, 1989.
Kasahara, Tokushi: *A Hundred Days in the Nanjing International Refugee Zone*, Asahi Shimbunsha, 1990.[3]

I must also mention some other valuable testimony from the Japanese side, Shimozato Masaki's *The Hidden Regimental History* (Aoki Shoten, two volumes). In addition, we have Hata Ikuhiko's *The Nanjing Incident* (Chūō Shinsho, 1986), which expresses fundamental doubts about definitions and the number of victims, and he points out that parts of the materials are unclear, but we should probably appreciate the fact that he informs the Japanese people that the Nanjing Incident was not, as the deniers say, a "fabrication."

The paperback edition of *The Road to Nanjing* has come into being with these circumstances in the background. It has now been eighteen years since I first visited China to gather material for what we might think of as its sister book, *Journey to China*. During that time, the Nanjing Massacre became something of a social problem, partly due to the textbook controversy. The textbook authorization trial (the third Ienaga trial)[2] was a formal objection to those who argued for authorization while distorting and minimizing the description of the Nanjing Massacre. If the school textbooks do not treat such a major incident correctly, our young people, unlike those in Germany, will not know their own history, and when they go abroad, they will in fact suffer the embarrassment of having to learn of it from foreigners. In this sense, this book and others like it may be thought of as a substitute for something that the nation itself ought to do.

Honda Katsuichi
Shiga Kōgen
October 24, 1989

---

2. Japanese schools have traditionally operated under a centralized system of textbook selection. Ienaga Saburō is a historian who has brought three lawsuits against the Ministry of Education challenging the constitutionality of the system. —Trans.

3. Materials from this book were later incorporated in *The Nanjing Incident* published by Kasahara in 1997. —Ed.

COMMENTARY

Honda Katsuichi's activities as a journalist have been many and varied. Since beginning his career at *Asahi Shimbun* in 1958, he has produced an immense number of works, not only in his original field of feature writing, but also in social commentary. His works may be divided into several broad categories. The early writings, such as *A Record of Setting Out on a Journey*, *The Longed-for Himalayas*, and *Thinking about Mountains*, dealt with mountaineering and exploration. Then came the books about minority peoples living close to nature: *The Canadian Eskimos*, *The New Guinea Highlanders*, *The Arab Nomads*, *The United States of America*, and *The Ainu People*. Beginning with *The Village on the Battlefield* and continuing through *Journey to Cambodia*, he wrote about the Vietnam and Cambodia wars. Finally, we have the works that substantiate the facts about Japanese military atrocities during the invasion of China, beginning with *Journey to China*. Outside of these main themes, he has also written a number of works of criticism concerning education and journalism, as well as discussions of stylistics and rhetoric. Still, his most notable reportage is that aimed at uncovering the history of World War II through on-site investigations.

The Road to Nanjing is among Honda's more recent works concerning the invasion of China. It is based on interviews conducted in China in November and December of 1983, and it first appeared in serialized form in *Asahi Journal* between April 13 and October 5, 1984. In January 1987, Asahi Shimbunsha published it in book form.

Honda's investigations in China began in 1971. With the reestablishment of diplomatic relations between Japan and China in the offing, he spent June and July traveling through China, aiming to get at the facts about the Japanese invasion. The results were serialized in four parts in *Asahi Shimbun* between August and December, and they were also carried in the magazines *Asahi Journal*, *Shūkan Asahi*, and *Asahi Graph*. In March 1972, Asahi Shimbunsha published the collected articles in book form as *Journey to China* (a paperback edition came out later).

The appearance of *Journey to China* caused serious repercussions, because it exposed the massacres perpetrated by the Japanese military and forced the Japanese people to take note of the problem of responsibility for the havoc inflicted on China in the last war. Since earlier criticism of World War II had been based on the idea of the Japanese people as victims, these ar-

ticles were a huge shock to *Asahi*'s readers. Of course, there had been confessions and descriptions of Japanese atrocities before this, but they had been
published by small presses in small runs and had thus lacked impact. In contrast, these reports were not only published in the mass-circulation *Asahi
Shimbun,* but also shook readers with the seriousness of the facts laid out and
the author's clear and sincere way of letting these facts speak for themselves.

At the same time, however, that these articles were making such a great
impression on the public, both Honda as an individual and Asahi as a company were the targets of intense criticism. Right wingers who want to affirm
Japan's role in the war asked if Honda and Asahi Shimbunsha were deliberately trying to sully Japan's history by exposing the military's atrocities. They
also criticized Honda for writing a one-sided account that presented only the
Chinese version.

In September 1972, diplomatic relations with China were normalized, and
a joint declaration was issued in which Japan "painfully acknowledged and
deeply regretted the damage it had inflicted upon the Chinese people." This
provoked the right-wing forces who had been justifying and glorifying Japan's
role in the war and opposing the resumption of diplomatic relations, and they
set out to attack Honda and Asahi. They concentrated on disproving the
Nanjing Massacre, which had been mentioned as the greatest of the atrocities.

The magazines *Bungei Shunjū* and *Shokun!* became the venues for the
right wing's attacks on Honda and their assertions that the Nanjing Massacre
had never happened. The criticism of Honda centered on efforts by Yamamoto
Shichihei and Suzuki Akira to prove that the "contest to cut down a hundred," a small part of the account of the Nanjing Massacre in *Journey to
China,* was unsubstantiated. They extended these arguments to deny the entire Nanjing Massacre, even though they were unable to offer any proof.
However, as sensational headlines blazed across magazine covers and
eye-catching subway advertisements proclaiming the critics' views, the general public was deluded into thinking that the truth of the Nanjing Massacre
really was debatable.

Naturally, Honda put up a spirited counterattack to these criticisms from
the right wing. His opponents, who had either spoken out of complete igno-
rance or falsified their materials, were unable to respond to his counter arguments. All they could do was keep repeating, "It never happened."

The account of the so-called Nanjing Incident takes up only a small portion of Chapter 16 of *Journey to China.* With cries of "myth" and "fabrication" arising from right-wing quarters, Honda must have wanted to conduct
more detailed on-site investigations, but his immediate motivation for putting those plans into action was the textbook controversy of 1982. In June of

that year, newspapers reported on the realities of the history textbook approval committee for elementary and secondary schools. The public learned that the "invasion" of China had been changed to an "advance," and that references to the 1931 Movement and the Nanjing Massacre had been modified, resulting in a sanitized portrayal of the era. Criticisms poured in from all over Asia, and China and South Korea filed formal protests with the Japanese government, which promised to rectify the situation. This intensified the reaction from the right wing, as they demanded to know why Japanese textbooks should be revised through diplomatic negotiations with foreign countries. Once again, we heard strident claims that the Nanjing Massacre had been overblown or that it had never happened at all.

Honda's first trip to China to gather materials for *The Road to Nanjing* occurred at the end of 1983, just when the unenlightened arguments of the right wing were at their height. He first conducted his investigations on the north shore of Hangzhou Bay, where the 10th Army had landed, and then he followed the trail of the Shanghai Expeditionary Force through Shanghai, Suzhou, Wuxi, Changzhou, Jurong, Zhenjiang, and Nanjing. At the end of 1984, he followed the trail of the 10th Army through Jiaxing, Huzhou, Guangde, Wuhu, and Hangzhou. These were the "roads" taken by the 10th Army (commanded by Lieutenant General Yanagawa Heisuke) and the Shanghai Expeditionary Force (commanded by Prince Asaka).

The clash of the Japanese and Chinese armies in the Marco Polo Bridge Incident of July 7, 1937, provided the opportunity for Japan to try to resolve the long-standing conflict between the two countries with a decisive blow. With the strong-arm tactics of the imperial guards and the infantry, Japan was well on its way to expansion of the war. In August 1937, the government issued its Declaration for Punishing Chinese Tyranny and dispatched the Shanghai Expeditionary Force, launching a total war. Given the fierce resistance of the Chinese forces, however, the fighting was unrelentingly heavy. After three months, the Shanghai Expeditionary Force was pinned down north of Shanghai, suffering heavy losses. The 10th Army was sent as reinforcements to land at Hangzhou Bay, and by attacking the Chinese from the rear, it was gradually able to break the stalemate. The Japanese Army thus began a war of pursuit toward Nanjing. As this book makes clear, the area along the route between Hangzhou Bay and Nanjing was subjected to a horrific campaign of looting, arson, mass murder, and rape, both in the cities and in the countryside.

Why did this happen? In fact, the Japanese Army's original battle plans contained no arrangement for a drive toward Nanjing, and there were no preparations for supplies from the rear, so the troops were directed to have their provisions supplied "by the enemy." In other words, they were to obtain their supplies by looting, which they referred to as "requisitioning." The troops split up into small units to conduct house-to-house searches for provisions, and this led not only to looting and arson, but also to worse crimes. With their disinclination to respect human rights, their strong contempt for the Chinese people, and their victor's pride at having turned the tide of war, the troops committed mass murder. Nor were the upper echelons of the military inclined to observe the rules: ignoring international law and human considerations, they ordered the slaughter of prisoners of war instead of treating them properly. In order to keep troop morale high, they also gave tacit approval to looting and rape.

Thus, these incidents of looting and rape did not suddenly begin occurring upon the capture of Nanjing. Rather, they happened continually all along the road to Nanjing from Shanghai and Hangzhou. Similarly, the massacres were not confined to the Nanjing city limits but occurred over a wide area between there and the coast. The significance of this book lies in providing the facts to prove the scope of the atrocities.

We can most likely say that Honda has shattered the protestations of Yamamoto Shichihei, author of *The Japanese Army Within Me*, and Tanaka Masaaki, author of the *The Fabrication of the Great Nanjing Massacre*, both of whom insist that the massacre never happened. *The Great Nanjing Massacre Judged*, in which Honda compiled the opinions and testimony about the Nanjing Massacre from the third Ienaga Textbook Trial, was published in 1989 by Banmeisha, and we can state that it is the last word against those who deny the massacre.

Now that they can no longer say that the Nanjing Massacre never happened, the deniers have changed their approach by declaring that the figure of 300,000 victims claimed by the Chinese is impossible. Judging from the population of Nanjing and the numbers of troops in the city at the time, they say, there could never have been that many victims. There were at most a few thousand or a few tens of thousands, they insist, so it is a mistake to speak of a "Great Massacre."

This insistence glosses over the essence of the problem. Of course it is necessary to settle the question of how much of a massacre occurred and how many victims there were within the city and in the surrounding areas during the assault on Nanjing. At the same time, it is clear that, based on the results of verified research to date, the small numbers that the deniers insist on are incorrect. But I must repeat: the Great Nanjing Massacre was not confined to the city of Nanjing itself. As this book testifies, the very road to Nanjing saw huge massacres.

To claim a small number of victims within the city, to deny the existence of a "Great Massacre" on that basis, and, by extension, to minimize the atrocities of the Japanese military in China, is a trick of the right-wing journalists and conservative politicians who take a positive view of the war and who try to absolve themselves of the responsibility for it. Even so, no matter how much they try to distort the history of the invasion, they cannot erase the truth. The fact that Japan's war of invasion was a crushing burden to China for fifteen years and led to repeated massacres and rapes everywhere has been proven by the testimony of countless witnesses.

This book presents these facts with accounts taken directly from people who lived through the actual events. In this way, it shows that the Nanjing Massacre was just one episode in the invasion of China, just one example of the atrocities committed. Creating a clear picture of the war as a whole as we continue to shed light on the Nanjing Massacre is one of our duties as Japanese people.

Fujiwara Akira
Professor, Kagawa Nutrition College

APPENDIX

Editor's Note: The following passages include interviews with both Chinese victims of the Massacre and with Japanese soldiers from some of the units involved. One selection was taken from *Chugoku no Tabi* (Journey to China, 1971), Honda's earlier book in which he first exposed the Japanese Army's atrocities. Four selections, taken from Honda's *Nankin Daigyakusatsu* (The Nanjing Massacre, 1997), in addition to victim interviews, quote from diaries, and reminiscences of Japanese soldiers, some of whom the author interviewed as late as 1994. Although taken from Honda's later writings on the subject, he wished them included in the English edition because of their significance.

EXCERPT FROM *CHUGOKU NO TABI*

Chen Degui (age 53) is now a cargo handler for the Xiaguan Transport Company in Nanjing. At the time the Japanese army occupied Nanjing, Chen and many other citizens of Nanjing fled to an area known as the Baota Refugee Zone,[1] located outside the walls northwest of the city. In the district was a British-managed meat processing plant called Heji yangxiang, which still exists to this day. Since the area was a British concession, the people hoped that the Japanese wouldn't be able to barge in freely.

"About that time, a so-called 'support committee' made up of mostly wealthy Chinese collaborators[2] was formed," Chen explained, tilting his closely cropped head. "In order to avoid the harsh treatment that was meted out to ordinary people, they had declared themselves to be the 'running dogs' of the Japanese military. One morning at the end of December, more than twenty members of the support committee formed a 'welcoming committee' and set out for the Japanese army's Meitan Harbor barracks to gauge their mood. Wearing their support committee armbands and carrying the Rising Sun flag, they apparently passed some information along to the troops, and that afternoon, seven or eight Japanese cavalrymen came to the Refugee Zone." Chen added that the cavalrymen merely walked around the refugee district and then withdrew after finishing their reconnaissance.

The next morning, at least 200 Japanese soldiers appeared, and with the help of the support committee they began hunting down all the adult

---

1. According to the records of the Tokyo War Crimes Trial, "In December, 1937, when the Nationalist Chinese government withdrew from Nanjing, an International Committee was organized by Chinese and foreign merchants and missionaries. The Japanese authorities agreed to let the area west of North Zhongshan Road and north of Hangzhong Road be an International Refugee Zone, and the Red Swastika Society was allowed to manage relief activities in that zone." However, the zone referred to here, the Baotaqiao Refugee Zone in the British concession outside the city walls, was a different location. The Japanese also invaded the International Refugee Zone.

2. The collaborators, or *Hanjian*. The general meaning of the word is "traitor to China," but under the Japanese military occupation, it typically referred to the "support committees," who became the cat's paws of the occupiers in order to escape the fate that their fellow Chinese suffered.

males. There were several thousand people in the quarter, and about 2,000 young men were discovered and rounded up.

The Japanese soldiers first lined the men up in four rows and made them give up their watches and coins before conducting a clothing and body search to find any remaining valuables. Anyone found with anything had it confiscated and was beaten severely. When the inspection was over, all the men were forced to kneel on the ground.

Maintaining this posture was extremely painful, but there was nothing the men could do, not when surrounded by watchful Japanese troops.

At about 4:30 in the afternoon, they were arranged in a column four men across and forced to walk along the banks of the Yangtze in the direction of Meitan Harbor. The end of the wharf there was used mostly for unloading coal, and there was a large warehouse along the pier, with guards and machine guns at the entrance. The approximately 2,000 men were marched into the warehouse.

(Chen later heard that the evening after the young men were rounded up, the Japanese soldiers returned to the Refugee Zone and abducted as many young women as they could find. All were raped, and a quite a few of those who resisted were killed.)

The 2,000 men spent the night packed into the warehouse like rush-hour commuters. At about eight the next morning, an exit door was opened on the wharf side, opposite the entrance.

"Now you're going to go the workshop and work," the Japanese told the men through an interpreter. "Arrange yourselves in groups of ten and come on out." Soldiers suddenly grabbed ten of the men nearest the door and pushed them outside. Then the door was closed. Soon the remaining men could hear gunfire coming from somewhere outside. When the doors opened again, the order came for the next ten men to come, so they gathered together and went out. More gunfire. Chen was in the third group.

When his group of ten emerged from the warehouse, they saw two rows of Japanese soldiers lined up facing each other, their bayonets ready. A soldier behind them yelled, "Run!" and they began running through a tunnel of bayonets.

Chen was the fourth man from the front. The way through the gauntlet of soldiers was about 100 meters long, heading alongside Bifeng Harbor[3] to the main channel of the Yangtze. As he ran toward the river, Chen could see about thirty Japanese military men in what appeared to be the dark uniforms

---

3. Bifeng Harbor: an artificial inlet dug at a right angle from the main channel of the Yangtze. It was used as a storm port and resting place for fishing boats and transport ships.

Ten men at a time were sent out through this warehouse door to be shot.

of the Imperial Navy, standing with their rifles raised behind the far end of the warehouse along the embankment. At that instant, Chen realized that the Japanese intended to shoot everyone dead, but there was no time to hesitate, because he could hear voices behind him yelling, "Run quickly!" and "Jump into the water!" At that very moment, shots rang out. Men flipped over or flew through the air as they tumbled into the water.

Luckily, Chen was not hit, and he was also a strong swimmer. He jumped into the river and stayed submerged, determined to travel as far as he could under water. Taking care to avoid the entrance to Bifeng Harbor, he came across a small Japanese vessel, perhaps a gunboat or patrol boat. He continued underwater along the length of the vessel until he reached the end of another wharf. There were warehouses and a railroad sidetrack here, too, and at the end of the track were some railroad cars that had run off the wharf still linked together, the remnant of an incident in which some of Chiang Kai-shek's troops had fled in panic aboard a train and ended up running it into the Yangtze.

When Chen reached this point, which was opposite the site of the ongoing massacre, he swam into a space where the floors of the derailed cars were suspended a bit above the water and poked his head above the surface, keeping the rest of his body submerged and in the shadow of the cars. He clung to a hydraulic brake pipe but didn't dare emerge completely from the water for fear of the Japanese soldiers who were loitering about.

The massacre continued as Chen watched. As each group of ten men came running out, the first of three or four rows of Japanese soldiers fired at them. The second row immediately finished off anyone who wasn't killed

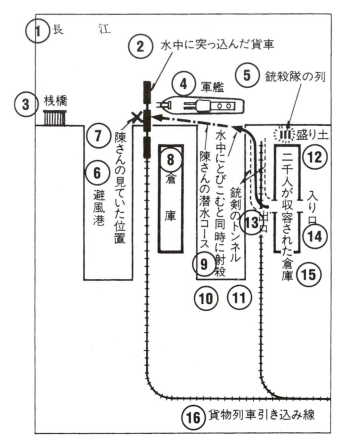

1. The Yangtze
2. Railroad cars that had been run into the water
3. Pier
4. Japanese vessel
5. Rows of riflemen
6. Bifeng Harbor
7. The position from which Chen watched
8. Warehouse
9. Where Chen swam underwater
10. Where the men were shot as they jumped into the water
11. The tunnel of bayonets
12. Embankment
13. Exit
14. Entrance
15. The warehouse where 2,000 men were held
16. Sidetrack for railroad cars

outright. As the corpses accumulated at the river's edge, the Japanese vessel revved up its propellers, creating turbulence in the muddy waters of the Yangtze and flushing the bodies into the main current of the river. Then the vessel, which had been pushed slightly forward by the action of its propeller, moved back to its original position, the next ten men came running out, more shots rang out, and the propeller revved up again.

This assembly-line massacre continued throughout the day. As it grew dark the Japanese vessel pulled away from the wharf and went off somewhere. The riflemen and the soldiers who had formed the tunnel of bayonets also left, evidently for some nearby barracks. Some sentries remained, however, and there seemed to be still more Chinese locked up in the warehouse. By this time, Chen was chilled to the bone from being submerged so long, and he was sure that he would die of exposure if he stayed in the water, but fear of the sentries kept him from climbing up onto the shore.

About 60 meters upstream there was a pier attached to a different wharf, and Chen dog-paddled there along the shoreline. The pier stood on a series of wooden supports, the front ones in the water and the others on dry land. Corpses, which seemed to be the victims of a different massacre than the one Chen had witnessed, were floating in the water around the pier, and others had been washed up on the riverbank. Chen carefully crept out of the water and found a ragged blanket lying on the shore. Wrapping himself in the blanket, he lay down amid the bodies, hoping to be mistaken for a corpse if he was spotted. As he lay there, he could occasionally hear the footsteps of sentries on the pier.

Some Japanese soldiers (maybe only one; Chen wasn't sure) came along early the next morning and tossed a hand grenade among the bodies that were floating along the shore. Chen assumes that all the bodies were clumped together and that the soldier was trying to disperse them so that they would float away. Then that soldier, or perhaps another one, came down from the pier to where the support pillars rested on land.

"I was shivering slightly due to the morning chill, "Chen recalled. "I was all curled up with both hands between my thighs, and I don't know whether the soldier noticed me shivering, but anyway, he shot me with a pistol and hit me right where I had my hands between my thighs. The bullet passed through the inner side of both thighs and through my ring finger. The pain was almost unbearable, but I somehow endured it and kept still."

The soldier must have thought either that Chen was already dead or that the shot had killed him, because he simply left.

Although Chen couldn't see what was happening, he could hear shots coming from the direction where the massacre had taken place. Apparently the Japanese were continuing the massacre by finishing off the men they hadn't been able to kill the previous day. Chen assumed that there would be no hope for him if the Japanese came back, so he moved from his position under the pier to a point just at the edge of the water. He then hid by taking three nearby bodies and piling them on top of himself.

The following afternoon, after Chen had lain awake a second night, some Japanese showed up with members of the "support committee" and some

The ten men who came out of the warehouse (near the railroad car at the right) were made to run alongside the warehouse toward the banks of the Yangtze, where they were shot. At the left is the water of Bifeng Harbor.

Chen points out the spot where the men were shot as they jumped into the water.

Chinese laborers to dispose of the bodies. The laborers begin lugging away the corpses that were piled on the ground, and eventually, they took the three that were lying on top of Chen. Then it was Chen's turn, but as soon as the laborers picked him up, they cried out, "He's still alive!" The members of the support committee took notice and asked who he was. When Chen told them what part of the city he was from, they asked him suspiciously, "How did you end up here?"

Chen said that he had been led here from the Refugee Zone and that he had been injured, but he insisted that he was a "law-abiding citizen." The laborers backed him up: "He's definitely a good person." The Japanese did not inflict any further harm on him, and he was relieved, two days after the massacre, to find things in a calmer mood.

"Get out of here then!" the Japanese ordered, and they had the support committee's interpreter write him a safe conduct pass.

The trip back to the Refugee Zone was not easy. Wounded in both legs, Chen was unable to stand up straight, and he walked hunched over, supporting the backs of his knees with his hands. When he returned to

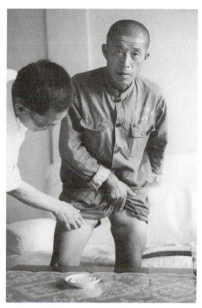

Chen showing the scars of the wounds he received when he was shot while lying among the dead bodies.

the Refugee Zone, he found it overflowing with people who had been burned out of their homes, so there was no hope of getting any medical attention. Instead, he took the advice that someone gave him, bathing his wounds in tea every other day and swabbing them with powdered bone. After forty days, during which he subsisted on two bowls of rice gruel per day, his injuries were more or less healed, and he returned to his home in the Gongmenkou section of the city.

Before the invasion, Chen had been an apprentice at a bicycle repair shop. Even after his injuries had healed, he had to ride his bicycle hunched over, because he still couldn't fully straighten his legs and body. One day, however, he fell off his bicycle and reopened the wounds. This time, they healed in a way that allowed him to stand normally.

After he had finished telling his story. Chen rolled up his pants legs and showed us the scars he still carried from those times.

The type of mass slaughter that Chen experienced occurred in many other places, including massacres that took place on a smaller scale in peasant villages far from the urban areas in and around Nanjing. One of them was experienced by Mei Futang (age 50), a peasant who was part of the Meishan Brigade of the Yuhuatai Xishanqiao People's Commune when I interviewed him.

Tears streamed down Mei's face as he told me about how nine people from his village, including seven members of his family, had been slaughtered with almost casual brutality, and eventually he broke down into sobs. The interview was further complicated by the fact that Mei spoke the peasant dialect of the Nanjing area, and there were many parts that my interpreter, Mr. Chao, a northeasterner, was unable to interpret. We ended up having to conduct a sort of two-stage interpretation, with the cooperation of an employee of the local China Travel Agency who was accompanying us, as Mei told us about what he had lived through as a sixteen-year-old.

"Our village was small, with only twenty people in six households, so everyone was related—fathers and sons and brothers—all with the surname of Mei. I think it was about three o'clock in the afternoon one day in December 1937 when a lone Japanese soldier came riding into our village on a horse, a sword at his side. The soldier yelled something in Japanese. He seemed to be saying, "Come outside!" and when all of us came running out, startled, he yelled something else. His gestures seemed to indicate that he was saying "Line up," so we lined up huddled together. Then he got off his horse and looked inside the houses, but he left pretty soon after that. But about ten minutes later, he came back with about 200 infantrymen. It turned out that he had been on a reconnaissance mission. He told us that the troops were going to spend the night here, so we should offer our houses."

All the people in all the households were beaten and kicked as they were thrown out of their houses. When night fell, the Japanese collected all the women and locked them up together in one room, with six or seven guards assigned to watch them. The twelve men and one elderly woman were locked up in a different room. However, the guards fell asleep after midnight, so all the women were able to flee.

On the morning after 200 soldiers had spent the night in the tiny village, everything was naturally in confusion. At dawn, the Japanese noticed that the women were gone and began interrogating the men, "Where did they run away to?" Having been locked in all night, the men didn't know and couldn't answer, so the Japanese lined them up and began punching them in the face and kicking them across the room.

There was an irrigation pond in the village where the villagers raised fish. The Japanese threw hand grenades into the pond to kill the fish so that they could eat them with their rice. They poked the village men with their bayonets as they ordered them to strip naked in the December chill and retrieve the dead fish that were floating on the surface of the pond.

Mei's oldest brother had been taken away to the next village to help cook for the soldiers. and his second oldest brother was suffering from a high fever caused by a typhus-like disease. When the second brother came out of the pond, he was extremely thirsty, and he went over to the Japanese soldiers' campfire and picked up a tea kettle that lay there—it was, in fact, the Mei family's own tea kettle. He poured some water out into a teacup, but just as he was raising the cup to his lips, a Japanese soldier grabbed it away and smashed it against his head. Pieces of the shattered teacup cut into his face, which bled profusely.

Just then, Mei heard the sharp sound of ripping cloth coming from inside his house. Soon the soldiers assembled the twelve members of the Mei family and marched them into the terraced rice paddy, which had a small mound about 10 meters in diameter in the middle. The twelve Chinese were made to assemble on the oppo-

Mei was hit at the base of the ear and at the base of the tongue.

site side of this mound from the Japanese and told to stand in a circle facing outward. Immediately, a soldier came with strips of cloth—quilting material from Mei's house that he had heard being ripped apart—and bound the twelve people hand to hand.

After binding the circle of people, the two or three soldiers withdrew to the opposite side of the mound. Then they tossed a hand grenade into the middle of the circle.

At that instant, the circle of twelve people became a ring of bloody, dismembered figures. Mei surmises that only a few people actually died instantly, because as he lay on the ground, he could hear several people screaming, and the voice of his fourteen-year-old nephew rent the air with particular intensity. A Japanese came running and killed Mei's screaming nephew by stabbing him in the throat with his bayonet. One after another, the other screams were also stilled by bayonets.

When the grenade exploded, Mei was hit at the base of ear, in the chin, and at the base of the tongue. Then the Japanese stabbed him twice in the chest and once in the buttocks, but this jab did not go all the way through, and luckily, the jabs to his chest did not hit any vital organs.

Nine out of the twelve people died, including Mei's grandmother, father, second older brother, nephew, and three cousins. Two others besides Mei sustained serious injuries but survived.

The Japanese moved on, apparently believing that everyone was dead. As they left the village at about ten in the morning, they set fire to all the houses.

When Mei's oldest brother, the one who had been taken to a neighboring village, saw that his own community was on fire, he became alarmed and hurried back with someone from the next village. All the houses were nearly destroyed, and only their smoldering frameworks remained. As the oldest brother and his companion from the other village searched the area, the companion found the site of the massacre first. "Over here!" he called. The oldest brother ran sobbing to where his family lay, and when Mei heard him, he tried to call out, "Brother, don't cry. I'm not dead yet." But since his tongue was injured, he could barely make himself heard.

His brother ran to him, untied the strips of cloth, and raised Mei to a sitting position. Having lost so much blood, Mei was extremely thirsty, and he gestured as he tried to say, "I want some water." He tried to drink some water from a teacup as his brother held his head up, but he couldn't on account of the grenade injuries to his tongue and lips. All his brother could do was to painstakingly pour a little water down his throat at a time.

Mei's brother and the man from the neighboring village pondered their situation as they stared absently at the smoldering ruins of the houses. If they were to return to the neighboring village with the survivor of a massacre, they would be discovered by the Japanese and suffer the consequences, so they decided to hide for a while. With the help of the man from the neighboring village, Mei's brother laid him on a board and carried him off into the hills. In order to avoid being found by the Japanese, they changed their position every two or three days for about twenty days, until Mei's life was no longer in danger. That's when the oldest brother returned to the village and disposed of the bodies of his family members, weeping as he dug seven graves.

EXCERPT FROM CHAPTER 4 OF NANKIN DAIGYAKUSATSU: "HOT PURSUIT OF THE DEFEATED ENEMY AT JIAXING"

Facing the 10th Army, the Nationalists were in a sparsely scattered battle array, unlike the situation in Shanghai, so they were under considerable pressure from the superior Japanese forces. On November 11, six days after the landing. Jiashan, 40 kilometers to the west, quickly fell under Japanese occupation. The eyewitness accounts of Jiashan residents presented here were collected during my 1984 visit.

Zhu Nianci was twenty years old at the time of the invasion and working as an elementary school teacher in Jiashan. In those days, the population of Jiashan County was about two million, and its central town was Weitangzhen, a commercial center with five hundred years of history and a population of ten thousand. According to Zhu, the Japanese Air Force began bombing the area on November 8 and continued for three days, causing the residents to flee to the surrounding countryside. On the tenth, the Japanese reached Fengjingzhen, about 10 kilometers to the east of Jiashan, and two days later, they came to Jiashan itself. Almost all the Chinese troops had retreated by this time, but a small contingent put up a bit of resistance near the railroad bridge (or Bridge 67) at the west gate before caving in.

Within the city of Jiashan, the county government offices, the Nationalist Party headquarters, the library, and the newspaper office had already been destroyed by the bombing, and most of the private homes had either been destroyed or sustained damage. When the Japanese came, only about a hundred people, most of them disabled, elderly, or ill, who had been unable to flee, remained in town, and almost all of them were killed. The bodies were disposed of by a member of the "support committee" named Shen Jinsheng and others, who told Zhu that most of the dead seemed to have been bayoneted. The bodies were buried at Liuzhou Pavilion outside the north gate of

Zhu Nianci.

the city. The townspeople began returning about two weeks after the Japanese arrived and found themselves being governed by the "support committee" that the Japanese pacification squads had set up. When Zhu Nianci returned about a month after the invasion, he found that the apartment building where he had been living was completely destroyed.

The morning edition of the *Asahi Shimbun* for November 13, 1937, carried a report from the Shanghai Special Forces dated November 12 and bearing headlines which crowed: "Nanshi, Nanxiang Completely Occupied—An Area Stretching for Fifty Tortuous *Li* from Luodian in the North to Jiashan in the South Has Come Under the Control of the Imperial Army."

Southwest of Jiashan is the major city of the region, Jiaxing, and one of its eastern suburbs is a small village called Dongzhazhen. At the time of the Japanese invasion, Wu Liangbi was a twenty-eight-year-old civil servant working in the village office. Here is what he told me about his experiences.

Jiaxing was first bombed on October 6, and trains from both Shanghai

Wu Liangbi.

and Hangzhou happened to be at the station just at that time. When the station was bombed, the Deyilou Tea House in front of it was also hit, killing many of the customers; pieces of their bodies—arms and legs—were found hanging tangled in the electrical wires.

Two days later, on the morning of October 8, the city was strafed with machine gun fire from the air. The passenger ship that regularly traveled up and down the canal between Jiaxing County and Pinghu County was hit; two

The fork in the canal that links Jiaxing and Pinghu. This is where the passenger ship was subjected to an unprovoked Japanese bombing attack.

This is the spot where a splendid temple called Sanguandian once stood. The Japanese burned it when they invaded Xinfengzhen, and the only remaining traces are these two gingko trees, believed to be 560 years old.

passengers died instantly and four more were severely injured. The ship took refuge at Dongzhazhen, and the residents of Jiaxing began evacuating to the countryside. Even the village office where Wu Liangbi was employed was relocated to Xinshengzhen, about 15 kilometers away.

Wu's parents' home was in Xinfengzhen, about 16 kilometers east of Jiaxing, and he himself fled to Zhulinxiang, a village about 20 kilometers

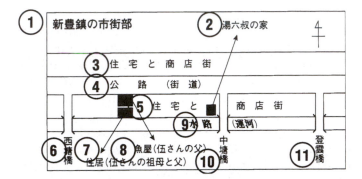

1. The commercial area of Xinfengzhen
2. Yu Liushu's house
3. Houses and shops
4. Road (highway)
5. Houses and shops
6. Xitang Bridge
7. The home of Wu Liangbi's father and grandmother
8. The fish store owned by Wu's father
9. Canal
10. Zhongtang Bridge
11. Dengyun Bridge

south of that town. Unfortunately, both Xinfengzhen and Zhulinxiang were on the road between Jinshanwei, where the Japanese had landed, and Jiaxing.

On October 13, the main street of Xinfengzhen was strafed with machine gun fire, but no one was killed, and the only aftereffect was that the street was littered with cartridges. On the 14th, there was a bombing raid, but the bombs fell on a vacant lot, the site of the present Xinfengzhen Elementary School, creating a crater 2 meters across and 3 meters deep. No one was killed or injured, but like the people of Jiaxing, the residents of Xinfengzhen began to flee to the surrounding countryside. The only ones who remained were shopkeepers and others who wanted to guard their property. Since there were no Chinese troops in the vicinity, a power vacuum existed, with no government and no plans for defense. It was to this unprotected town that the Japanese came a month later.

It started raining on the morning of November 16, but the skies cleared up around noon of the 17th. That evening, the Japanese invaded Xinfengzhen from the southeast. At the edge of town, near Dengyun Bridge, one of the town's three bridges, stood the five-room house of Lu Liuqiang. Although the Lu family had already fled, a coal dealer named Jin Bingxian was staying there with five other family members, including his wife, his mother, his two sons, ages twelve and three, the wife of his younger brother, and her three-year-old son. Like most other residents of the area, they had no information about Japanese troop movements, so they had just holed up somewhere that seemed safe. One of the first things the Japanese did as they entered the city was to kill the entire family.

That evening, Wu's father, Wu Baoxian, age fifty-seven, and his maternal grandmother, Ying Wangshi,[1] were at their home, a two-story building with its back to the canal and facing the main street, with the family's fish shop jutting out in front in a one-story addition. Directly off the fish shop was the household's kitchen, and beyond that was the guest room. Wu's father's room was far in back, facing on the canal, and Wu's grandmother's room was on the second floor.

The two of them were already asleep when Ying Wangshi was awakened by unusual noises, for she still had her hearing, although Wu Baoxian was slightly deaf. Taking a lantern, she came down from the second floor and asked Wu Baoxian to go see what was happening.

When Wu's father went into the shop, he found that the door, which should have been closed, was wide open. The three fish that should have been in the tank were gone, and the 5 kilograms of rice that had been stored in a container on the lid of the fish tank were gone as well. Wu Baoxian surmised that the store had been robbed, so he simply locked the door tightly and went back to bed.

The next morning, Xu Ade, a young man who worked for the Wu family, returned from Chenfenqiao, 3 kilometers to the north, where he had fled after the bombing. He reported that the Japanese had come to Chenfenqiao the previous night and massacred a lot of the residents. When Wu's father came out the front door, he saw the body of Fen Laoer, a musician who often played the flute or drum at weddings and funerals, lying in the street. It was at that point that he realized that the Japanese had come to Xinfengzhen as well, and that they had been last night's "burglars." He decided to take his mother-in-law and young Xu and leave town.

As the Japanese entered Xinfengzhen, a small group went to Beizhuang village, south of town, and killed three peasants: Shen Heliu, Shen Amei, and Chen Zhangshu. Then they went to the neighboring village of Yuantangli, where Wu Shanxian, Wu Liangbi's uncle from Xinfengzhen, had fled to Zhu Baosheng's house. The Japanese showed up when the villagers were in the midst of threshing. Although everyone fled immediately, three women, Wu Shanxian's wife, Wu Shenshi, along with Zhong Gaoshi and Li Wangshi, were unable to run very fast because of their bound feet. They were shot as they jumped into a stream. Zhu Baosheng's younger brother, Zhu Yusheng, was also shot along the riverbank.

---

1. The "Wangshi" part of her name shows that her maiden name was Wang. In those days, women from the poorer classes had no legal given names. When they were born, they were simply given a "baby name," and they were called that until marriage, when they took their husband's family name followed by the surname of their birth family and the title *shi*.

The canal that flows through Xinfengzhen, viewed from the Dengyun Bridge, looking west.

The road at the eastern edge of Xinfengzhen (Jiaping Highway). The man is pointing in the direction that the Japanese army came from.

Back in Xinfengzhen, a candy store owner named Wang Jinguan was watching over his house when he was shot and killed as soon as the Japanese came through his door. At the east end of Zhongtang Bridge, the middle of the town's three bridges, a mentally retarded man named Shi Guanchang was shot dead. In the same neighborhood, a white-haired, seventy-year-old tea shop owner named Yu Liushu was killed inside his shop. Under the bridge, a man named Li Asan was stabbed to death.

Slightly to the north of Xinfengzhen is a village called Hejiaqiao, home to a man named Cao and his two daughters, Cao Guiying, age nineteen, and Cao Tianbao, age sixteen. All three were killed, and their bodies were thrown

The Dengyun Bridge today. At the time of the invasion, it was a stone bridge.

into a nearby stream. The nineteen-year-old was raped before she was killed. Wu Liangbi saw the site of the murders after the Japanese had left, and he reports that Cao Guiying was found naked below the waist, a military sword stuck up her vagina and poking through her belly, so that her intestines spilled out.

Xue Adi was thirty years old at the time of the invasion. Her husband's older brother, Zhu Arong, ran a noodle shop, and she and her seven-year-old daughter and four-year-old son were living with him, along with a friend of her brother-in-law and the shop's apprentice, a total of six people. Xue's husband was not home at the time, having gone to Jiashan to work.

Once she heard that the Japanese were approaching, Xue lost no time in fleeing, because her children were still small. At about four on the afternoon of the 17th, she ran away to a village called Hudongbin (now called Hehuabin), just south of town. When she came back the next day, she found that her brother-in-law, his friend, and the apprentice had been killed. The brother-in-law was found just outside the

Xue Adi.

Xu Yuguan.

gate of a bathhouse, wrapped in a quilt. Evidently, he had been killed in the course of running away. Xue's guess is that the other two were killed inside the house at about ten in the evening.

Xu Yuguan was ten years old during the invasion, but in 1952, he served as mayor of Xinfengzhen. According to him, Xinfengzhen had been known as "Little Shanghai," and it was famous for its highly developed system of canals and its production of ginger and silkworms. Before the Japanese invasion, the population consisted of 400 households with 1,800 people, living in 3,000 rooms. Of these, 1,018 rooms were burned by the Japanese, and 100 more were demolished and used for firewood. Only 23 rooms in 8 households were left undamaged. Most of the residents were able to flee, but 86 of them were killed.

After the Tenth Army passed through the towns and villages in this way, it attacked and captured Jiaxing on November 19. The morning edition of the *Asahi Shimbun* for November 20, 1937, carried the following article under the headline "Changre and Jiaxing Secured at a Single Blow."

> Special correspondents Imai and Kodama reporting from Jinshan, November 19: After the _____Unit of the Shanghai Southern Army fought through heavy rains, Jiaxing, the third encampment and most vital defense point of the resisting Chinese forces, fell at six o'clock on the morning of the 19th. Our troops had already surrounded Jiaxing by the 18th, and from the evening of the 18th till dawn on the 19th, our _____units, the main force of the Kataoka, Kozakai, Nozoe, and ___ [2] yama Units cooperated in the concentrated bombardments by the _____Units from Shuangqiaozhen in the north to the vicinity of Jiulihui in the west. and the last forces defending Hangzhou fell into our hands. At six o'clock on the morning of the 19th, we flew the Rising Sun flag from the highest point in the city of Jiaxing.

---

2. This part is illegible on the original document.

EXCERPT FROM CHAPTER 8 OF NANKIN DAIGYAKUSATSU: "A MAD RUSH INTO THE CITY OF HUZHOU"

In Chapter 4, I mentioned a bit about what happened to the 10th Army between the time it landed at Hangzhou Bay and the time it arrived at Jiaxing. The next major city as one moves west from Jiaxing is Huzhou, but on the way there along the canal are such towns as Pingwangzhen, Zhenzezhen, and Nanxunzhen. I'd like to relate to you some of the experiences that survivors from the Nanxunzhen area told me about when I went there to interview them.

Fan Xiren was fifteen years old on November 15, when the Japanese occupied Pingwangzhen, and he says that even people in Nanxunzhen, 24 kilometers away, could here the sound of gunfire. The shopkeepers immediately

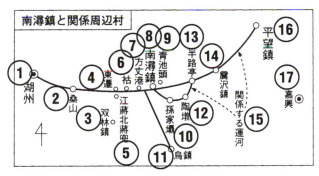

Nanxunzhen and its surroundings.

1. Huzhou	10. Cunjiaba
2. Sangshan	11. Wuzhen
3. Shuang linzhen	12. Taodun
4. Dongqian	13. Banluting
5. Jiangjiangbeijiangdou	14. Zhenzezhen
6. Gu	15. The canal connecting
7. Fangzhanggang	them
8. Nanxunzhen	16. Pingwangzhen
9. Qingchitou	17. Jiaxing

Fan Xiren.

closed up their shops and began fleeing. They didn't have far to go: most of them were headed for small peasant villages scattered throughout the countryside.

Fan's house was located along the Huangyu River, somewhat removed from the center of the city. His father, Fan Xiaosan, made his living as an artist, and the rest of the family consisted of Fan's mother, his two older brothers, his younger sister, and two younger brothers, eight people in all. On this particular day, Fan and his father remained in the city to guard their house, while the other six members of the family fled to Yansan, a small peasant village two kilometers to the southwest.

On the 18th, Fan and his father began

The city of Nanxunzhen

1. The part that was burned	7. Baijianlou	14. Nanshihe
2. Beishihe	8–9. Guandimiao	15. Huangyuhe
3. Beiza	10. Great Bridge	16. New Bridge
4. Highway	11. New Bridge	17. Dongzha
5. Yonganqiao Street	12. Canal	18. Nanzha
6. Kaolaowan	13. Merchants' association	

to hear gunfire from the east. His father went outside to look around, and he came back to report, "It looks as if the Japanese army's in town. Let's get out of here right away." Carrying cane baskets and bundles of clothes and shoes, they headed for the village where the rest of the family had fled. The sun was already setting, but as the two of them left the city and looked back, they could see the sky lit up by large tongues of flame.

Since Fan Xiren stayed away for a while, he did not directly witness the hellish slaughter that took place when the Japanese attacked Nanxunzhen, but according to the written records and to what he heard later, the Japanese first came from the direction of Pingwangzhen along the canal, and then at Banluting, where the canal forked, they headed south in a roundabout way and took the two villages of Taodun and Cunjiaba before entering Nanxunzhen from the south. Other Japanese troops came from the east along the highway, and at about four in the afternoon, they engaged a small unit of Nationalist Chinese troops from the Guangxi Army east of town at Dongzha. The Nationalists fought for only a short time before being routed.

Once the two groups of Japanese soldiers met, they started in on a round of arson and killing. First the houses on either end of the new bridge at the east end of town were burned, followed by the houses on either end of the main bridge and the western main street, and they kept smoldering until noon of the next day. About half the town was burned, and even many of the surrounding villages lost buildings. It was a full ten days before all the fires were brought under control. According to a survey conducted the following

The place where the Japanese landed.

The canal at the eastern edge of Nanxunzhen. The highway can be seen in the distance.

March, a total of 4,493 rooms were burned, about half on the north side of the canal and half on the south side.

Zhou Shiye had fled from Shanghai to his hometown of Nanxunzhen, and between the attack and the end of December, he tabulated the number of dead and wrote up a report that gave the number of bodies as about 400. He himself saw an elementary school teacher named Zhuang Kaibuo and his son being killed. In addition, Zhang Hefu, an elderly laborer who died in 1982, determined that the dead included about a hundred Nationalist soldiers who had been unable to get away, about eighty townspeople, and about two hundred peasants from nearby villages. The villagers were mostly people who had been forced into labor by the Japanese or those who had relatives in the city and had come to help them move their belongings.

According to eyewitnesses, corpses lay scattered throughout the streets of the city, but the worst places were the area from Ximuxiang to Xizha in the west and the Tangjiadou and Kaolaowan neighborhoods in the center of town. Baijianlou was the site of a massacre of thirty people, witnessed by the family of the engineer Cui Xuexing.

Shen Baowen was twenty-seven years old and newly married. After the Nationalists blew up the bridge across the canal, he fled to Xinantai, the village next to Shuanglinzhen, where his family had already fled a week earlier.

When he returned to town about two weeks later, he found that two of his relatives, his mother's older brother Shen Jinbao and his wife's older brother, Zai Yunsheng, were missing. Both had been residents of the northeastern suburb of Qingchitou, and they were among eleven people from that area whose fate was unknown. What had happened became clear when Shen's brother-in-law reappeared some time later.

Shen Baowen.

The eleven who were rounded up by the Japanese were all peasants, including some young men, and just as the soldiers were about to kill them en masse, a boat full of other Japanese soldiers happened by. Coincidentally, the Chinese man who had been drafted to row the boat was an acquaintance of both Shen Jinbao and Zai Yunsheng. He told the Japanese that he couldn't quite handle the boat by himself, and he asked for permission to have Shen and Zai come aboard and help him.

The massacre took place immediately afterward right in front of Shen and Zai. One of the nine remaining people tried to run away and was shot down. The rest were stabbed to death one after another with bayonets. After witnessing this, Shen Jinbao became mentally disturbed, and he hanged himself about half a year later.

Shen Baowen also heard about the following victims from his brother-in-law:

> A Yin: A man who was found dead in an irrigation ditch.

> Zhen Bao: A man whose throat was cut while he was sitting in a privy.

> Zai Aizhen: A woman in her twenties who was raped and stabbed. When found, she was naked from the waist down and had been stabbed seven times.

> A Feng and Gong Yun: Two women in their twenties who were raped but survived.

> Zai Caisheng: A man who was shot while rowing a boat and died about a week later.

Zhu Congliang.

Zhu Congliang was twenty-four years old and living in Fangzhanggang, a village about 4.5 kilometers from Nanxunzhen. Almost all the villagers had fled, but Zhu, his mother, and his older brother had remained behind, since they had no relatives in other villages to whom they could go for refuge and were so poor that they didn't have any extra money to support themselves while they were gone. They decided to wait till just before the Japanese arrived and try to make a break for it then.

On the evening of the 18th, the first Japanese troops came into the village from the south and began ripping the doors off the houses and carrying them down to the canal. Their intention was to build a temporary bridge to replace the Jiuli Bridge that the retreating Nationalist troops had blown up.

Seeing the Japanese, the Zhu family sneaked out of their house, with the two brothers carrying bundles and the mother carrying a thermos bottle. They walked north for half a li, about 250 meters, until they came to a small Confucian temple where the wealthy people and the more prosperous peasants honored their ancestors. This is where they hid.

After what was apparently a engineering unit had built the temporary bridge, several hundred Japanese troops came pouring into town in order to spend the night. They left the next morning. When the Zhu family returned to see what had happened, they found that about half the hundred rooms in the village had been torn down and burned for firewood, although their own house was undamaged. The undamaged houses were full of traces of the soldier's stay, including cooked food, all of which had been left lying there.

One of the villagers, a fifty-five-year-old man named Shen Mazi, had been captured in his home. Judging from appearances, the Japanese must have spent the night in his home and forced him to help with the cooking. However, before they left, they tied his hands, threw him into a large pot of hot water, and boiled him to death.

On the evening of the next day, the 19th, Zhu's cousin, the son of his father's older brother, a forty-eight-year-old man named Zhu Yuntang. was on his way back from his place of refuge, Wuzhen, by boat, when he was captured by the Japanese at Gucun. Of the three people in the boat, one jumped into the water and escaped, and according to him, the other two were

The old houses along the canal at the southern end of Nanxunzhen.

taken to the riverbank and shot. The body of Zhu's cousin was retrieved from a manure storage vessel near the site of the shooting.

Zhang Tianchi was twenty-seven years old that year. Zhang's family and his wife's brother's family lived in a village called Jiangjiangbeijiangdou. By the time the Japanese came on the 18th, nearly everyone had already left, but Chen Jiadong, age fifty-five, who worked in the shop owned by Zhang's brother-in-law, decided to stay behind and guard the house. "I'm old already, so nothing bad will happen to me," he said. "When the Japanese come, I'll just offer them some chickens or some-

Zhang Tianchi.

thing, and everything will be fine." A few other older people also chose to stay behind.

Three days later, on the 21st, some troops stationed at Dongqian, immediately north of the village, showed up. However, they weren't after chickens;

they were after *hua guniang*, young women. According to some of the other old people who stayed behind, when the Japanese caught Chen Jiadong, they had him guide them around the village, going from house to house looking for women, but there were none to be found. In reprisal, they took Chen to the side of the canal and killed him.

When the villagers returned home, they found Chen's body in a kneeling position. They were convinced that they had him to thank for the fact that their houses were not burned. If Chen had not been there to guide them, the Japanese probably would have set fire to the whole village in hopes of capturing any women who might come running out of the burning buildings. Even though Chen was not a native of the village, the people held an emotional funeral for him.

It was on November 24 that the Japanese charged into Huzhou. The morning edition of the *Asahi Shimbun* for November 25, 1937, carried the following report under the headline "A Mad Rush into the City of Huzhou."

> Jiaxing, November 24, Domei—At 11:00 A.M. on the 24th, part of the Nagano and Yamada units made a mad rush into the city of Huzhou (Wuxing), but about 3,000 enemy troops were holed up in the houses and put up stubborn resistance, leading to fierce street fighting.

Yang Zhongren was a forty-three-year-old laborer living in Meijiawan, a residential area containing about 200 houses, in the northern part of Huzhou. After the reports that the Japanese had landed at Hangzhou Bay, seven of the twelve members of his family fled, including his wife, their three children, and his younger brother with his wife and child. They ended up in a village 5 kilometers to the west called Zhaowan lungbaosi. The five who remained behind were Yang, his younger brother, his uncle (his father's younger brother) and his wife, and his aunt's father.

During the morning of that day, word that the *Dongyang gui*, or "Eastern devils," had come spread throughout the city of Huzhou, although people were skeptical, because no one had actually seen any Japanese soldiers. The Yang family had planned to slaughter some pigs that day, so with the help of two hired men, they started in with the butchering operations at about eight in the morning. They worked fast and finished around ten, and although the usual custom was to feed the hired men after the work was done, the men decided regretfully to forego the privilege, owing to the uncertain conditions.

After the helpers had left, Yang and his relatives were laying the fresh meat out on the table when they heard a terrific pounding at the door. Something told them that these were no ordinary visitors but a Japanese raiding party, so they panicked and hid under the beds. However, a saw came poking through the crack between the double doors and began cutting away at the wooden bolt. Realizing the danger, Yang and his family came out from under the beds and left by the back door. However, his aunt's father, Cui Pinggui, was already very old and remained in the house while the other four scattered in all directions. His uncle, Yang Laosi, climbed over a bamboo fence and ran about 10 meters before he was shot down. He cried out for help, and although both his wife and father-in-law heard him, they were in no position to rescue him. His wife went and hid in a mulberry orchard.

Yang Zhongren.

Yang Zhongren and his younger brother ran westward, hoping to reach the village where the rest of their family was. But all of a sudden they found themselves face to face with some Japanese soldiers who had sat down to rest. Making some vague gestures, the soldiers spoke to them. Yang and his brother didn't really understand, but they thought the soldiers might be saying, "Get out of here." Yang's younger brother therefore turned around and began walking home, but he hadn't gone 7 meters before one of the soldiers shot and killed him without even getting up.

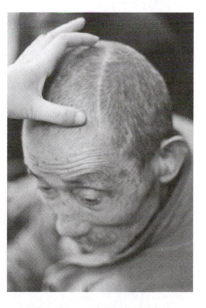

Yang Zhongren still bears the scars of being hit with a rifle butt.

Next the soldier took aim at Yang himself. (Author's note: It may have been half in jest.) Thinking that he was about to killed just like his brother, Yang had no idea what to do and simply froze. Then one of the soldiers knocked him on the head with the butt of his rifle, and he lost consciousness.

A man named Lu who was hiding in a pile of straw happened to witness this scene. According to him, Yang was hit three times and bled profusely. This happened all happened around noon, and the soldiers left at three o'clock, evidently certain that they had killed Yang. Lu went to Yang's home to find his aunt and the aunt's father, who were unharmed, and he told them what had happened. The three of them moved the still-unconscious Yang back to the house. They also fetched the bodies of Yang's younger brother and uncle.

Three days later, the family bought coffins for their dead and buried them in a vacant lot behind the house. After the incident, Yang was bedridden for about two years.

When he gave me this account of his experiences, Yang Zhongren was already quite old, and since he was rather hard of hearing, his son, Yang Xiaolong, acted as a sort of interpreter and helped tell the story.

Bai Denggao was nine years old. He lived in Chuangqian in the southern part of Huzhou with his father, who was a rickshaw man, his mother, and his two-year-old sister.

The Japanese showed up around lunchtime. The family could hear someone pounding heavily on doors across the 5-meter-wide canal. Still a child, Bai was not at all wary and didn't quite realize that the Japanese had come, so he went outside to look. Noticing the boy, the soldiers crossed the canal via a nearby bridge and headed toward the Bai house.

Bai Denggao.

When the soldiers came into the house, they found Bai's father right away and checked for signs that he had worn a military cap. Even though they ascertained that he was not a Chinese soldier, they led him away and made him serve as a water carrier at their base camp in the Dingjia Gardens.

That day, there were still a lot of Chinese troops hiding around town, since the Japanese had invaded the city much earlier than anyone had expected, and the Guangxi Unit, led by Li Zhongren, had been unable to retreat in time. The Japanese went around the city rooting out the stragglers, who were still wearing their army uniforms.

The canal at Huzhou.

The building across the canal from Bai's house was an uninhabited build-ing referred to as "the Liu family temple." Next to it was a vacant lot, and this is where the prisoners of war were assembled. Young Bai watched through a crack in the front door of his house as the prisoners were made to line up along the canal and strip naked. Then the Japanese threatened them with bayonets to make them jump into the water. The canal was not very deep, so the prisoners were unlikely to drown, but because of the winter cold, it was undoubtedly an unpleasant experience for them, and the Japanese simply wanted to torment them a bit.

Then the Japanese made the prisoners come out of the water and go back to the vacant lot, where the massacre began. The soldiers led the naked pris-oners to where three or four of their comrades waited with swords ready. The prisoners were made to sit down and then were beheaded from behind by the swordsmen. Fifty or sixty prisoners were killed in this way.

Three days later, a neighbor boy a year older than Bai was running and playing alongside the canal when a Japanese soldier took aim and shot him dead. His father, Chen, saw this and ran out, but just before he reached his son's body, he, too, was shot dead.

Bai's father returned from the Japanese camp after about a week, but two years later, in 1939, he was again taken away. After two years of forced

Wu Shenggen.

labor, he returned home in a broken-down and exhausted state, and he died eleven days later.

Wu Shenggen was twenty-five years old and a carpenter like his father. The other family members were his mother, his older brother, his wife, and their six-year-old son and two-year-old daughter. His other two older brothers lived elsewhere, and his older sister was married. The family home was located just outside the south gate of the wall.

After the Japanese landing at Hangzhou Bay, Wu's mother had fled with Wu's six-year-old son to her married daughter's home in Dingshanzhen, Yixing County, Jiangsu Province.

Just as the Japanese were about to attack Huzhou, Wu's wife took their two-year-old daughter and hid in the grass at the edge of a pond about one kilometer away. She ended up spending the night with her legs in the water. Thus the only people left at home were Wu, his father, and his older brother.

At seven in the evening, the house next door burst into flames. Surprised, Wu's father went out to look and was immediately found by the Japanese and shot in the stomach. A neighbor, A Si, carried Wu's father, who was on the point of death, into his own house. But the Japanese followed behind and set fire to A Si's house. A Si and his family managed to escape, but they were unable to save Wu's severely wounded father, who burned to death.

The next day, when Wu's older brother went to look for their father's body, he was found by the Japanese and led away, never to be seen again. Wu is certain that he was killed. After Wu's wife had hidden in the pond for a second day, the mother of Wu Huaigui, an acquaintance, found her and kept her for a while.

In March of the following year, Wu was caught up in a mass slaughter and forced to dig the holes where victims were buried alive, but since this happened after the Nanjing Massacre itself, I will not relate the incident.

The next city to the west of Huzhou is Changxing, but on the way there is a village called Lijiaxiang. What happened here also happened after the Nanjing Massacre, but an unusually large number of rapes occurred here, so I will tell about some of them.

In March of 1938, Cheng Guanfa, thirteen years old, was and staying in Gongqiao, about four kilometers to the northeast of Lijiaxiang, as a refugee. He was playing in the yard in front of the house when about thirty Japanese soldiers suddenly appeared, asking for *hua guniang* and searching house to house. In the house next door, they found a seventeen-year-old girl, and four soldiers dragged her away. He didn't see what happened next, but later the adults told him that she had been gang-raped.

Cheng Guanfa.

That evening, the girl drowned herself in the river. Cheng was there when her body was pulled out of the water.

In June of that year, Cheng and his younger brother were back in Lijiaxiang and staying with Xu Liangfa and his wife and ten-year-old daughter.

At about one in the afternoon on a June day, four drunk Japanese soldiers came by, looking for *hua guniang* as usual. Cheng's parents, who were laborers, were away, and so was Xu Liangfa, so only Xu's wife, a woman in her thirties, whom I shall call Wang Meijie, was home, along with the two boys.

The house, two rooms and a kitchen built around a dirt courtyard, belonged to an absentee landlord, and the two families were renting it together. When the soldiers caught Wang Meijie in her room, the boys could hear her screaming *"Jiu ming!"* (Help!). But she was gang-raped on the spot.

After that, Wang Meijie took to her bed and refused to get up for several days.

EXCERPTS FROM CHAPTER 9 OF
NANKIN DAIGYAKUSATSU:
"WE'VE TAKEN CHANGXING . . . AND
GUANGDE . . . AND WUHU"

After Huzhou, the 10th Army split up, and each division took a different route to Nanjing. The 24th Division went via Changxing, Yixing, Liyang, and Lishui. The 6th Division went through Guangde, the eastern suburbs of Langxi, and Gonglanbu. The Kunisaki Detachment went through Guangde, Langxi, Shuiyangzhen, Taiping (Dangtu), and Ma'anshan; crossed the Yangtze; and continued to Wujiangzhen. The 18th Division proceeded through Guangde, Xuancheng (Guoning), and Wuhu.

The *Asahi Shimbun* reported on the occupation of Changxing in the following manner, under the headline "Changxing Also Falls at Dawn."

> Shanghai, special telegram, the 26th: The Nagano, Yamada, Okamoto and other units, having occupied Huzhou and now pursuing the defeated enemy to the northwest, occupied Changxing, 40 kilometers northwest of Huzhou, at dawn. Furthermore, the units that occupied Wuxi are heading further in the direction of Changzhou and continuing their advance.

> Huzhou, the 26th, Domei—The Nagano, Yamada, and Okamoto units met with fierce fighting from artillery units as they rushed into Changxing, which serves as an enemy base in the foothills of Wushan, and they shifted to a bold dawn attack. By the time the day dawned, they had already occupied Changxing. They raised the Rising Sun flag at the highest point of the city wall, and all the troops gave three *banzai* cheers that shook the land south of the Yangtze.

Ye Yintian was twenty-nine years old, working as a reporter for the local newspaper, the *Changxing ribao*, and living in an area called Xiaodongmen near the train station.

Ye was the son of a man who owned a store that sold bamboo products and employed a few dozen people, but almost all of them had fled, and only the people over sixty remained. Since 97 to 98 percent of the population of Changxing had evacuated, only 2 to 3 percent remained, mostly the elderly, or so-called "stubborn people," or those who had simply failed to leave in time. Ye's father was among those who had gone, so Ye and two employees were the only ones still in the shop.

At about seven that morning, he saw flames rising from a house some 30 meters from his own, and immediately afterward, he heard gunfire. However, he hadn't expected the Japanese to arrive so quickly, so it never occurred to him that they were responsible.

Ye Yintian.

One of the employees told Ye, "I'm going to see if anyone's selling cigarettes," and went outside. Soon there was more gunfire, and when Ye looked out the second-story window, he saw that a lot of Japanese soldiers were standing in front of the shop and that the employee had been shot and was lying in the street, still alive and moving. One of the soldiers was wearing a vest and carrying a battle flag with its staff planted on the ground.

Shocked, Ye ran downstairs and escaped through the back door. He fled to a village 3 kilometers to the north, called Nibudun. (Later he fled to another village, less than another kilometer away, called Chezhuli, and, he was away from home for a month altogether.) That's why he didn't learn everything that had happened until later.

After taking Lijiaxiang, the Japanese troops gathered a large force together at Changxing Station and advanced westward along the following three routes:

1. Meishan—Baixian—Mianling—Yixing
2. Xiazhuan—Wuhu
3. Directly to Nanjing

Once inside the city of Changxing, the troops proceeded to a neighborhood about 100 meters from the train station and split into two groups, one of which attacked Xiaodongmen and the other Huangjiawan. They set fire to buildings, beginning with a large pawn shop called Yihedang. Since Changxing was the site of a Chinese air base, it was considered an important target, so Japanese Air Force planes began bombing the area across from the station, largely destroying the Chenghuang Temple and killing more than ten people. Once they had conquered the city, the Japanese military command moved into the home of a rich man named Yang Jusan in the Zhichengzhen neighborhood near the center of town.

After staying away for about ten days, Ye apprehensively returned to town to see if his house was all right. He took the long way, circling around the north end of the city, and since the houses had been burned, he had a good view for reconnoitering. He saw that the soldiers camped there were out and around between seven and nine in the morning and then took a short break, so he took advantage of that time to go check up on his house. Unfortunately, he found that it had been burned as well.

Since the Japanese were in the center of the city, they didn't go out into the county districts, but Ye sometimes sneaked outside the walls at night to have a look around. There were rumors going around that the Japanese had cut off women's bound feet and stacked them up at the Jinlian Bridge, so Ye and three companions set out at six one morning to see if the rumors were true. They arrived at the bridge, which was 700 meters north-northwest of the station, at about eight, having acquired several more companions on the way, until they ended up with a party of ten.

The Jinlian Bridge was a fairly large bridge over the canal on the way to the Jinlian Temple, but the the rumored pile of bound feet was actually at the Little Jinlian Bridge, a single slab of stone about 1½ meters long and 60 or 70 centimeters wide, laid across a branch of the same canal. The feet were piled up not on the bridge itself, but on the road next to it. The pile was of the same diameter as the road and in a cone shape several dozen centimeters high. The cone had been shaped with remarkable care, with a single foot at its apex. Some feet still wore shoes of many colors or decorated with embroidery, while others were bare, and still others were so covered with blood that it was impossible to tell whether they wore shoes or not. Because of the cold, the flesh had not yet started to decay, and there was little odor. Ye and his companions stood around the pile of feet, terrified, pale, and trembling.

Ye soon joined up with Chiang Kai-shek's Nationalists. About two years later, a party leaders' training session was held at Tianmu Mountain in Deqing County, about 100 *li* (50 kilometers) from Changxing, and that was where Ye met a Japanese prisoner of war who had been captured by Nationalist guerrillas. The prisoner had originally been a carpenter, and since he had been a prisoner for a long time, he could speak some Chinese. When Ye asked him about the bound feet, he replied, "Those feet are a novelty in Japan, and we'd never seen them before, so we cut them off. I didn't do that myself, but other people did."

According to the old people who re-mained in the city, most of the women whose feet were cut off bled to death.

Ma Gonglin was nineteen years old in 1937. Before telling me about his ex-periences, he admitted, "I don't like to talk about the past. When I do, I start crying, with my parents being killed and everything. But since you've come here to investigate the crimes that were com-mitted during the Japanese invasion, I'll make the effort."

Ma Gonglin's family were peasants in Zhuangjia, a village about 10 kilometers from Changxing. Their house was perhaps 100 meters from the road, in the middle of

Ma Gonglin.

the fields. There were four people in the family, including his fifty-three-year-old father, his forty-five-year-old mother, and his twelve-year-old sis-ter. Ma mentioned that, around that time, he had something wrong with his foot and couldn't work much.

About three days before the Japanese came, Ma and his sister were to be sent to the home of their father's younger sister in Changdou, and their thirty-six-year-old cousin came to take them the 3 kilometers by boat. The parents were supposed to leave a bit later, but because the Japanese came so much sooner than they had anticipated, it was too late for them.

Ma himself did not witness what happened next, but when he returned from his refuge about a month later, this is what the other villagers told him.

His parents were hiding in a cemetery about 200 meters from their house. Here and there, they could see smoke rising from burning houses. Ma's mother could not stand not knowing what was happening to her own house, so she moved to a position that afforded a better view. The Japanese caught her and raped her in a field in front of the house. She was later found dead, naked from the waist down and with an ax lodged in her.

When his wife did not return, Ma's father also left the cemetery, but he evidently saw from afar that she was surrounded by Japanese soldiers. Vil-lage residents saw him running off to the west, half-crazed and weeping, perhaps trying to join his children at their refuge. However, at Yaojia Bridge, about 2 kilometers away, the Japanese caught and beheaded him.

News of his father's tragic fate soon reached the place where Ma was staying. Two or three days later, when the Japanese had left the area around Yaojia Bridge, Ma, who was still unable to walk well, had his cousin go and retrieve his father's body.

Villagers covered the pathetic remains of Ma's mother with straw after the Japanese left, but a couple of days later, some more Japanese showed up and set fire to the straw. When Ma came back with a coffin about a month later, he found his mother's body with the clothing and hair burned away.

In June of the following year, fifteen people were steamed to death in the area, but since this happened after the Nanjing Massacre, I will not tell the full story.

Zhou Shuxin was eleven years old. He came from a peasant family in a village called Qiaoxi, about 4 kilometers southeast of Changxing. The day the Japanese came through, he fled to the home of his married sister in

Zhou Shuxin.

Wangbin, but after returning home, he heard the following account from his aunt, the wife of his father's elder brother.

The Japanese came at about three in the afternoon. In the home of the Tu family was a ninety-eight-year-old woman who had remained behind when the rest of the family fled. The soldiers knocked on the gate of the bamboo fence around the family yard, and when the old woman went to open it, they shot her dead. At about the same time, a peasant named Xu Ahei, age forty, tried to run away from the soldiers and was also shot and killed.

Since the Japanese left, Zhou returned to Qiaoxi, but more soldiers showed up during the afternoon of the following day. He fled to a small lake in the village of Fangjiabin, which was on the other side of the highway, and hid in the deep grasses along the edge.

In the village of Fangjiabin was a young peasant from Henan named Ping Maotou who lived with his twenty-five-year-old wife and three-year-old daughter. When three Japanese suddenly showed up at his house, Ping was able to escape, but the soldiers caught his wife.

When Ping went back in the evening, he found that his house had been burned, and his wife was lying dead outside, having been raped and stabbed in the belly with a bayonet. Their three-year-old daughter was also dead, lying on top of her mother's body and stabbed through the heart. The villagers surmised that the little girl must have followed along, clinging to her mother as she was dragged away.

Stunned by the tragic fate of his wife and daughter, Ping drowned himself in the lake. One of Ping's neighbors, Chen Qianzhong, witnessed the suicide and told Zhou about it afterward.

The morning edition of *Asahi Shimbun* for December 1, 1937, reported the following under the headline "Guangde Also Occupied, Imperial Army Invincible."

> Shanghai, special report, the 30th—As the northern lines of battle are extended, the units along the southern battle lines are also reaping increasing results and extending along the west side of Tai Hu Lake. They have entered a mountainous region along the border between Zhejiang and Anhui provinces and are advancing westward from Huzhou. Early in the evening of the 29th, the Fujiyama and Yamada units, which captured Sianzhen, occupied Guangde in Anhui Province. Guangde occupied an important position in the three provinces of Jiangsu, Zhejiang, and Anhui, and it is easy to defend and difficult to attack, but it has been considered a vital area from the very beginning. For this reason, the Nanjing government is said to have recently hurried to lay out branch rail lines from Xuancheng to Guangde along the Jinggan Railroad. Furthermore, the year before last, a large airport was established here, and along with Nanchang, it was the Chinese Air Force's most important base. The Chinese could not have imagined that the war would expand all the way to this area, and they have recently established military bases farther west of Guangde. Since the enemy's previous general command headquarters were here, losing the battles in the southeastern portion of Anhui, together with the attacks from the direction of Jinggan, means that the threat of the Chinese army is increasing. The fate of Nanjing is like that of a flame in the wind.

Wang Shicheng (seventy-two at the time of the interview) was twenty-five in 1937 and had a small general store in the Xiaodongmen neighborhood of Guangde. The 24th day of the tenth month, according to the old peasant calendar (November 26, 1937), began with an air raid by Japanese planes. Wang happened to be behind a Catholic church when the bombing occurred, and he saw a young woman who had been hit and was lying there with her internal organs spilling out. Throughout the city, there were bodies with the limbs blown off.

Wang Shicheng.

Wang's family, including his wife, soon fled to the suburb of Xixiang, but Wang himself stayed behind to guard the shop.

However, on the 26th day of the tenth month (November 28), just before the Japanese came into the city, Wang also fled to Xixiang. A week later, as he was on his way home, he saw a pile of about 100 corpses under the large bridge at the west gate of the city. Because it was winter, there wasn't much water in the river, which was about 30 meters wide and 2 meters deep, and he could see that all the bodies, some of which were those of elderly women and children, wore typical peasant clothing, There wasn't a single body in a Nationalist uniform. He later heard that all these people had been shot. When he returned home, he found that his house had been burned.

He saw and heard of a number of rape-murders. For example, in Wuchangxiang, the sixty-year-old wife of an acquaintance of his, Zhang Zhili, was raped by Japanese soldiers and then shot. Afterward, they stuck a stalk of Chinese cabbage up her vagina. In a house in front of the Catholic church, a seventy-year-old woman was stripped naked, raped, and shot. The family of Li Dingyuan, both parents and five children, was completely wiped out.

Advancing westward from Guangde, the Japanese occupied Xuancheng on December 7, and on the following day, they took over Wanzhizhen. However, according to Cheng Yongshu, eighteen at the time (65 at the time of the interview), Wanzhizhen was invaded by Japanese troops on December 4, after being bombed by four planes on December 2, although these troops went on to somewhere else on the evening of December 6. Then they—or perhaps a different unit— came back on December 8. These troops stayed until February 27, 1945, near the end of the war.

Right after the bombing, Cheng fled to Nanling County, about 20 kilometers to the southwest. The soldiers of the Nationalist army also fled at the same time, but without burning any houses or otherwise destroying things. On the morning of December 7, Cheng went to see his house on Sanjia Street and found that the whole area, including his house, had been burned out, and that there were five or six bodies nearby. (The town had a population of over 30,000, but it was largely abandoned during the war, and even in 1945, its population was only about 6,000.)

That same day, Cheng heard stories from an old man named Li Dezhang, who lived near a Catholic church slightly uphill and 40 meters away from a pawnshop on Bajia Street. The church flew the French flag and was presided over by a Spanish priest whose Chinese name was "Na." Old Li told him that the pawnbroker's large mansion, which was about 100 meters from the site of Cheng's house, had been the scene of rapes and massacres.

The pawnbroker's mansion was made of brick, a castle-like building of 660 square meters built around a central gar-

Cheng Yongshu.

den. Its 9-meter [sic] outer walls had a front and a back entrance, and the part around the front entrance was three stories high, while the rest of the complex was two stories high. The front door was made of iron.

The Japanese locked two or three hundred Chinese into this building, spread kerosene around, and set it on fire. Then they machine-gunned anyone who tried to escape.

Having heard this story from Old Li, Cheng went to see the burned-out ruins for himself. The most pathetic of the corpses he saw was that of a naked woman who lay near the rear door with her feet burned black. According to Old Li, this was the approximately thirty-year-old wife of a man named Du, and she had been thrown into the fire after being raped and killed.

Even though the front door of the mansion was covered with iron on the outside, the inside was wood, and this had burned and collapsed. There were said to be more bodies inside, but the idea of going in and seeing more gruesome sights terrified Cheng. Before the day was over, he fled back to Nanling County and stayed there until the war was over.

Wan Xuansheng (61 at the time of the interview, 14 years old in 1937) lived in a house on Bajia Street about 300 meters from the pawnbroker's mansion. On December 6, his six-room, 130-square-meter house was burned,

Wan Xuansheng.

although by that time, the family had already fled to his parents' home region, a rural area of Hanshan County. According to what he heard from his uncle, his father's third younger brother, his sixty-year-old grandmother, Zhu Laidi, was raped and killed just after the Japanese came into town. In 1941, Wan's twenty-seven-year-old brother, Wan Xuanlu, was beaten to death by the Japanese on some pretext or other.

It was on the evening of December 9 that the Eighteenth Division of the Tenth Army burst into Wuhu, a city on the banks of the Yangtze, but there isn't much information about it, because at that time, the mass media were focusing their attention on other military units, which were moving into positions surrounding Nanjing, and the papers and broadcasts were full of declarations that Nanjing would fall today or the next day. In the morning edition of *Yomiuri Shimbun* for December 10, for example, we find only the following short article under the headline, "The Rising Sun Flag Flies Over the City of Wuhu."

> Xuancheng, December 9, Domei—The Kataoka, Kozakai, Nozoe, and Fujiyama units took invincible positions on the 9th and pressed upon Wuhu, shifting to an all-out attack at five in the afternoon. Bursting into the city in the evening, they flew the inspiring Rising Sun flag over the city. As of six in the evening, they were carrying out mopping-up operations within the city.

Ge Zhengkun (63 at the time of interview) was fifteen years old, the son of a poor longshoreman living in the Sanming'an area of Wuhu. Most of the residents of Wuhu had fled across the Yangtze as the Japanese approached, but Ge's family couldn't afford to pay the fare on the boats that were ferrying people over. He was living with his mother, younger brother, and younger sister—their father was working for the Nationalists as a longshoreman and had moved on with them as they left.

The Japanese showed up at four or five in the afternoon, but since the Chinese army had already withdrawn, there was no fighting. Young Ge had never seen Japanese soldiers before, so he was watching them from the window with great curiosity. There were about nine or ten of them, some on foot and some on horseback, heading down the street led by a soldier with a battle flag. Ge innocently ran outside to get a better look, but when he was within 5 or 6 meters of the soldiers, the one right behind the flag bearer tried to stab him with a bayonet, grazing his left arm. Shocked, he ran back into the house. "It's the Eastern devils!" his mother cried, and she hid him deep inside the house. They decided to leave as soon as possible, and waiting for nightfall, they set out at eight o'clock, headed for Guanyu, a place about 20 kilometers northwest of the city.

Ge Zhengkun.

Ge's family stayed on in Guanyu, but in March of 1938, he returned to Wuhu to see what had happened to their house, even though it was just a humble house with a thatched roof. While in town, he was captured by the soldiers based nearby and put to work picking up the manure from the cavalry horses with his bare hands. He was beaten frequently, sometimes while hung from the ceiling by both wrists.

Zhou Yongsong (61 at the time of the interview) was fourteen in 1937. On December 5, before the Japanese came into Wuhu, three of their planes bombed Taihe Wharf along the Yangtze. Hearing that some ships were on fire, Zhou went to Zhaoshangju Wharf (now called the Number Eight Wharf) to watch. There he saw a passenger ship called the *Dehe* engulfed in flames. It had just pulled away from the docks carrying 3,000 passengers, all of them refugees bound for Wuhan. Only people who could afford the fare had been allowed on, and all the entrances had been sealed so that poor people would not be

Zhou Yongsong.

The *Asahi Shimbun* reported that "The all-out assault on Nanjing began with a volley of large shells from our rows of artillery positions at 1:00 P.M. on the 7th." Below that is an article about the naval bombardment and fall of Wuhu, and it says, "The troops arrived in Wuhu after cutting through lakes and marshes. Smoke was still rising from the places that had been bombed the previous day. Retreating enemy stragglers have poured into Wuhu from Nanjing. Prepare for bombardment! As we watch, all the bombs that we have are thrown at the city and its large buildings."

able to force their way on board without paying.

Evidently, however, a bomb fell through the smokestack and exploded inside the ship, and a huge fire broke out as the ship floated 200 meters from the riverbank. The people on the decks jumped into the river, but those inside were doomed, since most of the doors were locked, and almost all of them burned to death. Zhou could hear screams and cries for help. Yet, rumor had it that the Nationalists were transporting munitions in the hold, so the people on the riverbank just stood by for fear that the whole ship might go up in a massive explosion. However, they did toss pieces of wood into the river so that the people who had jumped in would have something to grab onto. Some of Zhou's acquaintances were saved in this way, including the sixty-year-old owner of a furniture store named Tang Guangtai.

The ship had already been burning for five hours [sic] by the time Zhou went to look, and it burned for two more hours before sinking. It is believed that 2,000 people perished in the disaster.

Long after the war, in 1978, the *Dehe* was raised from the bottom of the Yangtze, and in addition to a multitude of skeletons, searchers found a large amount of money.

Yan Daoxi (age 65) was eighteen years old in 1937 and living with his parents and three brothers in the Xihuayuan area of Wuhu. They tried to evacuate to their hometown north of the Yangtze, but there were no boats available, so they fled to a hospital run by an American church organization, where Yan's uncle, his father's younger brother, had already gone. However, their neighbors, a young man named Gan Laosan (age 28), who made his living plucking ducks [sic], and his twenty-year-old wife remained behind.

The young couple lived right along the river bank, and their house like all the other houses in that location, had a deck to the water's edge. When the river was high, there was water all the way to the house, and when the river was low, there was dry land underneath. Since the river was low, this is where they hid when the Japanese came.

As Gan Laosan tells it, the Japanese found them. He doesn't remember how many soldiers there were, but they forced him into a corner and then surrounded his wife and raped her. From about ten o'clock in the morning to six in the evening, soldiers took turns with her, new ones showing up when others left. Her cries eventually stopped, as if she had lost consciousness. When the soldiers finally left, Gan picked

Yan Daoxi.

her up and carried her to the hospital. Although she seemed to have no external injuries, she died soon after. Yan remembers seeing her body.

Sun Zhaoyang (age 60) was thirteen years old. He lived in Fangcun, just outside of Wuhu, one of the eight villages in Wuhu County. There were only twenty households in the village, and only two family names, Sun and Xu. As the villagers made their plans to escape before the Japanese came, they

Sun Zhaoyang.

decided that one household of men from each clan should remain behind. Sun Zhaoyang and his father were chosen to "represent" the Sun clan and take care of the village's possessions and cattle. A man named Xu Xifang also stayed behind as the "representative" of the Xu clan.

The Sichuan Army of the Nationalist forces had been in the area, and in the course of their retreat they had blown up the so-called Milk Bridge, which crossed the Qingyi River west of town. However, a small group of Nationalist soldiers had been unable to retreat in time, and they were in a hamlet called Shahekou about 2.5 kilometers south along the river from Fangcun.

Cavalrymen led the Japanese troops who came to the village in the evening, followed by foot soldiers, and they all spent the night. At about eight the next morning, some soldiers showed up at Sun's house, took young Zhaoyang, and ordered him to swim across the river with a rope. As he swam, he saw that there were five or six hundred bodies in the river, both Nationalist army stragglers and ordinary peasants. However, the peasants were evidently refugees from somewhere else, because he didn't know any of them.

Once young Sun was across the river, he strung the rope, and after that, the Japanese lashed three tubs together with boards on top and made a raft. Five or six soldiers got onto the raft, pulled themselves across the river with the rope, and retrieved boats that were on the opposite bank.

However, two or three days later, some more troops came through town in pursuit of retreating Chinese soldiers, and in the course of doing so, they burned eight houses, including Sun's, and shot the cattle. The pigs also died in the fires. Sun and his father wanted to flee, but they couldn't as long as the Japanese were in town.

Two or three days later, two Japanese soldiers came to town at about nine in the morning, accosted Xu Xifang, and said something to him. Sun and his father saw the soldiers shoot Xu, who could not have known what they were saying. Alarmed, the older Sun hid his son in a pile of straw, but the two soldiers found him anyway. They were about to bayonet him, but his father knelt down and begged, "This is my son. Please spare him." The soldiers hit the father with the butts of their rifles and then kicked the boy in the buttocks so hard that he flew through the air. "I still have the scars from that time," Sun told me.

The father and son soon realized that the Japanese soldiers had come to look for women and that Xu had been killed because he hadn't responded to their demands. The soldiers found a fourteen-year-old girl who had unfortunately returned to the village and raped her.

That evening, Sun and his father left the village.

Forty kilometers north of Wuhu on the way to Nanjing is the industrial city of Ma'anshan. Part of the Tenth Army passed through this region on their way to Nanjing.

About 10 *li* (5 kilometers) west of Ma'anshan along the Yangtze is the village of Caishiji, where there was once a large temple called Jiuhuamiao. Normally, thirty or forty monks lived there with a distinguished Buddhist teacher named Changji, but they had been joined by a large number of monks who had fled there for refuge from other smaller temples in the area.

Sun Ziming (age 61) was thirteen at the time. He lived at the west end of Caishiji with his family (his parents, younger sister, older brother, and sister-in-law), who were peasants. One evening at eight or nine o'clock, he heard gunfire coming from the direction of Jiuhuamiao, which stood on a hill a short way from the family home. When he went outside to look, he saw the

Sun Ziming.

temple in flames, casting a red glow over the whole sky. At about midnight, his entire family left the house and went to hide in a 3- or 4-square-meter cave about 1 *li* northwest of the village, which had been hollowed out of a rock to use as an-air raid shelter.

The following morning, they returned home, and about half an hour after they arrived, Sun's mother's cousin (the son of her father's sister), Tao Laosi, showed up. Tao, who was about twenty-seven or twenty-eight, had worked at the temple as a servant for two years, but that morning, his clothes were filthy with what looked like muddy water. Obviously terrified, he told the terrible story of what had happened at Jiuhuamiao.

The previous evening, twenty or thirty Japanese soldiers had burst into the temple to find the monks at prayer next to a flame called the "Buddha lamp." A soldier wielding a sword pointed at the flame and said something. It wasn't clear what he was saying, but he seemed to want them to extinguish the flame. Now this Buddha lamp was a special flame, fueled by oil that devout peasants had contributed. It burned in a large jar that held 300 or 400 kilograms of oil, covered with boards (a floating frame), with a wick in the middle. It was not supposed to be extinguished, day or night.

Assuming that the monks were ignoring their orders, the soldiers started killing the praying monks with their swords. (Tao Laosi saw all this as he hid in the drain near the entrance. Some say that the monks were killed with both bayonets and swords, but Tao insists that the soldiers used only swords.) Afterward, the soldiers threw altar fittings and other wooden items into the jar to feed the flame. Finally, they broke the jar, causing the the flaming oil to spill out and set fire to the temple. As the flames rose, Tao Laosi was afraid that the soldiers would discover him, so he escaped through the underground sewer.

He was the only person connected with Jiuhuamiao who was not killed.

This is all I will recount of the course of the Tenth Army's assault on China before reaching Nanjing. . . .

As I followed the course of the Shanghai Expeditionary Force, I heard many reports from survivors of massacres involving 100 people or more, but I did not have the opportunity to collect any such stories from survivors along the route of the 10th Army. That does not mean that there were no such large-scale massacres along its route. Here's an example from the confessions of a Japanese soldier, a field artillery squad leader from the 6th Division (Kumamoto), a man who wrote under the name of Nakagawa

Seiichiro (*To the Generations Who Don't Know War,* "The Yangtze Is Weeping—A Record of the Kumamoto 6th Division Landing Force," published by Daisan 8).

> On the way, we caught a Chinese straggler, and thinking that there must be more, we searched for them. About 200 more stragglers emerged, waving white flags of surrender, as the first prisoner summoned them. . . . [1] There we transferred the prisoners to the infantry, and we in the field artillery proceeded to our destination, but a few days later, I heard that all the prisoners had been killed. I also heard that on the previous day, nearly 300 stragglers and civilians had been taken prisoner, lined up along the railroad tracks, and wiped out by machine gun fire.

---

1. This happened on the way to Wuhu, and a construction party of twenty-five men had gone to a nearby village to find civilians who could be drafted as laborers to construct housing for the Japanese.

The ellipses in the passage quoted represent the following account: "When the twenty-five of us led the prisoners to an infantry camp, the senior officer there shouted at us, 'How can you guys fight a war when you're leading those prisoners around?' That's why we had to hand the prisoners over to the infantrymen. At that point, a young Chinese soldier about twenty years old made a break for it. Several of the infantry men took off their bayonets, aimed at him, and shot, and most of the shots missed, but one found its target. The young Chinese fell without making a sound and lay still."

EXCERPT FROM CHAPTER 22 OF NANKIN DAIGYAKUSATSU: "APPROXIMATELY 20,000 PEOPLE HELD AT THE SITE OF THE MASSACRE"

A photograph owned by Masao Shirato, who was part of the 65th Regiment, 8th Company Infantry, and shown as it appears in his photo album. The inscription above the photograph, "Outside Nanjing, Mufu Mountain, prisoners of war," was written by Shirato himself. You can clearly see that the prisoners are being led along with their hands tied behind their backs. Taken from *Soldiers of the Imperial Army Who Recorded the Great Nanjing Massacre*, edited by Ono Kenji and others.

What Niu Xianming surmised in his *Return to the Secular Life* was correct, namely that "Since there is no reason to kill 20,000 people at once, they must have divided them up and killed them in groups." It is extremely likely that they were divided into two, or even more likely, at least three groups. Let's take a look at the following primary source materials and eye-witness accounts.

From the field diary of Miyamoto Shogo:

> December 17, light snow—Today for part of the day I participated in the triumphal entry into Nanjing, but for the most part I was charged with disposing of prisoners. We left at 8:30 and marched to Nanjing and took part in the triumphal entry under clear skies in the afternoon. I was able to see the magnificent historic scene all around.
>
> In the evening, we finally returned, and we soon helped dispose of the prisoners and left. It was over 20,000. In the end, there was a great fiasco. We ended up wounding and killing a number of friendly troops. Our company suffered one dead, two wounded.

From the field diary of Endo Takaaki:

> December 17, clear—At 7:00 A.M. sent nine men to the summit of Mufu Mountain as guards. In order to participate in the triumphal entry into Nanjing, I had men from the R[egiment?] representing the 13th D[ivision?] form a line, and at 8:00 A.M., I left with ten soldiers from the platoon, and entered the city through the Heping Gate. In front of the Central Military Officers' Training School on the Nationalist Government Road, we were reviewed by His Excellency Army Commander Matsui. On the way, we saw them pressing seals to commemorate the founding of the field post office. I sent postcards to _____ko and Kan. I returned to my quarters at 5:30 P.M. Since it was 3 *li* from my quarters to the ceremonial site, I was tired. In the evening, I sent five men to punish more than 10,000 prisoners. I discovered the Tonichi[?] branch office in Nanjing today. When I asked after Takebushi, I heard that he is visiting someone in northern China. The wind has come up, and it's cold.

From the field diary of Sugeno Yoshio:

> (December) 17—I participated in the unprecedentedly grand ceremony of the triumphal entry. The ceremony began at 1:30. Prince Asaka and His Excellency Army Commander Matsui reviewed the troops. I joined in gunning down the remaining 10,000 or more prisoners.

From the field diary of Meguro Tomiharu:

> December 17, clear, outside the walls of Nanjing—I left the billeting area at 9:00 A.M. and participated in the Army Commander's triumphal entry into Nanjing, a history-making grand ceremony. At 5:00 P.M. I was put to work shooting about 13,000 enemy soldiers. Over two days, the Yamada Unit shot nearly 20,000. It seems that all the prisoners of every unit are to be shot.

Then we have the field diary of Saito Jiro, who evidently did not participate in the killing but wrote about the day as follows:

> Since today was the triumphal entry into Nanjing, it was decided that every squad should participate, except for the people who were on duty. At the supply unit, we divided everything up, and I, _____, Takeda, and Okamoto decided to be on duty while everyone else left at 8:00 A.M. During the morning, I left my post and went to requisition feed for the horses. Ten or more of our planes were participating in the triumphal entry, and roaring mightily they flew above us in formation, a stirring sight. Today was the old oil-pressing festival, the 15th, and we got together with _____ from the cavalry and the five of us made sweet red beans. We ate them sitting around the campfire, talking about various things, and wishing we were back home. There's talk that we will soon go over to the opposite bank of the Yangtze, march 10 or more *li* and be posted to a garrison. I've seen how things are for the refugees, and they're really in a pathetic state. No matter what happens, I don't want Japan to become a defeated country. In the evening, a reserve unit of about 150 men arrived. I saw Ando Fusao and Hashimoto Saburo from _____, and I asked for news of Kinkichi. They said he's with some troops that have been ordered to remain behind.

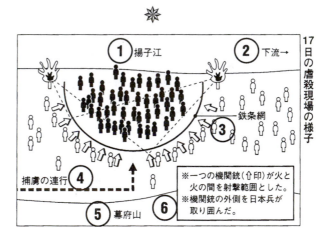

The site of the December 17 massacre

1. Yangtze River	6. Each machine gun (indicated by
2. Downstream	arrows) shot within the range
3. Barbed wire	between the fires.
4. The route that the prisoners took	7. Soldiers stood around behind the
5. Mufu Mountain	machine guns.

Among the survivors of the Morozumi Unit, there are some old soldiers who have given accounts of what happened then. Ono Kenji, who painstakingly unearthed these field diaries, introduced me to two of these veterans in 1994, fifty-seven years after the events, and I visited them at their homes.

They were Kurosu Tadanobu, age eighty-three, from the 13th Division, Mountain Artillery Regiment, 3d Battalion, Yamada Detachment, and Komatsu Taro, age eighty-seven, a transport soldier from the Morozumi Unit, 1st Battalion. I have not used their real names, because veterans who give this sort of testimony are often subjected to crank phone calls and hate mail.

It was on July 13, 1994, that I visited both of them at their respective homes, but what follows is compiled not only from their accounts but also from what Ono had heard and from the field diaries. Kurosu took part in the massacre on the 16th, while Kobayashi was involved on both the 16th and 17th. Since my informants were already well along in years, it was, in a sense, hopeless to expect that they would recall scenes from fifty years before in any detail, but the main points of what they said are valuable testimony, and I appreciated their accounts as such.

It was on October 3, 1937, that Kurosu landed at Wusong at the mouth of the Yangtze near Shanghai. Since they were in staggered rows in an artillery unit, they incurred some casualties as they went along, although not as much as the front-line combat units. It seems that the atrocities they committed along the way were carried out in a spirit of revenge for the unexpectedly heavy fighting they had encountered near Shanghai and for the many men who had been killed. Even so, the atrocities were horrendous.

"When we stayed overnight in a certain village, we'd take all the men behind the houses and kill them with bayonets or knives. Then we'd lock up the women and children in a single house and rape them at night. I didn't do that myself, but I think the other soldiers did quite a bit of raping. Then, before we left the next morning, we'd kill all the women and children, and to top it off, we'd set fire to the houses, so that even if anyone came back, they wouldn't have a place to live. That's how we advanced through China. I thought it was strange, and when I asked why we had to do such things, I was told that we were under orders to kill everyone, because this region had shown such fierce resistance to us. They were saying we had no option but to kill everyone, so we went through the war amassing a record of arson, looting, rape, murder, and every other sort of crime."

Thus all the men were killed, and all the women and children were killed after being raped. In other words, they killed all the residents of the villages where they stayed, so we must understand that the massacres were not limited to Nanjing.

As they approached Nanjing, increasing numbers of Chinese stragglers surrendered, and Kurosu remembers hearing that the number of prisoners was up to 90,000. The Morozumi Unit had charge of about 20,000 prisoners, and it kept them in twenty old barracks with a straw-thatched roof and earthen walls at the foot of Mufu Mountain. Among the prisoners were some twelve-

or thirteen-year-old boys who had been recruited to dig trenches and even some wrinkled old men.

On December 14, the day after the fall of Nanjing, Kurosu and his comrades were billeted in Dongwai Village.

December 15 was a day of rest, but on the afternoon of the 16th, the men billeted in the village were told to line up in formation. Those in the front were sent to tour the city of Nanjing, while those in the back were ordered to "mop up stragglers." Since Kurosu's row was in the back, he and his fellows were supposed to join in the "mopping up," but since they didn't have enough guns, they used some that had been confiscated from the Chinese.

As ordered by their superiors, they went to the prisoner holding area at the foot of Mufu Mountain. The open space in front of the barracks was surrounded by light and heavy machine guns. The first thing the soldiers did upon arrival was to take the prisoners and tie them together in pairs with their hands behind their backs. Kurosu heard that there were 5,000 men in all, and because of this, there wasn't enough rope to tie them all. They tore the clothes of the Chinese soldiers to make cords and also used their puttees. However, there were some Japanese soldiers who were most interested in stealing the Chinese men's watches and gold.

The evening moon was already out by the time the 5,000 men were tied up. The pairs of prisoners were made to line up and march off, with gun-wielding Japanese soldiers stationed every few meters. The procession set out in the direction of the Yangtze, and even Kurosu, who was somewhere near the middle, had no idea exactly where they were going.

Despite the moonlight, some men stumbled as they walked along the narrow road, and of course, they also dragged down the man they were bound to. If they could not get up quickly, the men behind them also fell on top of them. When that happened, the Japanese soldiers bayoneted them. The startled men behind them took the long way around to avoid being caught up in the mess.

There was a small hamlet about halfway to their destination, an hour from their starting point. That's where Kurosu encountered Second Lieutenant M, an acquaintance from his hometown, who was standing and talking with two companions. Kurosu had heard that M had been drafted, but this was the first time he had met up with him in China.

"I'm going to go do this," Kurosu said, pantomiming the act of stabbing someone with his bayonet.

"I have to do that, too," M replied. But they split up, and the procession proceeded to the banks of the Yangtze.

The open space where the prisoners were eventually collected faced on the Yangtze, and there was a sunken area surrounded by a stone fence more than 10 meters high. However, the sunken area was not filled with water; rather, it was a narrow beach leading down to the river. Behind the open space were some two- or three-layer concrete buildings, which were referred to as the "customs buildings." Kurosu later found out that these buildings had holes in the walls and that machine guns were aimed out these holes and at the open space.

Once the prisoners had arrived at the open space, a lot of soldiers began carrying out "test killings" in the surrounding fields: soldiers who had swords pulled prisoners out of the line and beheaded them. Others "tested" their bayonets. It was a scene like one of those temple paintings of demons tormenting the souls in hell, but none of the soldiers seemed to realize the situation was anything out of the ordinary. In fact, it almost seemed as if they were killing people so that they would have something exciting to talk about afterward.

Kurosu had never cut off anyone's head before, so he borrowed a sword from a sergeant-major and gave it a try. When he brought the sword down on the neck of a prisoner who was already lying dead on the ground, he found that it was harder to behead someone than he had expected: the sword went only halfway through.

While all this commotion was going on, a great cry sounding like one voice resounded from the gathering of prisoners, mingling with the sound of the machine guns starting their mopping-up operations. Kurosu also tried shooting at the prisoners with his rifle, but he stopped, since he was afraid of accidentally hitting another Japanese soldier.

Soon the prisoners were all lying on the ground, but even though the group had been swept with machine gun fire, not all of them had been hit. Seeing that there were still a lot of survivors, the soldiers walked around on the pile of dead and living prisoners, stabbing them with bayonets. Kurosu tried joining in, but since he was using a Chinese army rifle, his Japanese bayonet didn't fit. He borrowed another soldier's rifle, strapped the Chinese rifle to his back, and went around stabbing at the bodies.

When he stabbed one prisoner, the bayonet went into his mouth, and what's more, the prisoner was still alive and grabbed at Kurosu's rifle with both hands. Kurosu was surprised and unsettled, but he didn't have any second thoughts. The idea foremost in his mind was that this man was an enemy of his comrades. About a hundred Japanese soldiers participated in the stabbings, and Kurosu estimates that he stabbed about three hundred prisoners in the space of ten minutes. Of that number, only two or three were clearly still alive.

None of the prisoners got up and tried to run away, but Kurosu thinks that if any had run away, they would have done so immediately after the machine guns began firing. Evidently, not many prisoners made the attempt, and even if they had, they would have run into the Japanese soldiers who were standing at the foot of the high stone wall.

It was about eight in the evening when Kurosu returned to his billet. The next day, his arm was so sore that he couldn't raise it.

The supply soldier Kobayashi took place in the mass "disposal" of prisoners on both the 16th and 17th, and he thinks about three thousand were killed on the first day. However, he didn't have any part in tying them up at the barracks. His role began with the march toward the riverbank, which was explained to the prisoners in these terms: "We're going to transport you by boat to Shanghai, where you'll be well treated."

However, once the "test killings" began and the harrowing scene unfolded, the prisoners raised both hands and gave three cries that seemed to correspond to *banzai*. Just as they were lowering their hands, the machine guns began sweeping the area. Some shrapnel hit the palm of Kobayashi's left hand, but he remembers that it didn't hit him hard enough to cause any real injury. Since he didn't have a rifle, all he did was watch. He took no part in stabbing the victims, either, and withdrew at eight in the evening.

He didn't have any part in tying up the prisoners on the 17th, either, and began by assisting in their transfer. But this day's "disposal" was of a different scale, with fourteen or fifteen thousand prisoners.

The site of this massacre was Dawanzi, 2 or 3 kilometers downstream from the previous day's site, Yulaiying. Kobayashi walked behind the huge procession as a guard, this time carrying a bayonet. Occasionally prisoners tried to break free, but almost all of them were shot. Kobayashi himself saw a prisoner about 50 meters ahead attempting to escape, but with his hands tied behind his back, he couldn't run very fast, and he was summarily shot.

The march to Dawanzi took an hour or an hour and a half, but with the large number of prisoners being moved, it took even longer for them all to assemble in the open space. The sky grew dark, and since it was cloudy, there was no moon that night.

As Kobayashi recalls, the machine guns began spraying the group of prisoners at around 7:00 P.M. Again and again the guns fired, with short pauses in between, until it seemed that a pile of over ten thousand bodies had risen out of the depths of hell. Afterwards, as on the previous night, the soldiers walked around stabbing the bodies with their bayonets.

Kobayashi, of course, had never done anything like this before, but he had heard that it wasn't easy to pull a bayonet out of a body. In fact, he found that he could easily pull the bayonet out of a person's trunk, although once he had trouble pulling it out of someone's hip. When he tried stabbing a prisoner in the head, he found that the bayonet made a clicking sound and bounced right back. Walking around on the pile of bodies felt like walking around in the mud of a rice paddy or through a gelatinous piece of *konnyaku* root. Some prisoners who were still alive grabbed onto the soldiers' rifles in their final desperation, so it was dangerous to carry out this task unless another soldier was nearby.

As a matter of fact, this operation yielded about ten Japanese "casualties," either killed or wounded, as prisoners grabbed swords or bayonets from their tormentors and struck back, and Kobayashi knows of two or three cases where Japanese soldiers struck at each other in the confusion. He witnessed one incident in which a soldier who had accidentally stabbed a comrade picked up the victim piggyback and said, "If you die, I'll die, too." After being warned not to waste time saying stupid things to the injured man, he left with his charge.

Second Lieutenant M also "died in battle" that night. As Kobayashi recalls, it was 11:00 P.M., and since the soldiers were already out stabbing the victims, one could have supposed that the machine guns had stopped shooting. Whether the gunner panicked or couldn't see, or for whatever reason, Kobayashi heard a call of "To your right!" followed by the "rat-a-tat-tat" of machine gun fire just seconds later. He barely had time to think before throwing himself down to the left. Of course, if he had waited till he heard the gun firing, it would have been too late. Less than 2 meters away from him lay another soldier, Watanabe from Sukagawa, a young man two or three years younger than Kobayashi, looking almost as if he, too, had thrown himself on the ground. But he had been killed instantly, his belly ripped open. Kobayashi didn't actually see Second Lieutenant M get killed, but at midnight, he heard someone calling his name.

After all the confusion was over, the soldiers poured gasoline on the mountain of corpses and set it on fire. However, since they didn't have much gasoline, the fire was insignificant.

It was perhaps 1:00 A.M. when Kobayashi left the scene.

Thus the two-day massacre ended, but some of the field diaries, including the diary of Meguro Tomiharu, suggest that it continued on the 18th. If Meguro is referring to another site, this means that the massacres occurred over three days at three different sites.

In any case, the massacres produced huge piles of bodies, and disposing of them took another two days. Here are some diary entries for December 18 and 19.

From the diary of Miyamoto Shogo:

(December) 18, cloudy—After yesterday's events, I was finally able to go to bed around dawn. Soon after I got up, it was time for lunch.

In the afternoon, we disposed of the enemy bodies, and we hadn't finished by the time it got dark. Deciding to finish up tomorrow, we withdrew. The wind is cold.

(December) 19—Starting early in the morning, we continued disposing of the corpses left over from yesterday. It took till four in the afternoon.

A fire got out of control as we were disposing of the prisoners' clothes. We tried to make sure that it didn't spread to the barracks, and we were able to stop it. Tomorrow we are supposed to cross the river, and the soldiers stayed up late getting ready.

We got our first rations of rice and miso in a long time, and we even fried up some beef. We prepared food for tomorrow.

The wind is cold, and the levees along the Yangtze are beginning to look wintry.

From the diary of Endo Takaaki:

December 18—At 1:00 A.M., the punishment still was not over, and there were still some surviving prisoners. We were ordered to the execution ground to straighten things up. The wind blew fiercely, and beginning around 3:00 A.M., there was blowing snow. I was chilled to the bone, and words can't express how eager I was to see the dawn. We finished at 8:30. The wind died down, and the weather recovered. The soldiers guarding Mufu Mountain returned to quarters. Six soldiers went to tour Nanjing. I napped for an hour during the morning. We were each given an apple, something I hadn't tasted in a long time. At noon, nine of the fourth set of reinforcements were assigned. From 2:00 to 7:30 P.M., I sent 25 men to dispose of the more than 10,000 bodies at the execution ground.

December 19—At 8:00 A.M. I sent 15 men to continue disposing of the bodies. The regiment was ordered to load materials for crossing the Yangtze. At 1:00 P.M. I went to check in at the command post at the anchorage at the Zhongshan wharf. It was about 1.5 *li*. The riding horse we procured has a bad leg and is of no use. We decided to leave it behind. Twelve men went to tour Nanjing and brought back bean jam and canned Mandarin oranges for us. I had one glass of the treasured Akadama wine I'd brought along. Masuda Ryu is in the hospital in the city.

From a field memo of Sugeno Yoshio:

(December) 18—A light snow started falling in the morning. We went to dispose of the enemy who had been shot. The stench was terrible.

(December) 19— They went to dispose of bodies today, too. I did not go.

From the diary of Meguro Tomiharu:

December 18, clear skies, outside Nanjing—Beginning at 3:00 A.M. a wind came up and it rained. When I woke up, I saw that all the mountains were white with snow. It was the first snow. The number of units gathered inside and outside the walls of Nanjing is ten divisions. I rested. At 5:00 A.M. we shot about 13,000 enemy stragglers.

December 19, clear skies, outside Nanjing—Expecting to have some time off, I got up at 6:00 A.M. We threw the bodies of the over 10,000 enemy we shot yesterday into the Yangtze. Until 1:00 P.M., we prepared to depart in the afternoon, including the garrison command.

The source with the most details about disposing of the bodies is the diary of Sato Jiro:

> December 18, cloudy, cold—At midnight, the order came for us to go on duty to dispose of the bodies of the enemy stragglers. The entire transport unit set out. On the way we walked among countless enemy corpses. The wind smelled like blood and seemed murderous. We shot about _____ prisoners on the banks of the Yangtze. The moon, which shone brightly until yesterday, is clouded over, so the light was faint, and a misty rain was falling. The north wind was cold enough to hurt my ears. A comrade from the 12th Company who went to shoot the prisoners was hit in the stomach by a stray bullet and is near death. His dying moans are heart-rending, and I am filled with pity. At 3:00 A.M., we returned to quarters, went to bed. I took it easy in the morning, performed my morning rituals, made breakfast, and went to visit Nanjing with _____, Okamoto, and _____. We were amazed at the immensity of the construction of the wall surrounding the city. The height of the wall is three or four *jō* , and about 14 or 15 *ken* across [sic—Could he have the height and width reversed?]. The city proper has been either burned or destroyed, so there's nothing to see, and it's in a pathetic state. There are a lot of bodies of what may be enemy soldiers, their uniforms off, and their belongings scattered along the roadside. We returned near evening. I went to bed at 9:00.
>
> (Marginal note) Disposing of the bodies of the prisoners who were shot (midnight on the 18th)—I thought it was cold last night, and this morning there's a severe frost and ice forming. When I washed my face, the cold water stung. After breakfast, I went to the field post office at Nanjing Wharf and sent postcards to my family, to Nakazawa Eijiro, Murata Hajime, Yasuda Sosaku, Kageyama Yoshiharu, Sato Kin'ichiro, Omori Katsujiro, Suzuki Shigechika, Yamagiwa Eitaro, _____, Michiyama Kuniharu, the village office at _____, and the local chapter of military men at home. I had them stamped with a seal commemorating the fall of Nanjing. This evening was relaxed, with no sounds of artillery or gunfire. I went to bed. Yesterday morning, snow could be seen on the mountains near Nanjing, but it melted by about 9:00. My supplies were not as I thought they should be, so I went to the transport unit, and once again I was able to get rice dumplings from Watanabe and Ariga. What a coincidence. I took rice dumplings when I entered this unit, and now I've been able to obtain some rice dumplings. My feet are still in bad shape, and I wonder if they will get better soon. If we're able to settle down somewhere, I'll take care of them.

INDEX